Listen to what others are saying about TIME OFF!

"I wish I could be Mayor of San Francisco forever but even us politicos need a break once and awhile. *Time Off!* has given me a wealth of ideas for enjoying life after City Hall and the book beautifully represents San Francisco. It will greatly assist my staff and me in getting the most out of our leisure time."

~Mayor Willie L. Brown, Jr., a.k.a. "Da Mayor"

"My generation of young adults has experience with not working. In the middle '90s, we took long breaks between jobs because employers needed us more than we needed them. Now the tables have turned. The jobs we used to leave are now leaving us. Regardless of why we're not working, it's time to seize the full potential of that opportunity. *Time Off!* encourages you to take your leisure time seriously—to expand your mind and invest in friendships and family—the important things in life that no employer can ever take away. Take this book to heart and you'll someday start the story of losing your last job with this sentence: 'You know, that was the best thing that ever happened to me.'"

~Ethan Watters, San Francisco writer, author of *Urban Tribes: A Generation Redefines Friendship, Family and Commitment*

"Forget the GNP, think of your own *personal* GNP: what is going to add to your life, bring you more joy and less stress? *Time Off! The Unemployed Guide to San Francisco* is a great first step to getting your life on track, your priorities in place, and your panties (or boxers) out of a bunch! Whether you're employed or unemployed, this guide will improve the quality of your life."

~Bridget Fonger, co-author of *The Lazy Woman's Guide to Just About Everything*, and self-proclaimed "lazy woman"

"The biggest little book on the littlest big city."

~Ben Marcus, writer, surf scribe, and San Francisco "bon savant"

"This book will make you want to quit your job."

~Tom Haan, founder, Bojon.com (www.bojon.com)

"*Time Off!* is full of practical ideas and thoughtful medicine, delivered with a big, funny spoonful of sugar. I'm jealous—why does San Francisco get all the fun? Every city needs one of these! I'm rooting for The Leisure Team against The Workaholics in the Superbowl of real life.

~John de Graaf, national coordinator, Take Back Your Time Day and co-author, *Affluenza*

"Hands down, the San Francisco Bay Area is one of the most brilliant playgrounds in the world, both natural and urban. Get off your duff and get out and enjoy it! And keep this book in your back pocket. It's a fantastic resource for the cost-conscious, the lifestyle-conscious, and the 'soul' conscious."

~Susan MacTavish Best, founder and editor, *Posthoc San Francisco* (www.posthoc.com)

"If you're not working (and really, who works anymore?), you may as well sit down with a good book. A good book about not working? Hell, that's even better."

~Camper English, San Francisco writer and man-about-town

"Leaving work behind to travel and reconnect with the spirit and core values has always been an essential part of my life and is what led to the creation of 'Mister SF.' For locals and travelers alike, San Francisco is an epicenter of joy and imagination. *Time Off!* is all about enjoying the city as San Franciscans do—with leisure as a top priority!"

~Hank "Mister SF" Donat, San Francisco's "Heart of the City" columnist (www.MisterSF.com)

"I wholeheartedly believe that leisure is critical for romantic success; in our hurry-up world, what could be more meaningful than slowing down to enjoy life with the person you love? Leisure Team has created an amazing resource, jam-packed with suggestions and inside tips... which makes it that much easier to have fun!"

~Jennifer Jeffrey, writer, co-founder, "Sex and the Kitchen" (www.sexandthekitchen.com)

"As someone who's always looking for both a good time and a good deal, I think this book is a great reference. I just hope it won't make my favorite secret places too popular!"

~Marcus Ronaldi, filmmaker, event planner (www.marcusronaldi.com)

TIME OFF!

THE UNEMPLOYED GUIDE TO SAN FRANCISCO

TIME OFF!

THE UNEMPLOYED GUIDE TO SAN FRANCISCO

DEAN LATOURRETTE
KRISTINE ENEA

leisure team™ productions

Time Off! The Unemployed Guide to San Francisco
 Published by Leisure Team Productions, LLC. First printing 2004.

10 8 6 4 2 1 3 5 7 9

ISBN 0-9741084-0-5
Library of Congress Control Number: 2003092844

Edited by Ellen Clair Lamb
Proofed by Jennifer Birch
Cover and Illustration by Jamie Leap Designs
Additional Illustration by Sara Irvin
Printed and bound in the United States by Malloy Incorporated

To order online, visit us at www.leisureteam.com. To talk leisure, debate leisure principles, or just complain about your job, e-mail us at info@leisureteam.com. For bulk orders, please call our office at 415-564-9894 or e-mail your inquiry to us at orders@leisureteam.com.

This book is dedicated to
all of San Francisco's leisure seekers.

FOREWORD

BY HARRY DENTON

HAIL the benefits of leisure? I think I've been celebrating this credo throughout my blessed life. If anyone has learned the advantages of a leisurely lifestyle over the years, I have. In fact, the pursuit of leisure is what led me to open my first bar in San Francisco in 1986—Harry's on Fillmore.

Hell, it's no secret—I love a great party!

Leisure in Life

It may seem obvious that taking time for yourself is paramount to healthy living. Yet, I've seen so many people around me ignore this basic premise. For me, it's all about having fun, whether at work or at play. If I'm not having fun, then I'm doing something wrong.

Leisure to me equates to enjoyment, whether that means traveling the world, throwing a four star gala, or (gulp) working in an office. (I'll take the party, thank you!) It also means taking breaks, and I must say I've taken my fair share.

Every January for the past six years I've taken off and gone to Rio. It's pure pleasure—the weather is perfect and the people are beautiful and sexy—such a perfect locale for leisure! I take my coffee on the beach every morning, drink fresh juices and summer cocktails, and nap in the afternoons. So relaxing. In the evenings, it's dinner and then—guess what? Bring on the nightlife! The best part is, no shoes, ties, or pants. Or sometimes any *other* clothes!

Have I ever looked back and wished I hadn't stopped working to pursue a leisurely endeavor? Never.

Money = Love

I have friends who live solely for the day they will retire; I see people who work and work to add to their financial scorecard. Money to me is a three letter word… F-U-N.

If I'm not having fun then the money I make is irrelevant. Conversely, fun will bring in the money. It has for me, and I base many of my financial decisions on whether or not the outcome will bring more enjoyment to my life—not just more money.

As far as the age-old tradition of squirreling away all of your nuts for winter, I prefer a different philosophy: take time off while you're young. Why wait until retirement to see the world? And when you're older, go back to work! My mother got a new job at 75—no better way for her to stay motivated and keep her mind sharp. She worked at age 80 and plans to continue at 90! Mom is now 88, looks 65, swims everyday, and does yoga twice a week. She is an inspiration to me.

San Francisco: Leisure City

I can't think of a place in this world more appropriate for enjoying time off than San Francisco—it's what drew me here in the first place.

I came here from Idaho back in 1965 with $110 in my pocket (I sold all my cashmere sweaters) and never left. In 1972, I began working as a waiter and bartender in a variety of restaurants around town—was that ever a crazy time!

My first job was Henry Africa's. It was in my neighborhood and the owner said I should come to work for him and learn the business. Best decision of my life. It was such a detailed saloon—Tiffany shades, Gucci outfits for the waitresses. I learned so much about details. I began as a maitre d', then I played the piano at cocktail hour, and finally stepped up to waiting tables and bartending. I had never been in the restaurant and bar industry before but within six weeks, I knew I wanted my own business.

Many of the stories from that era would make you blush but I knew then what I know now: that the City was the perfect backdrop for wild and crazy antics, and that it was home to me.

Take the Book to Heart

What I like about *Time Off!* is that it not only captures my life philosophy, but it makes a convincing case for the crucial need for all of us to take breaks from work. I'm one of the fortunate few who really *does* love his job, but that doesn't mean I don't need lots of time to play. And I *do* know how to play.

So go out and enjoy, seize the day, night, and everything else you can get your hands on. Celebrate all that is San Francisco and make leisure a priority in your life.

Remember to be thankful for what you have, don't worry about what you don't have, and enjoy *every single day.*

TABLE OF CONTENTS

INTRODUCTION

YES, you *can* take time off from work and still enjoy life. Your life *can* and *should* flourish while you're not slaving away at a job. You'll need to be smart with your finances and rid yourself of self-imposed "unemployment guilt"—then just embrace the wide open, captivating world of unemployment around you!

Can you contribute to society when you are not working? Can you be fiscally responsible between jobs? Can taking time off transform you and everyone around you?

The simple answer to these questions is an unequivocal and resounding, "YES!" But the story doesn't stop there. *Time Off! The Unemployed Guide to San Francisco* ventures well beyond the simple answer to tell you how you can make the most of your free time. It's part philosophy, part "how to," and part guidebook. It hails the benefits of working less and playing more, explains how (and why) to take time off, and guides you to the best of the City. Most important, it helps you redefine and celebrate unemployment itself.

WHO THIS BOOK IS FOR

You don't have to be unemployed—at least in the conventional sense of the word—to read this book. San Francisco is an ideal stomping ground for anyone with any amount of free time.

But if you *are* out of a job, you're now perfectly poised to rediscover your home town. If you merely aspire to be unemployed, we hope to tip the scales in favor of gaining a new perspective on the familiar.

Maybe you have a job but it's part-time or project-based. If you're not into hustling 60 hours a week for The Man and would rather save some daylight hours for feeding your own soul, this book is for you too. And if you're lucky enough to like your job, or have a secure job and want to keep it—well, what's wrong with playing a little hooky now and then? Even workaholics need a vacation day once in a while.

Whether you were "downsized" or are gainfully employed, living here or just visiting, this book will offer you hundreds of ideas on how to savor your free time in San Francisco.

By the way, you don't have to be a millionaire to live well here. If you have a few dollars saved, that's a good start. We'll share some ideas on how to manage your money to squeeze out another month or two of relaxing. If you don't, not to worry; you can find plenty of fun in this city without a big price tag and we can tell you where. *Time Off!* is all about enjoying San Francisco the way a local would and should, at a relaxed pace and without burning through piles of money.

UNEMPLOYED, ON SABBATICAL—WHAT'S THE DIFFERENCE?

America hardly embraces unemployment. Unlike cultures where downtime is an integral part of a balanced life, our culture dismisses any kind of time off as an anomaly, a tragedy for the unmotivated, or a gift for the spoiled. The stereotypes are miserable! But why should unemployment have such a bad rap?

The very fact that there's no good word for "unemployed by choice and loving it" hints at a greater societal ill—*over*-employment. Someone who slaves 60+ hours a week at work is not only accepted but revered. That's crazy!

So, forget the stigma. We admire the unemployed. "Unemployed" means so much more than not having a job. In the broadest sense, it covers any down time at all, especially time not owed to an employer. In the best sense, it connotes a period of renewal, reflection and meandering creativity that produces original and lasting contributions to humanity. Even an unexpected layoff can lead to personal growth.

It's time to jettison the mindset that you're freeloading or unworthy if you're not contributing to the gross national product. The gross national product can't measure the value of the arts, volunteering, or any other low- or non-wage-earning activity. Ironically, too much time "producing" means not enough time to explore, create or invent—and without creativity or innovation, growth and prosperity disappear.

Ask anyone in San Francisco, "Who's unemployed?" and they'll tell you, "Half the people in this bar," or "Everyone at my gym." Some lost their jobs and others quit but they're all in the same boat. Almost everyone *could* be considered unemployed at some point and, in our opinion, everyone *should* be.

SAN FRANCISCO

Ah, San Francisco! A city that needs no introduction... or does it?

Most tourists have heard of the Golden Gate Bridge and cable cars, Fisherman's Wharf, Alcatraz—even the Great Earthquake of 1906. Fewer know San Francisco as "Baghdad by the Bay," a city that encompasses more than 800,000 residents in its 47 square miles and that served as the backdrop for such classic films as *The Maltese Falcon* and *Vertigo*.

History buffs know that Spanish colonists rechristened the small town of Yerba Buena after St. Francis on June 26, 1776, and that the United States won the city from Mexico in 1846. San Francisco's Spanish-language heritage endures in the present-day city motto, *"Oro en Paz, Fierro en Guerra"* (Gold in Peace, Iron in War). Serious San Franciscans can even name our City Colors, City Tree, City Flower, and City Bird. (City Bird? Find out in Chapter 4!) If any of this is news to you, maybe it's time to rediscover San Francisco!

The City has been the world's favorite tourist destination for decades. It has inspired immortals of literature, music and the arts, whose memories linger in place names such as Jack Kerouac Alley or Dashiell Hammett Street. San Francisco is famous for its tolerance and liberalism, welcoming those who would be outcasts elsewhere. It never stops inviting novelty, culture, and adventure. Financiers, entrepreneurs, strippers, hippies—all call San Francisco home.

San Francisco is all these things and more. It is also, at the turn of the 21st century, the site of one of the biggest economic crashes in history.

UNEMPLOYMENT IN SAN FRANCISCO

Unemployment has hit the Bay Area harder than almost anywhere in the country. The effects of the "Dot Bomb" still resonate, as San Franciscans continue to get laid off from one company after another.

At the epicenter of an unprecedented technology boom in the late 1990s, San Francisco saw its unemployment rate nearly triple in the subsequent bust, from a low of 2.4% in December 1999 to a high of 7.3% in January 2002. Although the City isn't suffering the country's highest unemployment rate, it ranks right up there—or rather, down there—with others hit hard by the crash.

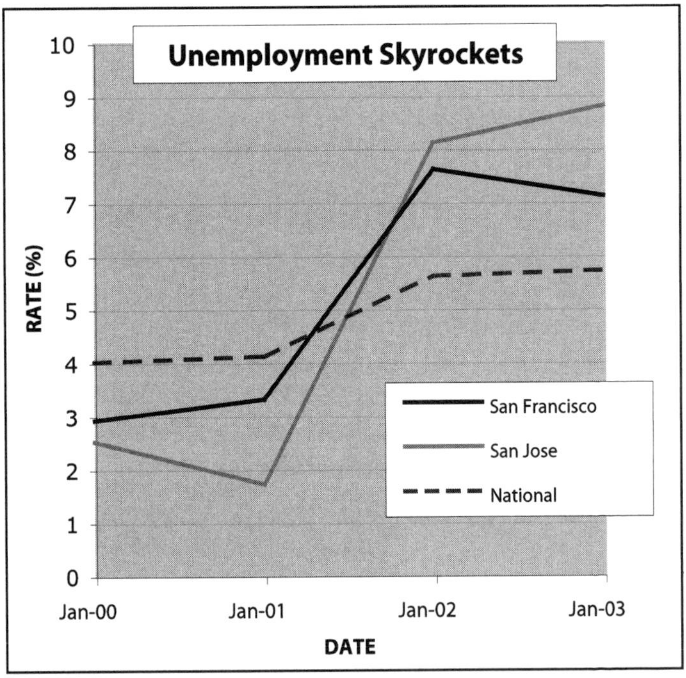

Nat'l and San Jose Metro rates from the Bureau of Labor Statistics (*www.bls.gov*). SF County rate from the California EDD (*www.calmis.ca.gov*).

As high as it is, San Francisco's official unemployment rate certainly understates the actual job loss. No rate can measure *misemployment* (being forced to change careers or take temporary work just to pay the bills) or count those who've moved away from the City altogether.

The government's eligibility rules for unemployment insurance add insult to injury by excluding: (1) anyone on a payroll—even if they work only one hour a week, (2) people who work but don't make any money (who needs that pesky paycheck anyway?), and (3) certain people who aren't working at all. Given those quirks of the system, it's safe to assume that more San Franciscans are feeling the pain than the "official" numbers show, particularly within the technology sector. Besides, we don't need precise numbers to know that plenty of our friends and neighbors are out of work or close to it.

But if there's one characteristic that has always defined San Francisco, it's resilience. No city in America has more vitality, from corner to corner. Many of the people interviewed for this book, hung over from excessive, hyper-economic living, are pausing to re-balance the work and the personal, stepping back to look around, and taking the time to fully appreciate their environs.

What's more, many are doing this by choice. Of the people we interviewed, at least a quarter were unemployed not because they were laid off but because they quit their jobs for various reasons, including traveling, spending time with family, and going back to school. The Employment Development Department figures that nearly 10% of California's total unemployed population are "job leavers." It's hard to quantify voluntary versus involuntary unemployment but clearly a good number of workers want to explore life outside the office. San Francisco companies lead the nation in offering *sabbaticals* (see **Leisure Lingo**) and many San Franciscans are taking them.

an ugly story

"PG&E Declares Bankruptcy" "San Jose Symphony Shuts Down" "United Closes its San Francisco Reservation Centers"

The dire headlines go on and on. Technology giants including Hewlett Packard, Applied Materials, and Cisco have slashed headcount repeatedly. Hopeful startups WebVan and Pets.com closed altogether. Even brick-and-mortar stalwarts such as Schwab, Gap, and ChevronTexaco have cut at least 10% apiece; the job loss at Schwab totaled 25% in 2001 alone.

Want details? Running tallies are available from several sources, including ***Forbes.com's "Layoff Tracker"*** (*www.forbes.com*, rather gruesomely subfiled under "bodycountarchive") and the locally developed ***World News Map*** website (*www.mapreport.com*, search for "Job Cut Timeline").

And why not? Unemployment can be fun! Not to make light of anyone's personal crisis but San Francisco offers so much to explore at such little cost, you might find that going back to work would just get in the way of your real life. Which brings us to another word...

LEISURE

"Time free from the necessities of work," said Aristotle. "Time which one can spend as one pleases," says the *Oxford English Dictionary.* Some scholars view leisure as a distinct period of time, to be enjoyed only as a luxury or by an elite leisure class; others see it more as an attitude and a lifestyle.

Many Americans believe that leisure awaits them only in retirement. After the second World War, we Americans somehow lost our way on the path to more leisure while the Europeans continued to increase theirs. Something's gone wrong here!

What does leisure mean to you? Two weeks a year in Hawaii? A Saturday afternoon nap?

For a growing number of Americans, leisure means something deeper—a way to live life to the fullest, and closer to the heart. More and more of us believe in the merits of adding more leisure to our lives. It was this belief that spawned Leisure Team Productions, and it is the reckless pursuit of leisure in San Francisco that is the focus of this book.

FORMAT OF THE BOOK

Time Off! is divided into three parts: contemplating and preparing for leisure, making the most of your free time, and transitioning back to work (don't do it!).

Part One, "Charting Your Course," makes the case for being unemployed or wanting to be, and sets the stage for breathing easier about your particular goals and situation.

Part Two seeks to whet your appetite for San Francisco during your *unemployed odyssey,* with recommendations for local sites and activities, events, dining & nightlife, and (believe it or not!) shopping while unemployed. Besides rediscovering your hometown, you can travel, explore unemployment on the edge, boost your health and fitness, and get to know your friends and family better.

Part Three focuses on "Sharing The Leisure" through volunteering, pursuing higher education, finding more balance in job hunting, and incorporating more moments of leisure into a working world.

Spread throughout the book are celebrations of **Great Moments in Unemployment**. If you see an italicized term that you're not familiar with, edify yourself with our **Leisure Lingo** glossary in the back of the book.

Most of the sites, shops, and other resources we recommend are in San Francisco—except for a few irresistible ones within easy striking distance. Each recommended resource is listed **in bold** within the body of the book as well as indexed alphabetically in the back.

Time Off! is not a guide to job hunting, although we do share some unconventional means for landing one. It's not "San Francisco on the Cheap," although we *are* big fans of free fun. And it's not a traditional San Francisco guidebook, although we'll give you plenty of unconventional and intriguing information on the City.

It *is* full of ideas on making the most of San Francisco while you're unemployed or aspiring to be, all designed to enrich your time off journey and propel you forward into the wonderful world of leisure.

UPDATES

The information in *Time Off!* was current as of the publication date but it's always a good idea to call ahead to see if hours, locations, or other information has changed. If you have updates, ideas, or discoveries to share, we'd love to hear from you—please send us an e-mail at unemployedguide@leisureteam.com. We'll publish the breaking news on our website, www.leisureteam.com.

Enjoy, and share the leisure!

Leisure Team Productions, LLC

LEISURE CITY
MAP
to
LEISURE School

PART ONE

CHARTING YOUR COURSE

CHAPTER 1
THE ART OF LEISURE

Linda Emery: A philosophy major? Now, what can you do with a philosophy major?

Bruce Lee: You can think deep thoughts about being unemployed.

~Dragon: the Bruce Lee Story

MASTERING the *art of leisure* promises something that everyone wants—greater peace of mind. We, the leisure faithful, encourage everyone to seek it, and we encourage you to take a break from work to do so.

How is this possible? Doesn't joblessness *create* stress?

Not necessarily. When you work day in and day out just to pay the bills, how hard do you wish for more free time? Imagine, for a moment, that your wish has been granted. Wouldn't it be a crime not to enjoy it?

Embrace the peace that this extra time can bring you. *Believe* in the power of leisure.

Are you interested? Read on!

THE LEISURE COMMANDMENTS

- Thou shalt enjoy at least one sustained period of unemployment during thy career.
- Thou shalt switch careers to do something thou really enjoyest, even if it means taking a pay cut.
- Thou shalt pursue one secret childhood dream without regard to status or the judgment of others.
- Thou shalt party until dawn on at least one weeknight.
- Thou shalt lounge around thy house in thy pajamas.
- Thou shalt create, experiment, and ponder.
- Thou shalt reconnect with thy community.
- Thou shalt partake of the great outdoors.
- Thou shalt travel and explore, beginning with thine own hometown.

Subscribe to these commandments and you'll reap rewards on this earth:

- Get to know yourself better.
- Connect with your friends, family and community.
- Become a *leisure connoisseur.*
- Launch your *unemployed odyssey.*

DEEP THOUGHTS ON YOURSELF

First, let's talk about you. What do *you* think about you? More important, what do you think about you without a job?

Take a deep breath and repeat this mantra: "I am *not* my job. *I* am not *my job.*"

In a culture that so values work and the concept of working hard, what does it mean to be unemployed? In Japan, another society that takes its work ethic to the extreme, the literal English translation for the statement, "I work for Nissan" is "I *am* Nissan." Never mind getting too caught up in your work—in Japan, apparently you *are* your work!

You are definitely not alone if you identify closely with your job. It's part of our culture, the so-called *Protestant work ethic* that says wasting time is evil. A host of proverbs support this: "idle hands are the Devil's workshop," "he that sleeps in harvest is a son that causes shame," and more of the same.

Beyond that, our culture deeply believes that material success somehow equates to divine favor, which suggests that our only purpose on earth is to work—for work's sake.

identity check

How many of the following statements do you identify with? More seriously, how many have you actually said?

- I can't say no to more work.
- I feel guilty if I'm not working.
- Each time I finish a project, I panic that I'll never work again.
- Promotions equal success.
- I am what I do.

If your answer is "one or more," you need help. Let us reveal two fundamental truths of the *art of leisure.*

Self-worth ≠ net worth.
Life is not a competition, at least not in that sense. You're still the same person—maybe even a better person—if you're not employed or if you're what society considers *underemployed.*

You ≠ your job.
Not having a job makes you no less smart, attractive, funny, kind, or any of the other things that define you. Not having a job can give you the time to discover what you really enjoy doing and what you'd change about how and where you work. Unemployment presents an opportunity to discover and reinvent your best self. Others have done it—you can too.

This sounds pretty bogus to us, unless your work is your passion. If that's the case—if your passion came first and now you get paid for it—bravo. You're either more talented, more skilled, or luckier than 98% of the population. But if work is merely what you do to pay the rent and feed yourself (although these are hardly small things), you need to make sure that work stays in its place.

Once you've earned enough to survive, every extra hour that you work is an hour that you don't spend playing, singing, dancing, learning new things, or helping others. It's an hour that you're not spending on an experience that you choose purely for the sake of having that experience, whether or not anyone rewards you for it.

All work and no play is—and this ain't no lie—dull, dull, dull. Why would anyone want to talk to you? Why would you even want to talk to yourself? You need mental space to create and grow. You *need* leisure.

RECOVERING FROM BURNOUT

How many of these statements have applied to you?

I became someone I didn't like.
I wouldn't have hung out with myself.
I wasn't at the top of my game.
I couldn't balance work and family.
I never had enough time.
I was so tired I couldn't think straight.
I had no life.

This pattern of conflict and stress almost always leads to burnout. You can't focus; you can't get your work done; you can't bring yourself to care. Your inability to get your work done makes it impossible to enjoy your time outside the office.

But here's one of the mysteries of the art of leisure—you get more work done if you let yourself take meaningful time off.

The more stressful your job is, the more you need to treasure the precious commodity of leisure time. Unemployment can be an unexpected blessing to the burned-out, because it gives you the leisure time you need to re-center yourself and re-focus on the things that are really important to you.

Unemployment gives you the time to imagine an entirely new future for yourself—maybe a future that's the polar opposite of what you've been doing. If you were miserable behind a desk, maybe you should leave it for something more adventurous—commercial fishing, substitute teaching, or your own freelance business. If your financial situation requires you to find another job in the same less-than-ideal field, you can still take some time to identify the lessons you learned from your last position, and figure out what worked for you and what didn't.

ROLES AND RELATIONSHIPS

Are work relationships more important to you than your relationships with your family and friends? More important than being a good citizen of your community? Are you a different person at work than at home?

Your job may not define you, but it does put you into certain relationships with other people, and many people allow their relationships with work and co-workers to overshadow everything else. Working hard may have helped you advance financially or climb a corporate ladder but what effect did it have on your family, your neighborhood, or your broader community?

If you've been sacrificing your personal relationships to the false idol of Work, you'll need to replace it with something when it topples. Unemployment presents an ideal opportunity to figure out who you are and how you relate to the people around you, whether they're former colleagues or family members. You can also give more thought to where your efforts will be most productive in the long term.

wasted leisure time

Too often, the burned out ooze home, spend four unproductive hours in front of the television, and drag themselves back to the office the next morning. Work becomes an escape from home and home an escape from work.

"I kept going for more money," former work-junkie Mary Mangold told us. "I got a really nice apartment, lived in a good neighborhood, bought designer clothes, with no energy to do anything. When I came home it was time to sleep. I might as well have been living in a closet."

This is not a minor problem. This is a tragedy, and the underlying syndrome has been dubbed *wasted leisure time*. Inoculate yourself!

The skills you learn in the workplace are useful in many other aspects of your life. Management and organizational skills can help you run a civic league, coach a softball team, even run for local office. Negotiating skills can help you start your own business, serve as a youth counselor, be a Big Brother or Big Sister. Likewise, the energy you used to direct towards work will now seem like a tremendous gift to your family and your friends.

It's all about balance. Unemployment can be your chance to reset the scales and find the balance that works for you.

DEEP THOUGHTS ON LEISURE

As a student of leisure, you may want to explore its long history to fully understand its awesome power. In the wrong hands, leisure can be a dangerous weapon used to sedate the masses. In the right hands, leisure has been responsible for many of the glories of civilization. We're not the only purveyors of leisure—you'll learn in **Chapter 10** where you can even earn a degree in Leisure Studies!

What is Leisure?

Leisure means different things to different people. Scholars believe that leisure did not exist until we humans, as a species, were able to meet our basic survival needs. While anthropologists have observed tribes that mix work and leisure across every aspect of life, most societies create a sharp distinction between the two.

Most people would agree that work is what we *must* do; leisure is what we *want* to do, which explains why some employers see leisure as a threat. Given the means, they fear, employees would never show up to work. "How can we compete with leisure?" Henry Ford once asked. How indeed!

When it's not positioned as work's enemy, leisure is sometimes seen as the ultimate reward. Ask people what they would do if they won the lottery and the answers are usually leisure-related—traveling, going on cruises, eating in fancy restaurants, going to the theater. Not working. On television, the stars of soap operas and sitcoms do the same things—again, not working. These leisure images, however, tend to be cost-intensive and often promise an enhanced social and sexual status for their consumers.

In many languages, the word that means "leisure" connotes laziness, suggesting that leisure is something shameful. We beg to differ. Our definition of leisure is something else altogether:

The Leisure Faithful's
DEFINITION OF LEISURE

A state of fulfillment, freedom, intrinsic motivation, and non-instrumentality.

• • •

Zen, "flow," or "being in the zone."

• • •

Any activity chosen for its own sake, for the experience itself.

Leisure Is Not Laziness

We strongly support lounging around—in fact, it's one of our commandments—but we don't agree that lounging around is unproductive. Research has repeatedly found that people who spend less time at the office are more productive than those who spend extra hours at work. We believe that the leisurely are more productive in all facets of their lives.

Today's leisure activities demand both attention and effort. Taking a class, volunteering, starting a home-based business, or playing a competitive game of racquetball takes time, skill, and energy, and produces visible results. Even pure loafing can "produce" a newly-refreshed self.

When you understand the energy that leisure demands, you see that the distinction between "have to" and "want to" isn't valid, and shouldn't be. The best work is work you want to do; the best leisure is a conscious decision to improve your life, or at least your state of mind. At its best, leisure is choosing what fulfills you, and then pursuing it for all you're worth—and that's *self*-worth, not net worth. Which brings us to another misconception about leisure.

Leisure Doesn't Require Big Bank

The consumer-economy version of leisure is fine for what it is and at times can hit the spot as conveniently as Club Med or a Starbucks

we're number one!
(but do we want to be?)

Americans now have longer work weeks and less vacation time than workers in any other industrialized country, according to the United Nation's International Labor Organization.

That's right, we work harder—by almost two weeks a year—than the Japanese. American workers average almost 2000 hours a year. This substantially exceeds the work weeks of industrial Europe: the British work 1,731 hours a year, the French 1,656, the famously industrious Germans only 1,560 hours a year, and those lucky Norwegians work only 1,399 hours!

The countries with work weeks most similar to ours are the developing nations—Sri Lanka, Thailand, Malaysia—where underpaid workers are scrambling to improve their quality of life to reach our level. We, on the other hand, have no such excuse.

So much for "first world" evolution!

double latté, but you can always find leisure without spending much money. Researchers say that most leisure takes place in and around the home, and they confirm that what's most important to people are interactions with their loved ones and activities they've invested time in. You don't need much money in order to spend time with your family and friends, learn a musical instrument, or improve your basketball game. Just like love, many of your greatest leisure moments will be things that money just can't buy.

Nor is leisure something to do after you've taken care of your basic needs. As far as we're concerned, leisure *is* a basic need—it's crucial to progress and the evolution of advanced society. The great achievements of civilization require large amounts of downtime to generate new ideas.

In the words of *The Story of Leisure* authors, "Free time, constructively used, advances society, enriches individual life, and produces massive cultural development over time." All major arts and sciences, especially the humanities, developed from the creative use of leisure.

Leisure Is For The People

We reject the ancient Greek philosophers' view that leisure should be available only to the elite few. We say that leisure is available everywhere and to everyone, by the masses and for the masses—especially for the unemployed, and especially in San Francisco.

GREAT MOMENTS IN UNEMPLOYMENT

GAME AFTER GAME

During the Depression years of the early 1930s, an unemployed salesman living in Pennsylvania developed a strange new board game while struggling with odd jobs to support his family. The inventor? Charles Darrow. The game? None other than Monopoly. Parker Brothers bought the rights to Monopoly in 1936, but Darrow shrewdly negotiated a royalty payment for every game sold. Darrow's entrepreneurial instinct and refusal to buckle despite being out of steady work made him a millionaire, the first game developer ever to have made as much money. • • • The game Scrabble came from similar origins. Alfred M. Butts, an unemployed architect looking to play a game that required equal skill as chance, created the predecessor to Scrabble in 1931. It would take until 1948 for him and his business partner to get the word out and begin manufacturing Scrabble in its modern form. The game has since become an international phenomenon—over 100 million sets have been sold in 121 countries—and early royalties to Butts allowed him to retire. Although Butts enjoyed playing the popular board game until his death in 1993, he wasn't a particularly good player. The reason? Por speling.

A BRIEF HISTORY OF LEISURE

Those Greek philosophers were among the first apostles of leisure, although they reserved it for a lucky few. In Greek society, which glorified learning and contemplation, the elite were supposed to use their leisure (gained at others' expense) to govern. Leisure came with great responsibility.

Romans democratized leisure with the Circus Maximus but, paradoxically, only to pursue the goals of the political elite. Mass entertainment ("bread and circuses") was a tool to divert social protest and control the masses.

Although Thorstein Veblen popularized the concept of leisure in 1899 in *The Theory of the Leisure Class,* some would argue that our philosophy of leisure hasn't changed much since ancient times. Mindless activities like television, recreational shopping, and computer gaming can sap energy from endeavors that are potentially more satisfying and more significant, such as hobbies, sports, or political involvement.

And the sad truth is, we have even *less* free time than our ancestors did. The year-round work week is a modern invention, introduced during the Industrial Revolution. Pre-industrial societies may have been less wealthy but they were far more relaxed. Check out these work calendars:

SOCIETY	TIME OFF
Medieval England	One-third of the year, including long vacations at Christmas, Easter and midsummer; numerous saints and rest days; weeks-long "ales" to celebrate marriages, deaths, harvests, and other occasions
Medieval France	52 Sundays, 90 rest days, 38 holidays
Medieval Spain	Five months every year
Late Rome (mid-4th century C.E.)	175 public festival days every year
Ancient Rome	109 of 355 days designated "unlawful for judicial and political business"
Ancient Athens	50 to 60 holidays

Adapted from *The Overworked American* by Juliet Schor.

After industrialization, the American work week began to decline again, ultimately to half its Industrial Revolution peak. Henry Ford was the first major industrialist to institute a 40-hour work week and labor union activism in the U.S. and Europe cut working hours further, with the decline continuing through the Great Depression.

The end of the Second World War, however, created a new boom not only in the standard of living but also in the working hours required to achieve it. It's not an exaggeration to say that we'd reached a crisis of leisure time by the end of the 20th century.

IT'S A CRISIS—DO SOMETHING!

So what are you going to do about your own leisure crisis? Act now to save the endangered leisure race!

We're not overstating it. Between 1969 and 1987, the average employee added almost a month to the working year. Maintaining our standard of living has demanded that we work more and more hours. Most Americans now work more than 55 hours a week, not counting housework or child care. A late 1990s Harris Poll found that leisure time, conversely, had dropped almost 40 percent, to slightly less than 17 hours a week.

How can this be when we have all this technology that's supposed to make our lives easier?

LEISURE FAITHFUL TO THE RESCUE

Why *are* we working so hard? One answer is obvious: to buy stuff.

It's not the only reason, but it's clear that "keeping up with the Joneses" requires us to value money and material goods over time and experience—the key ingredients of leisure. Acquiring an abundance of goods almost always means sacrificing leisure time.

On the bright side, once you identify the source of a problem, it's easier to address it. And more good news is that the leisure movement *is* showing signs of strength. A September 2002 Harris Poll found that for the first time in almost 30 years, Americans were working significantly less—only 47 hours a week in 2001 as opposed to 50 hours a week in 2000. (Curiously, leisure hours didn't go up as work hours went down; since 1999, leisure time has held steady at 20 hours a week.)

The rising unemployment rate certainly had something to do with this. Did it take an economic downturn to pry people away from their desks? For whatever reason, our society is just now reawakening to the value of leisure, and rightfully craving more of it.

simplicity

More a community than a political movement, voluntary simplicity caught hold in the Pacific Northwest in the early 1990s and has moved across the country. The Trends Research Institute estimates that between 10-12% of Americans now practice some form of voluntary simplicity and predicts that this number will continue to rise.

Some practitioners believe that simplicity requires the rejection of consumerist ideals, a commitment to social justice, or the embracing of a low-environmental impact lifestyle. We prefer—well, a *simpler* view of simplicity, like the way the ***Simplicity Network*** (*www.simpleliving.net*) describes it:

"Simple living… is not about poverty or deprivation. It is about discovering what is 'enough' in your life—based upon thoughtful analysis of your lifestyle and values—and discarding the rest."

Even those of us who *have* jobs are beginning to tire of spinning their wheels just to get more stuff. The work-spend cycle is exhausting. The powerful systemic forces pressuring individuals to work so hard (take for example, our current President's solution to turning around our economy: everybody just go shopping!) are forces that only political action can countervail. But for many of us, especially in San Francisco, that philosophy comes with political underpinnings that we reject. The political elements that favor less work, less stuff, and more inner peace never really left San Francisco, and they're now poised for a major revival.

THE WORLDWIDE LEISURE MOVEMENT

A revolt of sorts is taking place around the world—a revolt against non-stop, all-consuming work. If 40 hours a week is full-time, what is 60 hours a week? Young Japanese called "Freeters" don't want to know. Neither do the "Happy Unemployed" in Germany.

Yet, the U.S. lags behind in this leisure movement. More than any other citizenry, we have the potential to shorten work hours and increase leisure. Employees like it and employers don't seem to lose productivity because of it. Given all that, you have to ask—why don't we?

There are a few shining rays of hope—promising proponents Joe Robinson, author of *Work to Live*; the Shorter Work Hours Movement; the Simplicity Movement; Take Back Your Time Day—all lead the charge. More are sure to follow.

Climb on board, the leisure locomotive is leaving the station...

CHAPTER 2
COMING TO GRIPS

Leisure is the most challenging responsibility a man can be offered.

~William Russell

So you're unemployed, or you're thinking about taking the big unemployment plunge. Allow us to be the first to say, welcome. Congratulations, even.

Take a deep breath and relax, for you've reached a zone that's at once exhilarating and unsettling. Your first challenge will be coming to grips with your new status. Getting past guilt or feelings of inadequacy, however, is easier said than done.

Feeling ill at ease with the concept of taking time off is perfectly normal in our work-centric society. Remember, taking the friction out of *frictional unemployment* doesn't mean that you're planning on never working again. It does mean that until you're ready to work again—and work is ready for you—you can unwind, have fun, and make good use of your freedom. So put your watch away, chuck your Palm Pilot into a drawer, and learn to embrace your life off the clock.

FREE YOUR MIND

Eric Bannister's dad (name changed) got laid off and decided to stay *retired.* He got so bored he was often spotted outside vacuuming his driveway—with the hose attachment! At the other end of the spectrum, Axel Gregoriou (name changed) rapidly wound himself into a ball of angst, convinced he'd lose his home and family before he found another job. Neither found much joy in unemployment—at least initially.

While some people take time off in stride, those who don't hit the strike zone right away are definitely not alone. Most people go through some sort of grieving process to get over the shock of joblessness.

Five Steps of Unemployment Grieving

Ever heard of "The Five Stages of Grief" from Elisabeth Kubler-Ross's book, *On Death and Dying,* or seen the movie "All That Jazz"? If you feel like you're going through a similar mourning process, it's because you are. You're mourning your former employed self.

The good news is, the unemployment grieving process has a much happier ending. It goes something like this:

DENIAL

I'm not unemployed—I'm simply "between jobs."

Denial is fairly common in people who feel pressure to be working constantly and feel unproductive if they're not. Some people lie to themselves; others experience such shame that even if they don't outright lie to family and friends, they conveniently fail to mention that they've quit or been laid off.

ANGER

That @&%$ Employer!
I never liked working there anyway.
*I hope that f****** organization goes under.*

Some people get angry about their predicament, lashing out at former employers, the economy, the government, or anyone else in range. Instead of embracing and enjoying time off, they expend a great deal of energy being mad at the world.

BARGAINING
I'll trade you half my old salary for my previous job.

Many try to bargain their way out of unemployment, either by trying to hang on to their old job under less desirable circumstances or settling for a job that's beneath their abilities and pay scale.

DEPRESSION
This sucks—I'll never find another job.

Depression afflicts the newly-unemployed more than any other emotion. Don't fall for it! See "Cures for the Blues" later in this chapter.

ACCEPTANCE
I'm at peace with my non-working status. Now, please pass the hookah.

Acceptance is your goal if you want to get the most from your non-working time. It's a Zen thing that will come fairly naturally when you've become versed in the *art of leisure.*

Dealing with Guilt

Guilt is evil. Guilt is your enemy. Guilt stands between you and your happiness and could be your greatest obstacle in reaching unemployed enlightenment. You must fight it off at all costs! We implore you, do not let it grab hold of your psyche; it can spoil an otherwise savory time of relaxation and self-fulfillment, and cause you to cut this precious time short.

my company is f'd...

During the wave of technology layoffs that followed the demise of the "dot-com bubble," many former employees reacted with anger at the sudden and sometimes callous ways in which companies handled the layoffs. Talk about *frictional unemployment*! Some of the laid-off created websites as "venting" vehicles for this resentment, the most famous of which was *www.fuckedcompany.com.**

The site began as a clever point-scoring game where visitors could report on companies that were currently or soon to be "fucked" but quickly evolved (or de-volved, some would say) into a place where bitter employees or ex-employees aired their company's woes. Postings often revealed internal documents and memos that highlighted company mismanagement or disclosed embarrassing information about company executives.

The site peaked in the fall of 2001, with a reported 300+ new postings each day.

** F'd Company has a new book:* ***F'd Companies: Spectacular Dot-Com Flameouts,*** *by Philip Kaplan.*

Give yourself a break, both figuratively and literally. This is your time and your life. As long as you can maintain financial stability (see **Chapter 3**), you're entitled to do as you please. Transitional times are tough enough without putting unnecessary pressure on yourself.

Liberate yourself from the "must-work" mentality and instead of berating yourself for your current status, congratulate yourself. *Sit* for a while. Celebrate your standing in the unemployed world!

The Unemployment Time-Space Continuum

The Unemployment Time-Space Continuum is a loosely formed concept that goes something like this:

1. You will be late.
2. You will forget non-essential appointments.
3. It's okay.

Time becomes much more fluid when you're not working, and you'll find yourself on a completely different clock. Don't be alarmed if you're convinced it's Monday when it's really Tuesday. A severe case will have you thinking it's a weekend when it's not. Just don't look for any sympathy from your working friends!

It's also normal that you won't make it to every appointment or task that you set for yourself. The reality is, you don't *have* to do anything—at least, not in a work sense—and human nature tends to breed apathy in the absence of necessity.

This is, again, okay. Don't get overly upset or feel guilty, but do monitor your personal flake factor. Skipping out on your friends or colleagues is hardly anything to aspire to during a sabbatical.

AVOID THE COMPLEX

Guilt is one of the most common emotions associated with unemployment, says Rochelle Teising, co-founder of the San Francisco-based consulting group Success at Work. "It's really hard for people to see the gift in not working," she says, "because they often think that they've done something wrong. They don't let themselves enjoy the time off." Many of her clients try to alleviate this guilt by immersing themselves entirely in their job search, not allowing time for leisurely activities, and driving themselves crazy in the process. Don't let that be you!

HOUSEKEEPING

Psychological challenges aside, you should deal with several logistical issues right away. Unemployment can trip up the unsuspecting neophyte. Here are a few tips to smooth your transition.

Severance

Did you negotiate a severance package when you were hired (or in *aspiring retired* mode)? It might not be too late either to start from scratch or to improve the one you have. Your severance package should cover not only the severance amount but also things like benefit continuation, prorated bonus, and vesting of a portion of any stock or options—as well as spelling out the circumstances under which you'll be entitled to receive severance in the first place.

know your rights

Do you suspect you were unfairly laid off? ***Nolo Press*** (950 Parker Street, Berkeley, 510-704-2248, 800-728-3555, *www.nolo.com*) recently released the sixth edition of the popular book, *Your Rights in the Workplace,* by Barbara Kate Repa.

Nolo offers a few nuggets of free legal advice on their website, too.

Consulting either of these sources might help you size up whether your employer followed all the rules when sizing down.

how i found out i was laid off

During the recent burst of the high tech "bubble," apocryphal stories of layoffs abounded in the Bay Area. The scary stories weren't *all* true, but these are:

Andrew Riley, who was working for a small technology firm, told us that his boss had the nerve to invite him to his favorite bar for a beer—and then lay him off between sips!

Mary Mangold, a former account executive for E*TRADE, didn't have the comfort of her neighborhood watering hole to soften the blow. She simply arrived at her office one morning to find her computer gone and her desk cleared. "That was my first clue," she said wryly, "that something wasn't quite right."

Layoffs didn't take Joel by surprise. He got tipped off that they were coming the next day, so he brought a disposable camera to work to document the scene. "I hid the camera under the table while the flash was warming up," he told us. "The shots didn't turn out too clear but they sure caused a stir." Management kept complaining that Joel was trying to "make a case"—for who knows what!

And a whole group of unlucky employees who got laid off from a small tech company in one fell swoop were then marched over to a table in the corner where the *San Francisco Chronicle* was offering a special deal: half-price on new subscriptions for the recently unemployed.

Get it in writing. Severance can occur after a takeover, a new boss, an economic downturn or any other job-changing event, and can be paid either as a lump sum or a salary continuation.

Healthcare

Unless you're willing to roll the cosmic dice, you'll need insurance to protect yourself against major injury or illness.

If you've recently left a company that offered a health insurance plan, you qualify for COBRA, the national program designed to ensure continued coverage for workers after they leave a company. Paying a monthly premium will guarantee you the same coverage you were receiving *before* you left for up to 18 months *after* you leave. The rub: you'll have just a brief window of time to decide whether you want COBRA coverage. For tips on whether to elect COBRA or some other kind of insurance, see **Chapter 3**.

Retirement Plans

If you had a 401(k) or some other retirement plan with your former employer, you might be forced to do something with the funds. Many plans or companies will continue to administer your retirement funds if they exceed a minimum threshold amount. Otherwise, you should probably roll over the funds into an IRA to avoid early withdrawal penalties. See **Chapter 3** for more information on retirement plans.

Stock Options

You'll normally have a fixed amount of time to exercise vested, unexercised stock options after you leave a company, or forfeit them altogether.

For publicly traded stock, your decision will be straightforward: if the current stock price is higher than your option "strike" price, exercise the options. You can then either sell them all immediately and bank the profits; sell just enough to cover the cost of exercise (a partial-sale); or, if you can afford it, hold all the stock until you want to sell.

If the company is pre-IPO, the choice is less obvious. To exercise the options, you'll have to cut your company a check with no immediate chance to recover any costs by selling. If the company never goes public, the stock could end up being worthless. Double-check your paperwork to verify how much time you'll have to decide. You may want to wait until the last minute to see how the company is faring—particularly if you left as part of a large layoff!

Keep in mind that exercising stock options represents a taxable

pink slip: fact or fiction?

The term "pink slip" has long been used to refer to an employee's termination. It's even in most dictionaries. But where did the term come from?

The traditional theory is that once upon a time, companies issued employee termination notices on pink slips of paper. At the Henry Ford Motor Company, managers reputedly placed slips of paper in workers' cubbyholes at the end of each day—white meant their work was acceptable, pink meant they were out the door.

Neither theory has been verified, according to ***Snopes.com***, a popular website that researches urban legends. Snopes reports that Peter Liebhold, a curator at the Smithsonian Institution's National Museum of American History, has searched for ten years to find an actual pink slip but so far hasn't found one. While the concept of "getting the pink slip" is very real to certain unlucky workers, the origins of the term remain a mystery.

event, whether the company is publicly traded or privately held. That means you could have a substantial tax liability even *before* you sell. Your tax burden will depend on the fair market value of the stock on the date that the options are exercised and whether your options are qualified ("ISOs") or non-qualified ("NSOs"). You'll want to consult a tax adviser, preferably one who has experience with stock options (not all do). Remember to keep exact records of when you exercise

BEFORE TURNING IN YOUR BADGE

If you're facing an impending layoff or have just plain had it with your job, take these important steps before you walk out the door:

• ***Transfer Your Contacts.*** Whether it's a pile of old business cards or a comprehensive database, your contact information could be the most important asset you leave work with. Backup this information so that you can access it once you're no longer with the company—provided, of course, that your employer's confidentiality policy allows you to do so.

• ***Transfer Your Personal Files.*** If you're like most workers, you have personal files mixed in with business files. Separate them out and take them with you. Security policies might apply here, especially if you're walking out the door with a box of documents.

• ***Set Up a Personal E-mail Account.*** If you haven't already, get a personal e-mail account and let friends and associates know before you leave that your contact information will change.

• ***Settle All Financial Reimbursements.*** If you can, have the company cut you a check for any money they owe you before you walk out that door. This includes salary, travel expenses, or any other reimbursable expenses you've incurred.

• ***Don't Sign Anything!*** Don't sign a parting agreement—including a severance package—that you're unsure about until you've had a chance to review it thoroughly. At a minimum, take it home with you to evaluate outside of your work environment. Better yet, have a lawyer look it over and advise you on how to proceed.

your options, and how many shares you bought. For more on taxes, see **Chapter 3**.

Direct Deposit

If your former employer deposited your paycheck directly into your bank account, you may get socked with monthly fees once those direct deposits end (curses to fake-free-checking banks!). A quick phone call can let you know whether your bank will be charging you fees and whether you can avoid them by switching to a different type of account.

AFTER THE HONEYMOON

If you're like most unemployed people, it's been a long time since you've had your weekdays free. After a few weeks of pure enjoyment (the *unemployed honeymoon*), waking up with boundless energy, you might start to wonder what retired people do with their whole day. You run the risk of losing motivation, getting too much sleep and (doh!) actually watching daytime television. Here are better options.

Things to Do

Ever wished you had a personal assistant? Now you do—yourself. Spend some time on personal life maintenance.

Start with getting "stuff" done. Clean the closets. Shine your shoes. Alphabetize the spice rack if you've been wanting to. Everyone keeps a running tally of "nice to dos" that aren't urgent but can stack up like dishes in a sink. Checking them off of your list will clear your mind (or at least the table!) for more advanced leisure pursuits.

sf specials

Motor on over to Howard Street and challenge those parking tickets. Few people take the time, but those who do are often rewarded to the tune of 50% off of the total fines owed—just for showing up! Get the skinny on how and where from:

San Francisco Department of Parking and Traffic
1380 Howard
415-255-3900 for citations
www.ci.sf.ca.us/dpt

Any small claims you'd like to collect? Perhaps a pesky misdemeanor or two to clear up? The ***Superior Court of California, County of San Francisco*** (*www.ci.sf.ca.us/courts*) can guide you through solving your "problem." (I drank. I fell down. What's the problem?)

Chris Hession took to the ambitious task of organizing his CD collection, first by alphabetizing the entire set and then by cataloguing a playlist of several hundred of his favorites—indexed by title and number—to keep active in his enormous CD player. Try tackling *that* project while you're working full-time!

Are your weekdays suddenly free? Then you'll have plenty of time for court appearances and runs to the DMV. Even jury duty might become a weekday "to do"—you can't really say no to it now! Make medical appointments, dental appointments, or any other appointment that you'd normally have to squeeze into your lunch hour and cross them off of your list.

When you run out of errands to take care of for yourself, run daytime errands for your friends and neighbors: pick up their dry cleaning, walk their dog, or watch their kids. You'll score big-time brownie points. If they later offer to help you out by, say, buying you dinner, it'll be more like reciprocation and less like charity. Of course, when you tire of running errands (which will happen quite quickly, trust us), take the time to really enjoy yourself. See **Part Two** for a plethora of ideas.

Setting Goals

Once you've come down from the initial euphoria of your freedom from work, you may want to set some goals for yourself. If this sounds a bit ambitious, keep in mind that worthy unemployed goals can range from such lofty pursuits as travel or reading as many books as possible, to hanging a hammock in the backyard!

The point is—and you've heard the saying before—time flies when you're having fun. Before you know it, you'll be facing the prospect of work again. So outline what you'd like to accomplish, however grandiose or simple it may be, and prioritize your leisure.

PREPARING FOR CHALLENGES

Talking To Your Family

Families can be a real challenge when it comes to unemployment. Consciously or unconsciously, most families expect financial and career success of their members, and don't see taking time off as furthering those goals.

Are your parents on your case? Maybe they were raised in an era when unemployment carried even more of a stigma than it does today. To them and their generation, work was a large part of a person's identity and it was uncommon to leave a job without having a new one. For the most part, that generation didn't face the level of layoffs and employee turnover that characterize today's working environment. Constant change became a way of life towards the end of the baby boom—the U.S. Bureau of Labor Statistics reports that people born between 1957 and 1964 changed jobs an average of 10 times by

CURES FOR THE BLUES

Being unemployed can open up new worlds of freedom for you. Or, you might just find yourself sleeping too much, missing appointments and letting your laundry pile up. Beware! While we are all in favor of moving a little to the right on the *Unemployment Time-Space Continuum* (see p. 26), we do want you to feel like a million bucks, even if you don't actually *have* a million bucks.

Everyone's got a favorite cure for the blues. Working out is one—all forms of regular exercise combat depression, anxiety, stress, and sleeplessness through a massive release of the same chemicals in the brain that produce "runner's high" (see ***Chapter 7*** for fitness ideas).

Taking responsibility for another living creature also works. Marsha Converse got a dog. "It's not for the faint of heart," she told us, "and it was a long-term commitment, but it got me out and about in the neighborhood every single day."

Career counselor Rochelle Teising recommends music and dance, observing, "You cannot be depressed when you're dancing." And Rob DeWaters went to the beach once a week, weather permitting. "Seeing San Francisco's beautiful women in various forms of undress always had a way of keeping my spirits up," he told us.

If you just can't break out of a funk, you might need some professional help. We can't make that call but mental health specialists can. They'll help you see the *layoff blues* for what they are—tired old tunes that you can do without.

the time they were 36 years old. It's a new type of generation gap, one that can leave you feeling like a disappointment to your parents.

Being married can also make unemployment more stressful. Many who are newly-unemployed fear that their spouses will see them as lazy or inept. Whether real or imagined, this perception can create barriers, conflict and even resentment between partners.

Add kids and the obligation to support them into the mix, and you could have real disaster. Career counselor Rochelle Teising says that communication within families is often poor during times of unemployment. Some of her clients are so ashamed of losing their jobs that they keep it a secret! The irony, says Teising, is that these people need to connect with friends and family more than ever.

So, take your family to leisure school! Explain to them your goals and intentions. Tell them why you're taking time off—even if it *is* largely to goof off. Your goal is to make them more comfortable with your not working, even if they don't necessarily agree with the concept, and to circumvent those awkward moments at the dinner table. For more about unemployment-in-the-family, see **Chapter 8**.

What To Say To Friends

Chances are, your friends will be more understanding than your family when it comes to taking time off. Ted Witt, a 33-year-old operations director until the summer of 2001, claimed that most of his friends were happy for him when he lost his job. "They knew I was miserable at work, and that I wanted to go and travel anyway. My parents, on the other hand, didn't quite see it the same way."

KEEP THE OLD

Don't let unemployment come between you and your friends; use it to re-connect. Not only will you have more flexibility but you'll be getting reacquainted with your non-work self—the self that your friends might have been missing.

Eileen and Alexia had fallen out of touch after college but they picked up right where they left off after Alexia quit her demanding day-job. "Eileen's a single mother," Alexia told us, "so she's got a lot of good ideas about how to have fun during the school day."

Get even more social with the ideas in ***Chapter 8***.

In many instances, however, even your true friends will say (or think), "You should be working like me," or "When are you going to go out and get a job? *Coaster!*" Being open with them is the best way to combat this resentment. Without explanation, your friends could translate "not working" into "lazy," "spoiled" or both! They might jump to the conclusion that you have a large trust fund or gift from your family, for example, when in reality, you were smart with your money and saved. Or maybe you do have a *leisure patron*—offer to help find them one too! (See **Chapter 3** for tips on how.) Who knows, you might even convince one of them to join you on your *unemployed odyssey*.

♪...Tell me why, I don't like Mondays--tell me why!

~Boomtown Rats
"I Don't Like Mondays"

Mondays

Conventional wisdom holds that Mondays are the toughest day of the week for the working set. Yet, Mondays can be strange for the non-working, too. Others go off to work, but not you, friend. Your weekend simply continues.

Nearly all of the people we spoke with who used to work nine-to-five experienced some sort of anxiety around Mondays. "Sometimes it's the best day and sometimes it's the worst day," says Dave Casuto, a recruiter from San Francisco who was unemployed for about six months in 2002. "It's the worst day because everyone's going to work, and you feel kind of useless. It's the best day because on Sunday night, you get that instinctive pang about work the next day, until you realize, 'Oh yeah, I don't have to go to work tomorrow.'"

Fiona Rogers (name changed), a software executive who quit her job to take a year off to travel and relax, says the first few Mondays were the weirdest. "I used to continue to wake up early and wonder what on earth people could do before 6am on a weekday—laundry? Working out? You can't really make any noise, because most other people who aren't up and going to work are still sleeping." Gradually, however, her restlessness subsided and soon she was able to enjoy her Monday mornings stress free.

Turn what could be the worst day of the week into the best. Make it your bonus day. Go to your favorite café and read a good book. Partake in your preferred workout. Do whatever it is you care to do, and set the tone for the rest of the week.

Having free Mondays is not only okay, it's cause for celebration. Embrace it! Revel in it! If you can conquer the Monday Blues, you'll be well on your way to reaching a higher unemployment plateau.

??????????

"what do you do?"

This all too familiar inquiry haunts the *leisure seeker*. Perhaps no other question is more indicative of our workaholic and often judgmental culture. It might come during a first meeting at a cocktail party or from an uncle at your brother's wedding but it always implies the same thing: what do you do *for work?*

The "what do you do" question clearly subscribes to the age-old "work as identity" doctrine. "We have become walking resumes," Geoffrey Godbey of Penn State once told the *New York Times*. "If you're not doing something, you're not creating and not defining who you are."

Next time someone asks you what you do, whether you're unemployed or not, try answering, "I enjoy life. And what do *you* do?"

Holidays and Special Occasions

Ah yes, the holidays. If ever a time was ripe for societal and familial pressures, this would be it. Over the holidays, you should be working, you should be dating, you should be marrying, you should be having kids! Whatever you should be doing, you should be doing it doubly over the holidays, making November through January your most challenging unemployed months.

If you can avoid succumbing to traditional pressures, however, the holidays can actually be a great time to be unemployed. Think about the bright side—stress-free Christmas shopping! Leslie Gonsalves, a recruiter who was out of work for four months beginning one November, savored the holiday season. While her friends could take off only an afternoon here and there, she could shop every day, enjoying the company of a different friend each time.

Beware of special occasions too. Birthdays and weddings can unite you with extended relatives and friends, but they'll want to know "what you're up to" or will throw out the infamous, "What do you do?"

Because holidays and special occasions can be such trying times, we recommend these tactics to minimize the damage:

• **Stay Out of the Corner**: Watch for family traps like the inevitable two-on-one gang-up. The minute you sense the conversation at the dinner table turning against you, bob and weave, anticipate and avert. Change topics quickly and deflect questions about your time off with your own questions in return.

Your mother:
*So, are you even **looking** for a job?*

You:
Mom, this cranberry sauce is fantastic. Did you make it from scratch?

• **Be Proactive**: The best defense is a good offense. Being the aggressor (in a leisurely manner, of course) means you won't get caught off guard and sound defensive. Have stock answers ready for questions about your transitional time, and offer information to head off awkward lines of questioning. It's "nothingness" that makes people uncomfortable.

Transitioning between careers, or thinking about it?
—I'm taking a class.
—I'm doing some research.

No such ambitions?
—I'm exploring my creativity.
—I'm writing my memoirs.

preemptive strike

One unemployed gentleman we know took the bull by the horns, as had always been his secret yen (you'll see...).

He was so tired of fielding questions on what he was doing for work, what his plans were for the future, etc., that, in anticipation of a friend's wedding, he drafted a one-page personal fact sheet. The sheet mockingly explained that he had left his last job to "pursue other interests," including his "dream to someday be a rodeo clown."

He handed out copies at the beginning of the reception, forcing everyone in attendance to focus on other areas of interest in his life—whether they wanted to or not! While it might not have dramatically changed anyone's opinion of him, he did manage to score a date with a cute coed.

• **Know Your Allies**: Know who will rush to your defense in tight situations. Your protectors are usually the people who know you best, and they can help fend off the work-centric attacker from advancing within your comfort zone. Defense in numbers is almost always more effective than a solitary defense. Unite with the Leisure Team!

The January Effect

January is to the year what Monday is to the week. The holidays are over. Vacations have ended. People have gone back to work. But not you, and this can be unsettling. Although Leslie Gonsalves enjoyed having time off during the holidays, the opposite was true once January rolled around. Low on funds and with potential employers back at work, she no longer had any excuse to put off her job search efforts.

Stand fast and do not waver, for yours is a mission of quality of life, not of logging in as many work hours as you can. January can be the month to use your flexible schedule to set personal goals and decide how you want to spend your free time.

Tailor your New Year's resolutions to what you want to accomplish over the coming months: pledge to transition to a new career by taking classes or applying to graduate school, for example, or just resolve to enjoy your time off!

Losing Friends from Work

One potential side effect of being job-free is losing your friends from work. You could be surprised to discover that your relationships with these people you spent so much time with were bound by the job and not much else.

This realization can be unpleasant, particularly if much of your social life was wrapped around your workplace. We talked to several people who had difficulty filling the void left by their work-friends, because they had spent so much time at work that their non-work relationships had languished.

Be prepared to confront this issue by making an extra effort to keep in touch with former co-workers. This is your chance to put more energy into friendships outside of work, too (see **Chapter 8** for ideas).

Too Much Sleep

Sleeping too much can leave you drowsy all day and lead to depression. Try to get up on the early side and start your day with something physically active to get your blood pumping. While there's no need to imitate the army (you know—getting more done before 9am than most people do all day), there's nothing wrong with getting one thing done early—wash last night's beer mugs, maybe?—or at least take a shower!

SURPRISE!

Don't worry, unemployment also brings plenty of pleasant surprises. Besides having more time to catch up with old friends, you'll feel more relaxed and you'll probably become a kinder, gentler person. Your refreshed demeanor can lead to many other subtle benefits, such as improved restaurant service, better rapport with law enforcement officials ("You don't really need to write me that ticket, do you officer?"), and smiles from strangers on the street.

HOW MUCH TIME?

Wondering how long to stay unemployed? That's easy—as long as possible! If you have financial stability, peace of mind, and a good story to go with it, you can justify almost any length of time away from work. Employers are changing their attitudes towards extended breaks and that's something we can all be glad for.

top ten accomplishments of the recently unemployed

The recently unemployed have some impressive stories. Here are our ten faves:

10 Ann Marsh, a writer going through a career transition, went on more than 100 dates in six months, and found her man!

9 Andrew Riley scored a much coveted spot as Mr. May in the "Men of the Black Horse Bar" 2002 calendar—after being laid off in the very same bar.

8 Leslie Gonsalves got her carpets as "clean as they've ever been" by cleaning them for *three days straight*.

7 Steve Friedman, a former software VP, furnished his entire vacation house—with furniture he built by hand.

6 Anastasia Shilling moved to the central coast of California and became the local "chocolate fairy."

5 Heidi Wells learned Spanish on location in Xela, Guatemala, in just three months.

4 Dana Magenau, on a one-year trek around the world, climbed some of the world's highest peaks in Africa, South America, and Asia.

3 Scott Phillips, on a partially paid sabbatical, moved to his wife's hometown in Prague for a year, and road-tripped across Croatia along the way.

2 Jim Treman, with his girlfriend Jennifer, spent six months traveling and surfing his way through Indonesia, Africa, and Madagascar.

And the number one accomplishment of the recently unemployed... *[go on, flip the page!]*

1 Rob DeWaters, during a one-year stint of unemployment in San Francisco, managed to perfect the arts of newspaper reading, MP3 downloading, and tanning. **Congratulations, Rob!**

Jamie Alfaro, a human resources specialist and professional recruiter for the past ten years, says that the amount of time off employers view as "acceptable" depends on the circumstances. "In a challenging job market such as 2002," Jamie says, "hiring managers wouldn't even question a candidate whose job search took a year or more. In a red-hot economy, however, a candidate should have a very clear explanation for time off, and be able to talk intelligently about it."

In a stagnant economy, any time shorter than six months is almost self-explanatory. Between six months and a year, you should probably have a good story about why you haven't taken a job sooner.

Most employers consider travel a legitimate use of six months. Being able to afford your respite also sells well. Matt Green, a former software sales executive, says, "I always mentioned in interviews that I could afford to take time off. Once people heard that, they understood, and I also gained credibility that I had made a little money in my life."

After a year, according to most career experts, you'll be better off having either completed some kind of project or taken care of a medical or family situation. The good side of taking a year off is that you'll be thoroughly rested for your next job. The challenge will be finding a compelling way to describe it if you simply enjoyed yourself while living off your savings.

Did we mention savings? It's obviously a key factor. If you want to take a long leave but wonder whether it'll fly financially, don't give up too easily. Even if you have a financial goal beyond covering your cost of living—such as buying a house—set a minimum under which you won't let your savings drop, then enjoy yourself until then.

THE PIGGY BANK

Whatever you decide, you *will* need to get a solid grip on your expenses, because the fear of running low on cash or missing your financial goals can seriously bum your hiatus high. Read on for tips on how to cut costs, as well as generate some interim leisure bucks.

CHAPTER 3
FINANCES

Perchik: *Money is the world's curse.*
Tevye: *May the Lord smite me with it!*
And may I never recover!
~Fiddler on the Roof

They say money can't buy happiness?
Look at the smile on my face. Ear to ear, baby.
~Jim Young (Ben Affleck), Boiler Room

MONEY. Whether you can't get enough of it or think it's the root of all evil, probably no single factor troubles or eases the unemployed mind more. It's no fun to be unemployed and broke, so if you're going to take time off, you're going to need some money to do it—it's as simple as that.

In the best case scenario, financial planning for time off starts while you're still working. Saving money for a rainy day (or better yet, a sunny day!) is a critical step to enjoying your non-working time. A budget will come in handy whether or not you can plan ahead. The first section of this chapter, **Finance 101**, covers these topics.

In the worst case scenario, unemployment comes unexpectedly and sticks you in a financial bind. Don't panic. Even if you have just a small financial cushion, there are many ways to maximize your standard of living without a steady paycheck. You can scale back your discretionary expenses and, with a little more discipline, cut some of your fixed expenses too. You can even reduce your tax bill! If you have debt, you can deal with it proactively. **Finance 202** covers all of these ways to "play defense" and conserve your cash.

Finance 303 gets to the "offense:" bringing some funds your way. We include information on an array of funding sources—from severance packages and unemployment insurance to odd jobs—plus information on loans, grants, and proceeds from selling your things.

Be prepared—this is one looonnnnnng chapter. Give yourself plenty of time to digest it. It's dense, but it's important, so cancel all your plans and get your slide rule handy... Seriously, if you need a break, sneak a peek at the fun stuff in **Part Two: The Unemployed Odyssey**.

FINANCE FUNDAMENTALS

$ — Pay off as much debt as you can

$ — Build a cash reserve

$ — Line up several sources of credit, in case you need emergency funds

FINANCE 101

PLANNING & BUDGETING

Most financial advisors recommend stashing three to six months' salary in the bank to protect against the unexpected. How much do you have? How much will you need?

Your unemployed budget will depend on how long you want to take off and how you want to pass your time, especially if you want to travel. The good news is that the unemployed lifestyle costs less, so you'll be able to get by on less than you usually spend. This begs the question: how much do you usually spend?

Libraries are full of good books on personal financial planning. The recently published *Blindsided: Financial Advice For The Suddenly Unemployed,* by Edie Milligan, is a gem. We also recommend Stacy Johnson's *Life or Debt,* and the Federal Reserve Bank of Dallas's short yet free budgeting tutorial, "Building Wealth" (www.dallasfed.org, search for "Building Wealth"). If you want tips on how to plan a sabbatical, *Six Months Off* by Hope Dlugozima, James Scott, and David Sharp, is an excellent guide. Any of these resources can help you get a handle on your current spending, and they each offer ways to cut back.

Budgeting is fairly straightforward (and kind of a snore) but it does require some discipline. Are you up for the challenge? Keeping your goal in mind will help. If you're currently unemployed, you'll need to know how long you can milk your savings. If you're a member of the *aspiring unemployed,* you'll want to know just how long you'll have to save up before you can cut loose. In either case, budgeting is easier once you know how much you're currently spending.

Start by journaling your expenses for a full month. Track every last dime you spend—on morning coffee, afternoon snacks, cab fares, movie tickets, non-network ATM fees, everything. Include your housing and utilities costs, and make sure you record those "invisible" debit card charges by saving your receipts and tallying them up later. Save your credit card receipts too, and if you carry a revolving balance, budget for your minimum monthly credit card payments.

An Excel or Quicken spreadsheet can help show you where your money goes. You might also experiment with one of the free online financial calculators found at www.bankrate.com. Finally, even though it's a pain (and sometimes painful to see), remember to balance your checkbook.

With your expenses laid out on the table, you should be able to figure out where you spend your money. If you're curious how you compare to "average," see the table below. Then for a chuckle, compare your cost of living in San Francisco to the cost on October 20, 1904, when the *San Francisco Chronicle* reported that a family of 4 could get by on $14 a week, and rent ran a whopping $7 to $17 for a small three- to four-room flat.

Separate the necessary expenses from the discretionary ones, which are usually the easiest to cut and make the biggest impact on your budget. But you can reduce even your fixed expenses, as we'll explain, and you should cut them if you can. Wouldn't you rather spend that money on entertainment? Make realistic decisions and then stick to your new non-work budget.

THE LOCAL COST OF LIVING

In Spring 2002, San Francisco was only a hair less expensive to live in than Manhattan, according to the ACCRA Composite Index. The Index found that San Francisco was 84% more expensive than the average of 300 selected metropolitan areas in the United States. Only utility expenses were below average. Housing costs were way, way above average, so it's no surprise that housing typically consumes such a large proportion of a San Franciscan's budget.

AVERAGE SPENDING PROPORTIONS*

	Nationwide	San Francisco
Housing	28%	51%
Groceries	16%	12%
Healthcare	5%	4%
Utilities	8%	4%
Transportation	10%	7%
Other	33%	22%
TOTAL	100%	100%

*Approximate proportions, based on the spending proportions of the average American and on a 2002 cost of living index created by ACCRA (www.accra.org), now posted on various third party websites.

FINANCE 202

HOW TO CUT YOUR PERSONAL BURN RATE

Think of yourself as a company, with revenues and expenses as well as operating cash. If you're currently unemployed, your monthly revenue probably just dropped close to zero. You'll have to cut your expenses to make your operating cash last—which might sound strangely familiar to those of you who recently left a struggling startup! This means reducing the cost of things you need, and cutting the expenses you don't.

Alas, since some perks will have to get the axe, start with the small conveniences. Do you really need a cell phone *and* a landline? With call-waiting on both lines? Could you brew your own coffee instead of paying someone to brew it for you? Your nearest library branch probably has your favorite magazines and newspapers, so freeze or cancel your home subscriptions and spend some time amongst the book stacks instead. Consider putting your gym membership on hold too and get your exercise free by walking, biking, or running.

You get the idea. Each "convenience" charge may seem small on its own, but squandering two or three dollars here and there adds up over time. When you're feeling the pain of cutting back, call this truth to mind: every dollar of your savings that's spent on the luxury of convenience could be spent on extra time off instead.

start with the little things, finish rich

David Bach, a financial advisor and author of *Smart Couples Finish Rich*, told the Associated Press* that couples often stumble when the husband or wife loses a job. "They should be looking to cut their overhead 50 percent," Bach said. "But people don't do that. They cut back maybe by 5 percent, and the bills pile up."

**See "Advice for the Long-Term Unemployed" by Eileen Alt Powell, AP Business Writer*

renting roulette

The public can now rent former military housing in the ***Presidio*** (415-561-5454, *www.presidiotrust.gov*) and in ***The Villages on Treasure Island*** (415-834-0211, *www.homestore.com*). Low initial rents make this housing a great deal if you can live with some strings attached. For example: a two-bedroom, two-story townhouse with a yard rented for just $1650 a month on Treasure Island in 2002, but required a 12-month lease. Not all units are subject to rent control, either. You might also have to forego nearby amenities and suffer through a lengthy application process that can require "extras" such as a housing interest form, a large non-refundable deposit, or a criminal background check. Back in the positive column, some units in both locations have their own washer and dryer hookups, and tenants are generally allowed to keep one pet per household with an extra pet deposit. If all that suits your needs, renting at either locale could substantially reduce one of your biggest monthly expenses.

HOUSING

Running through half of the average San Francisco budget, housing is one area in which you can potentially save a bundle.

Reducing Rent

Are you a renter? Sixty-five percent of San Franciscans are. If you've lived in your place for a while, get up-to-date on what market rents are. They've gone down substantially as residential vacancies have gone up. "I moved to Alameda two years ago, at the height of the market," Claire Bannister, a legal assistant, told us. "Now I'm moving back. Rents in San Francisco are cheaper."

Many landlords have reduced rents when asked—some even *without* being asked. If your landlord isn't one of them, consider moving, especially if your place isn't subject to rent control (any place built after 1979 is exempt from the rules that put a cap on rent increases). With a large amount of vacant properties, you have a solid chance of finding one that's cheaper. Shaving even $100 off your $1,000/month rent could stretch your housing budget from nine months to ten. That's a full extra month of housing leisure!

Lowering Your Mortgage Payment

If you're fortunate enough to own your home, run—do not walk—to a lender to find out about refinancing. Mortgage rates are now at their lowest levels since the 1960s, but they're not likely to stay there for long.

A typical mortgage payment on the average home in San Francisco is about $4,000 a month; on the median SF home, it's $2,750. Talk to a lender to get an idea of whether or not refinancing will save you money. If you already have a reasonably low rate but your budget is still stretched, consider a variable rate. This type of refinancing might mean you only break even in the long run but it can reduce your payments now, when you really need the extra cash. You might also consider a cash-out refinance (see **Finance 303** for more details).

Buying a House Without Income

On Day Two of home ownership, Maureen Brown bought her first piece of hardware—a socket cover for 42 cents. She kept the receipt in case it was the wrong size. "I need the 42 cents," she said.

Needless to say, with zero income, you'll probably need savings to be able to purchase a home, but it can be done. When the building Maureen was living in came up for sale, she joined forces with her neighbors and bought it. She had enough savings to put down 25% plus cover the points and all the closing costs for the entire tenancy-in-common (TIC) partnership.

"With enough down, the lenders don't seem to care if you're not making any money," Maureen told us. Although her

**all i wanna do...
is have some fun!**

You might be in a real financial crisis. It would be simple to say, "Cut all discretionary expenses," but here's the problem: that's no fun. Now more than ever, you need a little fun.

Are you paying your mortgage with your credit card? Subsisting on rice and vegetables? Walking distances to rival Forrest Gump? If you don't see much humor in that, make sure you do find humor somewhere else.

Do not—repeat, do not—deprive yourself completely. Deprivation has a strange way of costing you extra in the long run.

Budget a monthly amount, small though it might be, for entertaining yourself. The investment you make in keeping up your spirits will surely pay off by keeping you motivated for other tasks—like resolving the crisis!

mortgage payments now consume almost 80% of the pay from her interim job, her down payment—combined with a superb credit report and the stated income of her partners ("who are not what I would call filthy rich")—allowed the TIC to take advantage of their lender's best rates.

Oh, and Maureen's mortgage broker didn't hurt. Catherine "The Loan Goddess" Tripp of **FiQuest Mortgage** (999 Brannan #206, 415-703-0990, www.fiquest.com) claims she can get anyone a loan. "If I can get an unemployed person a mortgage," she boasts, "I *must* be a Loan Goddess." And if you call after hours (ext. 16), that is indeed the greeting you'll hear.

there's no place like—*mom & dad's?*

When Mary Mangold realized that she was running out of savings, her bills were looming, and no jobs hovered on the horizon, she decided to move home.

"I was back in my old room with that ugly carpet and the horrible drapes that haven't changed in fifteen years," she said at the time. "I kept thinking, 'It's only going to last a month,' so I kept all my stuff in storage, but it's been over a year now and still counting."

The renter's market eventually rescued Mary; she's back in a one-bedroom apartment—at the same rent as she used to pay for a studio.

Moving Home With Mom and Dad

The drawbacks of moving back in with your parents are obvious: living under someone else's roof requires a sacrifice of a little independence and a lot of privacy. Still, more and more people are doing it.

If you're heading back to the nest yourself, prepare for some "casual" yet prying questions from your parents, particularly after you've spent a night out. Beware too of regressing to childlike and dependent behavior. Is your mom doing your laundry again? Your dad paying your phone bill? As well intentioned as they are, Mom and Dad can sap your drive to find work by making it too easy not to. You might want to keep track of any parental subsidies so you can pay them back later.

On the other hand, you might treasure the chance to spend quality time with your folks, especially if you've been living far away from them. "Moving back in was much to my mother's happiness," Mary confessed. "She never liked the idea of my moving away in the first place." Having someone to lean on financially might be just the break you need to stay afloat during your time off.

FOOD

Definitely one of the necessities of life.

Cooking at Home

Cooking at home can save you a lot of money. If this is not a new idea to you or you're already on your way to becoming a celebrity chef in your own right, guess who's coming for dinner?!

If you've had the inclination to cook but haven't had the time until now, this is the time to feed that desire (pun intended). At the extreme, someone who's used to having an expense account or in the habit of eating on the run might spend upwards of $1,000 a month on food. Eating every meal out, buying a couple of coffee drinks each day, and chipping in for cocktails with your friends can add up to a per diem of $50-plus, which might easily be as much as or more than your rent.

Shopping for your own food and cooking it at home can trim the fat from your food bill. See if you can match Marlo "The Balinese Gigolo" Sarmiento, who spent only $25 a week on food when he was in law school (see next page). That's less than the tip you might leave for a single dinner at Rubicon, a potential savings of $9,000+ a year. Now *that's* food for thought!

Budget Beveraging

Between mixed drinks, coffee drinks and bottled mystery waters, the beverages you consume can start consuming you, or at least your pocketbook. Save a few dollars through judicious imbibing.

It doesn't take heavy analysis to conclude that alcohol feeds you a lot of empty calories at a high expense. No need to teetotal—just partake a little less, or start your happy hour at home. When you're out, learn to nurse a single mixed drink all night or explore your affinity for warm, a.k.a. long-life, beer. Think of it as a survival skill that could come in handy if you return to a job that includes frequent office parties: while others become loose-lipped after too many cocktails, you'll be a model of decorum, and all ears for taking in intriguing inside information. If one drink per night is a little under your normal quota, let your employed friends pick up a couple of rounds—you can always even things out at a later date.

"Unleaded" drinks can cost just as much as the juiced-up ones. Are you addicted to caffeine? Do you spend $10 a day, $300 a month on coffee drinks? You will have more energy, more money and probably better health if you drink water instead. Skip the energy water, electrolyte water and other fitness drinks and try tap water. Carry a water bottle even. San Francisco tap water has tested at the highest quality levels for many years, thanks to our clean water source at Hetch Hetchy. That's something any budget beverager can be glad for.

Oh, okay, okay. Buy some beer or wine for drinking at home—as long as you shop wisely for it. Try **Beverages & more!** (3455 Geary, 415-933-8494, www.bevmo.com) or **Trader Joe's** (555 Ninth Street Retail Center, 415-863-1292; 3 Masonic @ Geary, 415-346-9964).

Food Budget Award Winner: THE BALINESE GIGOLO

Marlo Sarmiento ate on $25 a week by buying multi-purpose ingredients and catching his own fish. "Hey, if the people from the Mediterranean have been thriving on anchovy and sardines for millennia, why can't we?" he asks, noting that no license is required to fish off public piers like ***Fort Point***.

Marlo's weekly grocery bill included a $3 bag of rice, "not the Uncle Ben stuff," $4 on ground beef (or tofu), $2 on dry pasta, a $1 can of whole beans (pinto or kidney), $3 on fruit from Clement Street or Chinatown, $3 on onions & garlic, $3 on canned and fresh tomatoes, $2 on tortillas, $3 on cheese, and a buck on "miscellaneous" (spices, peppers).

With minimal investments in a crab net ($25), a rice cooker, a crock pot, and a cheap rod and reel set—"Gary at ***Sullivan's Sport Shop*** (5323 Geary, 415-751-7070) is really helpful in setting you up"—Marlo enjoyed a varied diet of spaghetti with fresh seafood sauce, fish tacos & burritos, chili, and seafood stir fry, supplemented with fresh fruit "as needed."

Marlo is currently living and working in Saipan, getting three eggs a day from his chickens Humu-humu, Nuku-nuku, and Apua'a, and tending to his coconut, papaya, and mango trees. "Fresh tuna, yellowfin, wahoo—all for $2/lb.," he reports. "Life is grand."

Drop Marlo a line for his recipes: *balinesegigolo@hotmail.com.*

Food Shopping

Even if you already cook at home, you can save more through judicious grocery shopping. Avoid the high-priced, small-volume specialty grocers, shop with a list to curtail impulse purchases, and escape huge markups on cleaning products by making your own, or even by shopping at a discount at a janitorial supply company (find one listed at www.thecityofsanfrancisco.org under "Janitorial Supply").

How about farmers' markets? Meals were a group effort not so long ago, when households shared refrigerators and stoves, and communal food-buying is enjoying a renaissance today. Farmers' markets offer fresh produce, open-air shopping and a casual place to socialize with your neighbors and the people who grow your food—not to mention the samples! Find details on market hours and location in the **Unemployed Shopping Guide**.

HEALTHCARE

Health Insurance

With healthcare costs on the rise and health insurance costs rising even faster, it might be time to consider whether you need all the HMO bells and whistles. If you're lucky enough to be in good health, look into "major medical" plans offered by providers such as Blue Cross of California, or HealthNet. These plans come with a high deductible—up to $5000 a year—and you'll have to pay for incidental checkups and prescriptions yourself, but you'll have the peace of mind that you will not have to deplete your own savings or bankrupt your family should some major accident befall you. Individual major medical plans can cost as little as $43 a month for both medical and dental coverage.

COBRA

Continuing healthcare coverage through your former employer's plan falls at the other end of the cost spectrum. COBRA, or the Consolidated Omnibus Budget Reconciliation Act (simply rolls off the tongue, doesn't it?), is the federal law that allows you to stay insured through your former employer for up to 18 months. The bad news is that you'll have to pay the premiums yourself, and they're usually expensive. The good news is that you have 60 days to decide whether you want to enroll. Within that period, coverage is retroactive—if you get sick on day 59, you can activate COBRA and be covered that same day.

If you're confident that you'll have a new job and therefore new health benefits within two months, you might skip paying for COBRA. But if you're not so sure or if you're going to be traveling out of the country (yeah!), don't wait. It's also not a good idea to wait if you have any preexisting conditions—a new insurer can refuse to cover treatment for that condition for up to a year if you can't prove that your coverage was continuous.

If you do elect for COBRA, you'll be legally entitled to health coverage through another company when your COBRA coverage expires, even if that same company refused to insure you before.

medi-cal

Medi-Cal might be an option for those who are low on income—even temporarily. Medi-Cal's government-imposed fee schedule is also low, though, which makes some doctors reluctant to see Medi-Cal patients. In a bind, Medi-Cal patients may have to seek medical care from a hospital emergency room.

See the online newsletter published by ***The Medi-Cal Policy Institute*** in Oakland (*www.medi-cal.org*) for the latest Medi-Cal news.

Community Health Clinics

San Francisco has at least twenty community health clinics. One of the more well known is the **Haight Ashbury Free Medical Clinic** (558 Clayton, 415-487-5632, www.hafmc.org), founded in 1967 by Dr. David E. Smith on the premise that health care is a right, not a privilege. It offers primary health care as well as specialties, and welcomes everyone who walks through the door. While they can't treat emergencies like broken bones or severe bleeding, they can provide you with referrals and community resource information.

Other clinics include the **Castro-Mission Health Center** (3850 17th Street, 415-487-7500) and the **Chinatown Public Health Center** (1490 Mason, 415-705-8500). For a more complete list, check the Haight Ashbury Free Medical Clinic's site (www.hafmc.org, click on "Community Clinics").

Staying Healthy

Various sources estimate that each dollar spent on prevention saves between three and seven dollars in treatment costs. Does that mean if you spent another $10 on prevention, you'd spend $20 to $60 less overall? That's how the math works, anyway. Yet prevention accounts for only three cents of each healthcare dollar spent in the United States. See if you can't save money by keeping yourself educated, preventing illness wherever you can, and staying in shape (see **Chapter 7**).

UTILITIES

Utility costs might not eat up a real big chunk of your budget but they can add up. So change a few habits and save a few bucks.

Shut off your cable subscription for a while and watch TV at a friend's instead, or offer to run a daytime errand for someone who's willing to tape your favorite show for you. Same goes for that new TiVo system. Save on your electricity bill by turning out the lights when you're not home. Turn off your computer when you're not using it. Avoid per-message text messaging charges on your cell phone by sending e-mails instead.

Live without a cell phone for a while, or think about how to combine it with your landline to better advantage. Most major mobile phone service providers offer plans that let you call long distance within their nationwide "network" at no extra charge. Make your long distance calls on the cell and all your local calls from home, or make long distance calls only when the rates are at their lowest. Or, as Jeffrey Yamaguchi, founder of workingfortheman.com suggests in Part 2 of his online "Laid Off 101" article: "Do the really smart thing and make your calls when you know people aren't going to be home. That way, people will

low income *is* low income...

If you're not generating much income (a strong probability when you're unemployed), you might qualify for reduced rate programs for phone, gas and garbage.

The income cutoff for these programs was $19,600 in 2003 and is adjusted each year to reflect changes in the average cost of living. If you qualify at the beginning of the year but end up earning more than the income cutoff, you'll owe the difference between the regular rate and what you already paid.

• • •

PHONE

SBC's (formerly Pacific Bell's) ***Universal Lifeline Telephone Service*** (800-310-2355) provides basic phone service at a reduced rate ($5.34 per month in 2003). You have to attest in writing to your annual income level.

[still dialing...]

[cont'd]

GAS & ELECTRIC

For qualifying households, the ***PG&E CARE Program*** (866-743-2273, *www.pge.com/care*) discounts the utility bill by 20%. Whether you're in the CARE program or not, PG&E can work out a payment schedule if you need more time to pay your bill. They'll also provide free energy education and weatherization to income-qualified customers. Call ***PG&E Customer Service*** (800-743-5000) for more details.

If you need one-time help to pay PG&E, contact the ***Salvation Army*** (800-933-9677) and ask about their ***REACH*** program: Relief for Energy Assistance through Community Help. When you're back in the green, you can help your neighbor by making a tax-deductible donation.

• • •

GARBAGE

Sunset Scavenger (415-330-1300) and ***Golden Gate Disposal & Recycling*** (415-626-4000) both offer certain households a 25% discount on basic garbage collection. Get an application by calling whichever collector serves your neighborhood.

return your calls and you'll escape long distance charges altogether."

More energy and water saving tips are available to members of the **San Francisco Community Power Cooperative** (1307 Evans, 415-550-7155, www.sfpower.org). If your income is low, you can join for only $5 a year.

Internet Access—Wired

There are any number of places to log on around the City, which can help you stay in touch with e-mail pals or apply for jobs online (but only if you have to!). You can pay by the hour (around $12 from Polk Street eastward, about $7 outside of the heart of downtown) via wired terminals serviced by providers like **ZRNetService** (www.zrnetservice.com) and **SurfandSip** (www.surfandsip.com).

However, we prefer our rates a little cheaper, as in gratis; complimentary; on the house. Free wired access isn't prevalent in San Francisco but it does exist.

If 15-20 minutes will do ya, stop by the **Main Library** (100 Larkin, 415-557-4400, www.sfpl.org) or one of the cafés that offer brief access with a purchase. If you get lucky and no one's waiting, your briefly-free minutes can go on indefinitely.

Comp USA (750 Market, 415-391-9778) offers untimed, unrestricted, and free wired access—be prepared to wait in line behind the local high schoolers. If you have a laptop with an Ethernet port, plug in at **Notes from Underground Café** (2399 Van Ness, 415-775-7638) instead.

And if you have the right purpose, you can log on at the **Kalmanovitz Medical Library** at UCSF (530 Parnassus at 3rd Avenue) for surfing related to the "missions of UCSF," or the **Foundation Center** (312 Sutter #606, 415-397-0902, www.fdncenter.org/sanfrancisco) if you're a non-profit or individual grant seeker.

FREE WIRED CAFES

- ***Cup-A-Joe Coffee House***
  1901 Hayes @ Ashbury, 415-221-3378
- ***701 Café***
  Yerba Buena Center, 701 Mission, 415-243-0930
- ***Samovar Tea Lounge***
  498 Sanchez @ 18th Street, 415-626-4700
- ***Internet Wired Café***
  1392 9th Avenue, 415-664-9293
- ***H Café***
  3801 17th Street @ Sanchez, 415-487-1661
  Bonus: H sells CDs for $1 so you can burn your own content to take home.

Internet Access—Wireless

Wireless access, on the other hand, is easier to obtain for free. Where it's not free, it's generally less expensive—as low as $5 a day for drop-in usage or $20 a month for a remote subscription plan.

Broadly speaking, wireless access is to Internet service what cell phones are to phone service—you're connected "over-the-air" versus over a physical line. To access it, your computer needs to be equipped with a wireless card, which you can procure for $50 or so (if it's not already built in). Then you can either pay for your own wireless "receiver" and subscription plan, or you can access someone else's.

Nearly two dozen cafés currently share their wireless subscriptions with their customers at no charge, with new hot spots cropping up every day. Other cafés host providers like **SurfandSip** (see

p. 254), **Deep Blue Wireless** (www.deepbluewireless.com), **Boingo** (www.boingo.com), or **T-Mobile** (at the ubiquitous Starbucks, www.tmobile.com).

A community group called **SF Wireless** (www.sfwireless.net) exists "to provide free wireless Internet access to those who need it." On their site, you'll find information on different access points or "nodes" throughout the City, and how to connect to them. The website www.80211hotspots.com lists nearly 100 SF cafes and hotels that offer wireless access (some free, some for a fee), and the truly intrepid can scout for signals elsewhere with the right equipment, or even share a wireless subscription with neighbors (this isn't necessarily legal, mind you; we're just saying it's been done).

FREE WIRELESS CAFES	
Cole Valley Café 701 Cole @ Waller, 415-668-5282	***Café International*** 508 Haight @ Fillmore, 415-552-7390
Samovar Tea Lounge 498 Sanchez @ 18th Street 415-626-4700	***Muddy Waters*** 1304 Valencia @ 24th Street 415-647-7994
Internet Wired Café 1392 9th Ave @ Judah, 415-664-9293	***Oakside Café*** 1195 Oak @ Broderick, 415-437-1985
H Café 3801 17th Street @ Sanchez 415-487-1661	***Royal Ground*** 2342 Clement @ 25th Avenue 415-387-5282
Jumpin' Java 139 Noe @ 14th Street, 415-431-5282	***Notes from Underground Café*** 2399 Van Ness @ Green, 415-775-7638
Mission Creek 968 Valencia @ 21st Street 415-641-0888	***The Canvas Gallery*** 1200 9th Avenue @ Lincoln 415-504-0060
Oh! Java Caffe 562 Central @ Grove, 415-776-5282	***Java Beach*** 1396 La Playa @ Judah, 415-665-5282
Javaholics 449 Balboa @ 6th Avenue 415-668-3434	***Venture Frogs*** 1000 Van Ness @ O'Farrell 415-409-2550
Rockin' Java 1821 Haight @ Stanyan, 415-831-8842	***Sacred Grounds*** 2095 Hayes @ Cole, 415-387-3859
Cup-A-Joe Coffee House 1901 Hayes @ Ashbury, 415-221-3378 896 Sutter @ Leavenworth 415-563-7745	***Central Coffee*** 1696 Hayes @ Central, 415-922-2008

TRANSPORTATION

In this expense category more than in others, saving money means spending time; the faster you want to get there, the more it'll cost. Slower paced travel does offer advantages beyond saving money though, such as getting outdoors to enjoy the City and even getting some exercise. You might help keep the air a little cleaner, too.

Drive Less

Gas is expensive. Insurance is expensive. Parking tickets—we won't even go there. Add in car payments and maintenance, and it becomes clear that giving up a private car could fund many extra months of leisure time. If you're really dedicated to cutting every cost and you have a car, sell it.

Does the mere thought of being without wheels give you the jitters? Then check out **City CarShare** (410 Jessie, Suite 503, 415-995-8588, www.citycarshare.org, and see "Sharing a Car" next page) or talk to a friend or neighbor about sharing a car. With a little planning and good communication, you can create your own car-share plan.

Cab Less

Door-to-door service without the hassle of parking is hard to forego, especially on a wet, foggy day. But cabs are pricey, and the January 2003 fare increase made them even more so. If you're not late for an appointment and you don't need a cab for safety, try another form of transport. As Natalia Lincoln, an unemployed dot-commer, told Jeffrey Yamaguchi in "Laid Off 101—Part 2": "The main thing to realize when unemployed is that you're very time-rich and money-poor. If you get home a half-hour later on the train than in a cab, it really doesn't matter as much."

Use Public Transportation

You can get almost everywhere in the City on **MUNI** (415-673-6864, www.sfmuni.com/home). Call them for point-to-point routing assistance. For trips to the East Bay, **BART** (Bay Area Rapid Transit, 415-989-2278, www.bart.gov) can now get you as far as Pittsburg. It can also (finally!) take you to SFO. If you need to get to the South Bay, **CalTrain** (800-660-4287, 4th & Townsend, www.caltrain.com/caltrain) offers a pleasant ride and is almost always on time, although it no longer runs on weekends. Trains do leave roughly on the hour during the week, with additional express trains at rush hour. Your best bet for getting to the North Bay is one of the dozens of bus lines operated by **Golden Gate Transit** (415-923-2000, www.goldengatetransit.org).

In addition to individual transit providers, a couple of online resources tie together the seemingly fragmented Bay Area travel network. One of them is **Rides** (800-755-7665, www.rides.org). Although Rides is geared towards commuters, there's no reason the unemployed can't also take advantage of their free commute consultation service. Another is the online **San Francisco Bay Area Transit Information** (www.transitinfo.org). Check out their site for comprehensive information on all of the Bay Area public transit options, including ferries, vans and shuttles. For really long-distance trips, call **Amtrak** (800-872-7245, www.amtrak.com) or **Greyhound** (800-231-2222, www.greyhound.com) and leave the driving to them.

SHARING A CAR

If you, like the average American, use your a car just a couple of hours a day, maybe you'd rather share a new lime green VW bug with 25 others instead. That's how many members share each of the vehicles maintained by ***City CarShare***, the nonprofit that launched its car-sharing program in San Francisco in March 2001.

The VWs and other models are parked at more than 20 San Francisco locations, or "pods," often in garage or lot spaces donated by the City. To use a car, you need only make a reservation online or via voice-activated phone line, then use your key fob to open the door and enable the ignition. An onboard computer automatically tracks your mileage and bills you monthly. If you need more gas, pay for it with the City CarShare gas card. Comprehensive insurance coverage is also included.

Makes sense, but does it make cents? Compare the fees to what you'd spend on your own car. Driving time with City CarShare—measured by reservation hours versus actual time on the road—runs $3.50 per hour and 37 cents a mile. Add to that a $30 application fee, a $10 monthly admin fee, and a $300 one-time, refundable damage deposit. If you decide you want to make the trade, you can apply online (if you're 25 years old with a valid California Driver's License and at least three years' driving history, that is). Before you know it, you'll be zipping around looking like a green gumdrop yourself!

Bike More

Since you've got more time on your hands (and feet), why not use them to ride a bike instead of driving? You'll save money on gas, and the extra exercise will help keep you fit. The City has official bicycle lanes and plenty of great bike routes (see **Chapter 7** for details).

For longer journeys, you can combine a bike with other public transportation. The **Bikes-on-Muni** program (call 415-673-6864 for a brochure) equips buses on about ten MUNI lines with double bike racks. Cyclists must load and unload their own rides. Bikes are allowed on most ferries (at the captain's discretion), on BART during non-commute hours, and in CalTrain's designated bike car. To travel between Oakland and San Francisco during commute hours, you can catch a ride on the Caltrans Bay Bridge Bike Shuttle for only $1.00 each way. This shuttle leaves San Francisco from the **Transbay Terminal** (on Mission between 1st Street & Fremont) and Oakland from the **MacArthur BART Station** (555 40th Street, Oakland).

ditching your car

No, we're not talking about launching your old clunker off a cliff *Dukes of Hazzard*-style (not that that wouldn't that be really cool), but donating your tired old vehicle to charity (see "Taxes" p. 65). Zillions of San Francisco non-profits will take it off your hands, including:

- ***Dolores Street Community Services***
  938 Valencia
  415-282-6209
  www.dscs.org
- ***San Francisco SPCA***
  2500 16th Street
  415-554-3000
  www.sfspca.org
- ***Juvenile Diabetes Research Foundation***
  121 2nd Street, 2nd Floor
  415-977-0360
  www.jdf-sfbay.org

Locate others or get assistance with the paperwork through ***America's Car Donation Charities Center*** (800-513-6560, *www.donateacar.com*).

Walk More

City planners take pride in the fact that, after Manhattan, San Francisco is the country's second most "dense" city, meaning that people can live, shop, and work without leaving their neighborhood. Pick one of SF's great commercial streets to explore (see the **Unemployed Shopping Guide**) and you might find that you can get all your errands done without the hassle of looking for parking, with the pleasure of strolling leisurely past store fronts instead.

OTHER

Not all of the expenses that fit into the "other" box are truly discretionary. Most dining and shopping are, though. Adopting frugal habits when it comes to entertainment and purchases will save you from having to cut them out completely.

Replace Expensive Outings With Activities That Are Free

No doubt, eating out fits nicely into a busy schedule and can also be fun. You can meet up with friends, have a bottle of nice wine, talk about how Masa's has real staying power in a city of fly-by-night Asian-Fusion-Americana-homestyle wanna-be's…

Or, if your life is now moving at a slower pace, you can entertain at home. Banish the image of chomping a bowl of cereal in the kitchen; morph that vision into a potluck dinner party with good friends, listening to music and drinking the bottle of fine wine that your friends brought (or the Two-Buck-Chuck that you bought at Trader Joe's!). Your friends will probably thank you for setting a low-cost trend. Plus, you'll have that much more incentive to keep your house clean.

As far as the music goes, before you go out and buy the latest Norah Jones CD, see if you can't borrow it from the library. Guess what? You can borrow cookbooks there too!

Throwing your own party is just one way to entertain yourself inexpensively. For evening events, look for house parties instead of bars. Skip concerts at Shoreline in favor of free music in Golden Gate Park. Want more frugal yet fun action? Find plenty of ideas in **Chapter 4** and **Fairs & Fests**.

Let Others Pay

San Franciscan Maureen Brown wasn't used to going on expensive outings after losing her job (especially after her savings were depleted to buy a house!) so when the bill came for a sushi dinner with an out-of-town friend, she told us she "looked at it and felt sick." Her friend offered to pay. "I said 'No, I'll pay,' but inside I was thinking, 'Oh god, yes, yes, please pay!'" And pay he did.

Don't be afraid to skip the suspense when your friends offer to pay. Just say, "Thanks, I'd appreciate that," and make a mental note to return the favor when you can. Same with Mom and Dad—if they want to treat you once in a while, let them.

What if you're unemployed and asked out? We think it's perfectly acceptable to let your date pick up the tab, men and women alike. This *is* the new millennium, after all.

Spend Less On What You Do Buy

What's that you say—no money to shop?

Well, for one, shopping doesn't necessarily mean buying. Two, you can't deprive yourself completely just because you might not have a stable income. Pick some lower priced items, such as music or books, and do a lot of looking before buying. Buy things on sale or secondhand. Go to garage sales (or sidewalk sales, or estate sales). Be aware of when you're shopping not for *things* but for instant gratification, and avoid major purchases for now—that's right, no plasma TV.

You can even out spartan living on the Friday after Thanksgiving, which was designated first by the British and then by the world as "**Buy Nothing Day**"—a day to either shop less and live more or to "conga against consumerism" (www.buynothingday.co.uk).

On the other days of the year, you can patronize the retailers listed in the **Unemployed Shopping Guide**, who offer the best values on items in the unemployed budget. If you do find yourself needing a major appliance (a vacuum cleaner, say), look for places that offer refurbished appliances, which often

simplicity in san francisco

The Simplicity Movement is alive and well in the Bay Area. Simple San Franciscans who want to learn from a guru can check out the work of ***Cecile Andrews*** (*www.cecileandrews.com*) or meet other simple folk at one of the ***Simplicity Forums*** (every fourth Monday evening at ***Pacific Heights Swedenborgian Church***, 2107 Lyon) that Cecile used to moderate. The books published by the ***Center for the New American Dream*** (in Maryland, 301-891-3683, *www.newdream.org*) are good reads—*More Fun, Less Stuff* or *Simplicity for the Holidays* can each help lengthen the life span of an unemployed budget.

Even if you aren't looking to save money, shedding some luxuries and their maintenance gives you the one thing that a true leisure seeker can never get enough of—more free time.

come with a limited warranty. They can cost less than half as much as new ones.

DEALING WITH DEBT

Unemployment isn't always fun and games, and pressing financial burdens can make it especially grim.

If you have debt but purchased unemployment protection insurance from your credit card carriers way back when, now would be a good time to file a claim. If your debt is still oppressive, you might find **Nolo Press** (950 Parker Street, Berkeley, 510-704-2248, www.nolo.com) a valuable resource. Nolo publishes Robin Leonard's *Money Troubles: Legal Strategies to Cope with Your Debts,* among other self-help legal titles, plus they are just good friendly people who offer a 40% discount to those who buy books and software in their Berkeley retail outlet. Other organizations in the Bay Area can help you alleviate financial strains or avoid financial crisis altogether (see below for some leads).

Avoiding Debt

The easiest way to get out of debt is, of course, not to get into it in the first place. As obvious as this is, most Americans spend 10% more than they make, and then spend 14% of what they make servicing their debts. Servicing debt without generating income can be a juggling act, especially if you weren't expecting to be out of work. If you're under a mountain of financial liabilities, you're definitely not alone.

But you can't afford to be average when you're unemployed, so first and foremost, control your credit cards. Adopt some simple habits—pay card balances in full each month, setting aside enough money in your prospective budget to cover each purchase. If you must make a major purchase while you're unemployed, budget and save for it before you make it, not after. The **Consumer Credit Counseling Service**

mortgage mulligans

If you can present them with proof that you can pick up where they left off, the ***Department of Social Services*** might help you catch up with your mortgage and utility payments by making a one-time-only, lump sum payment to you or your lender (or utility company). Government grants issued through local charities can do the same. Each requires that you show you have no other funds available, including a second mortgage lender (if you own a home).

of San Francisco (150 Post, 5th Floor, 800-777-PLAN, www.cccssf.org) can help you with debt management and other financial matters via phone, online, or at one of their many free or low-cost workshops. **Debtors Anonymous** (415-522-9099, www.debtorsanonymous.org) meets in San Francisco—to find out exactly where, call them, or mail a stamped, self-addressed envelope to: Northern California Debtors Anonymous Meeting List, P.O. Box 31224, San Francisco 94131.

Reducing Debt—Consolidation

Consolidate your debts if you can. A home equity loan can be a great way to go as it can come with the added benefit of a tax write-off. Another option is to transfer high-interest rate card balances to lower-rate cards. The average American's credit card debt is $8,500. Letting a balance this big revolve can cost you a seven-course dinner at Jardinière every month, depending on your rate (and your taste in wine). This is lost money that could be going to paying down your debt (or enjoying a succulent foie gras washed down with a '97 Cab).

To do that most efficiently, focus on paying off the highest rate debt first. Make minimum payments on everything else until that entire loan is paid off. Then move to the next highest rate, and so on. If you have good timing, you can float debt with teaser rates, transferring balances from card to card. You could probably find more exciting ways to spend your time though, and the card companies will catch on after a while; plus, you can damage your credit rating by opening up too many new accounts. On the other hand, your credit rating might be the least of your concerns, in which case we'll just note that federal interest rates are near a 40-year low—which means that other interest rates are low too—and likely will be for a while.

Reducing Debt—Negotiation

Americans carry consumer debt like no others. In true American fashion, entrepreneurs have capitalized on this by creating companies and services to get people out of the very debt that other companies helped get them into.

Debt reduction service providers will negotiate with creditors on your behalf to try to reduce your debt to 55-60% of what you currently owe, but you'll have to give them a cut of what they save you. If you're a good negotiator, you might try calling your creditors directly and negotiating yourself.

the negotiator

Marina Sarmiento highly recommends trying to strike a deal when you can't pay what you owe. "I've been out of work a bunch of times," says Marina. "At first, I couldn't pay my bills. Then I started negotiating with my creditors. I felt good about it. At least I was doing something."

Marina points out what the creditors know too: if they don't negotiate with you and you're forced to declare bankruptcy, they'll probably get just a small fraction of what you owe them. They also know that a collection lawsuit against you would be time-consuming and costly. Faced with these realities, savvy creditors will entertain reasonable offers. It's worth a shot!

Consumer credit counselors can also help you negotiate away some of your debt but unlike debt reduction servicers, credit counselors generally work for your *creditors,* not for you. If you decide to go this route, look for a non-profit agency such as the **Consumer Credit Counseling Service of San Francisco** (see previous page), which offers counseling for a sliding-scale fee.

Credit counseling has its pros and cons. Some lenders view it negatively, and won't lend to people who've recently used it. Other lenders are neutral; some even see it as a positive, figuring that you're at least taking a proactive approach instead of passively defaulting. The company that created the most widely used credit scoring formula ignores it; they discovered that consumers who use credit counseling are at no greater risk of default. Since credit counseling is not universally considered a negative (unlike bankruptcy), it might be something to explore.

Erasing Debt—Bankruptcy

You've probably heard that declaring bankruptcy can damage your credit rating—while you might solve some short-term financial problems, future landlords and lenders will be able to see "bankruptcy" on your credit report for up to ten years. But do you know all of your bankruptcy options? The bankruptcy code's Chapter 7, the "liquidation bankruptcy," (not to be confused with **Chapter 7** of *this* book, which is about Fitness and is a lot more fun!) allows debtors to walk away from their debts only after handing over all of their assets to a trustee, who will sell them and divide the proceeds among the creditors. The code's Chapter 13, however, the "wage earner plan," allows debtors to continue to own and operate a freelance consulting business. That could come in handy for the *self-unemployed.*

Find more free information online—from **WebLocator**'s detailed comparison of the different types of consumer bankruptcy (www.weblocator.com, select "California" then "California Law Guide" then "Bankruptcy") to **FreeAdvice.com**'s answers to such important questions as, "Can I go to jail for filing bankruptcy?" (the answer is no—see http://law.freeadvice.com under "Consumer Bankruptcy").

Consider your options carefully. If you need a lawyer, the **California State Bar** (180 Howard, 415-538-2000, www.calbar.ca.gov) can point you to several certified referral services. Although The State Bar cannot itself refer you to a lawyer, it *can* tell you whether the one you have found has the required bankruptcy specialty certification. The Bar Association of San Francisco (415-989-1616, www.sfbar.org) also has a lawyer referral program.

TAXES

Below, we pass on selected general tax information (found on official websites or from the experts we consulted) that seems—to our novice eyes—to be specific to the *unemployed, self-employed* or *self-unemployed* (see **Leisure Lingo**). We also point out a few local organizations that will gladly accept your charitable contributions, should making them be on your agenda. This information is certainly not exhaustive and it may have changed by the time you read this, so please confirm with the powers that be that you're doing everything right.

What's Taxable

You, like Odd Todd (read his story in **Finance 303**), might receive gifts or donations when you're unemployed, and you might be relieved to know that they are generally not taxable. Unemployment insurance payments are, however, and what's more, the Employment Develop-

the authorities

Both the ***Internal Revenue Service*** (IRS, 866-860-4259, *www.irs.gov*) and the ***Franchise Tax Board*** (FTB, 800-338-0505 or 916-845-7057, *www.ftb.ca.gov*) will answer your tax-related questions over the phone. Each provides downloadable forms and instructions on its website and makes them available in hard copy at most post offices.

TAX-AID (3 Embarcadero Center, Suite 2000, 415-733-8633, *www.tax-aid.org*) connects low income individuals with attorneys and CPAs who will assist in preparing their tax returns.

As always, we recommend consulting professionals for individualized financial and legal advice.

ment Department will report them to the IRS. The EDD will withhold federal taxes from your unemployment check, if you want, which can save you an unpleasant surprise at tax time. On the other hand, you can increase your cash flow now by planning to pay a lump sum later on.

Also taxable is all bartering "income" and self-employment income if you've earned more than $400 of it. Self-employment tax isn't easy to calculate—it's an "above the line" deduction and you'll owe higher-than-normal social security and Medicare taxes, but then you can deduct them as business expenses.... Good luck with it!

What's Deductible

"Attend tax planning seminar" might not top your "to do" list but you might learn something worth your while. Some are even free! Mike Robertson, a former San Francisco resident and current Lake Tahoe real estate agent and "alpine specialist," came back wide-eyed from one such seminar saying, *"Everything* is deductible!"

IRS Publication 501 discusses whether you should itemize your deductions but we won't here. We'll just point out that if you do want to itemize, save your receipts. Also worth investigating is whether you're eligible to deduct student loan interest—an "above the line" deduction that can adjust your income even if you don't itemize other deductions.

• **Job Search Expenses:** Tax attorney Heather Emigh explains, "If you're out of work and you're looking for new employment, you can deduct your job search expenses. For example, if you travel to New Orleans and apply for a job when you're there, you can deduct some of the meals, lodging, and travel expenses. The rules say you're supposed to divide your trip into that portion that was for pleasure and that portion that was to apply for the job, and you can deduct the job portion."

war story

A tax advisor who requests anonymity relates a tactic he's seen more than once—people deducting a portion of their expenses for every vacation they go on. As he tells it:

"They just get a local paper from the city where they're vacationing and when they get home, they mail a resume to one of the employers who advertised in that paper. They choose a 'high profile' employer like GM so they're sure to get a rejection letter. That letter, they assume, would serve as proof to the IRS—in the event of an audit—that they were actually looking for a job in that city."

GOOD DEEDS THAT ARE ALSO GOOD DEALS

Year after year, you can donate to certain local charities and record your own assessed value on the blank receipt they provide. Worthy beneficiaries include ***Goodwill*** (1500 Mission, 415-575-2100, *www.sfgoodwill.org*), the ***Salvation Army*** (*www.salvationarmy.org* or *www.satruck.org*) and ***Community Thrift*** (623-625 Valencia, 415-861-4910), which will give the non-profit of your choice a percentage of the proceeds from selling your donated items. Note that Community Thrift can't accept personal computers or software.

Drop-Off Locations	
Goodwill	**Salvation Army**
1500 Mission	1500 Valencia, 415-643-8000
629 Hyde	1185 Sutter, 415-771-3818
2350 Noriega	Crissy Field
large item pickup 888-446-6394	

• **Charitable Donations:** Gifts to tax-exempt charitable and religious groups might be deductible for you. Straight from the horse's mouth (a.k.a., the **IRS** website, www.irs.gov) is the following guideline: "The tax benefit for charitable contributions is only available for taxpayers who itemize deductions—about one-third of all filers. Those who take a standard deduction receive no additional tax benefit for their contributions." You can include only those contributions actually made during the calendar year. Ask for a receipt—you'll need a written acknowledgement from the charity for any single gift of $250 or more.

• **Business Expenses:** If you're self-employed or running your own business, you might be able to deduct certain business expenses, including a portion of what you spend to outfit a home office. Determining the right proportion can be tricky and you'll have to fill out an IRS Schedule C. If you travel and earn some money on your trip, you can deduct a portion of your travel expenses if you "actively" work (spend 500 hours/year or more) in the field that corresponds to your deduction. If you're a self-employed snowboarding instructor, for example, then you might be able to deduct snowboarding expenses from any money you earn as an instructor. Note that you can actively work in more than one field. If you're working as an independent contractor for someone else, you might be able to deduct certain non-reimbursed business expenses from your personal income.

Tax Credits

Whether or not you take deductions, you might be eligible for tax credits. While deductions can reduce your taxable income (which can in turn reduce your tax liability), credits reduce the amount of tax you owe dollar for dollar. In fact, some credits entitle you to a refund—even if you had no tax withheld and owe no tax! The Education Credit, the Earned Income Credit, and the California Renter's Credit all come to mind but there might be others you can use. The standing caveat applies here—please do your own research. The **IRS** website (www.irs.gov) is a good place to start.

Deferring Taxes

Want more time to file your return? You can get up to six more months by filing two different forms. IRS Form 4868 (*Application for Automatic Extension of Time to File U.S. Individual Income Tax Return*) extends the deadline from April 15 to August 15—no reason needed—and IRS Form 8809 (*Request for Extension of Time to File Information Returns*) extends it again, from August 15 to October 15. On this second form, you *will* need to state your reason, such as, "Additional time is needed to file a complete and accurate tax return."

The catch is that these are extensions to file, not extensions to pay. If you owe any taxes, the *payment* is still due by April 15. You'll have to estimate your tax liability reasonably well and pay a sufficient percentage of what you actually end up owing (90% for federal, 80% for California) to avoid penalties.

FINANCE 303
STASHING SOME CASH

Whew! Budgets, bankruptcy, and taxes—if you're still with us, we salute you. Now it's time to get out of the red and into the black by bringing in some much-needed cash.

UNEMPLOYMENT INSURANCE

The joint federal-state Unemployment Insurance Program, or "UI" for short, provides weekly payments to workers who lose their job "through no fault of their own." "Fault" is, of course, a subjective term but depending on your circumstances, you may be eligible for UI even if you quit your job or were fired. You can't apply for benefits until you are actually unemployed, even if you know you're about to get laid off, but you can apply if you're working part-time. While some part-time workers will be eligible for benefits, most self-employed workers will not. For an individualized assessment, contact California's **Employment Development Department** (800-300-5616, www.edd.ca.gov).

Filing a Claim

You can file a claim or an extension day or night if you file online or by mail, or during business hours by phone. Have your social security number handy plus the name, address, and phone number of your last employer. It will take the EDD about two weeks from the time your initial claim is filed to assess your eligibility for benefits, so file as quickly as you can. You must file your claim by Friday to get credit for that week.

odd todd, odd job

Check out one investigation of a guy you might have heard of: Todd M. Rosenberg, better known as "Odd Todd" of online fame. Rosenberg made $9,000 in cybertips from his animated cartoon, "Laid Off: A Day in the Life," at *www.oddtodd.com*. The trouble was, Rosenberg was also receiving unemployment benefits and the combination did not go over well with the New York State Department of Labor—at least initially.

The unemployed are generally not supposed to collect unemployment and earn money at the same time. They are supposed to be actively looking for work, not "kicking it on a couch, answering e-mails or drawing cartoons or getting interviewed on television about being unemployed."* It's also true, however, that the unemployed are generally allowed to accept donations. Luckily for Rosenberg, New York put his tips in that category and agreed that he didn't have to repay any benefits. Score one for the unemployed guy!

**See "Making Unemployment Work (Sort Of)" by Leslie Eaton, Home Front, February 24, 2002*

The EDD maintains an automated phone system (also at 800-300-5616) through which you can check on the status of an expected payment. To do so, you'll need to use this same system to create a PIN number. If you're eligible, benefits will start with the effective date of your claim, which will be the Sunday before the date your claim was filed. All claims have a one week waiting period, which is not a paid week and doesn't start until the claim is filed.

Maintaining Eligibility

Establishing your initial eligibility is just the first step. To continue to get paid, you'll have to maintain eligibility, which means that you must be "able to work," be "actively looking for work," and be "willing to accept a suitable job." You'll also have to mail in a completed and signed "Continued Claim Certification" every two weeks; a new form will arrive with each check. Regular benefits can last up to 26 weeks, although if statewide economic conditions justify a state or federal "extension of benefits" program, this period can stretch—up to 65 weeks in recent years.

Benefit Amounts

How much you'll receive each week depends on how much you earned during a "base period" year, which starts about 16 months before your claim is filed. Work and earnings from another state can be used to establish a claim. Although the maximum weekly benefit used to be a modest $230, recent legislation provided for decent annual cost-of-living increases, upping the max to $330 in 2002, on its way to $450 in 2005.

Special Programs

Claims are generally valid for one year after you've filed. Because the benefit amount can't change within that year, you might get stuck with an obsolete rate if you file towards the end of the year. Recognizing this, many people who are laid off in December wait until January to file their claims.

Enter the special programs approved by California or the Feds from time to time, such as retroactive benefits increases, backdating, and extended benefits. While each individual program is designed to fatten your check, you might need a Ph.D in math to figure out how they all intersect.

Fortunately, the EDD can tell you what's on the table at the moment and help you figure out whether you should apply. Keep in mind that the EDD might suspend your benefits while it completes its research and that electing to backdate could change your payout amount.

Going Out of Town

The EDD mails claim forms to your home address and requires your signature on each one. To be eligible for benefits, therefore, you (technically) need to be at home and actively looking for work (read: not traveling). Unfortunately, this means that if you travel even to pursue a professional opportunity, you might disqualify yourself for that time period's benefits—unless you can verify the purpose of your trip to the EDD's

a traveler's run at fooling the EDD

San Franciscan James Trudy (name changed) was laid off from his job as an architect, which coincided nicely with a pre-planned six-month trip around the world. He successfully filed for unemployment insurance following his layoff and decided to try and keep the ball rolling during his trip.

He had his address with the EDD changed to a friend's address, and had his friend forge his signature and send back the claim forms when they arrived. For bank deposits, he left deposit slips and addressed envelopes to his financial institution. The plan worked fine for several months, until the EDD randomly scheduled a phone interview to check on James' progress in "looking for work." As he wasn't available for the interview and unable to respond otherwise, his benefits were discontinued.

satisfaction. The silver lining is that if benefits are disallowed for any given time period, they are deferred, not lost altogether, until you're eligible again.

UI and Moonlighting

Not that any San Franciscans *would* cheat, but off-the-record surveys show that plenty of otherwise honest citizens earn cash on the side while collecting UI. Beware—the EDD is onto this and will try to ensnare you with the help of those calling their **Fraud Tip Hot Line** (800-229-6297).

If you're contemplating collecting a little "extra" unemployment insurance, you should know that falsifying unemployment claims may subject you to (at the very least) repaying all of your ill-gotten gains.

LEISURE LOANS

Depending on the circumstances, the concept of a "leisure loan" can be a good one: borrow money to fund more time off. This is not to say that we encourage you to accumulate large amounts of debt. But if the timing is right for you to take some time to yourself, yet you don't have the cash reserves, a small loan to support your leisure may be just what the financial doctor ordered. Particularly in a low interest rate environment, borrowing money to fund leisure can be a savvy investment in your well-being.

THE BANK OF MOM & DAD

Without significant assets such as a house or stocks, you might find that a loan from the Bank of Mom & Dad is the easiest to obtain, and carries the best interest rate (0% financing, anyone?). But any family loan comes with its own unique costs, usually in the form of unsolicited opinions and parental "guidance."

Some of you will find those hidden costs prohibitive. Others will reject the familial borrowing notion straight away out of pride. Be wary of "pride," however; it often represents little more than a false sense of obligation based on societally-imposed expectations.

Leisure loans can come in many forms, including personal loans from family or friends, a home equity loan if you're a home owner, or even a margin loan if you maintain an equity portfolio. Unfortunately, we were unable to find any banks out there that offered loans specifically with the intent to "fund leisure." We therefore call upon our nation's financial institutions: offer leisure loans as an investment in the balance and health of the American worker!

Home Equity Loans

If you're a home owner, a home equity loan may be a relatively secure way to borrow. As the name implies, these loans borrow against the value of your house. Home equity loans are usually available at lower rates than margin debt, and to the extent house values are more stable than stock values, your home will be a less risky asset to borrow against. Again, as with any borrowing situation, weigh the debt to equity ratio—in this case, compare the amount of the loan to the total value of the house, and consider total equity built up as well. The last thing you need is to jeopardize your home simply for a little extra cash.

Margin Loans

If you own a portfolio of stocks, why would you borrow against those very equities when you could sell them?

Well, for starters, if the markets are down, selling could net you a very poor price. You might be better off taking a

cash out mortgage

If you own a home and have built up some equity, refinancing might get you more than a lower rate or better terms. It might get you cash back—just like at the grocery store! With a "cash out" mortgage, you can pay off your existing first mortgage and have cash left over, up to the entire value of the equity in your home.

As appealing as that sounds, cash outs can be risky business. Around two-thirds of homeowners refinancing today are borrowing at least five percent more than they already owed, and using more than half of that cash to straighten out their bills, up from 30% just a couple of years ago.

In the words of one savvy San Francisco home owner, "It's really attractive to think you can refi and put some cash in your pocket. For some people, this might be more than they make in, say, six months—so the unemployed might find this attractive. But you really do not affect your monthly payments much, and you do not pay off your house any quicker."

short-term loan, then repaying it by selling when stock prices are higher. Brokerage houses make it very easy to borrow money; most offer checks that draw on automatically margined funds when written.

Neil Brown, Oakland-based CFA and financial services consultant, recommends that stockholding *leisure seekers* not borrow more than 20% of their total holdings, although the exact percentage would depend greatly on the composition of the portfolio. If you own only volatile equities such as small technology issues, for example, you probably shouldn't borrow against them at all.

Brown further cautions:

> *Margin borrowing should never become an addictive panacea for the chronic leisure seeker. Essentially, you are borrowing against the future earnings of your portfolio. At some point you will need to pay off the margin debt you have incurred with capital gains from the sale of winning positions, dividends, and/or interest earned from your investment portfolio (or if your portfolio goes nowhere, then cash from other sources). The worst words an equity borrower could ever hear are 'margin call.'*

RAIDING YOUR RETIREMENT FUND

Explore all your other options before you raid your nest egg. Look for more ways to cut expenses; reduce your debt as much as you can; even use a teaser-rate credit card to "borrow" money before you turn to your retirement fund.

If you're really in a bind, however, and you have an Individual Retirement Account ("IRA"), you can make an early withdrawal. Beware: you'll be subject to a 10% tax penalty, plus lose the real tax benefits of a retirement account.

Are there ways to avoid the penalty? Yes, a couple. You can withdraw up to $10,000 to buy your first home, or withdraw any amount to pay for "qualified higher education expenses." You'll owe ordinary income tax on these withdrawals, of course, but at least your tax hit will be in a year when you've probably received little other income.

If you have a 401(k), roll it over into an IRA, because you can't make an early withdrawal from a 401(k) without proving "undue hardship," and that's unduly hard. According to tax attorney Heather Emigh, "You have to write a letter to the IRS (it's not a form) and explain your situation—you're about to get evicted from your apartment, you can't afford to eat, and you can't find a job anywhere. If you can throw in some medical problems and/or starving kids, that would work even better." As if being unmonied weren't hardship enough!

Note, however, this small perk for the unemployed: the jobless can take money out of any qualified retirement plan, including an IRA, a 401(k), or 403(c), to pay for health insurance premiums.

SHOW ME THE MONEY

It's been said that free money is the best kind of money, although "free" is usually open to interpretation. Even as a gift, money rarely comes without strings attached. Still, you *can* find alternative sources of funding to finance time off.

Patronage

Explorers and artists of eras past were supported by the rich, powerful and royal. Famous sponsors flocked to Galileo, for example, and Shakespeare wrote some of his greatest plays and poems under the haven of patronage. Where are today's patrons?

Scholarships and grants are modern forms of patronage. Corporations are probably the single biggest patrons today, sponsoring such far-flung endeavors as science, athletics, and travel. How do you think the America's Cup yachting race with its multi-million dollar high-tech boats fills its sails? It may be a competition famous for its billionaire boys' club, but the America's Cup rakes in hundreds of millions of sponsorship dollars from corporations as well.

Coming out of graduate school, Internet and television producer Erik Olsen scored a sweet scholarship through the Rotary Club of Seattle, allowing him to travel and "work" in Chile for an entire year. His part of the bargain? Report back to the Rotaries on what he learned and tell them about his experiences—which, among other things, included meeting infamous Chilean dictator Augusto Pinochet.

The time-honored yet controversial concept of having a "sugar daddy" or "sugar momma" fund your leisure won't appeal to some, but its attractions have certainly withstood the test of time. Many a grand project has been funded through the "sweetness" of loved ones over the years. We're not here to pass judgment, only to present another option…

Such as explaining to your relatives or wealthy friends the concept of "patronage." Enlighten them as to how many great artists and philosophers have made world-changing contributions this way! Your modern leisure patron may come in the form of a rich uncle, a corporation, or perhaps even a government grant.

GREAT MOMENTS IN UNEMPLOYMENT

LANDING A LEISURE PATRON

It seems Karl Marx was the prototypical "slacker"—or so say those who report that he never did hold a real job. Rather, he found a wealthy benefactor, Friedrich Engels, who doled out a generous allowance while Marx maintained a lifestyle akin to today's perpetual graduate student. Marx did, however, manage to create a lifetime's worth of philosophical and political works in his leisure time, and—oh yeah—come up with the concept for that little thing called Communism. Score one for the proletariat slacker!

Regardless of where you find your funds, remember to share the leisure!

Grants and Scholarships

Scholarship and grant money (see **Chapter 10**) is often geared towards funding education—but not always. Numerous programs fund other goals in areas such as business, healthcare, or the delightfully nebulous "personal" category (we like! we like!).

An entire industry, not all of it ethical, exists to help you locate this money. Beware of get-rich-quick spins and advance-fee Internet offers unless you can verify the integrity of the organization another way.

Instead, see the book *Finding Funding: The Comprehensive Guide to Grant Writing* by Daniel M. Barber, which is, in fact, a comprehensive guide to finding grant money. You might also have luck with *I'll Grant You That* by local authors and teachers Jim Burke and Carol Ann Prater.

Another resource is **The Foundation Center** (312 Sutter #606, 415-397-0902, www.fdncenter.org/sanfrancisco), a San Francisco organization whose mission is "to support and improve philanthropy by promoting public understanding of the field and helping grant seekers succeed." Sounds good to us! Their free library and computer center houses an extensive grant database.

Do you have something more specific in mind? There are yet more sources that can help. The book *Six Months Off* includes information on grant money specifically geared towards sabbaticals. Writers and aspiring scribes should seek out the essential *Grants and Awards Available to American Writers* by John Morrone, Victoria Vinton, and Anna Jardine. Artists should look to the **California Arts Council** (800-201-6201, www.cac.ca.gov).

locals-only grants

Regional grants can be peculiarly specific. Take, for example, the Allgemeiner Deutscher Frauen-Hilfsverein, otherwise known as the ***German Ladies General Benevolent Society*** (P.O. Box 27101, 415-391-9947). The organization offers "temporary assistance to financially needy women and children of German descent who reside in the greater San Francisco Bay Area." Talk about specialized!

Another neighborly patron is ***New Langton Arts*** (1246 Folsom, 415-626-5416, *www.newlangtonarts.org*), which gives funds to artists for community-based art in the Bay Area.

Little-known, focused grants like these could be just your ticket.

bartering

If you have a useful talent or skill, consider bartering your services to others (no, we're not talking about anything sleazy!). If you're a photographer, for example, offer your work for trade-in-kind. You could get more in trade than you would in cash, and end up with a needed product or service.

If you're operating on a limited budget, perhaps bartering for a nice dinner out is just the ticket to spark your taste buds as well as your social life. So go on, make a deal!

SELLING YOUR STUFF

Offline

One of the smartest ways to shop isn't shopping at all. It's more like "reverse shopping"—trading or selling your used records, books or clothes for cash or store credit. "Buy-sell-trade" stores (see listings in the **Unemployed Shopping Guide**) will turn them over at a fair price, just as fair as the prices you'll pay for any used goods you buy there.

A word of warning: it can be humbling indeed to have some 16-year-old sprite pass harsh judgment on your clothing, or reject every single one of your used CDs—not that this has ever happened to us! For best results, tailor your wares to the venue, and present them clean, pressed, and on hangers.

Online

The Internet has become a grand virtual marketplace for buying and selling "stuff." This represents a boon to the leisure seeker because it offers a way to raise cash quickly by simply selling your junk. "People love junk," says Eddie Foronda, an experienced seller (see next page). "You can quote me on that." Thanks Eddie—we just did.

eBay (www.ebay.com), and the culture that has emerged from it, is at the center of this magnificent bazaar, where everything is for sale. In fact, as Adam Cohen talked about with *Book Magazine,* "the number of… users [of the more than 40 million users registered on eBay] who have quit their jobs and are now making a living solely as eBay traders is now measured in the hundreds of thousands."

Choose some non-essential items (furniture, sporting goods, and electronics are in particularly high demand) and put them up for auction to see what you can get for them. You'll have to arrange for payment and shipping of course, but this is pretty straightforward. Be honest, or buyers will use eBay's feedback system to ding you. "At first it doesn't seem like feedback is a big deal, but it's the biggest thing ever," Super Sale Eddie says (see below). "Even if you have 1,000 transactions and only one negative, people will look at the negative to see what it says." To support your local cybermarket, the site to see is **Craig's List** (www.craigslist.org) and its sale/wanted section.

Garage Sales, Flea Markets, Swap Meets

Garage or moving sales, if they're well-advertised, can pay off not only in money (no matter what the state of your finances), but also in reclaimed space in your closets and cupboards. Other people actually want your cast-offs—imagine that!

In addition to the typical places to list your garage sale, try posting flyers at a local college, especially in late summer. Don't forget your favorite café or pub, and sending a mass e-mail to your friends wouldn't hurt either. The point is, get the word out. Also important is not to advertise too early. For a Saturday sale, post to Craig's List ("no need to advertise in the paper," says sale maven Foronda) on Thursday, and don't let anyone show up early except your friends. On the other hand, be prepared to get bought out before your sale begins. "Some people just want the whole shebang, to see what they can get," Eddie has found. If you get an early request like this, entertain it. Be ready for business on time, with your wares tagged, plenty of change available, and some peppy music playing. Finally, sell cheap.

Flea markets and swap meets present a more consolidated market. First-timers should arrive early with their "mystery truckloads." For locations, see the **Unemployed Shopping Guide**.

EDDIE'S SUPER SALE OF MASS DEDUCTION

Not your typical sidewalk sale, Eddie Foronda's "Super Sale of Mass Deduction" is all about efficiency and high-tech advertising. He's got it down to a science, from "deciding the objectives of the sale" to "tying in the title to something relevant" (in this case, the U.S./Iraq conflict), to putting something new on there, "like a sealed USB printer."

In Eddie's case, "on there" means his own website, where he posts meticulously arranged photographs of every item to be sold (even the small stuff), along with item specs ("specs are very important") so that buyers will know exactly what to expect. Eddie thinks that even Colin Powell would agree: "Who needs proof with those low prices?" See the archived ad for Eddie's sale at *www.lostcastles.com/supersale.*

ODD JOBS

Willie Brown might not be hiring anymore, but you can find your own odd job in the classifieds of the *Chronicle, Bay Guardian,* or Craig's List. Some of those listings are downright wacky—serious *McJobs*!

You can also register with one of San Francisco's general temporary placement agencies, such as **Advanced Employment Services** (760 Market, Suite 458, 415-989-1188, www.advancedemployment.com) or the **Certified Employment Group** (111 Pine, Suite 710, 415-433-3600, www.certifiedemployment.com), or look for one that specializes in placement in your field, such as **PrintStaff** (785 Market, Suite 1700, 415-974-1078, www.printstaff.com) for print, copy and digital professionals.

You must have an unusual skill or two. Let people know that you're available for services like small business bookkeeping, freelance photography, bodywork, whatever. Put on your marketing hat and get creative! Better still, look around, see what people need, then figure out how to get it to them. Services like tutoring, yard work, house sitting, and housecleaning (we like "Spouses Do Houses") are always in demand.

SHORT-TERM GIGS?

Just to jolt your brain cells, consider these job titles:

• tutor ($27-80 an hour) • substitute teacher •
• personal assistant (to anyone who's always so busy!) •
• junior college professor (if you happen to have a master's degree) •
• child sitter • pet sitter (same thing? $20-$36 per night) •
• day trader • Amway/Mary Kay/Tupperware representative •
• house painter • handyman • launderer •
• tour guide (create a tour of your own!) •

Bartending and waiting tables might be reliable standbys in other cities, but you'll face stiff competition for those jobs in this food and drink town. On the other hand, San Francisco does have almost 4,000 restaurants, so someone's bound to have an opening.

Actors and extras earn $100-500 per day (800-260-3949 x3025). And don't forget—there's always *"consulting*!" (See **Leisure Lingo**.)

subbing

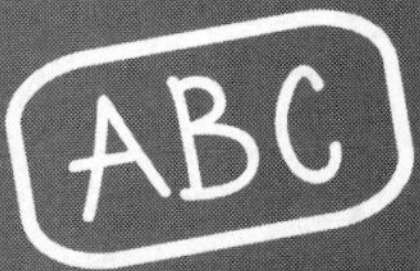

If you're after the big bucks and don't have nerves of steel, forget about substitute teaching, advises full-time classroom teacher Alayne Brand. "The sub jobs range anywhere from a highly enjoyable experience to possibly being the worst day in your whole life," she says. But if you can live with an erratic schedule, love working with the City's youth and want to be more visible in the school setting, go ahead and launch the five-month process of testing and documentation.

You'll need a bachelor's degree from a U.S. college, passing scores on the CBEST (California Basic Skills Test, $41, given seven times a year), fingerprinting, negative results on a TB test ($20) and a $100 cashier's check just to get the paperwork to apply to the ***San Francisco Unified School District*** (555 Franklin, 415-241-6101, *www.sfusd.edu*). If you survive the lengthy interview process and complete training and more paperwork, you can pay another $55 to receive your 30-Day Substitute Credential.

Don't worry too much about the "30-Day" part—if you land a longer-term position, the district will be able to bend the rules for you, if they like you. In fact, becoming liked and well-known at a couple of schools is the best way to get consistent, steady work. "A good, reliable sub is a gold mine," Alayne says. "You will be called almost daily if teachers like you and the students get their work done when you are in the classroom."

Although you won't receive employment benefits, you can earn between $121-200 per day subbing, sometimes more for long-term positions. If the lengthy and cumbersome application process discourages you, look into a district outside the City, where the hiring cycles are shorter.

If you'd prefer higher pay, consider attending the year of school you'll need for full-time work. Alayne did, and has found the intangible rewards amazing. "I have never for a moment regretted going into teaching," she says. "And it gets better each year."

For general information about teaching in California, check with:
California Commission on Teacher Credentialing
Sacramento
916-445-7254
www.ctc.ca.gov

HOW TO MAKE A BUCK

	How To Get The Job	How Much $$$
Balloon Maker	Buy some balloons and a dual air pump and set yourself up amidst the tourists and other street performers at Fisherman's Wharf, or contact ***Balloonabilities*** (800-350-8947, *www.balloonabilities.com*), a balloon-maker placement agency. Training is provided!	Up to $100 in tips during a 3-hour shift at Chevy's—more if you're supernaturally entertaining.
Day Labor Program	Have skills in child care, gardening, painting, janitorial work… the list goes on. Bring your desire to fuel this worker-run organization. (17th Street & Potrero, 415-252-5375 or 415-252-5376, *www.sfdaylabor.org*)	Workers receive 100% of all wages—from $12-$15/hr—plus meals, health care, classes in English and computers, and job-safety training.
Sperm or Egg Donor	Must be male or female. Sperm donors must be 21-35 with a high school diploma. Call ***Pacific Reproductive Services*** (444 De Haro, Suite 222, 415-487-2288, *www.pacrepro.com*) for more information on sperm. Eggs are a lot more involved (hence the handsome compensation). You must be 21-29, be willing to receive injections and be available for the full donor cycle, about three months.	For millions of sperm, $115-170 per "deposit." For one egg (or more, if the fertility drugs do their thing), $3500-5000 plus expenses.
Blood Donor	Must be human, at least 17 years old (or 16 with permission from your parents), weigh 110 pounds or more and be in good health. Don't do drugs or have AIDS, cancer, hepatitis or organ failure. For more information, check *www.bloodcenters.org*.	No dollars, but you will get a mini-physical (blood pressure, temperature, iron level and blood type), plus you can save a life without even going to med school!
Focus Groups	Ever wonder why a great movie like "The Shawshank Redemption" had such a weak name? The producers forgot to run a focus group, that's why. Bring your opinion and be an otherwise run-of-the-mill consumer, and you're in. Check *www.silentway.com/tips/sf/focus.html*.	$50-$150 for a one- or two-hour session.

WITHOUT MAKING A CAREER

How To Get The Job	How Much $$$	
Uh oh—the website says you need to be currently employed in your field. "Yes," says MB, "they *say* that you have to be working in your field, but I was indeed already laid off, as were many other teachers. They really have to say that to maintain reputability." Request application info online. 185 Berry, China Basin Landing Lobby 3, 800-448-6775 *www.universityofphoenix.com*	$800 per five-week course. The trick is to leverage your investment in prep time by teaching the same course repeatedly.	**Lecturer, University of Phoenix**
Desire to have "girl" in your job title. Selling and acting ability also helps, as does a fun and carefree attitude. You'll need a valid California Seller's Permit, which is free. You must be 21 or older. Try ***Peachy's Puffs*** (800-564-7833, *www.peachyspuffs.com*).	You pay a $25 security deposit. They provide your costume. Income will be, on average, $50-180 for a five-hour shift. Perks can include free admission to concerts at the Warfield!	**Cigarette & Candy Girl**
Be qualified for and willing to run the full course of a given study. Find UCSF program qualifications at *www.ucsf.edu* under "Research," then "Clinical Trials Seeking Volunteers." You can also find calls for research volunteers on ***Craig's List*** in the "Jobs" column under "et cetera jobs."	Payment ranges wildly, from fringe benefits only, to $1200 for completion of an antibiotic study involving seven I.V. doses, a bronchoscopy and five days in the hospital.	**Medical Research Studies**
Be aggressive; you'll be competing with a lot of seasoned walkers. Still, the pet industry *is* growing by 700% a year...	$9-$14/dog, 6-8 dogs/walk, 3-4 walks/day. That adds up to $2240 a week for a walker who's fully booked. Not bad, not bad at all.	**Dogwalker**
You probably know if you have a knack for helping other people get organized. Learn more about creating order from chaos from the San Francisco Bay Area Chapter of the ***National Association of Professional Organizers*** (*www.napo-sfba.org*).	Full-time or part-time available. Expect to earn between $10-$30/hr as a total "newbie," $30-$50 with some background (in office or project management, say), and $50-$70 if you've been in law or nursing. Experts command up to $150/hr.	**Professional Organizer**

MOM

PART TWO

THE UNEMPLOYED ODYSSEY

CHAPTER 4
REDISCOVERING SAN FRANCISCO

"One's destination is never a place but rather a new way of looking at things."

~Henry Miller

THINK you know your own town? You might be surprised. Did you know, for instance, that Lombard is *not* actually San Francisco's crookedest street? Vermont Street in Potrero Hill beats it, based on a complex calculation incorporating bends per yard combined with grade and angle. What's more, it has better views!

Spend your unemployed hours discovering SF's true highlights, as well as soaking up the culture and ambience that make living here so great. Rest assured that our City's boundless opportunities for urban adventure and exploration will entertain you as much as the tourists. "There's a reason why everyone moves here," says unemployed veteran Mary Mangold. "This is such a great city. Have as much fun as you can." Words to live by!

BECOME AN EXPERT ON YOUR OWN TOWN

San Francisco has always been proud of its distinctive character—and with good reason. Among our City's quirky claims to fame: we gave birth to the modern-day strip club (thank you, Carol Doda!), North Beach bathtubs served as LSD factories in the 1960s and '70s, and the Church of Satan was founded in the Richmond district. What local wouldn't be pleased to regale visitors with factoids like that?

With extra time on your hands, now's your chance to stock up your trivia drawer. San Francisco may not be quite as volatile as it once was, but it still houses an eclectic mix of personalities and goings-on, both above and below board, and they all await your rediscovery.

History and Trivia

Let's start with the original locals. The Ohlone Indians occupied what is now the San Francisco peninsula from about 10,000 years ago until the Europeans began displacing them in the late 18th century. The Ohlone were actually a collection of different tribes spread throughout the greater Bay Area. Like many modern-day San Franciscans, these tribes were nomadic and, by most accounts, lived very much in harmony with their natural environs. They clearly understood the concept of leisure, as they lived completely in the present, and enjoyed in abundance what the land provided.

Enter the Spaniards, who must have seen all this good living as a threat to their hard-working, Catholic way of life. These "civilized" settlers responded by attempting to enslave and convert the leisurely "heathens" to Christianity. To speed things up, they founded **Mission Dolores** (3321 16th Street) in 1776, marking the beginnings of modern-day San Francisco. That same year, the Presidio was formally established as a Spanish military outpost, and the early stages of a town began forming.

san francisco vitals

Population:	801,377
Namesake:	St. Francis of Assisi
Land Area:	46.7 square miles
Average Rainfall:	22.28 inches per year
Real Tall Building:	Transamerica Pyramid (260 meters/853 feet, 48 floors)

The Other Real Tall Building:	Bank of America Building (237 meters, 52 floors)
Famous Earthquake #1:	Great Earthquake, April 18, 1906, magnitude 8.25
Famous Earthquake #2:	Loma Prieta, October 17, 1989, magnitude 6.9
City & County Seal:	adopted on March 1, 1859
City Flower:	Dahlia
City Colors:	Black and Gold
City Bird:	California Quail
City Songs:	"San Francisco" & "I Left My Heart in San Francisco"
and finally, the City Tree:	a 100-foot Monterey Cypress in front of McLaren Lodge at Kennedy Drive

Now *that* is a vital city!

When Mexico won independence from Spain in the early 1800s, San Francisco returned to Mexican rule. But Californians were then an independent mix of Mexicans, Americans, native Americans, and Spaniards, who didn't exactly heed Mexico's head honcho.

Things really started cooking in 1846 with the outbreak of the Mexican-American War. San Francisco (then a small village known as Yerba Buena) officially passed from Mexican to American hands, and held its first municipal elections. In 1847, the town name was formally changed from Yerba Buena to San Francisco, after St. Francis of Assisi—and if you have any doubts about taking time off, note that our patron saint was also unemployed!

The discovery of gold on the American River in 1848 led to a temporary mass exodus from the City to the foothills of the Sierra Nevada. Soon after, however, San Francisco's population skyrocketed, soaring from 800 or so at the beginning of 1848 to an estimated 100,000 by the end of 1849. Most newbies arrived by sea, including thousands of immigrants from South America, the South Pacific, and Europe, as well as Americans from the Eastern United States.

Gambling, prostitution, and other assorted vices took root in the wake of gold fever, transporting the City into the heyday of the Barbary Coast, a seedy old waterfront area rife with crime. The **San Francisco Museum and Historical Society** (www.sfhistory.org) offers a historical walk of the area (www.barbarycoasttrail.com) for those wishing to delve into the underbelly of the City's past; the Barbary Coast is marked by a series of bronze medallions set in the sidewalks.

a garden for the ages

San Francisco boasts more than forty state historical landmarks, including the ***Golden Gate Bridge*** (State Historical Landmark No. 974), ***Union Square*** (No. 623), and ***Telegraph Hill*** (No. 91). Lesser known, but equally colorful, is ***Woodward's Gardens*** (No. 454) (corner of Mission & Duboce).

Robert B. Woodward moved to San Francisco in 1849 and made enough of a fortune from his popular hotel, *What Cheer House*, to buy a four-acre chunk of land on Mission Street. He transformed his new home into a private wonderland so entertaining that friends and neighbors soon clamored for invitations to visit. In 1883, he gave in and threw open his doors to the public.

more...

In 1872, the *San Francisco Real Estate Circular* arrogantly claimed, "San Francisco is in very little more danger of a disastrous earthquake than the Eastern States of being flooded by an overflow of the Atlantic ocean," and "San Francisco is in less danger from fire than any city of the East." Oops. Not only did the Great Earthquake rock the City's world in 1906, but the more destructive Great Fire was the seventh and worst in a series of Great Fires.

The completion of the Panama Canal in 1914 gave San Francisco the perfect excuse to throw a big-ass party—and invite the whole world. They did so with great fanfare at the Panama-Pacific International Exposition, spending more than $100 million to build 625 acres of lavish palaces, gardens, and other wonderlands. The legacy of this hugely ambitious undertaking remains the better part of the City's Marina district, including the Palace of Fine Arts, Crissy Field, the Marina Green, and most of the land along the northern waterfront.

1939 was a blockbuster year as well. San Francisco hosted the Golden Gate International Exposition (otherwise known as the World's Fair) on the newly created Treasure Island, to celebrate—among other things—the recent completion of the Golden Gate and Bay Bridges.

Not much of note went down in the '50s, except maybe Joe DiMaggio and Marilyn Monroe's wedding at City Hall—and the odd earthquake or two. The '60s and '70s, however, brought turbulent times to the City, with the emergence of pop music, drugs, youth culture, and activism, encapsulated by the Summer of Love in 1969. They also saw the rise of a politically active gay community, led by Supervisor Harvey Milk, who was assassinated along with Mayor George Moscone in 1978.

The outbreak of the AIDS epidemic dominated the 1980s. San Francisco became (and remains) a focal point in the treatment and politics surrounding the disease. A decade later, dot-com fever raged through city streets as wildly as the Great Earthquake and Fire, and ultimately might have left just as much destruction in its wake. The tremors from the "bubble burst" are still being felt today.

Whew! That's a lot of action in a relatively short time period. Interested historians can study up on SF history at the **Virtual Museum of the City of San Francisco** (www.sfmuseum.org), a superb site that would make most librarians proud. If you're looking for a more current perspective, introduce yourself to **Mister SF** (www.mistersf.com), and let him guide you through our fine city. Mister SF (columnist Hank Donat) has painstakingly scoured the streets of San Francisco, so you don't have to.

SAN FRANCISCO BACTERIA IS SPECIAL

Why is the uniquely tangy taste of San Francisco Sourdough impossible to cook up anywhere else? Because special types of the two most important ingredients grow here and only here: *Saccharomyces exiguus* (yeast), and *Lactobacillus sanfrancisco* (bacteria).

The yeast culture is something you can now buy in specialty shops around the country, but the bacteria (fortunately?) are not. This means that, unless you expose your fine loaf to our home-grown Bay Area bacilli, the flavor will always come out different.

...cont'd

Known as the "Barnum of the West," Woodward strove to provide ordinary folks with "Education, Recreation and Amusement." His gardens were a West Coast superlative in several respects: its largest and most comprehensive zoo, its first aquarium, and its largest rollerskating rink. Its attractions included ostriches, camels, and Japanese roosters with 25-foot tail-feathers; crystals, precious stones, and petrified fossils; hot-air balloon rides; and a 5000-seat octagon concert pavilion. For years running, it was San Francisco's most popular resort.

Woodward's land was split into 39 parcels after his death. Only one hint remains of what was: a gourmet restaurant of the same name.

Woodward's Garden
1700 Mission
415-621-7122

San Francisco's Wild Characters: Then and Now

The City by the Bay has long been home to crazy characters and personalities, from the highly eccentric "Emperor Norton" in the Gold Rush era, to "high priest" Timothy Leary in the 1960s, to Mayor Willie Lewis Brown—love him or hate him—spearheading city politics today. We honor the wildest throughout the rest of this chapter.

Although famous-folk sightings in San Francisco might be running a bit thin (where have you gone, Nicolas Cage and Wynona Ryder?), today's local luminaries are nonetheless approachable. You might, for example, find yourself pedaling the stationary bike next to Danny Glover at USF's **Koret Center** (see **Chapter 7**), or enjoying an Irish Coffee next to Sean Penn or Francis Ford Coppola at **Tosca** in North Beach (242 Columbus, 415-986-9651). And hey, George (Lucas, of course) is coming to town, bringing a portion of his Lucasfilm empire to the Presidio. Surely *that* will boost the wattage of the City's star power!

SAN FRANCISCO'S WILD CHARACTERS ★ Mayor Willie L. Brown, Jr. (born 1934) ★ NOW

THEN ★ Sally Stanford (1903-1982) ★

Sally, as in the song "I Wonder What's Become of Sally," and Stanford, as in the university (she liked the football team), became SF's most famous madam in the 1930s and '40s, operating brothels in Russian Hill, Nob Hill, and the Tenderloin. Her clientele included a who's who of City elite, and her one-time 1144 Pine Street address was known far and wide to taxi drivers and police alike. Despite her reckless youth, Sally grew to achieve popular mainstream status in both society and politics, giving up the "biz" in 1949 to move to Sausalito, where she opened the enduring **Valhalla Restaurant** (201 Bridgeway, 415-332-2777). Her election to the Sausalito city council in 1972, and mayor in 1976, earned her the nationwide moniker, "Madam Mayor."

"Da Mayor," for his part, is undeniably a character, from his fetish for feathered hats and Armani suits to his international expeditions to San Francisco sister cities with attractive assistants in tow (for a complete list of sister cities, see ***Chapter 5*** under "International Travel"). He's certainly shaken things up in a city that for many years was suffering from political gridlock, managing to get the job done where others have not. Put simply, Willie Brown makes San Francisco more interesting.

CINEMA SAN FRANCISCO

San Francisco has been a player in the movies since the beginnings of the industry itself. Although the majority of California's film production has long since moved south to Los Angeles, the City has fostered scores of notable filmmakers—Francis Ford Coppola, George Lucas, Kathryn Bigelow, Clint Eastwood, and Alfred Hitchcock among them—and has served as the studio backdrop to an abundance of celebrated films over the years.

Many of these films use San Francisco's distinct culture and topography as key plot and character elements, from the Mission Dolores setting of Hitchcock's psychologically twisted *Vertigo,* to the drag-queen undertones of Robin Williams' character in *Mrs. Doubtfire*. So fire up that DVD player, and explore the cinematic world of San Francisco.

the san francisco international film festival (www.sfiff.org)

Every Spring for 46 years and counting, San Francisco has hosted the increasingly popular two-week San Francisco International Film Festival. While star-gazing in the VIP rooms at the opening and closing night galas can be a hoot (Peter Coyote and Delroy Lindo are regulars), the films take center stage.

An expert programming staff brings more than 200 independent documentaries and films to the screens at the ***AMC Kabuki Theatre*** (1881 Post, 415-922-4262), which serves as ground zero for the festival; the illustrious ***Castro Theatre*** (429 Castro, 415-621-6120); and two out-of-area venues. Some of the best screenings are scheduled for weekday matinees—perfect for those living off the clock!

Find more film festivals listed in ***Fairs & Fests***.

Essential Viewing

Scott Trimble, a location manager and scout who manages **Northern California Movies** (www.norcalmovies.com, part of www.filminamerica.com), maintains a comprehensive list of the great films of San Francisco. Although his personal "can't miss" list includes some obscure flicks, such as *The Lady From Shanghai* (1948) and *Star Trek IV: The Voyage Home* (1986), he goes with *Vertigo* (1958) and *Bullitt* (1968) as "probably the most common films associated with San Francisco, the former for its picturesque views of the City and the latter for its famous car chase." We couldn't agree more, so after plenty of popcorn and soda, we chose eight more flicks for a top ten listing of San Francisco movie magic.

The Maltese Falcon

starring Humphrey Bogart, 1941

A film noir classic. Bogart stars as detective Sam Spade, with an office in downtown San Francisco at Sutter & Montgomery. Scenery highlights include a shiny new Bay Bridge, and the Ferry Building downtown.

Vertigo

starring James Stewart, 1958

Hitchcock loved San Francisco and Northern California, and it shows in this twisted and strange thriller. He throws in at least a handful of City landmarks: Mission Dolores, Fort Point, the Palace of the Legion of Honor, the Palace of Fine Arts, and Ernie's Restaurant at 847 Montgomery (reportedly one of Hitchcock's favorite drinking holes, but unfortunately no longer in existence).

Bullitt

starring Steve McQueen, 1968

By all counts a great film, and one of Steve McQueen's best. Not only does it feature one of the most famous car chase scenes ever, but it shows off some of

cops & chase scenes

For some unknown reason, San Francisco has had a film and television obsession with cops. Street cops, private detectives, homicide investigators, undercover narcotics, you name it—it's been done here. All this, in a city that's not particularly known for its crime, or even its police force. And for every cop movie or show, there is, of course, a cool chase scene, where the City transforms into a spectacular racecourse for chasing bad guys.

The fixation began when Bogart played "Sam Spade" in *The Maltese Falcon*, but the "SF cop" was immortalized forever in the 1970s TV crime drama *The Streets of San Francisco*, starring Michael Douglas and Karl Malden. Douglas returned to his City cop roots in 1992, in the saucy thriller *Basic Instinct*.

Other notable local cop portrayals include *Vertigo* (retired cop), *Dirty Harry* (five films total), *48 Hours*, *Jade*, *The Rock* (FBI), and the recent *Nash Bridges* (TV series). As for riveting chase scenes? While *Streets* and *Nash Bridges* offered them up weekly, top honors go to McQueen and his Mustang in *Bullitt*, followed closely by *The Dead Pool* (Dirty Harry), *Jade*, and *The Rock*.

For more information, go to *www.norcalmovies.com*.

the best of SF, including a beautiful home at 2700 Vallejo in Pacific Heights (still there), the Mark Hopkins Hotel, Grace Cathedral, and the Marina.

Dirty Harry

starring Clint Eastwood, 1971

Hometown boy Clint Eastwood (born in San Francisco in 1930) does his city proud in his Dirty Harry movies, with perhaps more on-location City shooting (of both the film and the gun variety!) than in any film before or after. The original story is, predictably, the best, but there are five in the series, spanning from 1971 to 1988 (in order): *Dirty Harry, Magnum Force, The Enforcer, Sudden Impact,* and *The Dead Pool.*

walk the walk like dirty harry

If you really get into cinema research, the ***Dirty Harry Walking Tour*** (*www.movietours.com/harry*) is for you. "Harry" fans (and fanatics?) can trace the steps of the City's most famous rule-bending movie cop, from the rooftop pool at the ***Chinese Cultural Center of San Francisco*** (see p. 129) where a woman was shot in the opening sequence of the film, to ***Kezar Stadium*** (Frederick & Stanyan) where Harry finally tracks down his psychotic suspect. Have fun with it, but please—leave the .44 Magnum at home.

Escape From Alcatraz

starring Clint Eastwood, 1979

Alcatraz co-stars with Eastwood in this suspenseful classic filmed on "The Rock." So what if hundreds of swimmers a year now make the long haul through the supposedly shark-infested waters in the swimming events of the same name? (see **Chapter 7**). Eastwood reminds us that making the crossing at night, with no training, no wetsuit, and in prison clothes would be no easy feat.

SAN FRANCISCO'S WILD CHARACTERS

O.J. Simpson (born 1947)

"The Juice" grew up in Potrero Hill before attending high school at Galileo in the Marina and junior college at City College of San Francisco. He went on to achieve college football fame at USC and pro football fame with the Buffalo Bills and 49ers before succumbing to the allure of Hollywood. And, well, you probably know the rest of the story from there.

matinee price, please

Whatever happened to the good old fashioned weekday matinee—has it gone the way of the drive-in? Almost, but not quite. A few survive, although unfortunately they seem to favor the multiplexes. But a matinee is a matinee, and once you're plunked down in a dark theatre smack-dab in the middle of the day, you're not likely to notice your surroundings.

Your best movie bargain about town is at the ***Balboa Theater*** (3630 Balboa, 415-221-8184, *www.thebalboa theater.com*). You won't necessarily see first-run blockbusters here, but matinees are only $5 every day of the week. You even get in free on your birthday—how cool is that? Kung Fu fans will like the nearby ***Four Star*** (2200 Clement, 415-666-3488), which also screens $5 matinees Monday–Friday before 4pm.

The Castro Theatre (next page) offers $5 matinees every Wednesday (in addition to Saturday & Sunday). ***The Red Vic*** (next page) and ***The Roxie*** (next page) offer the same schedule for less: just $4.50 and $4 a pop, respectively.

[next reel...]

48 Hours

starring Nick Nolte, Eddie Murphy, 1982

Okay, so this movie is less "classic" than the others. But Nolte and Murphy are at the top of their games, and an exciting bus chase scene shows us just how fast Muni *could* run if it had its act together.

Pacific Heights

starring Michael Keaton, 1990

Pacific Heights, Potrero Hill, what's the difference? As long as you've got a beautifully renovated Victorian, downtown city views, and a psycho tenant who's protected under a liberal San Francisco rent ordinance, you can't go wrong.

Basic Instinct

starring Michael Douglas, 1992

Michael Douglas and Sharon Stone in a sexually charged, kinky love/murder mystery—are you kidding? Dynamite stuff. Add to that a quintessential San Francisco chase scene where Douglas ends up swimming in the Bay, and this one will be a repeat rental.

Mrs. Doubtfire

starring Robin Williams, 1993

The authors personally witnessed the filming of this movie in 1992, and have to admit that Robin Williams looked pretty good in a dress. Excellent location shooting in Pac Heights and North Beach, along with Robin Williams at his best, make this a worthy rental.

The Rock
starring Nicolas Cage, 1996
Nicolas Cage flexes his muscle and Sean Connery grows hair extensions. Ouch! Still, *The Rock* does rock, from opening bell through to final knockout punch. Plus, it has one of the best modern car chase scenes ever (we're starting to think SF was designed for them), culminating in a spectacular local crowd-pleaser: a Department of Parking & Traffic three-wheeler gets blown sky high!

[...cont'd]

Finally, you'll find matinees in the multiplexes: at the ***AMC Kabuki 8*** (1881 Post, 415-922-4262) for $7 before 6pm, at the ***AMC 1000 Van Ness*** (1000 Van Ness, 415-922-4262) for $7.50 before 6pm, and at ***Loews Theatres at Metreon*** (101 4th Street, 415-369-6200) for $7 for the first show of the day.

The Dark Rooms

A disturbing trend is sprawling across the Bay Area and the nation: multiplexes are consuming the classic, single-screen theatre that projects character in addition to first-rate movies. That said, a few independents are hanging on in the City.

The Castro Theatre (429 Castro @ Market, 415-621-6120, www.thecastrotheatre.com) is the granddaddy of all independent cinema in San Francisco. If you haven't been to this grand palace, sat under the dramatic, mandala-like ceiling, and listened to the mighty Wurlitzer organ introduce a film, you have yet to truly experience the movies in the City. Another of our preferred film houses is the **United Artists Coronet** (3575 Geary, 415-752-6600), a towering big-screen venue out in the Richmond district that is unfortunately slated for conversion to a senior housing complex in Spring of 2004. Catch a flick there while you still can.

Other notable single-screens include:

The Bridge (3010 Geary, 415-352-0810)
United Artists Vogue (3290 Sacramento, 415-221-8183)
Clay Theatre (2261 Fillmore, 415-352-0810)
United Artists Metro (2055 Union, 415-931-1685)

If funky art-house is your style, check out **The Red Vic** (1727 Haight, 415-668-3994), where the draw is the atmosphere and unusual films, not the screen or sound quality; and **The Roxie** (3117 16th Street, 415-863-1087), a Mission district independent with plenty of moxie.

THE BEST THINGS TO DO FOR FREE IN SAN FRANCISCO

The City by the Bay presents endless opportunities for free fun. This is by no means an exhaustive list of gratis excursions—just (in our opinion) some of the best.

Take a Walk through Crissy Field

(www.crissyfield.org)

The new Crissy Field national park and recreation area, on the northern edge of the Presidio, is a gem. Opened in 2001, the newly created park is a combination of marshland, walking paths, sand dunes, and bay-front beaches. Start out at the Crissy Field Center on the southeast side of the park—equal parts museum, education center, and café/bookstore—and work your way west along the pathways. Walk all the way out to Fort Point, in the shadow of the Golden Gate Bridge, and watch the surfers and boats whisk by. The cozy café and warming hut on the waterfront makes an excellent pit stop. Amble back along the water and witness some of the best sailboarding and kiteboarding in the world.

Bike across the Golden Gate Bridge

Grab your mountain bike for a spin across the most beautiful bridge in the most beautiful city in the world. It never gets boring; the splendor of the scenery never wanes. Stop mid-way across and take in the City skyline, Alcatraz, and Angel Island on the Bay side, the Marin Headlands and the vast Pacific blue to the west. As a bonus, continue on the north side to the top of the Marin Headlands, where you can look back towards the Bridge with the City in the background—one of the most breathtaking vistas in the country, if not the world (see **Chapter 7** for more bike ride ideas).

Explore Sigmund Stern Grove

(Sloat & 19th Avenue, www.sterngrove.org)

Once home to the infamous Trocadero, a hotel and compound that was known as a raucous hideaway for the rich and elite at the turn of the century, Stern Grove is now a true jewel in the Sunset. Bound by

Sloat Boulevard to the south, Wawona Street to the north, 19th Avenue to the east and 34th Avenue to the west, "The Grove," together with Pine Lake, comprises some 63 acres of beautiful tree-lined recreation space. It comes complete with hiking trails, lawn bowling greens, croquet courts, golf putting greens, tennis courts, and horseshoe pits (see **Chapter 7** for more on fitness in The Grove). A well-equipped children's playground will keep the tykes smiling, too. As for the Trocadero? The original structure is still there, and although a bit tamer than in years past, it's still available for rent for social functions.

Stern Grove is said to be ten degrees warmer than the rest of the City, due to its wind-blocking eucalyptus trees—although we're prepared to dispute that claim! It certainly *is* warmer than the surrounding Sunset, particularly on windy, foggy days.

What's more, the trees and sloping terrain form a natural amphitheatre, which some have dubbed "nature's music box." The Grove has indeed gained fame for its eclectic (and free) summer music festivals. They are one of the best freebies in the City, so bring a picnic lunch, and be sure to arrive early for the best seating. Tip: You can reserve picnic table seating for up to six people by calling the **Recreation & Park Department** (415-831-5500) at 9am the Monday before each concert. Have your speed dialer ready. Go to www.sterngrove.org or see **Fairs & Fests** for the full scoop.

Spend an Afternoon in Golden Gate Park

Golden Gate Park is one of the world's greatest urban refuges. At 1,013 acres, it's the single largest man-made urban park in the U.S., larger even than New York's Central Park. Unlike Central Park, however, it remains a relatively safe place to visit.

Built in 1870 from little more than sand dunes, Golden Gate Park has nine lakes and more than a million trees within its borders. The park's diversity is nothing short of astonishing, home to (in no particular order): buffalo, soccer fields, fly-casting ponds, windmills, arboretums, Japanese gardens, museums, amphitheaters, golf courses, tennis courts, archery ranges, lawn bowling greens, pétanque courts, handball courts, horseshoe games, hiking trails, biking paths, skating areas, merry-go-rounds, baseball fields, softball fields, polo fields, and boating lakes. Take your pick of activities or locations, or simply bring a blanket and relax in a grassy meadow. For details on how to use the park as your very own gym, see **Chapter 7**.

SAN FRANCISCO'S WILD CHARACTERS ☆ Shanghai Kelly (19th century, dates unknown)

THEN

Perhaps a bit mythologized over the years, Shanghai Kelly was nonetheless a colorful personality from the Barbary Coast days. What we do know is this: James "Shanghai" Kelly, a fiery red-bearded character, owned a boarding house on either Pacific or Broadway, and later ran a saloon called the Boston House at Davis & Chamber. From there, the line between fact and fiction starts to blur.

Kelly was reportedly heavily involved in the practice of "shanghaiing," or kidnapping unsuspecting young souls and shipping them off to sea as crewmen on international voyages. Legends have him utilizing various deceits to capture his prey, including trapdoors in his saloon, drugged-up drinks at the bar, and opium-laced cigars made in Chinatown.

The most infamous tale has Kelly throwing himself a blowout "birthday" bash aboard a steamer on the Bay: inviting all on the waterfront for a night of free booze and revelry, then serving them drug-poisoned drinks—which were slurped up with pleasure. Kelly then unloaded his cargo of passed-out men onto three ships waiting outside the Golden Gate, collecting a tidy sum in return.

NOW

Good thing no such fate awaits you at *today's* bar!

Shanghai Kelly's
2064 Polk @ Broadway
415-771-3300

THE PERFECTLY FREE DAY

10am	Maritime Museum or free walking tour
12:15pm	picnic lunch @ Fort Mason, free Ghirardelli chocolate for dessert
2pm	Anchor Brewing Company tour
5pm	happy hour with free food
8pm	after dinner nap
10pm	no-cover dancing

Start your day with a walking tour led by **City Guides** (415-557-4266, www.sfcityguides.com). We like the year-round tour of Chinatown that meets at the Portsmouth Square flagpole, but take your pick of the many excellent walks they offer. If walking for two hours is just too much effort, confine your strolling to the floors of a museum, such as the **National Maritime Museum** (Aquatic Park) where admission is always free.

We'll call it a free lunch if you paid for it yesterday—or if you'll gladly pay Tuesday. Stop by the **Ghirardelli Chocolate Factory** (Ghirardelli Square, 900 Northpoint) to snag a free chocolate sample for dessert before you tote a picnic lunch over to the grassy expanse at nearby **Fort Mason** (corner of Marina & Buchanan).

Drinking as entertainment? You bet, as long as it's free and comes with education in hops, barley, and other parts of the beer-making process. **Anchor Brewing Company** (1705 Mariposa, 415-863-8350, www.anchorbrewing.com) hosts a 90-minute brewery tour at the company's Potrero Hill facility, which culminates in—you guessed it—ample tasting at the end of the tour.

Continuing the brewski theme, hit a bar that serves free food during happy hour. Given your inebriated state, no one will realize that you didn't actually buy your drinks *there*.

Try **Club Waziema** (543 Divisadero, 415-346-6641) any night of the week, or see **Dining & Nightlife** for more happy hour recommendations. Eat up, free grub!

After a refreshing evening nap, cap off the night in your boogie shoes at **Holy Cow** (see **Dining & Nightlife**), where there's "never a cover, always a party."

ANCHOR'S AWAY!

Although the building itself dates back to 1896, the brewery now known as ***Anchor Brewing Company*** (this page) was purchased by Fritz Maytag (yes, *the* Maytag's) in the 1960s, a transaction that marked the beginning of the modern microbrewing movement. Today's free plant tour begins with a lesson in ingredients, brewing methods for steam beer, porter, and ales—and the company's colorful history.

You'll generally need to book your reservations at least a month in advance, although you *could* tag along with a group of regulars. "We went every Friday when I got laid off," Mary Mangold told us, "and compared notes on how to fill out the unemployment forms."

We'll drink to that!

NINE TO FIVE

Nine to five? No, we're not talking about work (or the Dolly Parton movie), but about creative ways to occupy yourself during standard "business hours" Monday through Friday, while you're not working. You won't be able to enjoy these daytime activities once you go back to work—at least not very easily. So don't waste your day watching a soap opera, go out and create one of your own!

Ride Alongs

Always hankered to jump on the back of a screaming red fire engine? Citizens can hitch a ride with the **San Francisco Fire Department** (HQ: 698 2nd Street, 415-558-3200, 415-558-3403 for ride alongs). Although they reserve the right to limit the activities depending on the dangers involved, SFFD does accept informal ride along requests on a case-by-case basis. Be sure to make your "case" a special one.

WE'LL SEE YOU IN COURT

Step inside a courtroom and see justice in action. Some trials are downright fascinating! If you get a doozy, hey, it's not jury duty—step out at any time, or join the jury member who nods off during closing arguments.

Decide for yourself whether the lower courts erred when you hear the appeals at the ***United States Court of Appeals for the Ninth Circuit*** (95 7th Street, 415-556-9800, *www.ca9.uscourts.gov*). When the court is not in session here, take a public tour of the courthouse instead (on Tuesdays at 1pm, 415-556-9945, meet in front of the museum near the Seventh & Mission entrance).

The ***California Supreme Court*** (Earl Warren Building, 350 McAllister, 415-865-7000, *www.courtinfo.ca.gov/courts/supreme*) convenes for a good chunk of the year near the Civic Center, and ***Small Claims Court*** (Civic Center Courthouse, 400 McAllister, Room 103, 415-551-4000) is just across the street. Remember, no lawyers are allowed in Small Claims Court, which makes for some juicy if not always well-reasoned debates. Then again, lawyers aren't always the most logical creatures themselves...

Or, hitch a ride with local law enforcement. It's an eye-opener—really! You may spend more time drinking coffee than chasing bad guys but no matter. The SFPD knows good coffee (no diners and donuts for these folks).

The SFPD doesn't have a formal ride along program so call the **Citizens' Police Academy** (415-401-4701, www.sfgov.org/police, under "Citizens' Academy") and say you're looking for a ride along. The word on the street is that you can also arrange one informally through a friend on the force. If their request for you to ride is approved, you can tag along for four hours of their eight hour shift.

If you really get into all this police stuff, check out the full Citizens' Academy program, detailed in **Chapter 10**.

home entertainment

If you're of the couch potato variety, roll on down to the ***Home Entertainment Show*** (for location, check 410-769-8223, *www.HomeEntertainment-EXPO.com*). The four-day event showcases exclusive home theater, audio, and video, with live music performances from popular jazz, contemporary blues, and classical recording artists.

Brain Candy

Miss the intellectual stimulation of office life? Never fear. Stimulation for the brainy and outspoken is in no short supply in San Francisco.

The "Alerts" section of the weekly ***San Francisco Bay Guardian*** (135 Mississippi, 415-255-3100, www.sfbg.com), both in print and online, lists political events, lectures and community meetings, most of which are free. San Franciscans will protest anything. Find out how and where to join in.

Want to absorb valuable information that could help you change careers? Stop by an industry conference. Most are free for non-exhibitors. You can walk the floor, visit different vendors, people watch, and learn a ton—about what, of course, depends on the convention.

All events at the **Main Library** (100 Larkin @ Grove, 415-557-4400) are free, from internet classes to children's book readings. Pick up a Calendar of Events at the front information desk.

The **Moscone Center** (747 Howard, 415-974-4000, www.moscone.com) is the City's primary venue for big exhibitions. The annual **Macworld** (www.macworldexpo.com) in January is a local favorite: listen to Steve Jobs preach the Mac gospel and munch on all the latest Apple goodies.

what do we want? to protest!

The history of organized political protest in San Francisco dates back at least 150 years, to an 1852 "indignation meeting" at ***Portsmouth Plaza***, held to block the city council from purchasing the Jenny Lind Theatre and using it as the City's first city hall. The demonstrators failed.

Lost causes of modern times include:

- the 1969 cry that the shape of the Transamerica Pyramid "won't fit in the City."
- Jim Jones' march of 600 people across Golden Gate Bridge to call attention to the need for—get this—suicide barriers.
- Margo St. James' founding of COYOTE (Call Off Your Old Tired Ethics), a prostitutes' rights organization.

Win or lose, activist citizens will always feel at home in San Francisco, where former KFOG DJ Scoop Nissen used to say, "If you don't like the news, go out and make some of your own."

Getting Political

The idea of a democracy is that the people rule—but with everyone working so much, who has the energy?

You do. Whatever issue you're passionate about, now is the perfect time to get involved in SF's longstanding activist culture.

Many political organizations dealing with hot issues would love to have an intelligent, energetic volunteer like you. Start at *the* site for City politicos—**The Usual Suspects** (www.sfusualsuspects.com, check out "Political Links" under "Resources"). There you'll find info on a host of local organizations, elected officials, and media outlets.

An easy place to start is to voice your opinion about rent control or the homeless at City Hall. The Board of Supervisors' weekly meetings are open to the public, every Tuesday at 2pm. The agenda and schedule of special meetings are posted at www.sfgov.org.

Need a better understanding of city government structure before you go? Docent-led tours of **City Hall** (415-554-6139) are free. Sign in at the City Hall Docent Tour Kiosk on the Main Floor for this 45-60 minute tour, offered at 10am, noon and 2pm during the week (except on Mondays) and at 12:30pm on Saturdays. Groups of eight or more should call for a reservation.

If you're going to get political, be sure you're registered to vote. Contact the **Department of Elections** (415-554-4411, www.sfgov.org/election) to get yourself all squared away.

Wild Characters:
GOOD RIDDANCE!

James Jones (1931–1978)

The story of Jim Jones and the People's Temple is one of the darkest chapters of San Francisco history. Jones brought the headquarters of the infamous Temple to 1859 Geary Boulevard (now a post office) in the City's Fillmore district in 1971. The charismatic leader immediately established himself as a political power broker, ingratiating himself with California politicos Art Agnos, then-Governor Jerry Brown, and Willie Brown, among others. Indeed, Jones was said to have delivered Mayor George Moscone's victory in 1975 (amid allegations that the People's Temple committed voter fraud). Mayor Moscone later rewarded Jones with an official post: running San Francisco's Housing Commission.

Tragedy struck in November of 1978, when Bay Area Congressman Leo Ryan led an investigative mission to Georgetown, Guyana, seeking the compound where Jones and his followers had been living for over a year. Ryan and several reporters were gunned down at a Guyana airfield trying to rescue defectors. Later that same day, Jones ordered his congregation of roughly 1,000 to drink cyanide-laced Kool-Aid in the largest mass suicide in modern history.

TV or Radio Show Audience

Does all that civic stuff have you snoring? Then tune in to the great American pastime—TV. Only this time, get off the couch and into a live studio audience. Okay, so there aren't a *lot* of television studios in the Bay Area—you'd have to hop down to LA or out to NYC for the best selection—but there *are* a few random ones to look into.

If quiz shows and kids are an appeal, you can explore ***Peninsula Quiz Kids*** (1250 San Carlos Avenue, 2nd Floor, San Carlos, 650-637-1936, www.pentv.org/PQK/pqk.htm), where the audience reportedly "plays an important role in the show and is on television often," so there you go. The religiously tinged ***Soul Show*** (www.soulshow.tv) is another underground program, focused primarily on youths (ages 18-25). Check out their site for information on how to become an audience member.

LIGHTS, CAMERA, ACTION!

According to Edward Guthman, film critic for the ***San Francisco Chronicle,*** finding work as an extra isn't hard. You don't have to be an actor or a member of the Screen Actors' Guild, just look like a "real person" (we know, this is difficult for some of us). Keep in mind that the work isn't glamorous—the hours are long, there's a lot of sitting around, and you have to take orders all day. That said, getting behind the scenes can be a lot of fun.

To be an extra, you have to either answer a film company's "open call" or go through a casting company. Try out your act with one of the following:

★ ***Beau Bonneau Casting*** (84 1st Street, 415-346-2278, *www.beaubonneaucasting.com*) uses the SF Casting Network to procure extras. Their website explains how the whole process works.

★ ***Nancy Hayes Casting*** (1515 Vallejo, 415-567-2278, *www.hayescasting.com*) maintains an impressive list of projects.

★ ***Laura Folger Casting*** (450 Taraval, Suite 300, 415-664-3072). You'll need to pay a small registration fee, and supply a recent photo (clothes on, please).

It doesn't happen during the day and it'll cost you a little didge ($10), but if comedy's your thing, you can check out San Jose's *Stand-UP, It's Thursday Nite!*, taped at **Big Lil's Comedy Cabaret** (157 West San Fernando Street, San Jose, 408-295-7469 for tickets, www.biglils.com). Despite its name, the show currently broadcasts on Friday nights (Saturday mornings) at 1:30am on SF station KRON 4.

KQED Public Broadcasting (2601 Mariposa, 415-864-2000, www.kqed.org) doesn't have studio audience facilities, but they do offer free tours of their production facilities, which are pretty cool. Call their main number and ask for KQED Tours to arrange a group visit.

To get behind the camera, peer into **Artists' Television Access** (992 Valencia, 415-824-3890, www.atasite.org), whose mission is "to bring the tools of the mass media within reach." They provide cheap access to audio-visual equipment for artists, as well as a venue for a wacky mix of events. Suffice it to say you're bound to see performances here the likes of which you've never seen before. Check their website for a complete calendar.

Movie or TV Extra

Looking for an opportunity to claim your 15 minutes of fame? Or just interested in blowing off an afternoon and meeting some stars? Movies and television programs are constantly filming in San Francisco; you just need to know where to find them. They always need extras, hangers-on, groupies, or whatever you'd care to label yourself.

The **San Francisco Film Commission** (415-554-6244, www.ci.sf.ca.us/site/film_index.asp) will be able to tell you what movies are being filmed in the City at the moment. It pays to be extra nice to them on the phone. Their recorded hotline (415-554-4004) lists upcoming productions.

During a break between high-tech jobs, Russian Hill resident Joe Parente worked as an extra on the film *Bedazzled*. Although he calls the film itself "very forgettable," he felt it was still a great experience. "In addition to a couple of crowd scenes, I was also chosen to play a San Francisco Policeman in full uniform. I had the opportunity to meet Brendan Fraser, and I think—think—Elizabeth Hurley actually checked me out when I was in my uniform!" Joe could've sold his story to the tabloids, he says, but he chose instead to respect Liz's privacy. He received $71 for eleven hours of work. Woo-hoo! Drinks on Joe!

Get On a Boat!

With water in just about every direction, the San Francisco Bay Area is a boater's dream. So how can you enjoy the waterways of the Bay if you're not a yacht-owning tycoon? Start by hitting up those rich friends! But if boat-owning compadres are in short supply, you'll have to get a little more resourceful.

If you just want to soak up some nautical history, try touring the **S.S. Jeremiah O'Brien** (Pier 45, 415-544-0100, www.ssjeremiahobrien.org) in the heart of Fisherman's Wharf. It's a little touristy, but will set you back only seven of your leisure bucks. The people watching alone is worth the price of admission. While you're down there, jump aboard one of the **Blue and Gold Fleet** (Pier 41, 415-705-5555, www.blueandgoldfleet.com) and ferry over to Sausalito or Tiburon.

For a bigger adventure, rent a Boston Whaler from **Bay Adventures** (85 Liberty Ship Way, Sausalito, 415-331-0444, www.sfbayadventures.com). This is one of those rare activities you feel like you shouldn't be able to do: cruise a small motorboat anywhere you want in the Bay—under the Golden Gate Bridge, along the Marin Headlands, or around Angel and Alcatraz islands—for $75 to $125 an hour. It's spectacular! Boating experience is "required," but as long as you can start the motor, steer in forward or reverse, and dock the boat, you'll be fine. Be sure to consult the experts before setting out for info on tides, currents, and hazards.

Want to leave the motor behind and sail your way across the Bay? Start by visiting the **SFSailing** website (www.sfsailing.com), chock full of incredibly useful information on local sailing. The site's original and most useful purpose is to connect skippers with potential mates. That's right—you too can crew! The best part is, you don't even need any experience. Many captains actually seek out rookie crew members, so they can teach them the "right" way to sail. Of course, if you are an experienced sailor, there are skippers looking for you, too. The website's "crew" lists include Racing, Bay Cruising, Ocean Cruising, and Pick-up, and it also has a skippers list.

Local yacht clubs post crew opportunities on their bulletin boards too. The most buttoned-up of the bunch is the **St. Francis Yacht Club** (on the Marina waterfront, 415-563-6363, www.stfyc.com). Not far behind is the North Bay's **San Francisco Yacht Club** (98 Beach Road, Belvedere, 415-435-9133, www.sfyc.org). Both are blue blazer-type clubs, so wear your finest duds when you drop by.

Care for some formal instruction before putting out to sea? **SFSailing** (see above) lists companies that offer lessons in the Bay Area. Most are pretty pricey. A much less expensive alternative is **Sailing Education Adventures** (Fort Mason Center, Building E, Room 235, 415-775-8779, www.sailsea.org), a non-profit membership organization "dedicated to promoting sailing through competitively priced instruction and related educational and social activities." They offer reasonably priced adult lessons, boat rentals, a children's sailing camp, and volunteer opportunities (which may make your boat rentals that much cheaper). An annual membership costs $55 for individuals, $75 for families. It entitles you to benefits including eight free group sails per month—which by themselves are worth more than the price of membership.

BE A TOURIST IN YOUR OWN TOWN

If you've lived in the Bay Area for any length of time, you've no doubt visited tourist traps that are dull, cheesy, overpriced, or all of the above. So why bother? Because our City is full of treasures that are often taken for granted by all-too-jaded residents, places that are special whether you're a tourist from Des Moines or a fourth generation San Franciscan.

Make it your duty as a local to stay up-to-date on the City—or at least as up-to-date as the tourists are. Pick up your very own tourist packet at the **San Francisco Visitor Information Center** (Hallidie Plaza, 900 Market @ Powell, 415-391-2000, www.sfvisitor.org). The packet includes coupons and a guide to discount shopping (which is available at major hotels, too. For more stores, see the **Unemployed Shopping Guide**). Check the end of this chapter for other references that are good for tourists and great for locals. But you won't likely need your tourist packet to reconnect with these SF essentials.

Golden Gate Bridge

Ah yes, the Bridge. An obvious choice, but it's always attractive. Drive it, bike it, walk it—crawl it for all we care! Just take it all in.

Look up and imagine climbing one of the two towers, which crazed Berkeley students did, by the way, back in the '60s. Look down and imagine (morbid as it may be) plummeting to the frigid water below, as an estimated 25 people do each year. As graceful as it is, the Golden Gate Bridge holds the dubious distinction of being the number one suicide location in the world. Or maybe it's *because* of its beauty—experts believe that even the suicidal are partial to aesthetics. On a happier note, the Coast Guard reports that the number of deaths in recent years has decreased dramatically due to increased patrolling. Do everyone a favor—stay on the bridge while enjoying it.

THE ORIGINAL "LOCALS" ON THE ROCK

No one knows exactly how long ago the Ohlone Indians first landed at Alcatraz Island, only that they used it to isolate and ostracize those who had violated tribal law. (Sound familiar?) European settlers took it, along with the rest of San Francisco, from the Ohlone in the late 1700s.

In 1969, however, long after Alcatraz had closed its doors as a federal penitentiary, a group of Indians led by the charismatic Richard Oakes occupied the island and symbolically claimed it for the Indian people. The group remained there for almost two full years before the federal government moved in and removed them. Although the land never did officially return to the Indian people, the occupation is credited with giving birth to the modern Indian self-determination movement.

Alcatraz

Blue & Gold Fleet: 415-705-5555, www.nps.gov/alcatraz

Never been to "The Rock?" Shame on you! This is one San Francisco landmark that is as intriguing as it is spooky. It's managed by the GGNRA and the National Park Service, and they've done a wonderful job at preserving and re-creating the different historical incarnations of the island: prison, military installation, Indian reservation, and nature preserve. The Cell House recorded audio tour is guaranteed to raise the hair on the back of your neck. Don't get sold out—buy your ticket online ahead of time. Save a few clams by going in the (warmer) off-season—before July 1.

Cable Cars

www.sfcablecar.com

Sure, a cable car travels slow and you can no longer hop on and off it at will but Andrew Hallidie's invention is still a great way to roll. Pick up the California Street line from downtown and ride up to Nob Hill, then transfer to the Powell-Hyde line and ride down to Fisherman's Wharf. Other good places to catch a ride without waiting in line: top of Lombard Street (Lombard & Hyde) or at California and Van Ness. Best perk for locals: no $3 fare if you have a MUNI Fast Pass.

Ferry to Tiburon

Blue & Gold Fleet: 415-705-5555, www.blueandgoldfleet.com

Just being out on the San Francisco Bay is breathtaking enough. But boat across to the pleasant town of Tiburon, with its wonderful waterfront restaurants and spectacular City views, and you can almost fathom why Bay Area houses are the most expensive in the nation. Suck down a Sam's Smoothie (fully leaded) out on the deck and you'll swear you're in heaven. As a bonus, continue on the ferry to Angel Island for great hiking, biking, and picnicking (see **Chapter 7**).

Palace of Fine Arts and The Exploratorium

Originally conceived for the 1915 Panama-Pacific International Exposition by architect Bernard R. Maybeck, this strangely situated, seemingly out of place work of neo-Roman architecture is undeniably appealing. The Palace was reconstructed with modern materials in 1966 and, in 1969, a quirky new science and technology museum called **The Exploratorium** (3601 Lyon, 415-397-5673, www.exploratorium.edu) opened its doors to the public. According to the museum's own mission statement, "The Exploratorium was conceived to communicate a conviction that nature and people can be both understandable and full of newly discovered magic." We're down with that!

Union Square

Post, Stockton, Geary & Powell Streets

We know, we know, Union Square is crowded, jam-packed with tourists, and appears to be little more than a giant shopping mall. But trust us, it *is* cool if you know where to look, and you'll find just about any mainstream retail store you might need, if shopping is indeed your bag. It's also a great place to people watch—you're bound to make some new international friends among the throngs of sightseers who flock here from all over the globe.

Park at the **Sutter-Stockton Garage** (444 Stockton), one of the cheapest downtown. If you happen to stumble into the **E & O Trading Company** (314 Sutter, 415-693-0303, www.eotrading.com) on the way out of the garage, all the better. E & O houses a delicious Asian restaurant and brewpub rolled into one. Sounds a-okay to us!

POST

POWELL

WILD CHARACTERS
even *more* now

Marian and Vivian Brown (born ???*)

The City's favorite twins are often spotted parading through Union Square or the Financial District in matching '40s hair, hat and dress, but always with sensible shoes. Do they wear matching dress all the time? Yes, they say, and reportedly will only buy an outfit if they can find two identical pieces that they both like. This dynamic duo is also a favorite with Madison Avenue. With commercials for Virgin Atlantic, Joe Boxer, and the Chronicle among others, their fame continues to soar.

**You'll have to ask them!*

STOCKTON

GEARY

Upscale retailers Macy's, Saks Fifth Avenue, Tiffany's, and Neiman Marcus anchor the square (look for the prominent neon signs). Say what you will about the prices, these establishments are nonetheless elegant. Neiman's internal architecture alone makes it worth a visit.

If you feel like splurging, lunch with the Pacific Heights ladies in Neiman's top floor **Rotunda Restaurant** (150 Stockton, 415-362-4777).

Zip across the square to the **Westin St. Francis Hotel** (335 Powell, 415-397-7000) and into their great glass elevators to zoom up 31 floors for a panoramic eastward view.

To get off the main drag, take a stroll down the tranquil **Maiden Lane** (off Stockton between Post & Geary), formerly "Morton Street," one of the City's most notorious alleys for crime and prostitution. The street is now much more pedestrian—literally—during the day, with a variety of cafés, boutiques, and galleries nestled into its semi-chic single block.

Architecture buffs shouldn't miss the **Xanadu Tribal Art Gallery** (140 Maiden Lane, 415-392-9999)—its 1948 brick structure is the only Frank Lloyd Wright building in San Francisco.

THE ANIMAL KINGDOM

A surprising number of creatures—human and otherwise—mill about the Bay Area. Some are caged; others are just making their way out in the world.

connemara's escape

San Francisco sported numerous horse racetracks and even a few dog tracks back at the turn of the 20th century. According to Raymond H. Clary, who wrote *The Making of Golden Gate Park*, an independent-minded greyhound named Connemara decided he'd had enough of chasing mechanical rabbits.

After crossing the finish line of a race he'd won at a track in Ingleside, Connemara just kept on running, eventually all the way to Sutro Forest, near present-day UCSF. There he took up residence and became the leader of a pack of wild dogs who regularly terrorized cats, chickens, pigs, and even took out a few peacocks in Golden Gate Park. The valuable greyhound was never recaptured, preferring instead to live a life of leisure in the wilds of San Francisco.

A model of freedom for us all!

all filler, no killer

Although many of his proclaimed exploits have since been proven myths, Anton LaVey *was* the founder and High Priest of the Church of Satan—and that certainly counts for something.

His celebrity status during the '60s and '70s was based in large part on a self-created legend, a very clever PR campaign, and his ability to snow both the media and his "disciples." *The Satanic Bible*, authored by LaVey and the guiding work for the Church, was largely plagiarized from various sources, and was originally conceived as a commercial vehicle by Avalon Books.

Still, LaVey did manage to attract a loyal following, including Jayne Mansfield and Sammy Davis Jr., and many an SF notable attended satanic rituals at his notorious "Black House" at 6114 California Street—where he kept a pet lion chained in the back yard.

Free Zoo Day

Zoos aren't for everyone, sometimes not even the animals. The **San Francisco Zoo** (1 Zoo Road @ Sloat & Great Highway), 415-753-7080, www.sfzoo.org), for example, hardly served as a model of animal care—until recently.

Thanks to a large infusion of new funds, the Zoo has been imbued with new life and a welcome change in philosophy: it's now a "conservation zoo" that focuses on preservation and education. So far, the upshots have included new facilities for visitors and a new Lemur Forest in a large outdoor setting. Next up will be the creation of a multi-species African wildlife roaming exhibit, and the Great Ape Forest.

Mark your calendar: the first Wednesday of every month is free; otherwise you're looking at $10 admission ($8 for City residents).

Whale Watching

The Bay Area coastline is ideally situated for viewing the gray whale in its annual migration from arctic waters to Baja breeding grounds. December through May is the season, and the **Oceanic Society** (415-474-3385, www.oceanic-society.org, then "Whale Watch") is the vessel.

Day trips from SF cost $50 per person Fridays and Mondays, and $52 per person on weekends. San Francisco departures, however, are the most expensive and lengthy (six hours). If an entire day on a rocking and rolling diesel powered boat sounds a little much for you (several locals we spoke with found that it was), try driving north to **Bodega Bay** or south to **Half Moon Bay**, where trips run $34 and last about three hours.

Bird Watching

Point Reyes National Seashore (www.nps.gov/pore) is the pre-eminent bird-watching venue within easy striking distance from San Francisco (see **Chapter 5** for more). Its amazing selection of land and sea birds will satisfy beginner and expert birders alike.

Just south of Point Reyes is the **Bolinas Lagoon** (www.bolinaslagoon.org), long a top destination for coastal bird-watchers. **Audubon Canyon Ranch** (www.egret.org) manages the nearby Bolinas Lagoon Preserve as well as the Bouverie Preserve in Sonoma, which is home to over 130 species of birds and to 350 species of wildflowers.

But you don't have to leave home to find birds. Plenty of land birds and waterfowl can be sighted in **Golden Gate Park**, and the **Marin Headlands** within the **Golden Gate National Recreation Area** (www.nps.gov/goga) is the perfect place to view raptors, particularly in September and October.

LIONS & TOGARE & BABOONS—OH MY!

In one of the more bizarre tales involving a lion, a Satanist, and a baboon, an SF Zoo director was severely beaten by apes in 1968, and left bloody and unconscious in the ape cage.

It all started with a pet lion named Togare, who was owned by the notorious Satanist Anton LaVey, founder and leader of the Church of Satan. Togare was living at LaVey's infamous "Black House" in the Richmond until the City responded to neighbors' complaints by passing an ordinance banning lions in private homes. Togare was banished to the San Francisco Zoo. For reasons unknown, the zoo director took an extreme dislike to Togare and eventually had him shipped to Lion Country Safari in Southern California, never giving LaVey a chance to say goodbye.

Being a Satanist and all, LaVey was predictably angry. He supposedly channeled his anger into a curse, to be delivered through the Zoo's Egyptian crystal baboon. Not long after, when the zoo director wandered into their cage, the normally docile apes (led by a certain baboon) launched a vicious attack, brutally clawing and beating the director.

The moral? Damned if we know. Let Satanists be Satanists?

Bison, Peacocks and Other Fauna in Golden Gate Park

Not all of the animals who have made Golden Gate Park their home still live there, as the park's flora and fauna are ever-changing. But over the years, the park has hosted a zoo's-worth: wild peacocks, turtles, ducks, herons, hawks (and plenty of other birds), weasels, rabbits, snakes, quail, fox, feral cats—even grizzly bears! (They were in cages. Don't ask.) Did we mention the bison paddock? As Jurassic as it sounds, it's really quite docile, amounting to nothing more than a few grazing buffalo in a fenced in area. Fun? That depends. Just knowing they're there might be enough to float your boat.

Sea Lions at Pier 39

www.pier39restaurants.com/cam.htm

Yes, they smell. Yes, they're lazy. But are there any creatures more leisurely than those lounging lions (of the sea variety) that have made Pier 39 their own retirement community? Ray-catching and napping seem to be their prime daytime activities.

We suppose some of them have to go out and catch fish from time to time, but you wouldn't know it by watching them. Witness the alpha males staking their "docks," knocking others into the water, or the pups who can't quite find room to sun-tan—and keep falling into the drink! Watching the frolic may be one of the few good reasons to toss yourself into the mêlée that is Fisherman's Wharf.

People Watching

People are animals. Watch them and you'll see!

The males of the species bask in the sun at "Dolores Beach"—the affectionate nickname for the City-facing slope of **Mission Dolores Park** (20th Street @ Church)—stretching out, preening, and trying to attract a mate.

Many females, meanwhile, can be observed in their own native habitat: the shopping mall. The food court in the pit of **San Francisco Center** (865 Market @ 5th Street) places observers in prime position to analyze the bags-in to bags-out ratio as shoppers enter and exit the mall via the underground Powell Street BART station.

★ SAN FRANCISCO'S MILD CHARACTER ★ Herb Caen (1916-1997) ★

San Francisco's most beloved columnist in the 20th century, Herb Caen served as the City's heartbeat for nearly seven decades.

* * *

His quick-witted column was as humorous as it was newsworthy, but was often downright scathing. With a dot-dot-dot of his typewriter, he could as easily ruin a restaurant as launch a political career.

* * *

Caen could coin a phrase, too, receiving credit for San Francisco nicknames "Baghdad by the Bay" and "The City That Knows How" and terms including "beatniks."

* * *

Pals with Mayor Willie Brown and just about every other mayor through the years, Caen received a Pulitzer Prize in 1996 for his tireless work as the voice of San Francisco.

Human athleticism, competition and aggression are all on display during the Nordstrom Half-Yearly Sale. Doh! We *meant* to say in amateur sports and games. We suggest **Police League Soccer Games** at the fields in Golden Gate Park near Ocean Beach, or pickup basketball in the Panhandle, for the best combination of testosterone and colorful language.

Fisherman's Wharf features a crazy combination of indigenous and nomadic humans. Kick back on a bench near the audience for any street performer or balloon-folding clown at **Pier 39** to watch the circus unfold amongst high concentrations of non-natives. Another 80,000 migratory humans arrive by sea each year to the **Port of San Francisco** on twenty ships making an average of 45 calls.

Your study of human behavior can only come in handy once you're back in the workforce. How do you think Machiavelli got so good at politics? Haight Street, downtown at lunch hour, North Beach on a weekday afternoon, hotel lobbies and the airport—each provides a fine vantage point for observing humans in action. It's free, it's leisurely, and it can even further your career by helping you better understand your future boss or co-worker.

★ SAN FRANCISCO'S WILD CHARACTERS ★ **Alma Spreckels (1881-1968)** ★

An early model for the strong woman, "Big Alma" was equal parts beautiful, outrageous, provocative, and stubborn. Born on a farm in the Sunset district, she married wealthy sugar magnate Adolph Spreckels and proceeded to shake up San Francisco society with her liberated views. She gave them views of the scenic kind, too—inspired by the French Pavilion at the 1915 Panama Pacific International Exposition, she and her husband recreated the landmark by building the ***Palace of the Legion of Honor*** (100 34th Avenue, 415-863-3330, *www.famsf.org*). Alma was fervently involved with causes supporting war efforts during the two world wars. She posed for the risqué statue (still there) in Union Square, invented the garage sale (so they say), and at age 57(!) chartered a plane and eloped with a cowboy. A famous Alma one-liner: "I'd rather be an old man's darling than a young man's slave." You go, girl!

EXPLORING THE NEIGHBORHOODS

Everyone knows about Hunter's Point. Setting foot in it will lead to immediate death by gunfire (won't it?). The truth is, you're probably safer in Hunter's Point than in a cross-walk on Van Ness: for every murder in San Francisco, four pedestrians are killed by cars. Venture out that way and not only will you return alive, but you might stumble onto a find you would never have expected. A quirky café, perhaps, or a cool artist studio.

Anne Tesler (name changed) thought the time had come to check out Treasure Island. Little did she know that she'd picked the 25th Anniversary of the Treasure Island Museum as the day of her first visit. "I spent the whole afternoon there," she told us, "soaking up the incredible views of the City and exploring the museum. I even caught a short but fascinating old movie on the making of the Bay Bridge."

Even the tamest of neighborhoods harbors secrets. Peter Stein enjoyed them so much that he created an entire PBS series, *Neighborhoods: The Hidden Cities of San Francisco.* With time on your hands, explore a neighborhood you thought you knew, or choose a new neighborhood and poke around. Let us know what you find!

Neighborhood	Find
Alamo Square	Surely you've seen the postcard: a block of Victorian row houses (a.k.a., ***Painted Ladies***) set against the San Francisco skyline. Now go see them for yourself—on Steiner between Grove & Hayes. See if you can track down the shoe garden by the groundskeepers' shed while you're up there.
Pacific Heights	The ***Spreckels Mansion*** (2080 Washington @ Octavia), now Danielle Steel's house, was built in 1913 to be San Francisco's largest mansion. The house has 99 rooms. Yipes! That's gotta be some utility bill.
Marina	Stroll out to the end of the Yacht Road jetty at the St. Francis Yacht Harbor, north of Marina Boulevard, and amidst the honking of sea gulls you'll find a ***wave organ***, one of nature's own musical instruments.
Financial District	Just to prove it *is* all about money, the Financial District proudly presents you with the ***Museum of Money*** (in the basement of the Union Bank of California, 400 California) *and* the ***Federal Reserve Bank*** (101 Market, 415-974-3252), where the tours are free but the pallets of shrink-wrapped cash are not.
Hunter's Point	***Café Lola*** (702 Innes, 415-282-8091) is owned by Joanna Schneier and named after her pit bull, who runs around untethered indoors. Friendliest dog you'll ever meet. Savory brews and grub too!
Russian Hill	First track down the skinny ***Macondray Lane*** (off Leavenworth between Jones & Taylor), then amble over its stone pathway to the wooden ***Taylor Street Steps***, on display in the PBS miniseries based on Armistead Maupin's *Tales of the City.*
Telegraph Hill	The ***Wild Parrots of Telegraph Hill*** have been captured—on celluloid, in a movie of that same name. Are they escaped pets? Did they arrive via steamer from Africa? No one seems to know.
Chinatown	A statue of the ***Goddess of Democracy*** presides over the heart of Chinatown in what is now known as ***Portsmouth Square Park*** (Kearny between Clay & Washington), formerly known as ***Portsmouth Plaza*** (State Historical Landmark No. 119). As a plaza, the site saw a lot of action, including Sam Brannan's 1848 announcement of "gold in them thar hills" and California's first celebration of admission to the Union in 1850.

Street Murals

Guiding yourself on a tour of the City's street murals is another aesthetically pleasing way to get to know new places.

Mona Caron drew the **Duboce Bikeway Mural** (Duboce between Church & Market, Duboce Triangle area) in 1998, simply to spruce up the 360-foot stretch of roadway closed to cars but well-traveled by bikes and pedestrians. You can catch a glimpse of it from the south-facing windows of the N-Judah as you enter or exit the Market Street tunnel, but the colors are much more vibrant when you're up close and personal.

It took a whole cadre of muralists and "aerosol artists" led by muralist Ray Patlan to liven up **Balmy Alley** (Balmy Street between 24th & 25th Streets, parallel to Harrison & Treat, in the Mission). The outdoor gallery now features a mural on every building, wall, and garage door on the block, about thirty in all.

While it *is* the densest, Balmy Alley is but one of dozens and dozens of open-air museums in the Mission. No one is better-versed in them than the docents at the **Precita Eyes Mural Arts Center** (2981 24th Street, 415-285-2287, www.precitaeyes.org), a nonprofit mural-arts association that teaches mural-making and hosts numerous year-round tours via bus, bike or foot. Care to learn the history of murals? Precita Eyes' slide show will take you back 4,000 years to the murals of Egypt. If your style is more urban contemporary, commission one of their artists to decorate your home or office walls.

music in the city: a rocking tour

Don't have two hours to spare for a walking tour? That's okay, short is leisurely! Take your own mini-tour of rock'n'roll history in the Haight. Haight houses occupied by famous rockers include:

112 Lyon—Janis Joplin
142 Central—Jimi Hendrix
710 Ashbury—Grateful Deadhouse
130 Delmar—Jefferson Airplane
636 Cole—House of Manson

[and the beat goes on...]

Walking Tours

Like so many cities in Europe, San Francisco was made for walking. Sure, there are hills (43 named hills, in fact), and thus some really steep streets (the steepest blocks are Filbert between Hyde & Leavenworth, and 22nd Street between Church and Vicksburg, both 31.5% gradient).

But you'll steer around them all on the "Bawdy & Naughty" walking tour, covering only two flat blocks after leaving from the eastern Maiden Lane Gate. Explore the lives and "loves" of legendary parlor madams such as Belle Cora, Sally Stanford and Ah Toy starting at 11am on the first three Mondays of the month. Quite a topic that early in the day!

The non-profit **San Francisco City Guides** (100 Larkin, 415-557-4266, www.sfcityguides.org) is supported by more than 200 volunteers working under the auspices of the San Francisco Public Library, and hosts 125 free walking tours, plus an excellent web guide to the City. The **Visitor Information Center** (see "Best Resources for Locals" p. 138) includes the City Guides' *Free Walking Tours* pamphlet in their tourist packet.

[...and the beat goes on]

Round out this short survey by sharing your knowledge of our native musicians with your friends, or anyone else who happens to be hanging out in Buena Vista Park:

- ***Chris Isaak***—
  oft mistaken for Elvis
- ***Sheila E.***—
  lived the glamorous life with Prince, still jammin' with father Pete "Coke" Escovedo
- ***Courtney Love***—
  launched her musical career in our fair City, where she sang for about a week with Faith No More
- ***Joan Baez***—
  now hosting the dinner-circus-theater ***Teatro Zinzanni*** (Pier 29 at Embarcadero & Battery, 415-438-2668, *www.zinzanni.org*)

A final tidbit: the Beatles played their last live concert at (then-named) Candlestick Park on August 29, 1966—an odd choice of venue for the Fab Four!

NATURE IN THE CITY

San Francisco maintains a surprisingly large amount of open space for its small size. Blessed with the country's largest urban park and plenty of undeveloped, leftover military land, the City by the Bay boasts arguably the most beautiful recreation land of any city in the U.S. If you can't find yourself a favorite outdoor stomping ground here, then maybe urban nature just isn't your habitat.

Parks

San Francisco has made parks a priority since Golden Gate Park's founding in 1870. Its 230 "official" parks comprise roughly 3,500 acres, or nearly 12% of the total area within City limits—and we're going to list each one! Just kidding, only the best for you.

Land's End

El Camino del Mar near 32nd Avenue, or Point Lobos @ 48th Avenue

Land's End, the rugged and scenic stretch of coastline at the very northwest tip of the San Francisco peninsula, affords panoramic seascapes from both its hidden beach and its hiking trail. The trail can be entered from the west (near Point Lobos Avenue/Geary @ 48th Avenue) or the east (along El Camino del Mar near the California Palace of the Legion of Honor) and is a relatively easy two-mile walk. At the west end, follow the paths that lead down to the ocean, and you'll find yourself on a craggy, semi-private stretch of beach, perfect for some mid-week solitude.

site of the first U.S. dynamite factory

What must be one of the City's shortest lived business ventures (even by dot-com measures) has been memorialized in history for at least 60 times longer than it was in existence: the gunpowder and dynamite factory at what is now Glen Canyon Park (State Historical Landmark No. 1002).

The Giant Powder Company began America's first commercial manufacturing of dynamite on March 19, 1868. Just over twenty months later, the business ended with a bang: the factory exploded.

The obliteration of all of its buildings and even the surrounding fencing came to be known as the Glen Canyon or Rock Gulch explosion.

Glen Canyon Park

Bosworth @ O'Shaughnessy

Yes, there *are* true canyon lands in San Francisco, as this hidden oasis in Glen Park attests. Although not a huge space, it comes complete with a running creek, cool rock outcroppings, and a decent but short hiking trail. Dog walkers and nature enthusiasts will be happy here. Beware of the poison oak!

Huntington Park

Mason & California, top of Nob Hill

This urban park rests auspiciously atop prestigious Nob Hill, while Grace Cathedral, The Fairmont, and "The Mark" (Mark Hopkins Hotel) watch over it like patrician aunts and uncles. Nap on one of its sunny park benches, dream of playing Parcheesi at the haughty Pacific Union Club next door, and ponder the mindset of Charles Crocker when he surrounded his neighbor with a 40-foot tall fence to "encourage" him to sell Crocker his property. And just think—you can enjoy all this gentried splendor *without* having to be a railroad baron!

more parks to ferret out

• ***Buena Vista Park*** wooded and wild • ***McLaren Park*** 75 picnic tables, many private • ***Michelangelo Playground*** a North Beach oasis • ***Visitacion Valley Greenway*** formerly fenced parcels become garden spaces • ***Who Hei Yuen Park*** first new Chinatown park since the '50s • ***Precita Park*** cleaned-up and green • ***South Park*** ceded back to the homeless by short-lived startups • ***St. Mary's Square*** not just a garage • ***Pioneer Park*** hey, it's the space around Coit Tower!

The Presidio

415-561-4323, www.nps.gov/prsf

This former military base bordered by the Pacific Ocean, Lyon Street, West Pacific Avenue and the Bay is now a 1,480-acre public park with miles of hiking and biking trails, beaches, picnic sites, abandoned military barracks, artillery batteries, an army museum, and other assorted sites—even a pet cemetery and at least one major office development. **Fort Point** guards the foot of the Golden Gate Bridge. Find maps, books and other useful intelligence daily between 9am and 5pm at **The Presidio Visitors Center** (415-561-4323, temporarily located in the Officers' Club, Moraga & Graham).

Fort Funston

Skyline/Highway 35 near John Muir Drive

415-239-2366, www.nps.gov/goga/fofu/index.htm

Long a favored destination for dog walkers, Fort Funston and its surrounding turf invite cliff-hugging hikes, lost hours surveying the Pacific, and scampers down an uncrowded stretch of beach (chasing your pooch no doubt). Or leave Fido at home and just laze the afternoon away watching the hang-gliders launch off the glider port and then float along the coast.

Agua Vista Park

Mission Bay, next to Kelly's Mission Rock

Deep in the heart of Mission Bay lies a park you've probably never heard of: Agua Vista Park. Its specialty is ship repair. A little industrial, perhaps, but you can watch, listen, and learn. Then head over to **The Ramp** next door (855 China Basin, 415-621-2378) for a cheeseburger and a beer. You'll swear it's 1950 all over again.

Douglass Park & Playground

1100 Douglass @ 26th Street, Noe Valley, 415-695-5017

Tucked away in a corner of Noe Valley, Douglass Park is small and unassuming, dog- and kid-friendly. Its thrill du jour is a tall cement slide that's fun for grownups and kids alike. Sweet! **Carnaval San Francisco** (www.carnaval.com/sanfrancisco) shares this tip for maximum speed: "Bring your own cardboard and sprinkle a little sand on the slide before you push off." Watch out for the infamous park mud during the wintertime.

For More on Parks

Not enough park info here for you? Then you could use another friend. Good thing then there's **Friends of Recreation & Parks** (www.frp.org, use "Links & Resources"), where you can find all the rec-savvy friends a guy or gal could ever need. The City's official site is not a bad matchmaker, either: **Recreation & Park Department** (www.sfgov.org, click on "City Agencies" and then "Recreation and Park Department").

BEACHES

You won't find the cast from *Baywatch* here (nor David Hasselhoff, thank god), but San Francisco has coastline galore—some of it urban, other stretches delightfully removed from the hustle of the City. A heads up: the beaches are typically cold. Very cold. You'll need multiple layers to stay warm, sometimes even your winter parka.

Baker Beach

off Lincoln near 25th Avenue, www.nps.gov/prsf/places/bakerbch.htm

Catch San Francisco's premier sunbathing beach on a warm day and you may never want to leave the City again. This mile-long stretch of sand starts just west of the Golden Gate Bridge and sweeps along the Presidio towards the Seacliff neighborhood. The closer you get to the bridge (to the north), the less clothing you'll spot on your fellow bathers. The north end is also a popular gay beach. Solid swimmers can take a dip in the frigid water but should mind the wicked cross-currents and undertow, as well as the fact that San Francisco's only recorded great white shark attack occurred here in 1959—just 50 yards offshore.

China Beach

Seacliff & 28th Avenue

Just west of Baker Beach lies its baby sister, China. This small strip of sand, tucked into the walls of the Lincoln Park cliffs, is ideal for families and picnickers. It's probably the best beach in San Francisco for swimming—which isn't saying much, as it's still very cold water and bathers need to mind the sometimes-strong currents. But lifeguards are on duty (hey, is that Mitch Buchannon?) during the summer months to help the occasional swimmer in trouble.

NAPPING, RAYS & READING

Where to Soak Up Some Vitamin D	***Reading Factor***	***Sun Factor***	***Nap Factor***
Lafayette Park (Sacramento @ Laguna)	good	excellent, stay west	good, so long as you're not on the side with the dog run
Kalmanovitz Library (UCSF, Parnassus @ 3rd Avenue)	excellent	poor, but incredible views of the Golden Gate	superior, but beware: the comfortable leather chairs have been known to elicit heavy snoring
Main Library Outdoor Reading Room (100 Larkin, 6th floor)	excellent	superior, and no wind at all	poor, unless you're comfortable snoozing on a cement bench
Your Car (really!) (park up near the ***Sutro Towers*** or down at the ***Marina Green***)	excellent, lots of peace and quiet (provided your windows roll up)	totally at your discretion	depends on your cruiser
Washington Square Park (Columbus @ Union)	moderate	excellent	no good, possible for only the most tourist-inured

strybing arboretum

What the ***Strybing Arboretum*** (9th Avenue @ Lincoln, 415-661-5191, *www.strybing.org*) lacks in name recognition, it more than makes up for in spectacular flora.

A delightful backdrop for the average visitor, Strybing is a dream come true for the horticulturist, bursting with 70 acres of extravagant plants and flowers. It's a feast for all five of your senses. (You've had flower salads, haven't you?)

On your way out, stop by the quaint ***Strybing Botanical Bookstore*** to brush up on your knowledge of plants.

North Beach

neighborhood in northeast corner of the City

Okay, so it's not actually a beach—it's not even on the water anymore! But it once *was* waterfront, before landfill set in, and it remains one of the coolest neighborhoods in San Francisco. If you need to lay out, go bag some rays in **Washington Square Park**.

South Beach

Waterfront south of Bay Bridge

It ain't Miami, and South ain't any more of a beach than North, but the thriving waterfront neighborhood of South Beach features **SBC (Pac Bell) Park**, numerous new restaurants and bars, and the best weather in the City. Imagine laying out your beach towel between the ship docks and stripping down to your swimsuit without freezing!

Ocean Beach

(Great Highway from Point Lobos to Sloat, in the Sunset)

Ideal for running, biking, or exercising the dog (on a leash in most places), Ocean Beach is a massive natural playground spanning about four miles of western San Francisco. If you can handle the often-foggy conditions, you'll delight in this vastly underutilized recreational space. Don't count on swimming here, however, as waves can reach as high as 40 feet during the winter, and rip currents and rumbling whitewater constantly surge through the lineup.

Ocean Beach is *the* place in San Francisco to see the sun set. (They don't call it the Sunset district for nothing!) Even when the fog is in, the distant sky often magically clears just in time to watch a golden orb slip below the horizon. Grab a beach chair and a few beers (hide the glass bottles, they're not allowed), plant yourself somewhere along the spacious sand dunes, and savor a perfectly leisurely moment.

SECRET STAIRWAYS AND SPECTACULAR VIEWS

Vulcan Street Steps

(off 17th Street between Ord & Levant, Upper Market)

Serene and lined with pines, Vulcan Street ascends the southern slope of the Buena Vista hill. Look out over the Mission, and keep an eye out for paving stones from the area's original streets.

San Francisco Art Institute

(800 Chestnut, 415-749-4567)

Not only can you admire a Diego Riviera mural inside the Art Insitute, you can enjoy a fine, inexpensive lunch during the week. Then step onto the rooftop deck for a vista that extends past Coit Tower to Oakland.

Pemberton Stairway

(from Clayton & Corbett to the top of Corona Heights)

The renovated and redesigned upper section between Villa and Graystone Terraces and their accompanying gardens are the pride of Twin Peaks. Aficionados describe the views on the way up as "showstopping."

Harry Stairs

(Harry Street, from Laidley to Beacon in Glen Park)

This climb starts in Glen Park and summits at the bottom of Billy Goat Hill in Diamond Heights. If you're vertigo-free, take a peak back over your shoulder on the way up for sweeping views of Treasure Island. If you'd rather face forward, try to catch a glimpse of the charming cottages amidst the forest-like greenery. The stairs are mostly wooden, with a handrail.

Top of Quarry Hill

(Roosevelt @ Museum Way, near the Randall Museum)

Hitting the crest of the red rock mountain at Quarry Hill gives you that Planet of the Apes feeling—you know, when Charlton Heston's character finds the Statue of Liberty buried in the sand? The contrast between your immediate primitive landscape and the City skyline down below is just as startling (well, almost). Take a seat and crack open a beer. You'll deserve it after this short but steep trek.

MUSEUMS & ART GALLERIES

Ah yes, culture. We could all use a healthy dose of it, *n'est-ce pas?* Although San Francisco's art scene languished a bit in the late '90s, it's enjoying a refreshing renaissance now, with small galleries and studios sprouting up to fill the void left by collapsed startups. You can almost hear a collective sigh of relief blowing across the City. Add to that a thriving large-museum scene, and it all equates to a fine time to get yourself cultured.

Free Museum Days

Admission is free on the first Wednesday of every month at many San Francisco museums, including the **Exploratorium**, the **Asian Art Museum**, the **Academy of Sciences**, and all of the museums at Fort Mason. Other free museum days include the first Tuesday of every month for **SFMOMA**, the first Thursday of every month for the **Center for the Arts** at Yerba Buena Gardens, and every Tuesday for the **Legion of Honor**. Remember, a museum outing makes for an impressive date, and you don't need to spend a lot of money. No excuses!

MUSEUMS	
free first wed every month except as noted	**always free**
M. H. de Young Memorial Museum (under construction, will re-open in 2005 across the Music Concourse from the Academy of Sciences)	***de Young Arts Center*** (2501 Irving, 415-682-2481) Tues-Sat, 10am-5pm
Steinhart Aquarium ***Natural History Museum*** ***Morrison Planetarium*** (in California Academy of Sciences; will move temporarily to 875 Howard)	***National Maritime Museum*** (Aquatic Park, end of Polk Street *www.maritime.org*) open daily, 10am-5pm
Asian Art Museum (Larkin @ McAllister)	***World of Oil*** (555 Market) Mon-Fri, 8am-4:30pm
Museum of Modern Art (151 3rd Street) free first *Tuesday* of every month half price every *Thursday* 6pm-9pm	***Mission Dolores*** (16th Street @ Dolores) free *but* $2 donation expected open daily, 9am-4pm

Museum of Craft & Folk Art ***Mexican Museum*** ***Museo Ital-Americano*** ***MOMA Artists Gallery*** ***African-American Historical & Cultural Society*** (all located in Fort Mason)	***Chinese Cultural Center of San Francisco*** (750 Kearny, 3rd Floor, 415-986-1822, *www.c-c-c.org*) Tues-Sat, 1pm-4pm
Exploratorium (Bay & Lyon)	***North Beach Museum*** (in Eureka Bank, 1435 Stockton) Mon-Fri, 9am-4pm
Cartoon Art Museum (814 Mission)	***Cable Car Museum*** (1201 Mason) open daily, 10am-6pm
Center for the Arts Yerba Buena Gardens (701 Mission @ 3rd Street) free first *Thursday* of every month	***Chinese Historical Society*** (650 Commercial) Thu-Sat, 1pm-4pm
Legion of Honor 415-750-3600 (Lincoln Park, 34th Avenue off Clement) free *every* Tuesday	***Fire Department Museum*** (665 Presidio, 415-558-3546) Thu-Sat, 1pm-4pm
Golden Gate Railroad Museum (Naval Base at Hunter's Point 415-822-8728, *www.ggrm.org*) open weekends 10am-5pm M-F by appt. *no free days* but you can rent a locomotive—how cool is *that*?!	***Strybing Arboretum*** (Golden Gate Park) open daily, 10am-4pm
	Wells Fargo Museum (420 Montgomery) Mon-Fri, 9am-5pm

Artist's Open Studios

San Franciscans want to know—just what *does* go on inside all of those South of Market live-work lofts, anyway?

Finding an answer starts with the **San Francisco Bay Area Gallery Guide** (1369 Fulton, 415-921-1600), a bimonthly publication listing the City's current art shows. To get on their mailing list, send them a self-addressed, stamped envelope (ZIP is 94117). You can also pick up a guide at the **San Francisco Visitor Information Center** (at the cable car turnaround; find full contact info on p. 138).

San Francisco Open Studios (934 Brannan, 415-861-9838, www.sfopenstudios.com) is the oldest and largest open studio program in the country. Every October weekend, artists from throughout the City open their workspaces to the general public, enabling the artists to gain exposure and sell their artwork, and allowing the public to meet and interact with the artists.

The **Artists Guild** (601 Van Ness #E3-140, 415-835-0610, www.artistsguildsf.com) was founded to exhibit artists' work at outdoor venues across San Francisco. Often these are park sites such as Washington Square, the Marina Green, or Huntington Park. The Guild maintains a monthly exhibit schedule on its website, if you'd like to plan your art viewing for the month.

Don't miss the annual ***Spring Open Studio*** (415-387-5936, www.springopenstudio.com) presented by the Artists of Hunters Point Shipyard. Each spring, usually in May, the Shipyard artists open their studios to you, the general public. An added bonus: Spring Open Studio marks one of only two times per year the general public is allowed to roam the former U.S. Naval shipyard.

Looking for something to do on a Thursday night? First Thursdays are a running series of after-hour gallery showings sponsored by the **San Francisco Art Dealers Association** (www.sfada.com). They happen on—you guessed it, the first Thursday of every month, usually from 6-9pm (although times are fluid). Participating galleries are located primarily downtown, and several even welcome visitors with complimentary wine.

The **San Francisco Art Institute** (800 Chestnut, 415-771-7020, www.sfai.edu) serves as a nucleus for exhibitions and public programs, most of which are free. Heck, their website alone is worthy of a tour, and will lead you to a world of physical exhibits.

At any hour and for no admission, you can study up on the fine works of art displayed in the online version of the **San Francisco Airport Museums** (650-821-6700, www.sfoarts.org). Surf through eclectic and unexpected displays with themes drawn from science, history, design, and anthropology, or assess the new spaces created by the Airport's latest $3 billion expansion: a huge beast replete with moving sidewalks.

LEISURELY ENTERTAINMENT

You'll find plenty of food- and drink-based entertainment rolled into our special section, **Dining & Nightlife**. But for offbeat entertainment at little or no cost, where you won't need to tip the maitre d' or spring for a pricey round of drinks, read on right here.

The Spoken Word

Book and literary readings are usually free and, depending on the topic, can double as groovy social events. San Francisco maintains its literary tradition through a strong network of independent bookstores, as well as a series of ongoing literary events.

Stacey's Booksellers (581 Market, 415-421-4687, www.staceys.com) and **A Clean Well-Lighted Place for Books** (Opera Plaza, 601 Van Ness, 415-441-6670, www.bookstore.com) host more readings than anywhere else in the City, hands down. You can try your luck by just stopping by, or check their sites for current schedules. The **Booksmith** (1644 Haight, 415-863-8688, www.booksmith.com) and the famed **City Lights Bookstore** (261 Columbus, 415-362-8193, www.citylights.com) are both excellent venues and regular stops on the author's tour.

SAN FRANCISCO'S WILD CHARACTERS NOW Lawrence Ferlinghetti (born 1919)

Lawrence Ferlinghetti landed in SF in the 1950s and soon defined what it meant to be a liberal and literary activist. His City Lights Bookstore and publishing house fast became the focal point for the beat generation and the City's intellectuals. In 1956, he was arrested on obscenity charges for publishing Allen Ginsberg's *Howl*. The trial that followed drew national attention as a landmark First Amendment case, and further cemented Ferlinghetti's reputation as a leader in alternative publishing. Lucky for writers and book buyers, he was acquitted. In addition to promoting local talent, Ferlinghetti has published many of his own articles, poems, and books over the years, winning numerous literary awards. At age 84, he remains prolific as a writer and lecturer, and up until just recently wrote a regular column for the *San Francisco Chronicle*.

If the bookstore environment doesn't exactly get your blood pumping, look into one of the more social venues.

You can get your dose of Glenfiddich while listening to renowned authors at the proudly-literary **Edinburgh Castle Pub** (950 Geary, 415-885-4074, http://ecastlenews.homestead.com/ecastlehome.html), for example. The relatively new **Café Niebaum-Coppola** in North Beach (916 Kearny, 415-291-1700, www.cafecoppola.com) plays host to literary events but keeps it a bit hush-hush. Call them for details.

Discover even more artistic and literary venues at the excellent site by **SF Station** (www.sfstation.com, under "Literary Arts" then "Spoken Word Events"). Another solid resource is **Artist Resource** (www.artistresource.org, under "Writers Events"), which promotes and highlights the visual arts as well as the written word.

Ongoing literary events that will keep the creative juices flowing include the free and increasingly popular **Grotto Nights** (www.sfgrotto.org), held quarterly at the San Francisco Main Library and followed by an open-air party at **The Grotto** headquarters (26 Fell), all generously underwritten by The Grotto and various sponsors. **Porchlight** (www.porchlightsf.com) is a colorful storytelling series that's currently hosted at **Café du Nord** (2170 Market, 415-861-5016, www.cafedunord.com), normally on the third Monday of each month. For more information, e-mail info@porchlightsf.com.

Theatre

There's a reason people think of the theatre as a rich person's activity. Hurray for **TIX Bay Area** (www.theatrebayarea.org under "TIX Bay Area"), Theatre Bay Area's half-price, same-day ticket program. Buy tickets starting at noon for a performance that same night, in person only, at the **TIX Pavilion** (in Union Square on Powell between Geary & Post).

You can also find reasonably-priced seats at the **American Conservatory Theatre** (405 Geary, 415-749-2228, www.act-sfbay.org), a performance and education-oriented theatre group. Second balcony seats run for $15 on weeknights, $19 on weekends, and as little as $8 on special preview nights. Call for details.

Ballet, Opera and Symphony

The ballet is not just for Pacific Heights limo riders anymore. The **San Francisco Ballet** (455 Franklin, 415-861-5600/415-865-2000 for tickets,

san francisco's wild characters ✩ HARRY DENTON (just turned 21!)

Everybody in the City loves a party, and Harry is usually in the middle of it all. A local entrepreneur extraordinaire, Harry launched **Harry's on Fillmore** (2020 Fillmore, 415-921-1000) in 1986, and his "guests" there are still partying hard (even though it's under new ownership).

He's since opened numerous other nightspots, including Southside, Harry Denton's, the **Starlight Room** (atop the **Sir Francis Drake** hotel, 450 Powell @ Sutter, 415-395-8595), and **Rouge** (1500 Broadway @ Polk, 415-346-7683).

Harry's philanthropic contributions over the years have been legendary, as have his crazy antics. Through it all, he's managed to maintain his sense of humor and fundamental love of a great party. "Delusions of grandeur make me feel a lot better about myself," Harry says. He said it; we didn't!

www.sfballet.org), in its campaign to attract a younger, broader audience, now offers advanced-order balcony seats for as little as $8 for weekday performances, $10 for weekends.

There are two ways to get significantly discounted tickets for the **San Francisco Opera** (301 Van Ness, 415-861-4008/415-864-3330 box office, www.sfopera.com). You can stand in line for one of the two hundred $10 standing room tickets offered the day of each performance (cash only, one ticket per person). Tickets go on sale at 10am the day of the performance. Or—if you've still got a valid student ID (hold on to that City College card!)—you can buy any available ticket through the "student rush tickets" program. These tickets go on sale at the box office at 11am the day of a performance, and you can call ahead to check if tickets will be available. Balcony side seats are regularly $24 during the week, $26 on Fridays and weekends. Rather leave those little jeweled binoculars at home? You can hear live opera every Saturday for a song (the price of a cup of coffee) at **Caffe Trieste** (609 Vallejo, 415-982-2605, www.caffetrieste.com).

Getting in at a discount to hear the **San Francisco Symphony** (Davies Symphony Hall, 201 Van Ness, 415-864-6000 box office, www.sfsymphony.org) is a tougher nugget to crack. Select shows offer "center terrace seats" (seats that are sometimes occupied by a chorus just behind the stage), at $15-20 apiece. One hundred of these tickets are sold for non-chorus performances; 60 are available in advance, and 40 go on sale at the box office two hours before each show (cash only, two tickets per person). Student rush tickets are also available for $20 each on the day of a performance. Call the student rush hotline at 415-503-5577 for the skinny.

Open Rehearsals and Ushering

Many arts organizations will allow a limited audience for a dress rehearsal, or will occasionally advertise an "open" rehearsal. If you're interested in a particular show, don't be shy. Call and ask. If the director balks, mention that you are unemployed.

Ushering is another way to enjoy performances for free. Wear white on the top and black on the bottom, and you're nearly there. Once your job is done, you can relax, and enjoy whatever show you're ushering for free.

The **San Francisco Choral Society** (West Portal, 415-221-5590, www.sfchoral.org) welcomes volunteer ushers at any of their four annual concerts; many other choral groups do as well. Most of the 300+ volunteer ushers registered with **Cal Performances Volunteer**

FREE CONCERTS, PLAYS, AND DANCE

Sausalito Friday Night Summer Concerts
Escape the city fog and bike, ferry, or drive over to Sausalito for free concerts every Friday during the summer.

Shakespeare in the Park
September brings the San Francisco Shakespeare Festival, which is free on weekends. Take a blanket and picnic basket and enjoy (with luck) the Indian summer weather.

Free Noontime Concerts and Dance
Yerba Buena Gardens are alive with the sound of music all summer long.

Usher Program (101 Zellerbach Hall #4800, Berkeley, 510-643-6710, www.cpinfo.berkeley.edu, then "Job and Volunteer Opportunities") stuff programs or tear tickets at Zellerbach Hall, but a couple of the luckier ones caught one of Mikhail Baryshnikov's last performances at San Francisco's War Memorial Opera House.

SAN FRANCISCO'S WILD CHARACTERS

then:

James Lick (1796–1876)

Dubbed "California's Stingiest Man," Lick arrived in San Francisco in 1847 with a chest containing $30,000 in Peruvian gold and 600 pounds of Domingo Ghirardelli chocolate. He presciently poured his money into real estate; then the Gold Rush made him one of the wealthiest men in San Francisco. That didn't stop him from living like a pauper, however, and his reputation for wearing tattered clothing and fishing through garbage cans was legendary. His wealth also enabled him to become a philanthropist extraordinaire, and his name can still be found on Bay Area schools and university buildings, even a freeway. He was buried at Lick Observatory on Mount Hamilton, lying beneath the stars—and the telescope that bears his name.

THE LEISURE SEEKER'S DAY OFF

No day could be leisurely enough without sleeping in. Thus, our ideal morning schedule goes something like: 7am—sleep. 8am—sleep. 9am—sleep. 10:30am—rise only if unavoidable. Kick around all morning—read, cook, have sex, whatever—then think about food.

The **Ferry Plaza Farmer's Market** (see the **Unemployed Shopping Guide**) is now open four days a week and makes a great place to buy fresh fixings for dinner. With Union Square just two MUNI stops away, you can swing by after shopping to the **TIX Pavilion** to buy half-price tickets for an evening of live theatre (see "Theatre" p. 132).

If baseball's in season, spend the afternoon at a day game at **SBC** (formerly Pac Bell) **Park**. Next, catch the N-Judah (it stops just outside of the park) for convenient transport across town to the beach. You can even sightsee a bit on the way (see "Street Murals" p. 120).

If your day off is a non-game day, catch the N-Judah from the Powell Street Station instead and disembark at Carl & Stanyan, then trot

sbc (pac bell) park

Even the skeptical have been won over by this urban baseball stadium. Ben Marcus, a self-proclaimed Giants fanatic, recently spent the better part of a summer going to games there. "Pac Bell [now SBC] Park is the best-designed public facility I have ever seen," he says. "It's clean, convenient, safe, and somehow manages to be intimate for 40,000 people. Whoever designed and built the thing should be dipped in gold."

Ben funded his Club-Level tickets ($40–$65 a pop) through a combination of unemployment insurance and freelance writing gigs, but he also likes View Reserve seats ($18) on the first-base side for a great mix of game and Bay views. Bleacher seats and standing room only tickets are $10.

Other fans enjoy the game for free underneath the **Old Navy Splash Landing**. "If the crowd thickens," says stadium tour guide Steve Yung, "the Giants might ask those in front to clear the way every third inning or so." Otherwise, linger with the rest of the knot hole gang as long as you like, or invite yourself onto one of the various watercrafts (rowboats/kayaks/surfboards) floating the afternoon away in **McCovey Cove**, chasing down Barry Bonds' home run balls.

down to **Avenue Cyclery** (756 Stanyan, 415-387-3155) to rent a bike. The ride from there out to **Ocean Beach** is a leisurely one and the roll along the Great Highway sends you from the **Cliff House** (in its fifth incarnation) at the north end to the **San Francisco Zoo** at the south.

The luck of the Irish-Americans is with you as you ramble on into the Irish-run **Java Beach** (1396 Judah @ La Playa) with their tasty hot subs and beer specials throughout the week. Soak up the late afternoon sun on their outdoor patio, and/or pedal down to the **Beach Chalet** (1000 Great Highway @ Ocean Beach) for a microbrew.

Drop the bike off afterward if you need to, go home and take a nap, then cook up dinner. Then you're off to the theatre. Enjoy the show!

AND DON'T CALL IT "FRISCO!"

Joshua A. Norton (1819-1880)

San Francisco's original **WILD CHARACTER** and the City's only monarch (sort of), "Emperor Norton," as he was fondly known to San Franciscans, arrived in San Francisco via South Africa in 1849 with $40,000 in his pocket and a screw loose in his noggin. He made the first of his many bizarre declarations ten years later, by proclaiming himself the Emperor of the United States.

The City press loved him, and published his outlandish proclamations and "decrees" on a regular basis, as well as making up a few of their own and attributing them to Norton. In addition to proclaiming himself the Emperor, Norton also declared himself "Protector of Mexico," decreed that the United States be dissolved and the Democratic and Republican political parties abolished, and demanded that a suspension bridge be built between Oakland Point and Goat (Yerba Buena) Island, and then on to San Francisco. He later ordered the arrest of the Board of Supervisors for ignoring all of his decrees.

Norton was adamant about the correct usage of the City name, saying, "Whoever after due and proper warning shall be heard to utter the abominable word 'Frisco,' which has no linguistic or other warrant, shall be deemed guilty of a High Misdemeanor." Penalty for noncompliance was $25.

So say what you will about our City, but—*don't* call it "Frisco!"

BEST RESOURCES FOR LOCALS

San Francisco Visitor Information Center
(Hallidie Plaza, 900 Market @ Powell, 415-391-2000, www.sfvisitor.org)

Books
- *Lonely Planet San Francisco* (3rd Edition, 2003)
- *Time Out San Francisco* (4th Edition, 2002)

Newspapers and Magazines
- *7x7 Magazine* (www.7x7mag.com)
- *SF Weekly* (free weekly, www.sfweekly.com)
- *San Francisco Bay Guardian* (free weekly, www.sfbg.com)
- *San Francisco Chronicle Datebook* (Sundays, www.sfgate.com)
- *San Francisco Magazine* (www.sanfran.com)

Web
- **Carnaval San Francisco** (www.carnaval.com/sf)
- **Citysearch San Francisco** (http://sanfrancisco.citysearch.com)
- **Friends of Recreation & Parks** (www.frp.org)
- **Mister SF** (www.mistersf.com)
- **Planet SOMA** (www.planetsoma.com)
- **SF Station** (www.sfstation.com)
- **San Francisco Bay Area Transit Information** (www.transitinfo.org)
- **San Francisco City** website (www.sfgov.org)
- **Virtual Museum of the City of San Francisco** (www.sfmuseum.org)

FAIRS & FESTS

MORE than one hundred events recur in San Francisco each year, festooning everything from tall ships to tulips, and attracting millions of participants wearing anything from a g-string to a ball gown. If you'd like to witness one of these weird and wacky rituals, this list is for you.

With only the highest regard for the other fabulous fiestas hosted here each year, we highlight three that simply scream "San Francisco!"

Only in San Francisco #1

BAY TO BREAKERS

3rd Sunday in May, 415-359-2800, *www.baytobreakers.com*

The Bay to Breakers race is one of the best and most peculiarly San Francisco events of the year. Why? For starters, picture an 8'x10' "boat" stuffed with kegs, rolling the entire 12K course offering "Free beer to naked people!" Then count all the thirsty nude runners taking advantage of the handout even as they are trudging up the Hayes Street Hill—and that's just the tame action. The largest foot race in the world steers more than 80,000 costumed and, uh, un-costumed racers from the corner of Howard & Spear to the breakers of Ocean Beach, hurling flour tortillas all the way. The fastest finish in just over thirty minutes, with the Back of the Pack pedestrians reaching the checkered flag as late as noon (4 hours after the starting gun) and centipedes falling somewhere in between. Pre-race prep includes group exercise sessions, energy drinks, a pasta feed, and an oxygen bar. Don't miss the post-race Footstock festival at the Polo Field for live music, food and drinks, and even massage.

STREET FAIRS

San Francisco neighborhoods come alive each summer with the smell of roasted garlic, the reverberation of jazz and rock music, the fresh flow of draft beer, sometimes even the slapping of chapped leather on bare skin! Yes, the street fair tradition is a good one, and whether you're a button-up type looking to show off the latest summer fashions or a biker boy looking for a leather buddy, you'll find a fair to fit your needs. They bounce and jig their way through summertime weekends, and admission is free to all.

ANNUAL FESTIVALS

San Francisco Festivals are all about celebrating a particular culture, whether it's ethnic, vocational, culinary, or sexual. The important thing is they go on and on, all year 'round! Unlike at the street fairs, admission is not always free, but you'll always find food, revelry, and assorted entertainment.

If it's a celebration of food you're after, you can't go wrong at the **Crab Festival**, encompassing the whole month of February. Whether you prefer your local Dungeness in cioppino or freshly cracked with a little oil and vinegar, at your favorite restaurant or on a bay cruise, you'll eat your fill during this series of events. Most are ticketed, but the Walk on the Wharf is free—organized by the **San Francisco Convention & Visitors Bureau** (201 3rd Street, Suite 900, 415-391-2000).

On the other end of the flavor spectrum is the **Ghirardelli Square Chocolate Festival** (900 Northpoint, 415-775-5500, www.ghirardellisq.com) in early September. Not much to explain about this one. Bring the kids, save your appetite for the sundae eating contest and content yourself in knowing that proceeds benefit Project Open Hand.

The kids can also join you at the straightforwardly-named **Street Performers' Festival** (415-705-5500, www.pier39.com) at Pier 39 in August, or the **Winter Solstice Festival** (415-441-4093), which takes place in early December on Fillmore Street. Each features comedians, jugglers, unicyclists, and slack ropewalkers, among other "carni" delights.

the street	*the action*
Howard *(April)*	How weird! (Get it?) The amazing array of performance art at this South of Market fair includes butoh, belly dance, circus acts and stilt walkers. (415-371-8706, *www.howweird.org*)
Union (June)	A "see and be seen" affair in the Marina. Enjoy art, live music (classical and jazz) from two stages, a waiters' race and a kiddie area. (415-456-6455, 800-310-6563, *www.unionstreetfestival.com)*
Haight (June)	Hearken to the insistent Haight Street murmur of "Buds? Buds?" as you pass the face painters or either of the two live music stages. (415-863-3489, *www.haightstreetfair.org)*
Fillmore (July)	It's a jazz festival, really, with three stages of continuous jazz and other live music. (510-232-5030, 800-731-0003, *www.hartmannstudios.com)*
Dore (July)	Only Folsom Street wears more leather. This "Up Your Alley" fair features human masters and servants, raises bucks for charity and is quickly becoming as popular as its older brother, the Folsom Street Fair. (by SMMILE, 415-861-3247, *www.folsomstreetfair.com/alley)*
Third (August)	More music and family activities at this party in the developing stretch of the Bayview/Hunters Point district, benefiting community youth. (by MM&Associates, 510-237-5393)
Nihonmachi (August)	Lion dancers, Taiko drummers and children's events fete Japanese culture. (Japantown, 415-771-9861, *www.nihonmachistreetfair.org)*
Polk (September)	Basic and straightforward—music, arts & crafts, and multi-cultural cuisine—but the dancing in front of the swing stages keeps it be-boppin'. (415-383-3470)
Folsom (September)	It's the largest and the leathery-est. Adults only, please! Celebrates alternative lifestyles. All proceeds benefit local charities. (by SMMILE, 415-861-3247, *www.folsomstreetfair.com)*
Castro (October)	Dance, performances, and community groups help raise funds to benefit AIDS charities. (415-841-1824, *www.castrostreetfair.org)*

the dateline

Here's the whole ***Fairs & Fests*** shebang, with events listed by month.

For exact dates, check with the experts:

- ***San Francisco Visitor Information Center***
  Hallidie Plaza
  900 Market @ Powell
  415-391-2000
  www.sfvisitor.org

- ***Festivals.com***
  www.festivals.com
  a wonderful party resource

- ***Pier 39 Marina***
  www.pier39marina.com
  for events at Pier 39

...

january

Berlin and Beyond Film Festival

San Francisco International Art Expo

East-West Shrine Game

AMA Supercross Series

Sports and Boat Show

Mochi-Making for Japanese New Year

Anniversary of the Sea Lions' Arrival

Martin Luther King, Jr.'s Birthday

CULTURAL FESTIVALS

This assortment of cultural events doesn't capture *all* of SF's ethnicities, but if you make it to each of them, you'll have made a healthy beginning.

Kick the year off Slavic style at the mid-February **Russian Festival** (Richmond District, www.russiancentersf.com). Celebrate the renewal of spring two months later at the **Cherry Blossom Festival** (Japantown Center; call SF Visitor Information Center for more into, 415-391-2000), which runs for two consecutive weekends in mid-April.

Pay homage to all that is Korean with the **Min-Sok Festival** (by the Intercultural Institute of California and Korean Center, Inc., 415-441-1881, www.koreannet.org) in mid-May, centered around a forum of Korean Studies Scholars.

Grab a whole handful of cultures in June at the nationally-acclaimed **Ethnic Dance Festival** (Fort Mason Center, Building D, 415-474-3914, www.fortmason.org or www.worldartswest.org), which claims bragging rights as "one of the largest events of its kind in the country featuring real people, real dances and real music of Northern California communities." Herald Filipino culture—with more dancing—in early June at the **Fiesta Filipina** (Civic Center Plaza; call SF Visitor Information Center for more info, 415-391-2000).

The summer solstice wouldn't be complete without the flavors of Italy at the nation's oldest urban street fair—the mid-June **North Beach Festival** (Grant & Green, 415-989-2220, www.sfnorthbeach.com).

The **Juneteenth Festival** (at Kimball Park, bounded by Geary, Steiner, O'Farrell & Fillmore, 415-447-1330, www.juneteenth.com) celebrates June 19, 1863, the day African-Americans in the deep South learned of the Emancipation Proclamation.

Commemorate the French revolution on July 14th, **Bastille Day**, in the French Quarter near Union Square. Immerse yourself in Pacific Islanders' culture at the **Aloha Festival** (Parade Grounds in the Presidio, 415-281-0221, www.pica-org.org) in August, and in early September, head to Chinatown for the **Autumn Moon Festival** (Grant between California & Pacific, 415-982-6306, www.moonfestival.org).

Round out the year in honor of Latin American cultures. Celebrate art and independence at **Vivas Las Americas!** (Pier 39, 415-705-5500, www.pier39.com) and the **Latino Summer Fiesta** (Mission District and Civic Center Plaza, check www.latinbayarea.com under "Events"), both in mid-September, then join the candlelight processions through the Mission for **Día de los Muertos** (from 24th Street & Bryant to the altar at Garfield Square in Balmy Alley) on All Souls' Day, November 2nd.

CARNAVAL

Decide for yourself whether to bring your family to any of the many ethnic festivals throughout the year, but please, bring just your naughty adult self to ***Carnaval*** (Harrison between 16th & 22nd Streets, 415-920-0125 or 415-826-1401, *www.carnavalsf.com*).

Why San Francisco's version of Mardi Gras is held in late May and not on the days before Lent will remain a mystery to all but those who issue event permits, but no matter—it's one of the City's largest annual public events, featuring exotic dancers and pan-Latin jazz, salsa and samba. If it's got a beat, you can bet someone scantily clad will be dancing to it.

february

Crab Festival

Russian Festival

San Francisco
Independent Film Festival

Chinese New Year
Parade & Street Fair

The Great San Francisco
Crystal Fair

San Francisco Tribal
Folk & Textiles Arts Show

Pacific Orchid Exposition

Tulipmania

Fisherman's Wharf
Classic Car Exhibit

California
Antiquarian Book Fair

• • •

march

Tiburon
International Film Festival

San Francisco International
Asian American Film Festival

St. Patrick's Day Parade

Jewish Music Festival

Contemporary Crafts Market

Bouquets to Art

Flower & Garden Show

ALL THE WORLD'S ON STAGE

Art emerges organically at the **Exit Theatre** (156 Eddy) in September, as the producers of the **San Francisco Fringe Festival** (415-931-1094, www.sffringe.org) present nearly 300 performances of shows they have never seen before. Performers don't even have to audition (or sleep with anyone) to get their names in lights. All they have to do is be one of the first fifty applicants to meet the festival deadline. Really.

Artists from around the world take the stage for this non-juried and completely uncensored celebration of theater, sometimes with remarkable results. Kaliyuga Arts' *Beauty* toured internationally after premiering at Fringe in 1994. Although quality ranges from the up-and-coming to the just-plain-out-there, even a flop won't set you back more than $8.

Who says theater is dead?

FILM FESTIVALS

San Francisco is fast rising as a focal point for film festivals. The **San Francisco International Film Festival** (see next page) in late April is the City's largest and probably the most well known, but you can find movies to suit your own taste almost any other week of the year.

Berlin and Beyond Film Festival
January, Castro Theatre
415-263-8760
www.goethe.de/sanfrancisco

San Francisco Independent Film Festival
February, various locations
415-820-3907 or 415-421-TIXS
www.sfindie.com

- ***Tiburon International Film Festival***
  March, location TBA
  415-381-4123, *www.tiburonfilmfestival.com*

- ***San Francisco International Asian American Film Festival***
  March, Castro and Kabuki Theatres
  415-863-0814 x809, *www.naatanet.org*

- ***San Francisco International Film Festival***
  April, Kabuki, Castro and other theaters
  415-561-5000 or 415-931-FILM, *www.sffs.org*

- ***Urban Kidz Film Festival***
  May, 762 Fulton
  415-392-4400 or 800-965-4827, *www.ukff.org*

- ***San Francisco Black Film Festival***
  June, Delancey Street Theater
  415-771-9271 or 415-346-0199, *www.sfbff.org*

- ***San Francisco International Lesbian and Gay Film Festival***
  June, Castro Theater
  415-703-8650, *www.frameline.org*

- ***San Francisco Jewish Film Festival***
  July, Castro Theater
  925-866-9559/tickets and 415-621-0556/info, *www.sfjff.org*

- ***San Francisco Arab Film Festival***
  October, 2 Plaza Avenue
  415-564-1100, *www.aff.org*

- ***American Indian Film Festival***
  November, Palace of Fine Arts Theater
  415-554-0525, *www.aifisf.com*

- ***Film Arts Festival of Independent Cinema***
  November, various venues
  415-552-3456, *www.filmarts.org*

- ***Black/Lesbian/Gay/Bisexual/Transgender Film Festival***
  December, Rainbow Room, 1800 Market
  415-346-0199, *www.blacklgbtff.org*

april

Howard Street Fair

St. Stupid's Parade

Cherry Blossom Festival & Parade

Easter Parade & Festival

San Francisco International Film Festival

Opening Day on the Bay

Golden Gateway to Gems

Giants Opening Day

• • •

may

Bay to Breakers

Min-Sok Festival

Carnaval

Urban Kidz Film Festival

Cinco de Mayo Parade & Festival

Black & White Ball (biennial)

KFOG KaBoom!

San Francisco Youth Arts Festival

Rosie's Tap Jam

PARADES

Everyone loves a parade, especially tall people who can see over the heads of those who showed up early.

SF hosts a world-class marching spectacle almost every month. February's is the **Chinese New Year Parade** (2nd & Market to Columbus, 415-391-9680, www.chineseparade.com) which starts in early evening and caps three weeks of celebration that include a flower fair, the Miss Chinatown USA Pageant, and the Chinatown Community Street Fair.

The annual **St. Patrick's Day Parade** (2nd & Market to Civic Center, 415-675-9885) is in March, as it should be, and April's parades are several: **St. Stupid's** (Embarcadero Plaza to Washington Square), sponsored by The First Church of the Last Laugh on April Fool's Day; the **Cherry Blossom Parade** (at the Civic Center), which closes the Cherry Blossom Festival; and the **Easter Parade and Festival** (Union Street, 415-441-7055).

Cinco de Mayo (parade on Mission Street, festival in Civic Center Plaza, 415-826-1401, www.latinbayarea.com under "Events") highlights Mexican and Central American art and culture, and the **Gay Pride Parade** unites the queer community in late June. Parade season cedes to the street fairs until about October, when Italians, including Columbus, are feted on—where else?—Columbus Avenue, in the **Italian Heritage Parade** (Fisherman's Wharf & North Beach, 415-434-1492, www.sfcolumbusday.org). Two November parades wrap up the season just in time for Christmas: the **Veterans Day Parade** on Market Street, and the **Union Street Fantasy of Lights** ceremony and parade at the end of the month.

Only In San Francisco #2
GAY PRIDE PARADE
Market Street from the Embarcadero to the Civic Center
late June, 415-864-FREE, *www.sfpride.org*

A genuine slice of San Francisco, the Gay Pride Parade is for humans in all forms, as reflected in the event's official name: Lesbian/Gay/Bisexual/Transgender Pride Parade.

It's très political, attracting speakers from around the world and a host of groups carrying banners, as well as famous hosts (including Nancy Sinatra, Sir Ian McKellen, Sharon Gless, and Margaret Cho), the formerly-named ***Dykes on Bikes*** (who now ride under the much-watered-down, litigation-required handle of "San Francisco Women's Motorcycle Contingent"), the ***Sisters of Perpetual Indulgence*** (*www.thesisters.org*), the cross-dressed, and the undressed.

The weekend-long event officially kicks off with a Fag Friday party at the ***Endup*** (*www.fagfridays.com*). It continues with Pink Saturday and on Sunday consumes the entire Civic Center area during the post-parade festival, with a main stage and nine side stages.

Five hundred rainbow flags fly from lampposts the entire length of Market Street. The crowd numbered nearly one million in 2003 and attendance shows no signs of waning. Viva la Rainbow!

OCEANS OF FUN

No matter how cold the water is, plenty happens offshore in this town, especially when sailing season begins on **Opening Day on the Bay** (Pier 39, 415-823-6633, www.picya.org) at the end of April. Boats and fireworks abound at the **Fourth of July Waterfront Festival** (Pier 39 & Fisherman's Wharf, 415-705-5500, www.pier39.com), and in very late August, the **Tall Ships Festival** (www.sailsanfrancisco.org) hosts crews from all over the world. October brings sonic booms and combustion of a different kind, when the U.S. Navy's Blue Angels push aeronautics to the limits to close out **Fleet Week** (Embarcadero & Fisherman's Wharf, 415-979-4000, www.airshownetwork.com). Early December brings **Christmas at Sea** (Hyde Street Pier, 415-561-6662, www.maritime.org), when children board the historic *Balclutha* to 'fess up to Santa.

june

Union Street Art Fair

Haight Street Fair

Juneteenth Festival

Fiesta Filipina

North Beach Festival

Ethnic Dance Festival

San Francisco
Black Film Festival

San Francisco
International Lesbian and
Gay Film Festival

Gay Pride Parade

The Great San Francisco
Crystal Fair

Day of the Accordion

Stern Grove Festival

• • •

july

Third Street Fair

Dore "Up Your Alley" Fair

Fillmore Street
Jazz Festival

Bastille Day
in the French Quarter

Books by the Bay

San Francisco
Jewish Film Festival

BIG HUGE PARTIES

As far as we can tell, if you can't have fun at one of these parties, you'd better hang up your lampshade for good. Ticket prices can hit three digits, so it'll be up to you to make it money well spent.

"Money" is in fact the operative word at the biennial May's-end **Black & White Ball** (Civic Center & other venues, 415-864-6000, www.bwball.com). Thousands of Bay Area elite and want-to-be glams congregate at the B&W, the City's biggest black-tie block party.

By Labor Day weekend, the attitude (but not the quality) definitely tones down a bit for **A La Carte, A La Park** (Golden Gate Park, Sharon Meadow, 415-458-1988 info, 415-478-BASS tickets, www.eventswestca.com), where dozens of "ess eff chefs" pair their eats with fine wines and music.

Pump up the volume again for the trio of raucous affairs in October. To get the most out of **Oktoberfest By the Bay** (Fort Mason Center, Festival Pavilion, 888-746-7522, www.oktoberfestbythebay.com), wear your lederhosen and swim with the tide of traditional folk dancers, yodelers, nonstop German music, and (naturally) stein after stein of beer.

If you're still tipsy a few days later, that's okay—what better state of mind for enjoying an **Exotic Erotic Ball** (Cow Palace, 415-567-BALL, www.exoticeroticball.com), once in October, again on New Year's Eve. They're the largest adult indoor masquerades in the world, with truly outrageous costumes and nudity galore. Wait, maybe we're confusing it with **Halloween in the Castro**... No matter, the description applies equally to each.

tunes & giant jam sessions	
the music	***why it's better than a CD***
Jewish Music Festival (March) various locations San Francisco and East Bay 510-848-0237 *www.brjcc.org*	Have you ever heard klezmer music? (Have you ever even heard *of* klezmer music?) It's a trip. Makes for an ambitious first date.
KFOG KaBoom! (mid-May) Piers 30 & 32 415-995-6930 *www.kfog.com*	This free all-day concert sports three bands and plenty of food, and closes after dark with a state-of-the-art, rivaling-fourth-of-July fireworks show, synchronized to a KFOG soundtrack.
Stern Grove Festival (June, July, August) 19th Avenue & Sloat 415-252-6252 *www.sterngrove.org*	More than a music festival, the Sunday afternoon symphonic, ballet, Cuban dance, and even hula shows are free all summer long.
North Beach Jazz Festival (early August) throughout North Beach 415-252-8773 *www.nbjazzfest.org*	If sipping wine to a groovy vibe is your scene, you'll dig this annual fest.
San Francisco Blues Festival (late September) Great Meadow @ Fort Mason 415-979-5588 *www.sfblues.com*	The blues greats turn out for the oldest blues festival in America.
Reggae in the Park (early October) Sharon Meadow, in Golden Gate Park 415-458-1988 *www.eventswestca.com*	Enjoy ethnic arts, international food and Caribbean culture, as well as multicultural world-beat music.
San Francisco Jazz Festival (late October) locations throughout SF 415-788-7353 800-850-7353 (outside CA) *www.sfjazz.org*	One of San Francisco's biggest and best music festivals features numerous well-known jazz musicians, yet generally operates below the radar. Smooth moves for smooth grooves.

july cont'd

Fourth of July
Waterfront Festival

Cable Car Bell-Ringing
Competition

Stern Grove Festival

• • •

august

Nihonmachi (Japantown)
Street Fair

Pier 39
Street Performers' Festival

Aloha Festival

North Beach Jazz Festival

Sausalito Art Festival

Tall Ships Festival

ACC Craft Show

Comedy Day

Stern Grove Festival

• • •

september

Polk Street Fair

Folsom Street Fair

Ghirardelli Square
Chocolate Festival

Autumn Moon Festival

Vivas Las Americas!

Latino Summer Fiesta

Only In San Francisco #3

HALLOWEEN IN THE CASTRO

October 31st, intersection of Market & Castro

Although the City's official Halloween party has moved to the Civic Center, the real action at its former home down the street is legendary, a lot more grown-up, and won't cost you a dime.

You'll find drag queens in brilliant gowns, feathers galore (think headdresses and boas), tall hats and wigs—even a rubber catsuit here and there amidst the 300,000-person sea of humanity swimming down Castro Street.

Considering that the crowd can be packed like sardines, the atmosphere remains festive and friendly. Beware the balconies, though. It's better to be at the house party that spills onto one of them than it is to be walking underneath. Keep an eye out too for the hunks in hot pants and a little naughtiness. It's all quintessential San Francisco.

SPORTS AND CARS

January's **East-West Shrine Game** (Pacific Bell Park, 925-762-2277 tickets, 650-372-9300 info, www.shrinegame.com) is the prestigious groundbreaker of all of the university all-star football games, featuring America's best college seniors and benefiting the North American Shriners Hospitals for Children.

Same venue, January or February, is the **AMA Supercross Series** (Pacific Bell Park, 415-478-2277 tickets, 415-972-1800 info, www.sxgp.com), a race of the world's fastest and toughest track motorcycle riders. A third highlight is April's **Opening Day for the San Francisco Giants** (Pacific Bell Park, 800-544-2687 tickets, 415-972-2000 info, www.sfgiants.com).

Change gears—automatic or manual—at two car exhibits: from the time-tested and classic at the **Historic Fisherman's Wharf Classic Car Exhibit** (part of the Crab Festival in February, Pier 45, Shed A, 415-546-0800 for info, tickets available at the event), to the latest and greatest at the **San Francisco International Automobile Show** (November, Moscone Center, 415-331-4406, www.moscone.com).

AREN'T THERE COWS AT THE COW PALACE?

Yes indeedy, at least once a year at the ***Grand National Rodeo, Horse and Stock Show*** (415-404-4111, *www.grandnationalrodeo.com*) in late October. Then the heroic staff works like the dickens to get the giant barn-like structure smelling pretty in time for the ***Great Dickens Christmas Fair*** (415-392-4400, *www.dickensfair.com*), running each weekend between Thanksgiving and Christmas.

The ***Sports and Boat Show*** (415-931-2500, *www.sfboatshow.com*) hits the palace in January, and the ***Flower & Garden Show*** (415-771-6909, 800-829-9751, *www.gardenshow.com*) arrives in March, but it's the pre-Labor Day "greatest show on earth" that promises to bring out the kid in all of us: the ***Ringling Brothers and Barnum & Bailey Circus*** (415-478-BASS for tickets, *www.cowpalace.com*).

september cont'd

A La Carte, A La Park

San Francisco Blues Festival

Ringling Brothers and Barnum & Bailey Circus

Dragon Boat Races

International Vintage Poster Fair

Fringe Festival

• • •

october

Castro Street Fair

Italian Heritage Parade

Fleet Week

Oktoberfest By the Bay

Exotic Erotic Ball Halloween

Halloween in the Castro

Halloween San Francisco

Reggae in the Park

San Francisco Jazz Festival

The Great San Francisco Crystal Fair

San Francisco Arts Festival

Grand National Rodeo, Horse & Stock Show

Pier 30 Pumpkin Pandemonium

ARTS, CRAFTS & CRYSTALS

For a city that isn't known as particularly craftsy, San Francisco sure has a lot of crafts fairs. And those crystals! They're for sale at Fort Mason at least four times a year (Feb., June, Oct., Nov.) at **The Great San Francisco Crystal Fair** (Fort Mason Center, 415-383-7837, www.crystalfair.com) and again in August at the **Golden Gateway to Gems** (contact the Gem & Mineral Society for current location: 415-564-4230, www.sfgms.org).

The purely arts festivals are also plentiful. Start with January's modern and contemporary **San Francisco International Art Expo** (Fort Mason Center, Festival Pavilion, 877-734-2399, www.sfiae.com). Continue into February with the global **San Francisco Tribal, Folk & Textiles Arts Show** (Fort Mason Center, Festival Pavilion, 310-455-2886, www.caskeylees.com).

May brings the **San Francisco Youth Arts Festival** (at Zeum, Yerba Buena Gardens, 415-750-8630, www.sfyouth artsfestival.org), which showcases the artwork and music of San Francisco students in grades K-12. Participation and attendance for all Youth Arts events are free.

Jaunt across the Golden Gate in late August for the fine arts, music and food of the **Sausalito Art Festival** (415-331-3757, www.sausalitoartfest.org), then round out the year at the **San Francisco Arts Festival** (Bill Graham Civic Auditorium, Grove between Larkin & Polk) in October. With more than 15,000 original works, the San Francisco show is one of California's largest.

CRAFTS FAIRS

It's the subject of heated debate: what is "craft" and what is "art"? Decide for yourself at one of these bazaars of wearable art, home furnishings, ceramics, jewelry, stoneware bowls, silk scarves, and patterned quilts. Did we forget to mention the gourmet food? It would hardly qualify as a San Francisco event without it.

Contemporary Crafts Market (March)
Fort Mason Center, Festival Pavilion, 415-995-4925, *www.craftsource.org*

ACC Craft Show (August)
Fort Mason Center, 800-836-3470 or 415-896-5060, *www.craftcouncil.org*

Harvest Festival and Christmas Crafts Market (November)
Concourse Exhibition Center, 635 8th Street, 707-778-6300
www.harvestfestival.com

Celebration of Craftswomen (late November)
Fort Mason Center, Herbst Pavilion, 415-383-3470, *www.miramarevents.com*

KPFA Crafts Fair (December)
Concourse Exhibition Center, 635 8th Street, 510-848-6767, *www.kpfa.org*

flower power

Bet you didn't even know that San Francisco had an Orchid Society, did you? Brighten up the winter with three floral festivals starting in late February:

Pacific Orchid Exposition
Fort Mason Center, Festival Pavilion
415-665-2468, *www.orchidsanfrancisco.com*

Bouquets to Art annual fundraiser
California Place of the Legion of Honor
Lincoln Park, 415-750-3504, *www.famsf.org*

Tulipmania Festival
Pier 39, 415-705-5500
www.pier39.com

november

American Indian Film Festival

Film Arts Festival of Independent Cinema

Veterans Day Parade

Fantasy of Lights Parade

The Great San Francisco Crystal Fair

Harvest Festival and Christmas Crafts Market

Celebration of Craftswomen

San Francisco International Automobile Show

Great Dickens Christmas Fair

Embarcadero Center Lighting Ceremony

Pier 39 Tree Lighting

Yerba Buena Center Tree Lighting

Ghirardelli Center Tree Lighting

Fisherman's Wharf Tree Lighting

Official City Tree Lighting

Dia de los Muertos

OTHER COOL EVENTS

In A Category All Their Own

How's your herring? Ask any of the hundreds of sea lions basking on Pier 39's K-Dock at the **Anniversary of the Sea Lions' Arrival at Pier 39** (January 19th, 415-705-5500, www.pier39.com). Declared a "Watchable Wildlife" viewing area by the California Watchable Wildlife Project, this is where humans gape and sea lions honk, but there is noooooo feeding allowed.

Change your tune to "Happy Birthday" the next day as you're riding the **Freedom Train** (chartered by the Dr. Martin Luther King, Jr. Association of the Santa Clara Valley; for info, contact CalTrain, 800-660-4287, www.caltrain.com) up from the peninsula to march over to **Dr. Martin Luther King Jr.'s Birthday Celebration** (January 20th, Bill Graham Civic Auditorium and Yerba Buena Gardens, 510-268-3777).

Bookworms unite every other year at the California **Antiquarian Book Fair** (February, Concourse Exhibition Center, 415-551-5190, www.californiabookfair.com), the world's largest rare book fair. Convene again at **Books by the Bay** (mid-July, Yerba Buena Gardens, Mission @ 4th Street, www.booksbythebay.com), a celebration of independent bookselling with panels, signings and plenty of local literary stars.

If dancing's more your thang, click up your heels on National Tap Dance Day for **Rosie's Tap Jam** (May, The Cannery, 2801 Leavenworth, 415-771-3112, www.thecannery.com), featuring Rosie's bunion-inducing two mile "Tour de Tap" parade through Fisherman's Wharf.

Your experience of all that is officially San Franciscan just won't be complete until you attend the **Day of the Accordion** (June, The Cannery, 2801 Leavenworth, 415-771-3112, www.thecannery.com), a celebration of San Francisco's official musical instrument (don't ask) and an afternoon of Cajun, zydeco, conjunto, polka, and Parisian music. Doesn't ring your bell? Then how about the **Cable Car Bell-Ringing Competition** (July, Union Square Plaza; contact MUNI for info, 415-673-6864, www.sfmuni.com), where seasoned Muni operators vie for top honors, drawing on melodic as well as oral abilities.

You'll either laugh your guts out or throw Bronx cheers at the stand-ups of the decades-old **Comedy Day** (a Sunday afternoon in late summer, Golden Gate Park, Sharon Meadow, www.comedyday.com). No charge for the bellyache!

It's the same gratis entrance fee for spectators at the Northern California/International championship **Dragon Boat Races** and festival (September, North of Lake Merced at Skyline & Harding Road, www.cdba.org). Witness this ancient yet vibrant team sport at its best, where boats are decorated with dragon heads and tails, drummers don costumes and goofy hats, and the paddling rhythm keeps pace with the beats on a cedar and rawhide drum on the bow.

Less ancient but still vintage, American and European wares go on display at the **International Vintage Poster Fair** (September, Fort Mason Center, 650-548-6700, www.posterfair.com), the oldest and largest event of its kind in the world. For Halloween, you can peruse the pumpkins and parade around with the rest of the spooky crew at **Pumpkin Pandemonium** (October, Pier 39, www.pier39.com, 415-705-5500).

Traditional Irish and Scottish live music and dancing feet sound out at the **Celtic Christmas at the Cannery** during the first three weekends of December, while Santa comes to town nearby at **Ghirardelli Square's Jollyday Fair**. Not wintry enough for you? Then dash through the (indoor) snow at the **Metreon Center Winterland** (4th Street & Mission), which screens children's movies every December Saturday morning. Round out the holiday season at the hands-on **Mochi Making Ceremony** in Japantown, where the Masters of the Mochi demonstrate how to pound sweet rice into a gooey mass inside a hollow tree stump "bowl." You then get to try your own hand using mochi-pounding poles the size of a baseball bat. The yummy gum is rounded into balls, coated with soybean-sugar sauce and consumed as candy as a part of the traditional Japanese New Year celebration.

december

Winter Solstice Festival

Black/Lesbian/Gay/Bisexual/Transgender Film Festival

Christmas at Sea

Exotic Erotic Ball New Year's

KPFA Crafts Fair

Great Dickens Christmas Fair

Celtic Christmas at the Cannery

Ghirardelli Center's Jollyday Fair

Metreon Center Winterland

Skip the post-Thanksgiving shopping rush and get lit instead. No, not stinking drunk—lit up like a Christmas tree! Lighting ceremonies abound in November. They are beautiful to witness, for Pagan and Christian folk alike. In rough chronological order, the electricity flows thus: first at the ***Embarcadero Center*** (415-772-0200), where a late afternoon holiday fair leads up to the flipping of the switch on 17,000-odd bulbs that outline four skyscrapers against the night sky for the rest of the holiday season. The celebration includes fireworks, music, and an ice skating show in honor of the official opening of the rink. Then ***Pier 39*** (415-705-5500, *www.pier39.com*) turns it on with a day of face painting, street performers and magic tricks, closing with the illumination of 2,500 lights on a 65-foot tree. The ceremony at ***Yerba Buena Center*** (in the ***Esplanade Gardens***) includes entertainment, cocoa, cookies, and magic. ***Ghirardelli Square*** (415-775-5500, *www.ghirardellisq.com*) lights up the waterfront with a 50-foot tree, trimmed with Ghirardelli Chocolate and ribbons, and provides entertainment, caroling, dancing, and a visit from Mr. and Mrs. Santa Claus. ***Fisherman's Wharf*** lights a 50-foot tree at Taylor & Jefferson. Breakfast with Santa at Pier 39, then carol along the waterfront. Free motorized cable car rides, too! Finally, the ***Recreation & Park Department*** lights the Official City Tree, a magnificent Monterey Cypress, in front of the ***McLaren Lodge*** (Oak & Stanyan).

let there be light!

DINING & NIGHTLIFE

EAT, drink, and be merry, right? Well, right—but also, if you're a leisure seeker, watch your budget, connect with your community, and keep it real. It's about value, which doesn't necessarily mean bargains. You'll find value in a variety of price ranges and places, whether you're operating on $30 a day or $300 a day, a Mission tattoo artist or a Marina yuppie.

San Francisco establishments are as broad and diverse as the City itself. We found this out first-hand when our survey on "best value" restaurants turned up 75 different restaurants—out of 80 total responses! You'll have no shortage of choices.

How, then, did we select our own picks for this special section? Did we ever return that dart board we borrowed? No, really—in addition to your feedback, we made our choices using four criteria:

1—Value for the money
2—Connection with the community
3—Uniqueness or "funkiness factor"
4—Positive vibe and other "intangibles"

If this sounds like an inexact science, it was. In some cases, we gave people and places the nod just because we liked them. In others, we liked the kickback they gave us! Okay, this we're not kidding about: *none of these recommendations have been influenced by commercial arrangements in any way.* You won't necessarily agree with all our selections, but that's okay—you're not supposed to. Check it out for yourself. These locales all make the world, or at least our community, a better place to be. Either that, or they've just got really awesome noodles. Enjoy!

EATING OUT

Eating out on a limited budget can be a challenge, but fortunately San Francisco has a plethora of excellent lower-priced dining options. Restaurants recommended here range from spartan to upscale, and we've included some unusual categories in hopes of inspiring you to try something different, cuisine or otherwise. There's a variety of food-types for the most diverse of palates. What they share is exceptional value.

Five Cheap Restaurants You'll *Want* to Eat At

If you're operating on a limited budget, you want to know the bargain restaurants. The problem is, you want them to be good, not just cheap. Everyone has their favorite "cheap eats" joint, and San Francisco has many inexpensive restaurants, but these five rise above the pack.

I ***Shalimar*** *(532 Jones, Tenderloin, 415-928-0333)*
Good, cheap Pakistani cuisine in a sketchy section of the Tenderloin. Go for the food, not the atmosphere. You can eat comfortably here for $5, and like a king for $10.

II ***King of Thai Noodle House*** *(639 Clement, the Richmond, 415-752-5198)*
The food at King of Thai is good, spicy, cheap and, well, good. You won't find fancy nouveau California-influenced Thai food here, just straightforward, robust dishes like soup bowls, fried noodles, and pad Thai. The chain has six restaurants in all, but the original Clement Street location seems to do it the best.

III ***Yokoso Nippon*** *(314 Church, the Castro, no phone)*
More commonly known as "No Name Sushi," this sushi bar is marked by low prices, large portions, and a BYOB (Bring Your Own Beverage) policy. We like.

IV ***PPQ (Pho Phu Quoc)*** *(1816 Irving, the Sunset, 415-661-8869; 2332 Clement, the Richmond, 415-386-8266)*
PPQ is an insider's delight: inexpensive Vietnamese cuisine with great noodles, clay pot dishes, and curries. The lights may be a little bright, but hey—no one's complaining.

V ***Red's Java House*** *(Pier 30, South Beach, 415-777-5626)*
Enjoy burgers, dogs, and beers on the water at this San Francisco institution. Best enjoyed outdoors on a sunny day, but beware of the feisty pigeons. A burger and a Bud will run you $3.50. Daytime only.

Five Best Value Restaurants

These aren't the cheapest in town, but give serious bang for the buck:

I ***Chow*** *(215 Church, the Castro, 415-552-2469)*
Park Chow *(1240 9th Avenue, Inner Sunset, 415-665-9912)*

Perhaps the best value to be had in a San Francisco sit-down restaurant. You simply get a lot for your money here: good food and drink, nice atmosphere, and an extraordinarily friendly staff.

II ***Eric's Restaurant*** *(1500 Church, Noe Valley, 415-282-0919)*
Excellent Chinese cuisine comes with a California twist at this Noe Valley institution. Also try Eric's sister restaurant **Eliza's** (1457 18th Street, 415-648-9999 in Potrero Hill; 2877 California, 415-621-4819 in Pacific Heights), where the menu is curiously similar, but the décor decidedly different.

III ***Cha Cha Cha*** *(1801 Haight, Haight-Ashbury, 415-386-7670; 2327 Mission, the Mission, 415-648-0504)*

Long a popular choice for groups and big nights out, this Caribbean tapas joint is crowded, festive, and a good value. One word: sangria.

IV ***Ti Couz*** *(3108 16th Street, the Mission, 415-252-7373)*
Yes, it *is* French and they *do* serve mostly crepes, but Ti Couz is good. Real good. Looking for a date spot? Fellas, take note: chicks dig it.

V ***La Méditerranée*** *(2210 Fillmore, Pacific Heights, 415-921-2956; 288 Noe, the Castro, 415-431-7210)*

A cozy restaurant with a diverse menu, "La Med" is a popular date spot for those who don't want to break the bank.

fine dining value

If you're willing to roll the dice on some fancy food, "enroll" yourself in a gourmet dining experience at the ***California Culinary Academy's Carême Room*** (625 Polk, 415-292-8229 for reservations, *www.baychef.com*), where you can get four star cuisine at two star prices. Students prepare the food, and the extravagant buffets served on Thursdays and Fridays are the usually the best value. Food quality can be sporadic, depending on who's cooking, but they aim to please—don't miss dessert!

For a more tried-and-true meal, try ***Metro Cafe*** (311 Divisadero, 415-552-0903, *www.metrocafesf.net*), which serves a fixed-price three-course home-style French dinner for $15, $12.50 for early birds. Bring your own wine and pay the $10 corkage fee if you can't eat your food dry. Metro offers outdoor patio dining and is open seven nights a week, and for weekend brunch.

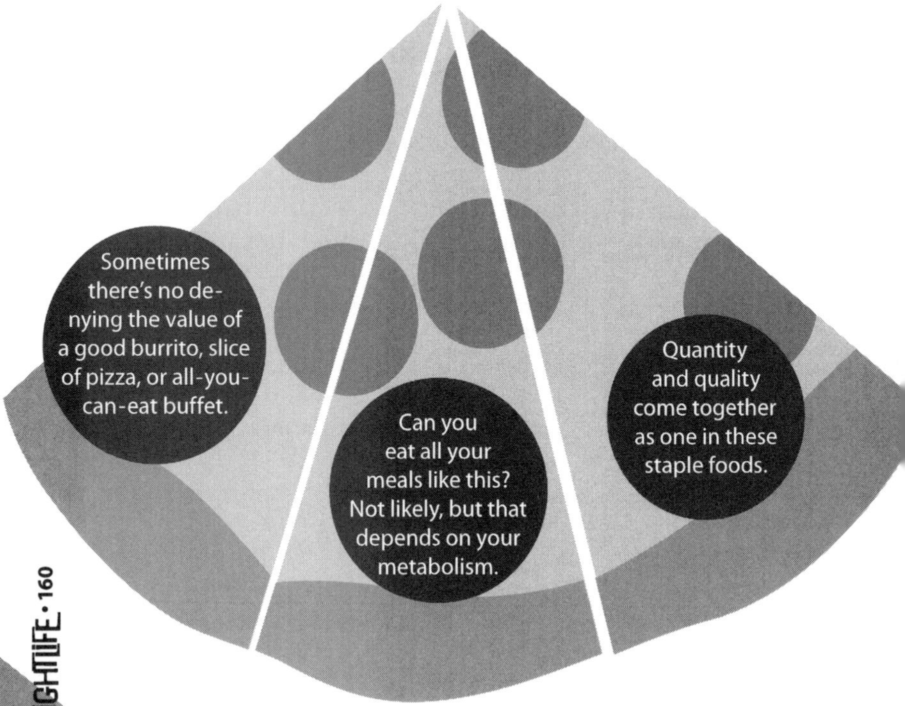

STAPLES OF THE UNEMPLOYED

The Slice

Pizza is not exactly one of San Francisco's specialties, taking a back seat to the slices in New York, Chicago, and other points east. Nevertheless, this Italian-influenced staple can be found in hundreds of local restaurants, which could number more than in all of Italy! Choose wisely, for quality varies significantly from place to place.

Escape From New York
1737 Haight, Upper Haight, 415-668-5577
508 Castro, the Castro, 415-252-1515
333 Bush, Financial District, 415-421-0700
Any of Escape From New York's three locations is a safe bet. So what if we had to steal from New York to get some decent pizza in this town? Although authenticity has its limits (you won't run into Snake Plissken, for example), this popular New York style pizzeria gets it right.

Goat Hill Pizza

300 Connecticut, Potrero Hill, 415-641-1440

Goat Hill serves savory pies in a festive atmosphere frequented by post-victory co-ed softball teams.

North Beach Pizza

1310 Grant, North Beach, 415-433-2444

Although North Beach Pizza now has five locations around San Francisco, their pizza is still as rich, cheesy and filling as ever. Seems that verging on big chain status has not managed to destroy the flavor—or improve the delivery speed!

Extreme Pizza

1980 Union, Cow Hollow, 415-929-8234
1730 Fillmore, Western Addition, 415-929-9900
1052 Folsom, SOMA, 415-701-9000
www.extremepizza.com

Extreme Pizza is another successful local startup, baking up good 'za at reasonable prices: most combinations cost less than $6 for an individual pizza.

Za Pizza

1919 Hyde, Russian Hill, 415-771-3100

Speaking of "za," we find Za a perennial favorite among tipsy Russian Hill revelers.

Pauline's Pizza

260 Valencia, the Mission, 415-552-2050

Pauline's is our final finalist. The most upscale joint on our list, Pauline's boasts the best gourmet pizza in the City. You might want to forego that accompanying brew-ha-ha here for a nice glass of vino.

all-you-can-eat buffets

Always a way to "pack in" value, buffets offer the hungry diner quantity for the money. Just don't expect to take home a doggy bag! Then again, stranger things have happened.

Bring your appetite and a friend or two and check out the buffet bars at these generous establishments:

Coriya Hot Pot City
852 Clement
The Richmond
415-387-7888

Not only is Coriya all-you-can-eat all the time, but it's cook-your-own-food as well!

The cuisine is a combination of Japanese shabu shabu and Korean barbecue. The fun of preparing your food at your own table makes this a great bargain date joint.

Cost per person at dinnertime is $11.99 Monday–Thursday, $12.99 Fridays and weekends, and that buys you sodas and desserts, too. The same spread at lunch (before 4pm) will run you $2 less, $9.99 and $10.99 respectively.

[mangia! mangia!...]

[...seconds, anyone?]

Funny how every single Indian restaurant offers a buffet lunch—or does it just seem that way? The food all goes down easy so we're not complaining. A couple of joints to stock up at are:

Star India
2127 Polk
Russian Hill
415-292-6699
3721 Geary
Inner Richmond
415-668-4466

Lunch buffet costs $6.95, served at the Polk Street location from 11:30am-3pm Monday-Friday and noon-3pm on weekends, and from 11am-3pm everyday at the Geary location. Decent Indian food comes in mass quantities at both locales.

•••

Taj Mahal
398 Eddy
Tenderloin
415-922-9055

This dicey enclave in the Tenderloin, like the other Indian joints in town, has a lunch buffet where you can eat until you're full, queasy, or both. It's offered seven days a week, for lunch from 11:30am–4pm and again for dinner from 6pm–10:30pm. The food rocks, as many will attest, and the buffet runs just $4.95.

[keep eating...]

The Burrito

Atop the unemployed food chain, so to speak, the "little burro" actually has a fascinating history, both in San Francisco and beyond. Its origins can be traced back to our friends the Aztecs who, when the Spaniards first arrived in Mexico in the 1500s, were already pounding out corn tortillas of various sizes, and filling them up with meat and beans. But it wasn't until the Europeans brought the gift of wheat that the flour tortilla was added to the mix, enabling the more modern, gut-busting versions so prevalent today.

San Francisco's first burrito migrated up from the deserts of Southern California during the gold rush era, but it wasn't until 1961 that the first actual retail burrito was sold, reportedly from a corner grocery store at 2399 Folsom Street named **El Faro**—a burrito shop to this day. The modern burrito was further internationalized with the "wrap" movement, which **World Wrapps** launched from San Francisco in the mid-1990s. Burrito blasphemy to some, wraps use international ingredients and a variety of flavored tortillas to achieve a healthier result.

San Francisco's Mission district is now burrito ground zero in the City, and the venerable **El Farolito** tops the burrito pyramid. As anyone who has sampled their carne asada burrito at 2am on a Sunday can attest, this could be as close to burrito nirvana as one can get.

Just a short stagger down the street is **La Taqueria**, where the tacos are as good as the burritos. No rice inside the tortilla means more meat per burrito, and, in the opinion of its loyal followers, more flavor.

Moving down to the popular 16th & Mission area, **Pancho Villa** is the aficionado's choice. With an assembly line that would make Henry Ford proud, this burrito factory may churn out more "product" than any burrito stand west of the Mississippi.

Good burritos can't all be located in the Mission. Good thing, then, that **La Canasta** pulls its weight in the Cow Hollow district. Watch the Marina SUVs line up in front of this to-go-only taqueria at suppertime.

Gordo Taqueria has long been known for making quality burritos in the Avenues. Try the Gordo Plates for a hearty alternative, and prepare to take a leisurely nap afterwards.

El Farolito
2779 Mission, 415-824-7877
2951 24th Street, 415-641-0758
4817 Mission, 415-337-5500

Gordo Taqueria
2252 Clement, 415-387-4484
5450 Geary, 415-668-8226
1239 9th Avenue, 415-566-6011

La Canasta
3006 Buchanan, 415-474-2627

La Taqueria
2889 Mission, 415-285-7117

Pancho Villa
3017 16th Street, 415-864-8840

World Wrapps
2012 Market, 415-987-7300
www.worldwrapps.com

[...munch, munch, munch}

At these prices, you could easily stick with Indian food each time you dine out. But variety is the spice of life, so sample spices from other regions—even the homeland—at these tasty venues:

Pride of the Mediterranean
1761 Fillmore
Fillmore District
415-567-1150

All-you-can-eat lunch buffet, 11am-3pm, seven days a week, $7.95. Middle-eastern cuisine. Stick around for the bellydancing at night.

...

Bottom of the Hill
1233 17th Street
Potrero Hill
415-621-4455

True, the Bottom of the Hill is better-known for its live music than for its food but on Sunday afternoons they offer one of the best values in town: all-you-can-eat (surprisingly good) barbecue and live music, all for seven bucks.

STOP *[I couldn't eat another bite!]*

CHEZ SAN FRANCISCO!

San Francisco is quirky, period. One way to explore its unusual side is through some of the restaurants and bars you're not likely to find anywhere else.

AsiaSF

201 9th Street, SOMA, 415-255-2742

www.asiasf.com

Exotic might be a tame word to describe the scene here. Gender illusion meets hip cocktail lounge meets sexy burlesque show. A true San Francisco original!

Hot 'n Hunky

4039 18th Street, the Castro, 415-621-6365

Where better to get your burgers "hot 'n hunky" than in San Francisco's Castro district?

El Rio

3158 Mission, Outer Mission, 415-282-3325

www.elriosf.com

Forget happy hours, how about happy *days?* In addition to being a downright wacky, diverse bar-o-fun, El Rio also represents pure bar value. A recent calendar check of their website revealed the following: Dollar Day on Mondays, with $1 well drinks and a $1 cover after 8pm for DJ music; $2 margaritas on Tuesdays; Happy Hour on Fridays with free oysters on the half-shell from 5-7pm; Salsa Sundays from 3pm and after, an $8 cover gets you live music and a free BBQ! (See "Spice Up The Week" on p. 184)

Beach Blanket Babylon/Club Fugazi

678 Green, North Beach, 415-421-4222

There's no food here, but this remains one of the most original shows around, and continues to re-invent itself year after year. While it's on the must-see list for tourists, locals need to get their hineys down to the Club Fugazi and check it out.

Pow!

101 6th Street, SOMA, 415-278-0940

No food here, either, but this is where the superheroes convene to discuss strategy. This eclectic, homo-erotic dive is kitsch at its finest, serving up complimentary candy and condoms, x-rated cartoons, and Sony Playstation games.

New Eritrea Restaurant

907 Irving, the Sunset, 415-681-1288

Never tried Eritrean food? Never even heard of Eritrean food? You're not alone. But where else besides San Francisco can you sit on the floor and eat with your hands a cuisine described as "similar to Ethiopian but more Italian-y" without raising an eyebrow?

LEAVE 'EM TO THE TOURISTS

Postrio

545 Post, Union Square, 415-776-7825

Long gone the way of Wolfgang Puck's now-franchised food empire, Postrio is expensive, impersonal, and lacks character.

Tonga Room & Hurricane Bar

950 Mason, Fairmont Hotel, Nob Hill, 415-772-5278

A strange combination of old-money San Francisco and tropical kitsch, this high-end tiki bar used to be a hoot. But these days, the service is abysmal (you'd be bitter, too, if you had to work at a "Pirates of the Caribbean" bar every night), and their "legendary" happy hour, from 5-7pm, is less than legendary, costing $7 per plate plus a one-drink minimum ($6-8 bucks).

Le Colonial

20 Cosmo Place, Union Square, 415-931-3600

The food's not bad, but it's terribly overpriced. Leave this one to the colonialists; have a drink at the fancy bar and network with Financial District types instead.

House of Nanking

919 Kearny, Chinatown, 415-421-1429

Long known as an inexpensive staple on the edge of Chinatown, locals gave up on this place years ago as it became too crowded, too impersonal, and the food quality suffered. Come to think of it, was the food ever that good here?

Fisherman's Grotto

2847 Taylor, Suite 9, Fisherman's Wharf, 415-673-7025

Crowded, expensive, and noisy, with below average food. Need we say more?

splurge

Okay, so these restaurants aren't cheap—and this really doesn't have anything to do with unemployment—but we couldn't resist picking our favorites. When you're ready to splurge or the parents are in town, consider these fine establishments:

Jardinière
300 Grove
Civic Center
415-861-5555

•••

Masa's
648 Bush
Union Square
415-989-7154

•••

Farallon
450 Post
Theatre District
415-956-6969

•••

Rubicon
558 Sacramento
Financial District
415-434-4100

•••

Slanted Door
100 Brannan
SOMA
415-861-8032

THE WAY-BACK MACHINE

These aren't necessarily the cheapest eateries and bars about town, but with them come history, tradition, and plenty of character. Step out of the 21st century and commune with the famous San Franciscans who sought leisure in days of yore.

Tosca Café *in North Beach*
242 Columbus, 415-986-9651
Tosca is all that a leisurely time off hangout should be: friendly, eclectic, diverse, cozy, and oozing with character. The local film crowd hangs there, plus the jukebox plays nothing but opera! It may have gained a little too much notoriety for its own good in recent years, leading to a slight tourist infusion (believe us, we realize we're adding to the exposure with this very listing), but it all still seems to work. Bohemians, stars, tourists, and plain old folk blend well in this colorful European style-bandit.

Balboa Cafe *in the Marina*
3199 Fillmore, 415-921-3944
This is one bar and restaurant that transcends old and new. First opened in 1913, it remains popular with old timers as well as young Marina singles on the prowl. The authors can personally attest to this but that's all we're saying. A lesser known fact about the Balboa is that the restaurant is particularly good (locals rave about the burgers) and very reasonably priced. Unemployed ruffians beware: the bartenders double as bouncers and can be seen hopping the bar with lightning speed at the first sign of trouble.

***Tadich Grill** in the Financial District*
240 California, 415-391-1849

As the oldest of the oldies, Tadich is steeped in folklore. If you really want to bone up on its history, read the book, *Tadich Grill: The Story of San Francisco's Oldest Restaurant*. Sit at the bar with a stiff cocktail and soak up the Gold Rush era nostalgia or enjoy a boozy seafood lunch and mingle with Financial District types taking a break from the office.

***The Saloon** in North Beach*
1232 Grant, 415-989-7666

The Saloon is dubbed the oldest bar in San Francisco, although it's hard to believe that no one could get a drink in this town until 1861. Originally known as Wagner's beer hall, this legendary blues dive packs a wallop, with live music every night of the week—a good place to go when you don't have to get up for work the next day, if you catch our drift. Leave your good shoes at home.

***Little Shamrock** in Inner Sunset*
807 Lincoln, 415-661-0060

Opened in 1893 primarily as a restaurant and watering hole for workers in Golden Gate Park, they call the Little Shamrock the second oldest bar in San Francisco. How could it have taken 32 years to open a second bar in the City? Ponder that question as you take a draw off a smooth Guinness—as long as the smell of stale beer doesn't put you off, that is.

other timeless joints

Buena Vista Café
2765 Hyde
Fisherman's Wharf
415-474-5044

A bit touristy, but they pour some two thousand Irish Coffees here a day.

•••

Vesuvio
255 Columbus Avenue
North Beach
415-362-3370

A classic, bohemian favorite from the '50s that still thrives today. Write your leisure memoirs here during your sabbatical.

•••

Gold Dust Lounge
247 Powell
Union Square
415-397-1695

Mingle with the tourists (heck, you're on vacation too!) and listen to live jazz seven days a week at this relic.

NIGHT OWL EATING

San Francisco can be a challenge for late night eats—a frustrating attribute to say the least, especially if you're inclined to stay out late on a school night. If you don't have anywhere to be the next morning (and there's a good chance you don't), your evening may be just getting started around 10pm. But if you haven't made up your dinner mind by then, you'll often find yourself SOL (and we don't mean "Sorry Or Lost"). Never fear; these digs allow you to dine into the wee hours.

Osha Thai Noodle Café *(696 Geary, Tenderloin, 415-673-2368)*
Open until 1am Sunday-Thursday, 2am Friday and Saturday, this Tenderloin diamond in the rough has great food and a hip scene.

Steps of Rome *(348 Columbus, North Beach, 415-397-0435)*
In fine Euro fashion, the Steps of Rome serves food at all hours. You can grab breakfast first thing in the morning and dinner or a snack until 2am during the week—3am on weekends. A perfect place to bleed off that midweek bar crawl, if for no reason other than that you can.

Brazen Head *(3166 Buchanan, Cow Hollow, 415-921-7600)*
Now this is what we're talking about. For 23 years, the Brazen Head has quietly served great food until 1am every night of the week. Darkened windows and cozy booths make it *the* place for that discreet affair. Add to that a classic, old-school bar, and you may be hitting up this hideaway at midnight several nights a week.

Emmy's Spaghetti Shack *(18 Virginia, the Mission, 415-206-2086)*
If you've found yourself cocktailing through the dinner hours in the Mission, a plate of Emmy's spaghetti and meatballs can be a welcome reprieve. This place puts the "F" in funk and you'll make friends fast here. Serving until midnight, it makes for a good one-two time off combo with **El Rio** (see "Chez San Francisco!" p. 164) just down the street.

Yuet Lee *(1300 Stockton, Chinatown, 415-982-6020)*
Not your typical Chinese, this late-night eatery serves up some unusual seafood dishes until three in the morning—perfect after you stumble out of a nearby North Beach watering hole.

CAFES OF THE CITY

The café is the unofficial home of the unemployed. If offers a connection point to your community (or, at a minimum, gets you out of the house), and loitering is encouraged—at least in some coffeehouses.

San Francisco maintains a strong café culture, with ample options varying by neighborhood, style, and ambience. Go in the morning and take pleasure in watching others scramble to work while you relax the morning away. Find one you like and make it your hangout, or pick a different one to visit each week, creating your own personal tour. For a comprehensive look at local cafés, see the beautifully published *The Cafes of San Francisco,* from TCB Cafe Publishing.

We've included our favorites here, using a highly sophisticated ranking system. All, by definition, have exceptional coffee and/or food, and a community orientation. Beyond that, we've rated them for other important features: (1) loitering friendliness, (2) conduciveness to work (the laptop factor), (3) pleasure orientation, and (4) uniqueness or funkiness. The "overall" rating is not an average, but a highly subjective recommendation based on a certain *je ne sais quoi.* Venues are listed by alphabetically-ordered neighborhood.

'hood/café	why it's a good place to spend time off	rankings				
		Overall	Loiter	Work	Pleasure	Funkiness
The Castro ***H Café*** (3801 17th Street, 415-487-1661)	This Internet-friendly café doubles as a cozy neighborhood hangout in the Castro. A row of wired terminals along with free wireless access for laptops will keep you connected, while the comfy couches are perfect for reading or even napping!	3	4	5	3	2
Cole Valley ***Reverie*** (848 Cole, 415-242-0200)	An excellent, community-oriented café with a back patio, soft music and a mean latté. The fountain in the back is sure to soothe the most frayed of nerves, and if you loiter long enough you're likely to run into local luminary Craig Newmark of Craig's List fame.	5	4	3	5	4
Cole Valley ***Cole Valley Café*** (701 Cole, 415-668-5382, *www.colevalleycafe.com*)	Another nugget in Cole Valley's "café alley," this coffeehouse is popular with the neighborhood home office crew. Good coffee, free wireless Internet access and excellent house music are reasons to set up shop at this staple.	4	5	5	3	2
Inner Sunset ***The Canvas*** (1200 9th Avenue, 415-504-0070, *www.thecanvasgallery.com*)	A fine addition to the Inner Sunset, The Canvas is an excellent "working" location at all hours of the day. It comes complete with free wireless Internet access and doubles as a hip evening destination with music and various artist events.	5	5	5	4	4

'hood/café	why it's a good place to spend time off	rankings				
		O	L	W	P	F
The Marina ***The Grove*** (2250 Chestnut, 415-474-4843; 2016 Fillmore, 415-474-1419)	*The* café and daytime hangout in the Marina, The Grove is the place to go to see and be seen, and not for the diversity of the people. A good locale to get you out of the home "office." Also check out their new location at Fillmore & Pine.	3	3	4	4	2
The Mission ***Café Macondo*** (3159 16th Street, 415-431-7516)	Home to the multi-cultural intellectual, Café Macondo has a lively, spirited vibe that lends itself more to conversation than study. It also offers a decent selection of paperbacks if you'd like to brush up on your reading.	4	5	2	4	5
Noe Valley ***Martha Brothers*** (1551 Church, 415-648-1166; multiple locations)* *Rankings apply to Church Street location	A hometown success story, this family-run coffeehouse has several locations. 24th Street is the original, but the nearby Church and Duncan site is the best, with more space for lounging the day away. Arguably the best-tasting coffee in the City.	4	5	3	4	3
North Beach ***Caffe Trieste*** (609 Vallejo, 415-392-6739, *www.caffetrieste.com*)	This North Beach institution is San Francisco's original bohemian café. Supposedly the first espresso house on the west coast, Trieste is old Italy meets beat poet meets screenwriter (Francis Ford Coppola reputedly wrote the screenplay for *The Godfather* here). For all its notoriety, it still manages to retain its Old World charm.	5	5	1	5	5
North Beach ***Café Prague*** (584 Pacific, 415-433-3811)	A Czech island in a sea of Italy? Filled with creative energy, this Eastern Bloc-style coffeehouse fits the bill for lounging or for lunching, and hosts live music on Friday and Saturday nights.	4	3	4	5	5

'hood/café	why it's a good place to spend time off	rankings				
		Overall	Loiter	Work	Pleasure	Funkiness
Outer Sunset ***Java Beach*** (1396 La Playa, 415-665-5282)	Known for its great location, eclectic patrons, and crusty staff, this beachside café is a popular hangout at any time of the day. Comfy couches, a nice outside patio and free wireless in addition to DSL terminals complete the scene.	4	5	3	4	4
Pacific Heights ***Peet's Coffee & Tea*** (2197 Fillmore, 415-563-9930)	A coffeehouse chain, yes, but Peet's is homegrown in the Bay Area. The coffee is second to none (hey, it's Peet's), and its Fillmore street location is one of the chain's best.	3	3	2	4	2
Potrero Hill ***Farley's Coffeehouse*** (1315 18th Street, 415-648-1545)	Farley's may be the best neighborhood coffeehouse in San Francisco. It has it all: great coffee, tea, and other assorted beverages; a diverse, friendly clientele; indoor/outdoor seating with great views—a true home away from home, and a great place to hang.	5	5	3	5	5
Potrero Hill ***Atlas Café*** (3049 20th Street, 415-648-1047)	Atlas makes an ideal place to nurse a beer on a Monday afternoon, with a diverse crowd and a spacious backyard patio. Look into the Sunday all-you-can-eat barbecue during the summertime.	4	5	2	4	5
Richmond ***Bazaar Café*** (5927 California, 415-831-5620, *www.bazaarcafe.com*)	An oasis in a cold, foggy stretch of the City, Bazaar's cozy atmosphere will keep you coming back. For those occasional sunny days, it boasts a protected back patio to chill on. It also hosts open mic nights for both musicians and comedians, writers' events, and even has released its own compilation CD. Need we say more?	5	5	3	4	5

'hood/café	why it's a good place to spend time of	rankings				
		O	L	W	P	F
Richmond ***Blue Danube Coffee House*** (306 Clement, 415-221-9041)	A wide open, south-facing window and sidewalk seating highlight this funky Clement Street café. DSL terminals and a wide selection of lunch foods round out the attractions.	4	4	2	4	4
Russian Hill ***Royal Ground*** (1605 Polk, 415-749-1731)	Lost amongst the bigger chains on Polk Street, this unassuming little café might actually be busier during midweek business hours than on the weekends. Strong coffee, fattening pastries, and an air of creativity make it the preferred leisurely café in Russian Hill.	3	4	3	3	3
SOMA ***Caffe Centro*** (102 South Park, 415-882-1500, *www.caffecentro.com*)	Despite the hi-tech crash (or perhaps because of it), this parkside café retains its charm. Good sandwiches at lunch are a highlight, and worth the lines.	3	2	3	4	3
Western Addition ***Café Abir*** (1300 Fulton, 415-567-7654)	A culturally diverse Arabic café that's popular with students and artists, and qualifies as an "any time of day" café. There's an adjoining magazine and smoke shop, and south-facing sidewalk seating on Fulton Street. Beware the water bowl for the dogs trotting home from nearby Alamo Square Park—and guard your muffin!	4	5	3	4	4
Western Addition ***Central Coffee*** (1696 Hayes, 415-922-2008)	This community-based coffeehouse is short on space but long on friendliness and great food. Park it in one of their comfy red booths, work on your laptop with free wireless access, and groove to their eclectic music selection, chosen and directed by the staff.	5	5	4	4	5

NIGHTLIFE

Nocturnal crawls are great benefits for those not tied to a set schedule (read: don't have to get up for work in the morning). Most nighttime events do, however, require some money, so be forewarned: nightlife can be a quick drain on the budget. But then again, when else will you be free to stay out until 3am on a school night? Pick your spots, and take advantage.

THE DIVIEST BARS (That You'll Still Want To Go To)

These salty dogs are short on appearances and long on, well, salt. Suffice it to say, there are a lot of dives in San Francisco, a sign of urban vitality if there ever was one. If you're looking to stretch your dollar a bit, keep these on your short list. Approach each establishment with caution depending on your individual tolerance level.

Our selection criteria? Extremely scientific: 1) Must be open on Monday nights—not only open, but thriving; 2) Bonus points given for attracting daytime clientele; 3) Extra bonus points given for a sign out front with a martini glass; 4) Super extra bonus points given if that sign is neon (see box next page).

Zeitgeist *(199 Valencia, the Mission, 415-255-7505)*
No martini sign here but this is by far the best biker bar in the City. The "dress code" is leather and black, and the doorman just might let you know it. If you're not the biker type, consider acting the part when walking through the door. A great backyard deck and barbecue area highlight this rugged haunt. And if you happen to get lucky? Live in the moment by checking into one of the little-known hotel rooms upstairs, just $30 per night.

Ha-Ra Club *(875 Geary, Tenderloin, 415-673-3148)*
The 'Loin is pretty much built on dive bars, and the Ha-Ra Club rises above (or sinks below) the pack. They offer, in their own words, "cheap cocktails served up low-end style." That more or less sums it up. Coax the bartender back inside to pour you a drink if he's out on a smoking break.

The Buccaneer *(2155 Polk, Russian Hill, 415-673-8023)*
Any bar with a name like this ought to live up to its reputation, and The Buccaneer certainly has the feel of a drunken Spanish galley. Happy hour pitchers of beer from 5-8pm daily are only $6. Hang on to your dinner as this ship rocks and rolls through the night.

Mauna Loa *(3009 Fillmore, Cow Hollow, 415-563-5137)*
Maybe not the roughest bar on this list, but a dive relative to its surroundings. A tropical oasis it ain't, but it does reek of, uh, character. One longtime bartender there recommends hitting it on weeknights to limit the "fraternity factor," and to wear your drinking shoes. Trust us, you don't want to ask.

Murio's Trophy Room *(1811 Haight, Upper Haight, 415-752-2971)*
What exactly *is* a trophy room? We're not sure, but it seems to work. Anything goes at this diverse watering hole. Tattoos meet students meet freaks meet hipsters. Word to the wise: steer clear of those inclined to brawl here as the night wears on.

500 Club *(500 Guerrero, the Mission, 415-861-2500)*
A rough-around-the-edges neighborhood bar that serves drink specials at all hours. This dive would just as easily fit in the happy hour section, as they run an extended one Monday-Thursday from 2pm-7pm, plus drink specials at midnight, just when you want (and need) them.

pink martini, anyone?

In our romps around the City, we found at least three bars with pink neon martini glass signs, a sign of a true dive if there ever was one. Coat up the stomach, and join us for a little rabble rousing.

Chances (298 Divisadero, Western Addition, 415-255-6101)
Go on, take a chance and enter the bar that Citysearch says could be "one of the most poorly decorated businesses on earth." We won't dispute this. Liquor is king here (drinks are stiff), and pool and foosball rule in the back.

Il Pirata (2007 16th Street, Potrero Hill, 415-626-2626, *www.ilpirata.com*)
"The Pirate" is run by the same family that used to manage Bottom of the Hill. Part watering hole, part hipster hangout, Il Pirata is a lot of things. But dive bar drinking is what it does best. You can listen to quality live and DJ music most nights of the week. Bonus: the really cool mermaid mural to stare at in your drunken stupor.

Delirium (3139 16th Street, the Mission, 415-552-5525)
"Service for the sick" rests adjacent to the pink martini glass on the sign out front. Just what the doctor ordered? Perhaps. A replacement for the beloved Albion, Delirium does its predecessor proud with a no-frills, strong-cocktail approach. Bonus: happy hour from 4-7pm every day means $1 off all draft beer—except Chimay (bastards!).

THE MARINA DIVE CRAWL?

A little known fact: Chestnut Street, in the upscale and wealthy Marina, has one of the highest dive bar densities of any street in the City—strange but true. Tucked in between Pottery Barn, Gap, and Noah's Bagels are some downright serious drinking establishments.

Starting on the western end and traveling east, begin your tour with ***Delaney's*** (2241 Chestnut). Consider ingratiating yourself with the locals by buying a round of drinks. Next up, if you've always wondered exactly what "beverages for adults" are, wander on into ***Windows*** (3259 Pierce @ Chestnut, 415-567-4466) and find out for yourself. Then stop by and say hi to Sculley at (Donahue's) ***Marina Lounge*** (2138 Chestnut, 415-922-1475), a locals' favorite. Further down the road, saddle on up to the ***Horseshoe Tavern*** (2024 Chestnut, 415-346-1430) for a cocktail and to shoot some stick.

If you're still standing at this point, there's nothing like finishing off a divey evening with some good old fashioned drunken karaoke. Sing your heart out at the nearby ***Silver Cloud,*** just off the Chestnut stroll (1994 Lombard @ Webster, 415-922-1977).

BEST DAYTIME DRINKING

Drink the afternoon away? Sure, why not? Try your favorite pub during the daytime. You'll get to meet the bartender, which almost always leads to free drinks. While any old place would probably do, choose a locale where you'll likely have some unemployed company:

Pier 23

Pier 23, the Embarcadero, 415-362-5125, www.pier23cafe.com

Where would San Francisco be without Pier 23? Probably a little less drunk on a Friday afternoon, that's where. This waterfront special has likely housed more outdoor daytime drinking over the last ten years than any other establishment in the City.

Lou's Pier 47

300 Jefferson, 415-771-5687, Fisherman's Wharf, www.louspier47.com

Live blues, all day, all the time. What more could you ask from this ode to New Orleans? Hang and drink with the vacationers from Des Moines, and show them how to be a tourist in your own town.

The Ramp

855 China Basin, in China Basin, 415-621-2378

This is the City's other great outdoor drinking establishment—on the waterfront, tucked away in innocuous China Basin. While Pier 23 may resemble a frat party, the Ramp (at least during daytime hours) maintains a far mellower vibe. Catch one of the frequent steel drum bands there during the summertime, and you'll likely begin plotting a boat escape to the Caribbean.

Harrington's Bar & Grill

245 Front, Financial District, 415-392-7595

Harrington's is what it is, and that is the real deal—a hearty, authentic, hard-drinking Irish pub and restaurant. Is it day or night? Do you care? Probably not, but your employed Financial District friends might if you meet them at this dark, dingy classic for lunch.

The Irish Bank

10 Mark Lane @ Bush, Financial District, 415-788-7152, www.theirishbank.com

This raucous pub achieves Irish authenticity, at least in the drinking sense. Many a worker and non-worker alike have lost their way in the halls of the Bank, only to emerge hours later wondering who turned off all the lights. A favorite for happy hour and after work (or non-work!).

Anchor Brewing Company

1705 Mariposa, China Basin, 415-863-8350, www.anchorbrewing.com

We've mentioned it before (see **Chapter 4** under "The Perfectly Free Day") but it *is* free. And it *is* good beer. Not only that, but it requires you to drink during the day. Enough said!

chinatown triple whammy

From the ***Buddha Bar*** (901 Grant, 415-362-1792) to ***Li Po*** (916 Grant, 415-982-0072) to the ***Bow Bow Cocktail Lounge*** (1155 Grant, 415-421-6730)—this trio of dives packs a worthy triple punch (you *will* feel the blows) and is a great tour to truck the out-of-towners on when you tire of sifting through trinkets or negotiating firecracker purchases. The Buddha Bar is the most hilarious of the three and features constant shouting in multiple languages and some top-notch peoplewatching.

keeping it real

Here's where to hang with the neighbors, and keep things down to earth:

Kezar Bar & Restaurant
900 Cole
Cole Valley
415-681-7678

A friendly staple in Cole Valley for dinner and drinks, you might find yourself sharing a stool with the house cat at this neighborhood haunt.

•••

Toronado
547 Haight
Lower Haight
415-863-2276

Beer, beer, and more beer highlight this gritty Lower Haight hangout, but it's surprisingly friendly inside. Toronado pours the largest selection in town, including a fine offering of Belgian ales.

•••

Hobson's Choice
1601 Haight
Upper Haight
415-621-5859

Swig some rum punch at this graduate school hangout, and order some food to match from the nearby ***Asqew Grill*** (1607 Haight, Upper Haight, 415-701-9301)—you can order from the Hobson bar and eat it on-site.

[another round?...]

BEST HAPPY HOURS

The good news is that happy hours have returned with gusto to San Francisco. It seems that a drastically altered economy has forced bars to actually try to attract customers—what a concept!

The bad news is that many of these so-called "happy hours" are little more than marketing ploys, with paltry drink discounts and zero food. What's so happy about that?

Some bars have nonetheless gotten with the program and offer a happy hour worth attending. And to those rare few that have always made good on their promises of happiness—kudos. We salute you!

Bamboo Hut
479 Broadway, North Beach, 415-989-8555
If you like your drinks fruity with umbrellas, this is your place. Thursday and Friday nights see half-price drinks until 8pm, and that includes the fancy ones. When the tiki statues begin circling around you, you'll know it's time to move on.

Jade
650 Gough, Hayes Valley, 415-869-1900
We searched long and hard for an upscale cocktail lounge with a decent happy hour, and finally found it at the newly-opened Jade. The space is smooth and comfortable, and it looks exactly like the type of place that will run you $8-10 per cocktail. But during weekday happy hours from 5-7:30pm, draft beers, well drinks, and certain specialty cocktails are all only two bucks! One of the best values in "hip" we've come across.

San Francisco Brewing Company

155 Columbus, North Beach, 415-434-3344, www.sfbrewing.com

It's not clear why, but this brewpub on a busy Columbus block in North Beach is often overlooked. Maybe it's because with all the mayhem of North Beach—the great restaurants, cafés, and bars—a brewpub just isn't the first thing that comes to mind. But if it was good enough for Jack Dempsey (he once worked here as a bouncer), it's good enough for us. In any event, SF Brewing delivers, and their happy hour is hard to beat. Every night of the week from 4-6pm and then again from midnight-1am, 10 oz. beer is a buck and pints are only $1.75! And that's for real… good… beer. Tip: try the Emperor Norton Lager for a brew with authentic San Francisco character (see "And Don't Call It 'Frisco!'" in **Chapter 4**).

[…this one's on us!]

The Bell Tower
1900 Polk
Russian Hill
415-567-9596

A great, sassy neighborhood stop. The owner, Barbara, will be in full support of your work break, and will likely contribute to your hangover to boot. Dinner is grand, but later in the evening the Bell becomes a serious drinking establishment.

• • •

Perry's
1944 Union
Cow Hollow
415-922-9022

Some call it a sports bar, but we're not buying it. People come here for the conversation, good burgers, and stiff drinks. Snag an outdoor table on a sunny afternoon and peoplewatch as the Union Street parade saunters by.

The Bitter End

441 Clement, Inner Richmond, 415-221-9538

Home of the famed Trivia Tuesdays, this Irish pub is good clean fun (well, not *that* clean). Tuesday nights aren't so much happy hours as they are an esteemed cultural event—drunken trivia. Once a week, seemingly hundreds of thirsty trivia hounds descend upon this unassuming pub to try their hand at competitive team trivia (the thin-skinned need not chime in). The $2.50 beer specials on a rotating selection of (good) beer each week don't hurt none, either.

The Lexington Club

3464 19th Street, the Mission, 415-863-2052, www.lexingtonclub.com

Even the ladies need their happy hours, and the Lexington provides same sex seekers with just that: $2 well drinks and domestic beers, and $2.50 drafts weekdays from 3-7pm. Men should arrive with a female friend, or give it a pass altogether.

Lost and Found Saloon

1353 Grant, North Beach, 415-981-9557

If you're looking to stretch your non-working dollars, put the **Lost and Found** on your short list. Two words: dollar beers. Their happy hour lasts until 9pm daily (including Saturday nights!) and they feature 2-for-1 beers as well as a beer of the month for $1.

Luna Lounge (Border Cantina)

1192 Folsom, SOMA, 415-626-6043

Perhaps our cousins south of the border are a little more hip to the concept of happy hour. Taco Tuesday is the draw here, with $2 tacos, $2 domestic beers, and $3 imports from 6-11pm—enough to get you full and feeling good for less than one yuppie coupon ($20). They also have a Thursday happy hour from 5-7pm, with $2 domestic drafts.

Kennedy's Irish Pub & Curry House

1040 Columbus, North Beach, 415-441-8855

www.kennedyspubcurryhouse.com

Irish pub and curry house in one? You bet, and drink specials galore. Happy hour runs from 4-8pm daily at this raucous pub, and is highlighted by two dollar Guinness. Five bucks gets you a pitcher of Pabst Blue Ribbon all day, all the time.

Mad Dog in the Fog

530 Haight, Lower Haight, 415-626-7279

A popular hangout with football (of the European variety) hooligans, this English-style pub has the right stuff. Happy hour runs Monday–Friday until 7pm with $2.50 pints (on all beer!). Drop in on one of their Tuesday specialty quiz nights and wrap your noodle around such colorful topics as *"The Simpsons"* or "1980s Trivia."

Club Waziema

543 Divisadero, Western Addition, 415-346-6641

Waza–who? This is another quality neighborhood joint that fits like a glove, serving beer, wine, and... Ethiopian food—what else? In addition to a weekday happy hour from 4-7pm, they have an all-you-can-eat happy hour from 4-9pm. Woo-hoo!

Special thanks to local happy hour expert* ***Marcus Ronaldi* *(www.marcusronaldi.com) for his input on this section.*

BEST TUNES FOR THE BUCK

While these stages don't see the biggest, most heavily promoted shows, they get a surprising number of quality acts, from underground local musicians to big name artists. Depending on the type of show, the cover charge generally will leave you enough money to buy a round of drinks for your friends.

♩ *Bottom of the Hill*

1233 17th Street, Potrero Hill, 415-621-4455

www.bottomofthehill.com

This club consistently manages to book the best up-and-coming indie rock bands before they become famous, from the Beastie Boys to Bad Religion, Joan Jett to Juliana Hatfield, Kid Rock to Korn. Ticket prices vary depending on the band, but average $8-10 for most shows. A back patio provides a much-needed safety valve on crowded nights, and their all-you-can-eat BBQ plus live show on Sundays is legendary (see "All-You-Can-Eat Buffets" p. 161).

♩ *Last Day Saloon*

406 Clement, Inner Richmond, 415-387-6343

www.lastdaysaloon.com

This "saloon" is actually a split-level venue, with a friendly bar downstairs and a spacious stage and open floor upstairs. The small club hosts an impressive lineup. It's not unusual to see some first-rate musicians come through here, particularly in the blues and rock genres. Ticket prices hover in the $5-10 range, a great value given the high level of talent.

♩ *Storyville*

1751 Fulton, Western Addition, 415-441-1751

Jazz turns to funk turns to hip-hop at this progressive club and restaurant. True, Storyville sponsors a lot of DJ nights, but the great hip-hop scene combined with the occasional live band makes this a worthy stop. Covers generally run from $5-10.

♩ *Cafe du Nord*

2170 Market, the Castro, 415-861-5016

www.cafedunord.com

This speakeasy holdover is a downright cool, swanky place to hang out. The live music is all over the map, from jazz to hip-hop to German punk, and tickets cost around $10.

♩ The Blue Lamp

561 Geary, Tenderloin, 415-885-1464
www.bluelamplounge.com

Heavy blues and stiff drinks are the draws of this Tenderloin haunt. This is not the place to go for a quiet date night. But if you're looking to get a little rowdy, particularly on a weeknight, the Blue Lamp definitely will fit the bill.

♩ Noe Valley Ministry

1021 Sanchez, Noe Valley, 415-282-2317
www.noevalleymusicseries.com

This venue is, as the name asserts, a ministry, located on an unassuming block of tranquil Noe Valley. As a "house of prayer and community," the ministry puts on an innovative music series that includes Bay Area and international performers. Folk is probably the most common, but the ministry has been host to virtually all types of music, as well as comedians and other performers. Concerts are usually on Saturday nights, and entry typically costs $15-20.

♩ Elbo Room

647 Valencia, the Mission, 415-552-7788
www.elbo.com

Long a staple in the live music scene in San Francisco, the Elbo Room delivers a non-pretentious vibe with bands most nights of the week. Like the Last Day Saloon, the club splits into a cool bar downstairs, and dance-friendly music upstairs. Reggae, rock, Latin, and hip-hop will all be heard here, as well as many other types of music. Tickets usually go for $5-10.

♩ Edinburgh Castle

950 Geary, Tenderloin, 415-885-4074

We weren't quite sure where to list this eclectic haunt, as it's part live music venue, part dive, part theatre—and part just good old-fashioned kickin' bar. You're equally likely to hear live music as a literary reading here. Cover charges are all over the map (the bar says they let the bands decide) but generally range from free to $10.

DANCE AND LATE NIGHT

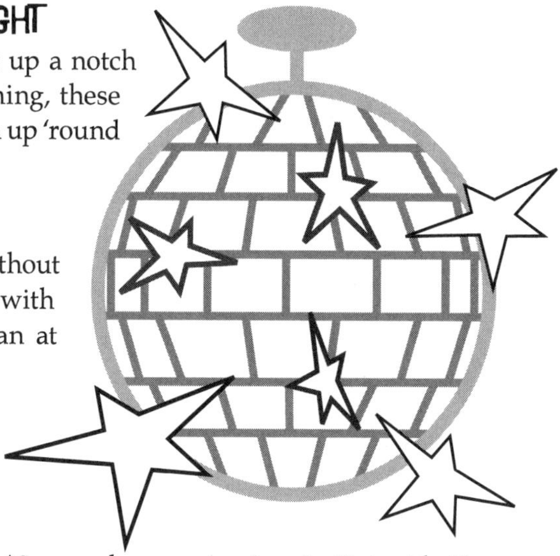

When it's time to kick it up a notch and roll on into the evening, these venues will escort you on up 'round midnight.

No-Cover Dance

Get your groove on without fronting any cash and with a tad more intimacy than at your average mega club.

Blondie's Bar & No Grill
540 Valencia, the Mission
415-864-2419
www.blondiesbar.com
Okay, we lied—there's a $2 cover here on weekends. But with 16 oz. martinis, you'll earn it back quickly on drink value, not to mention booty shaking on the dance floor.

The Monkey Club
2730 21st Street, the Mission, 415-647-6546
This "club" is actually more of a lounge, where DJ music sways the crowd into spontaneous dance as the evening wears on. Nab a coveted booth and you'll be styling. Beware: too many premium-priced drinks will quickly empty your wallet here.

Holy Cow
1535 Folsom, SOMA, 415-621-6087, www.theholycow.com
Okay, it might be a sweaty barn, but it don't cost nothin'! This San Francisco rite of passage is all about having fun. How can you go wrong with a motto like "never ever a cover"?

Wish
1539 Folsom, SOMA, 415-278-9474, www.wishsf.com
Like the Monkey Club, Wish is a lounge first and a dance venue second, but the music is so damn good, dancing seems to happen naturally.

Nickie's BBQ
460 Haight, Lower Haight, 415-621-6508, www.nickies.com
Well, Nickie's also charges a cover, but it's usually under $5 and the place brings it. You can dance to all kinds of music here, but funk is definitely at the core. One of the best sweaty dance halls in town.

miscellaneous fun

Ploy II Thai Cuisine
1770 Haight
Upper Haight
415-387-9224

Tucked away above Haight Street (2nd Floor), Ploy Thai provides a pleasant reprieve from the hustle and bustle of the Haight. Score a table by the window, order their $5 lunch special, and behold the colorful antics on the street below.

•••

Kan Zaman
1793 Haight
Upper Haight
415-751-9656

Enjoy nightly belly dancing, hookah pipes, and inexpensive cuisine at this delightful Middle Eastern eatery. Great for groups, but go early or prepare to wait.

•••

Make-Out Room
3225 22nd Street
the Mission
415-647-2888

A diverse crowd paints this all-purpose bar, good for drinking, lounging, or dancing. There's live music and events from time to time, so best to call ahead. Drink Pabst Blue Ribbon for $1 during happy hour, 6-8pm Monday-Thursday.

[could you possibly have any *more* fun?...]

Spice Up the Week

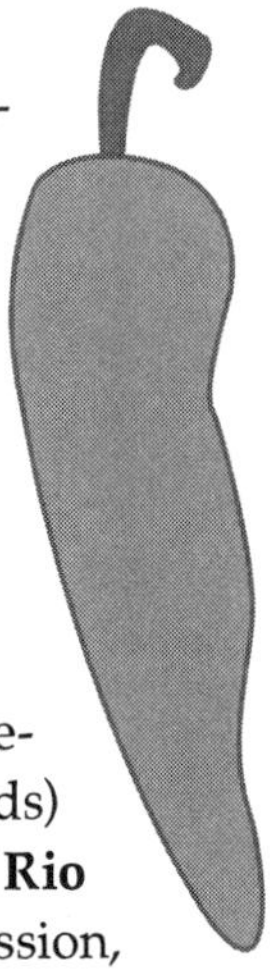

We can't quite put our fingers on it, but there's something quite leisurely about salsa dancing. It's just so... zesty. San Francisco has a surprisingly strong salsa scene, and in many cases it's happening in places you wouldn't suspect.

Salsa in San Francisco begins (and sometimes ends) with Salsa Sundays at **El Rio** (3158 Mission, Outer Mission, 415-282-3325, www.elriosf.com; also see "Chez San Francisco!" p. 164). Every Sunday afternoon in the Outer Mission, the dance floor at El Rio pulses to the rhythm of live salsa music and couples of every background imaginable gyrate and spin their way to bliss. The cover is $8 (which includes a BBQ), the doors open at 3pm, and a dance class for beginners is given at 3:15pm. That's pretty much all you need to know.

When you've graduated to more advanced dance, the place to go is **Roccapulco** (3140 Mission, Outer Mission, 415-648-6611, www.roccapulco.com), which is just down the street from El Rio. Hot Latino dancers tear up the dance floor here—particularly on weekends—and lessons are included in the cover charge.

Café Cocomo (650 Indiana, Potrero Hill, 415-824-6910, www.cafecocomo.com) hosts steamy salsa on Monday, Thursday, and Saturday nights. Beginner and intermediate lessons are offered at 7:30pm on Monday nights for $7.

Other notable salsa scenes include **Glas Kat (Ay Karamba)** (520 4th Street, SOMA, 415-495-6620, www.glaskat.com) on Tuesday nights with live music and lessons; **Elbo Room** (see "Best Tunes" p. 182) on Thursday nights with live music; **El Valenciano** (1153 Valencia, the Mission, 415- 826-9561) on Friday nights with lessons; and believe it or not, **The Ramp** (855 China Basin, China Basin, 415-621-2378) on Saturday afternoons, complete with an outdoor barbecue.

[...the best for last]

Trader Sam's
6150 Geary
the Richmond
415-221-0773

Unlikely you'll be walking a straight line after exiting this funky Polynesian bar. Arrange your ride ahead of time and come on in from the foggy cold at this Richmond treasure.

•••

Puerto Alegre
546 Valencia
the Mission
415-255-8201

If it's party-starting time in the Mission, Puerto Alegre is an inexpensive way to rev up, with strong margaritas and starchy Mexican food.

Karaoke

What sabbatical would be complete without a dose of karaoke tomfoolery? Here's where to totally embarrass yourself.

The Mint
1942 Market, the Castro, 415-626-4726
Many call it the City's best karaoke bar. Top singers combine with drunken first-timers and everyone has fun.

Silver Cloud
1994 Lombard @ Webster, 415-922-1977, see "The Marina Dive Crawl?" p. 176
The Marina's answer to karaoke has caught on quickly, and crooners pack the joint most nights.

Sachi Cocktail Lounge
1581 Webster #207, Japantown, 415-567-5866
This mostly-Asian hangout has private karaoke rooms for groups.

Tango Tango
1550 California, Nob Hill, 415-775-0442
Gay men and lesbians sing to their hearts' content at this Polk Gulch funhouse, which hosts karaoke Tuesday-Sunday nights.

Yet Wah Restaurant *(also known as **Karaoke Yw**)*
5238 Diamond Heights Boulevard, Diamond Heights, 415-282-0788
A Chinese restaurant in Diamond Heights with karaoke? Hey, we'll go with it. The fun begins at 9pm every night.

STAYING OUT REALLY LATE

Keep it going into the wee hours of the morning at these hip places where you can keep on dancing long past last call.

The Endup

401 6th Street, SOMA, 415-357-0827

www.theendup.com

In a town that generally goes to bed early, the Endup is the pillar of late-night debauchery. It's one of the few places that never really closes on the weekends, save for a few hours early Sunday when everyone stops to check their pulse. The Endup is, for lack of a better word, an institution. If you're going to let it all hang out while you're not owing time to an employer, this is the place to do it. Party on.

Club Six

60 6th Street, SOMA, 415-863-1221

www.clubsix1.com

Club Six is smack-dab in the middle of perhaps the diciest block in San Francisco but it is still one of the better late-night scenes in the City, with deep rhythmic dancing and relaxed lounging upstairs. Open until 4am.

Cat Club

1190 Folsom, SOMA, 415-431-3332

www.catclubsf.com

This edgy late-night club can be a wild scene. Drinking and dancing hard are the main focus here so leave your judgments at home. Sunday has always been a big night but check ahead of time as the scene varies nightly. Open until 4am.

Sno-Drift

1830 3rd Street, China Basin, 415-431-4766

www.sno-drift.com

Known for its quality hip-hop and other beats, Sno-Drift is off the beaten path in industrial China Basin—a late-night destination spot, as there's nothing else around. Open until 4am.

THE UNEMPLOYED SHOPPING GUIDE

SHOPPING while unemployed? Absolutely! True, the more you spend, the shorter your leisure, but trading a few bucks for some choice bargains is still a wise move. Books, music, and clothes to carouse in are all key ingredients of quality free time.

This shopping guide will help your dollars go the distance at a time when you need them to stretch, with tips on:

- where to swap your tired old things for what you really want
- secrets of veteran garage sale shoppers and cutting-edge online auctioneers
- finding good deals
- savoring the window-shopping experience
- transforming buying into recreation

No need to bust the piggy bank or surrender to impulse when you're shopping. Be selective. Keep a higher purpose in mind—lengthy leisure time—and you can resist the forces urging you to overspend. Plus, if you choose items with staying power, shopping becomes investing. There's a new skill for your resume!

buy • sell • trade

Some of the best places to buy are also places where you can sell or trade items you're ready to part with. Music, books and clothing stores top this list. With a little scouting, you can find many others, like sports equipment or furniture. Just don't buy back your own stuff!

USED MUSIC

Music is vital to the unemployed soul. Treat yourself to some fresh tunes now and again, especially if you can acquire them by trading in songs you've grown tired of.

Amoeba Records (1855 Haight, 415-831-1200, www.amoebamusic.com) is the prime dealer for recycled tunes. Prices are based on the title and condition of your submission—with the biggest bucks paid for what's rare, popular and in mint condition—and you'll get 20% more in trade than in cash.

Buying at Amoeba is as much fun as selling. Their selection of new and used music is the largest in the City—in fact, they're the largest indie record store in the country—and you can easily kill an afternoon perusing the stacks. Listening stations will come soon enough; they're already installed at the **Berkeley Amoeba**,

vinyl

Want to drop a request with your favorite DJ in a place where you can hear yourself think? Shop where the DJ's shop—in the Lower Haight. No less than five stores within three blocks (and one more just off the block) sell old-fashioned vinyl. From east to west, the spinners start at ***Rooky Ricardo's*** (448 Haight, 415-864-7526), which hosts a record swap the first Sunday of each month. Across the street, ***Zebra Records*** (475 Haight, 415-626-9094) provides ten stations where you can listen before you buy. Find more of the twelve-inch discs at:

Tweekin' Records 593 Haight 415-626-6995

Spundae Reckords 678 Haight 415-575-1580

Groove Merchant 687 Haight 415-252-5766

Jack's Record Cellar 254 Scott 415-431-3047

(2455 Telegraph Avenue, 510-549-1125). Meanwhile, enjoy free in-store performances (check their website for the schedule or join the Amoeba Music Newsletter), the $1 bin, and the special "used" CDs: never-been-played copies dropped off by promoters.

Recycled Records (1377 Haight, 415-626-4075) also buys and sells used vinyl and CDs. Ditto for **Record Finder** (258 Noe, 415-563-3775), **Open Mind** (342 Divisadero, 415-621-2244), **Streetlight Records** (2350 Market, 415-282-8000; 3979 24th Street, 415-282-3550) and the punked-out **Mission Records** (2263 Mission, 285-1550), which occasionally hosts afternoon shows in the back room.

DUDS TRADERS

Although clothing traders can be found throughout the City, upper Haight Street is the duds-trading epicenter.

Sell or swap at **Crossroads Trading Company** (1519 Haight, 415-355-0555; 1901 Fillmore, 415-775-8885; 2123 Market, 415-552-8743, www.crossroadstrading.com). You'll earn 40% of retail when you sell, and 50% when you trade. Ask about consignment, if that's the kind of transaction you'd prefer. **Buffalo Exchange** (1555 Haight, 415-431-7733; 1800 Polk, 415-346-5726, www.buffaloexchange.com) works much the same way, and they buy all day, with an eye towards vintage, punk and retro.

Wasteland (1660 Haight, 415-863-3150) or **Held Over** (1543 Haight, 415-864-0818) are other well-worn options, but your clothes had better be hip! To offload a more conservative wardrobe, try **Good Byes** (3483 Sacramento, 415-674-0151; 3464 Sacramento, 415-346-6388), which sells your clean and pressed clothing on consignment. You'll need to check back within 60 days to see if your finery has moved.

SHAVE AND A HAIRCUT

Lucky for the budget-conscious that Gene Hays at ***Mes Amis*** (193 Franklin, 415-558-7118) offers an affordable salon haircut: $45 for a quality do. "People are tired of dropping $80 at other salons, so they come to me," Gene says.

Hip haircuts can be had for even cheaper if you're willing to live on the razor's edge by volunteering to be a hair model. ***Blade Runners Hair Studio*** (1792 Haight, 415-751-1723, *www.bladerunnersstudio.com*) shears human guinea pigs for $15 instead of $55. You'll need an appointment on a Monday or Wednesday afternoon.

READ IT AGAIN, SAM

Those versed in the art of leisure have been known to read, read, then read some more, and when they're done, trade in those tomes for something new.

Their first stop on the book trade route is almost always **Green Apple Books and Music** (506 Clement, 415-387-2272, www.greenapplebooks.com). If Green Apple didn't invent the buy-sell-trade concept, they're certainly among the foremost experts, after logging more than 35 years in the biz.

If you'd rather sell to **Russian Hill Bookstore** (2234 Polk, 415-929-0997), call first to confirm when the buyer will be in, and bring your art, history, or religion titles.

West Portal Books (111 West Portal, 415-731-5291) buys, sells, and trades, and is open every day. **Bookmonger** (2411 Clement, 415-397-2332) sells used books, paperbacks, and magazines.

Forever After Books (1475 Haight, 415-431-8299) isn't buying too much at the moment, unless you have something they really want. It's still worth a try, as there are stacks and stacks of used books to peruse even if your offerings are rejected.

Columbus Books (540 Broadway, 415-986-3872) purchases more regularly—buying between noon and 6pm every day except Wednesday and Thursday—in exchange for store credit. It won't be too hard to walk out with a new-to-you paperback; there are two floors of them and they run just $2-3. You'll also earn a discount after $50 in purchases.

Final stop on the circuit: **Phoenix Books & Records** (3850 24th Street, 415-821-3477), trading in art and out of print, literary and new titles. Cash and trade are offered here and at sister store **Dog Eared Books** (900 Valencia, 415-282-1901, www.dogearedbooks.com). Sell them your CDs too, if they're good quality.

Didn't we read that somewhere before?

HOT OFF THE PRESSES

Used goods are great, but there's nothing quite like that new-book smell. Spend wisely: search behemoth **Amazon.com** first, read their customer reviews, then set out with a specific shopping list to keep you on track.

Excellent independent book stores abound in San Francisco, but none tops **City Lights Books** in North Beach (261 Columbus, 415-

362-8193, www.citylights.com). Founded in 1953 by Peter Martin and beat poet Lawrence Ferlinghetti, City Lights has supported local writers for 50 years, offering consignment sales for small presses and zines. If you're looking for world literature, poetry or SF history, make City Lights your first stop.

A close second is **A Clean Well-Lighted Place for Books** (Opera Plaza, 601 Van Ness, 415-441-6670, www.bookstore.com), where they're friendly and knowledgeable with a fine selection. Same goes for **Stacey's** (581 Market, 415-421-4687). **Booksmith** (1644 Haight, 415-863-8688) carries the same new books as the big chains, but adds small press, fetish, and edgier titles to the mix.

If you're after something even scarier, stop by **Borderlands Books** (866 Valencia, 415-824-8203, www.borderlands-books.com)—science fiction, fantasy, and horror only. Serious book lovers run this place and they've been known to invite their artist friends over to create art on site all day.

Looking for a gay or lesbian title? Drop by **Different Light** (489 Castro, 415-431-0891) for books, readings, and performances. It's a part of Castro history.

"b" is for book ("c" too)

- ***Books Inc.***
  2275 Market
  415-864-6777
  3515 California
  415-221-3666
  2251 Chestnut
  415-931-3633
  www.booksinc.com

- ***Bookmonger***
  2411 Clement
  415-387-2332

- ***Black Oak Books***
  540 Broadway
  415-986-3872
  630 Irving
  415-564-0877
  www.blackoakbooks.com

- ***Book Bay***
  Building C, Fort Mason
  415-771-1076

- ***Cover to Cover***
  1307 Castro
  415-282-8080
  www.covertocoversf.com

- ***Carroll's Books***
  633 Vallejo
  415-397-5267

Browser Books (2195 Fillmore, 415-567-8027) is hands down the best place to bide time while you're waiting for a movie at the **Clay Theatre** (see **Chapter 4**) or when you've left home on a Sunday morning without something to pore over while you sit and sip next door at **Peet's Coffee + Tea** (2197 Fillmore, 415-563-9930).

And for a really fresh selection, check out the new **Book Passage Bookstore** in the Ferry Building (Embarcadero @ Market, 415-835-1020; also 51 Tamal Vista Boulevard, Corte Madera, 800-999-7909, www.bookpassage.com), a welcome addition to the City and a staunch supporter of independent publishing.

MORE RETAIL ALTERNATIVES

With time on your side, you can afford to wait for sales at garages and sidewalks. "There's a whole science to it," says shopper Eileen Sendrey, who bought a perfectly good laser printer at a garage sale for $10. "You're looking for people who really do want to clear out their closets. Every now and then you'll hit a total jackpot."

After you check the "garage & moving sales" section of **Craig's List**, track down the freebie paper, *Classified Flea Market*, or the ***Chronicle*** classifieds (online at www.sfgate.com/classifieds under "garage sales"). Then scout out signs on the street on the weekend. "I learned to judge the quality of a sale by the quality of the sign," says Eileen. "If it's just a cardboard sign with an arrow, chances are it's a junky sale. If it's an estate sale, however, you don't want to miss it."

If flea markets are more your bag (circus?), check out your options at www.fleamarketguide.com. On Sundays, the **Alemany Farmers' Market** becomes the **Alemany Flea Market** (100 Alemany, 415-647-9423). The **San Francisco Flea Market** (1651 Mission) runs all weekend. Weekends are good for swapping too, at the **Geneva Swap Meet** (at Geneva Drive-In near the Cow Palace, Daly City).

TIPS FROM THE VETERANS

To get the best pickings of a flea market or sidewalk sale, forget about breakfast. Most "early birds" hit an 8am garage sale closer to 7am, and some of the best flea market loot doesn't even make it off the flatbed! Take the opposite approach if your definition of success means getting the lowest price. Most sellers don't want a shred of that stuff going back into their house, so they slash prices or even give things away at the end of the day.

More tips from the experts:

- Plan a route if you want to hit more than one sale.
- Be reasonable and respectful in bargaining, but don't be afraid to offer a price lower than what's marked.
- Carry money in small bills. Garage sellers will love you for it, plus it will be a lot easier to use the "I've only got $5" tactic if you don't yank a 20-spot out of your pocket.
- Ask to plug in anything electronic to make sure it works before you pay for it.
- If you're looking for something large, make sure you have the means to lug it home.

How about auctions? Join the mailing list of **A1 Auction Service** (www.a1auctionservice.com) for announcements of their live auctions, as well as instructions on how to hold your own auction—even a sound sample of the vocal skill peculiar to auctioneers: "chanting."

pre•shopping

There's no reason to put your cultural education on freeze frame just because you don't have a lot of disposable income. Purchase alternatives (no, we're not talking about the five-finger discount) will keep your fingers snappin' and your head buzzin' with the most up-to-date music and literature, plus enable you to suss out your sporting goods before paying full retail price.

Skip The "Buying" Part

Sample Music For Free

A wealth of music is still available for download off the Internet, despite the Napster meltdown. Dave Casuto suggests checking out new music at the listening stations at music stores like **Virgin Megastore** (2 Stockton @ Market, 415-397-4525, www.virgin.com/megastores/usa). "It's really rewarding, and it's free!" Find more listening stations at **Borders** (400 Post, 415-399-1633; Stonestown Galleria, 415-731-0665, www.bordersstores.com) or **Tower Records** (2525 Jones, 415-885-0500; 2280 Market, 415-621-0588 records, 415-255-5920 video; Stonestown Mall, 3205 20th Avenue, 2nd floor, 415-681-2001, www.towerrecords.com).

Borrow Your Sports Gear

Particularly if you're trying a new sport, borrow what you need from friends before you buy new gear. You'll get a much better idea of what you want if and when you decide to get your own stuff. And who knows, you may decide you don't even like the sport that much.

Shop While You Sip

The truly frugal can "shop" for books by becoming a regular at a café with a well-stocked bookshelf. Mexican- and revolution-inspired **Café Macondo** (3159 16th Street, 415-431-7516) has a good selection, as does the Arabian **Café Abir** (1300 Fulton, 415-567-7654).

Go To The Library

Be it for books, magazines, video, or audio, "shopping" at the library can offer you choices you never knew existed (like the 1962 *Dolphin Guide to San Francisco*). The newly renovated **San Francisco Main Library** (100 Larkin, 415-557-4400, www.sfpl.org) near the Civic Center is open seven days a week, and boasts beautiful architecture as well as pleasant places to read. Patronize any of the 25 local library branches—visit the website to find one near you.

unemployed discounts

Think the unemployed deserve a price break? Many businesses agree.

Several gyms offer discounted sign-up fees for those who bring in an unemployment insurance check stub. ***Funky Door Yoga*** (see "Mind and Body" in ***Chapter 7***) will work with you. We even heard about one guitar teacher who strums at reduced rates for those out of work. It never hurts to ask.

The President of ***Bum Card International*** (he's also a member! *www.bumcard.com*) is busy lining up discounts for the unemployed, too. Check out your low-price options for finding jobs in Alaska, boosting your cell phone reception or spiffing up your resume—when you're ready to find a job—in back issues of Bum Card Monthly, and get your very own Bum Card for only $2!

Discount Designs

Variously known as the warehouse district or the garment district, the large block South of Market between Brannan & Bryant, 2nd & 3rd Streets contains countless designer clothing outlets:

- Find $5 racks at the **Georgiou Outlet** (925 Bryant, 415-554-0150)
- The **Red Dot Outlet** (508 4th Street, 415-979-1597) features local designers and workout gear.
- Shop **Jeremy's** (2 South Park, 415-882-4929) if you absolutely must attend the Black and White Ball (see **Fairs & Fests**). They discount designer finery up to 50%.

Other Outlet Stores

Manufacturers' outlet stores can't advertise what they sell, but here's a hint: it's the same garb as at their retail stores, only it costs less. Some goods are new but slightly damaged, others are overstock or discontinued, but all of the leisure goods are covered and then some. Expect an odd cornucopia at awesome prices, although shopping fan Kelli Elliott advises, "It helps to know comparison pricing ahead of time."

Discount shopping guides are available at most major hotels, as are publications such as *The San Francisco Guide, Where,* and *Quickguide* that offer coupons and discounts. Or, if you'd like to take a shortcut, shop the **Nordstrom Rack** (555 9th Street, 415-934-1211) for clothes or **Books Inc. Outlet** (160 Folsom, 415-442-4830) for books.

If you don't find what you want within City limits, try the outlet malls: **Marina Square** (Marina Boulevard East exit off of I-880 in Oakland/San Leandro), **Petaluma Village Factory Outlets** (Petaluma Boulevard North, Old Redwood Highway exit off of US-101 in Petaluma, 707-778-9300), **Great Mall Of The Bay Area** (447 Great

SECONDHAND PRIZE PURCHASES

Jane shopped a garage sale and found a clean, intact and nearly-new 9'x12' area rug for only $10!

The worktable that Serafina bought at Busvan's going-out-of-business closeout sale cost only $5!

Foronda shopped at Goodwill and found a bag for his new laptop for 1/10th of what he would have paid even at a discount office supplies store. It was a perfect fit!

Mall Parkway in Milpitas, Montague Expressway exit off of Hwy 237, I-680, I-880 or US-101, 408-956-2033, 800-MALL-BAY), or the **Outlets at Gilroy** (Lleavesley Road exit off of US-101 in Gilroy, 408-842-3729, 800-866-5900).

SHOPPING ONLINE

Spot a garage sale item that's peanuts to you but would be a treasure to someone else? Don't be afraid to buy it now and then sell it online. Shop for new and used goods using online auction and community sites like ***Craig's List*** (*www.craigslist.org*), one of the most efficient ways to buy or sell just about anything you need.

The larger ***eBay*** (*www.ebay.com*) is a good place to shop for bargains as well as auction off your goods. EBay's little sister, ***half.com*** (*www.half.com*), markets others' used goods to you at substantial discounts. ***Amazon.com*** (*www.amazon.com*) sells much more than books, these days—scroll to the Bottom of the Page for special one-day deals on all sorts of stuff.

DVDs & video

Maintain your movie trivia files by choosing from 87,000(!) mainstream, independent, rare, and foreign films at ***Le Video*** (1231 9th Avenue, 415-566-3606). With a comparatively meager 14,000 titles, ***Dr. Video*** (1521 18th Street, 415-826-2900; 2810 Diamond, 415-333-7321) can also prescribe some choice flicks.

Head over to the ***Main Library*** (see p. 193) for foreign films, or to ***Naked Eye News and Video*** (607 Haight, 415-864-2985) for the Hong Kong genre. To have all of the above delivered to your doorstep (three at a time) with no late fees, rent DVDs online from ***Netflix*** (*www.netflix.com*).

Mechanics Institute Library (57 Post, 415-393-0105, 415-421-1768, *www.milibrary.org*) has a gargantuan selection of videos. As a bonus, joining the library automatically makes you a member of the chess club, too. Membership runs $60 a year.

Off-Price Clothes

A true shopper loves a bargain. For new clothes at fair prices, try:

- ***Ross Dress for Less***
  799 Market, 415-957-9222
  four more San Francisco locations
  see www.rossstores.com

- ***Old Navy Flagship***
  801 Market, 415-344-0376;
  Potrero Center, 2300 16th Street,
  415-255-6814, www.oldnavy.com

- ***Loehmann's***
  222 Sutter, 415-982-3215

- ***Marshall's***
  901 Market, 415-974-5368

- ***Burlington Coat Factory***
  899 Howard, 415-495-7234

- ***Shoe Pavilion***
  899 Howard, Suite 101, 415-974-1821
  three more San Francisco locations
  see www.shoepavilion.com

Used Clothes

Vintage, pre-owned and pre-antiqued clothes can be not only washed by the pound, but bought by the pound—or the bagful.

The Dollar Stretcher newsletter reports one shopper's "bag sale" score: "I saw a woman stuff two wedding dresses in a bag. She told her friend, 'My daughter is getting married and if she does not like either of them I will just sell them at my garage sale for $20 each.'" The shopper's cost? A mere $4!

Fill your own sack for $8 a pound at **Clothes Contact** (473 Valencia, 415-621-3212)—only slightly pricier than wash and fold! Smile pretty at the clerks; sometimes they'll give you an even greater discount. For more, hit the City's other used-clothing mecca: The Haight. The first-in-the-phonebook **Aaardvark's** (that's right, three a's) **Odd Ark** (1501 Haight, 415-621-3141) specializes in denim, leather and crazy polyester shirts & dresses.

Off the main drags, try **First Chop** (954 Irving, 415-564-7030) for women's consignment clothing, shoes and accessories in more rainbow colors and loud prints.

Thrifty Fillmore Street

Amidst tony home furnishing (read: furniture) and designer clothing stores, you'll find no less than six pre-owned goods dealers among the **Fillmore Street Shops** (www.fillmoreshop.com, a subset of www.sfbayshop.com):

- ***Next-To-New Shop***
  (run by the Junior League)
  2226 Fillmore, 415-567-1627
  Peddles fine clothing and even some used couture.

- ***Repeat Performance***
  (run by the San Francisco Symphony)
  2436 Fillmore, 415-563-3123

- ***Victorian House Thrift Shop***
  2033 Fillmore, 415-567-3478
  Benefits the California Pacific Medical Center.

- ***Goodwill***
  1700 Fillmore, 415-441-2159
  Sells all clothes and furniture at 50% off during occasional half-price Wednesday Sales.

- ***Departures from the Past***
  2028 Fillmore, 415-885-3377

- ***Seconds To Go***
  2252 Fillmore, 415-563-7806

furniture

With eight blocks of prime window shopping, from Steiner to Van Ness, Union Street is not exactly chock-full of budget-conscious stores. There are a few great values to be had, however, and they're not just at the sidewalk sales.

Our fave for affordable furniture is ***Sofa a la Carte*** (1528 Union, 415-474-4565), where all the seating is custom: choose your own size, shape, fill and covering, either slip or upholstered. Manager Jill Hackett sells us: "Our couches make people so comfortable at home, they will never want to go out and get another job!"

If all that choice paralyzes you, or if you need some furniture accessories—*and* if you can weather the lack of customer service—you can find unbelievable deals (such as a night stand for $15 or a sofa bed for $95) on used furniture from luxury hotels at ***National Furniture Liquidators*** (1110 Van Ness, 415-775-9999; 2301 Mission, 415-643-8888).

FOOD, GLORIOUS FOOD

All that bargain-hunting can sure work up an appetite! After you've studied the food-shopping techniques from the **Finance** chapter, put them to use at these fine food establishments, or just grow your own! (See "Grow Your Own" on p. 200.)

Grocery Stores

Trader Joe's (555 9th Street Retail Center, 415-863-1292; 3 Masonic @ Geary, 415-346-9964) is a good place to start. TJ's is all about good deals on food, which they extend by buying in large volume directly from suppliers and saving space, and therefore rent, with those funky check-out stands.

If you have the storage space, **Costco** (450 10th Street, 415-626-4388, www.costco.com) is great for bulk purchases—your savings should cover the $45 annual membership fee.

Leave some room in your pantry for the 20-lb. bag of rice, available at any of the Chinese groceries on Clement Street. Clement Street is likewise a great place to find inexpensive fresh produce.

One single-store discount grocer is **Discount Grocers** (1203 Polk, 415-929-7385). For live birds and fish, head to Stockton Street in Chinatown.

Food Co-Ops

Food cooperatives often buy food in bulk, saving money for members who take turns with food pickups, deliveries and other tasks. Unfortunately, we could find only two within city limits.

One, the **Other Avenues Community Food Store** (3930 Judah, 415-661-7475) is an Outer Sunset consumer cooperative with a mostly volunteer staff. The other, the **Rainbow Grocery Cooperative** (1745 Folsom, 415-863-0620, www.rainbowgrocery.org), has its own spin on the co-op concept: because its workers, rather than its shoppers, own and operate the business, you must apply for a job and be hired and then go through the rigors of their membership process to have a voice in decision making. Their food is organic and largely locally produced.

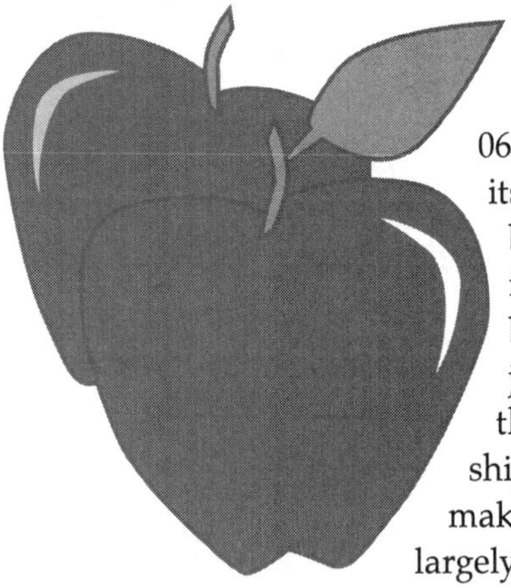

Farmers' Markets

Of the more than 3,000 farmers' markets in the state, San Francisco's **Ferry Plaza Farmers' Market** (One Ferry Plaza Building, Market & Embarcadero, 415-291-3276, www.ferryplazafarmersmarket.com) is one of the best. This market attracts more than 60 farmers even in the winter off-season, and more than 100 between April and November. Highlights include premium fruits and vegetables, plus a Saturday chef's program in summer that features live demonstrations from trendy local chefs, complete with samples for the audience. Since May 2003, this market has been open on Tuesdays (10am-2pm), Thursdays (2pm-6pm) and Saturdays (8am-2pm), plus there's a garden market on Sundays (9am-3pm). Permanent foodie shops (including Acme Bread, Cowgirl Creamery and Scharffen Berger Chocolate) are on their way.

The **Alemany Farmers' Market** (100 Alemany, 415-647-9423) is another San Francisco landmark, operating in its current location since 1947. Sicilian immigrant John Brucato, the "father of the Alemany Market," took on the grocery lobby and won in order to launch the forerunner of this market during World War II. You can now shop there on Saturdays from dawn to dusk (6am-5pm).

If Wednesdays (7am-5:30pm) or Sundays (7am-5pm) are your shopping days, head to the **Heart of the City** at Civic Center Plaza (Market between 7th and 8th Streets, 415-558-9455).

Grow Your Own

Crags Court, Michelangelo, White Crane Springs, Potrero del Sol and Hooker Alley. No, they're not new restaurants, they're San Francisco community gardens—places where neighbors and friends get together to make use of even the smallest patch of vacant land to grow-their-own.

Anyone can start a community garden, sometimes known as a "pea patch." For some coaching, check the website of the **San Francisco League of Urban Gardeners**, or **SLUG** (2088 Oakdale, 415-285-7584, www.slug-sf.org). The site lists the location of nearly fifty established gardens in which plots periodically open up. You can also send e-mail to SLUG's Garden Coordinator, who can guide you through the process of sowing a new one. SLUG offers free compost as well as gardening advice.

Even if you live in a yardless apartment, you can grow herbs in a window box. You could find one at a garage sale, or build one yourself. If you're lucky enough to have a yard, you can take an afternoon or two to plant a garden, and be grazing on fresh homegrown tomatoes and lettuce soon after that.

Dependable sources for seeds, dirt, and other supplies, including grown plants, are the **Sloat Garden Centers** (2700 Sloat, 415-566-4415; 327 3rd Avenue, 415-752-1614), with moderate prices and great selection; **The Garden Hound** (1921 Clement, 415-387-5608); and **Potrero Gardens** (1201 17th Street, 415-861-8220).

The **Bay Area Gardener** (www.gardens.com) catalogs a wealth of information on gardening classes, books, and stores. Need a reason to visit the City's smallest bookstore? Gardening's why. See **Strybing Botanical Bookstore** (9th Avenue & Lincoln, 415-661-5191).

WINDOW SHOPPING FOR THE NOSE

The scent of the bath and body shop ***Hydra*** (1919 Fillmore, 415-474-9372, *www.hydrasoap.com*) is as fragrant as an aromatherapy massage. Hang out for a while and enjoy the aroma, then buy a slab of soap to go.

The ***Scarlet Sage Herb Company*** (1173 Valencia, 415-821-0997, *www.scarletsageherb.com*) smells pretty too, and will even outfit you to create your own sweet-smelling beauty products. Think of it as window shopping for your nose!

TURN SHOPPING INTO RECREATION

Feeling the urge to create? Project stores such as the **Terra Mia Decorative Art Studio** (1314 Castro, 415-642-9911, www.terramia.net)—the original glaze-your-own ceramics store in Northern California—are good places to wile away some hours and leave with a functional piece of art, in proportion to your skill level, of course.

The do-it-yourself theme can apply to clothes as well as dishes if you've got the knack and a workable sewing machine. Find fabulous discounts on fabric and notions at:

- ***Fabrix***
  101 Clement, 415-221-4111
- ***Fabric Outlet***
  2109 Mission, 415-552-4525
- ***Discount Fabrics***
  1432 Haight, 415-621-5584
  4458 Mission, 415-586-8045
  2315 Irving, 415-564-7333
  warehouse & largest retail location:
  525 4th Street, 415-495-5337

beading

If your goal is to get a necklace for less, you probably won't save much money by beading it yourself, but if you size it up in terms of entertainment, you'll see that it's a much better value per hour than most movies. Six hours spent beading can be a valuable lesson in delayed gratification. You'll wind up with something personalized, to boot.

Surprise Party! (1900-A Fillmore, 415-771-8550) carries beads, shells, and small Chinese antiques. ***Gargoyle Beads*** (1310 Haight, 415-552-4274) hauls in their beads from all around the world. The stock at ***General Bead*** (637 Minna, 415-255-2323) fills two entire floors, yet perhaps the most gorgeous imported stones reside in the bins of the ***Bead Store*** (417 Castro, 415-861-7332).

Start with something simple if you need a refresher, like curtains or a duvet cover. Heck, sew two sheets together and get your duvet cover that way. Find them at the **Linen Factory Outlet** (1001 Clement @ 11th Avenue, 415-221-8598).

Maybe you're the craftier type. Scrounge up a project for yourself at **Scroungers' Center for Reusable Art Parts (SCRAP)** (801 Toland, entrance on Newcomb, 415-647-1746, www.scrap-sf.org), where the selection of paper, cloth, metal, wood, and glass bits changes daily, depending on what's been donated. Most parts are dirt cheap. **Pearl Arts and Crafts** (969 Market, 415-357-1400) might lead you to an artsy creation as well. We'd be remiss if we didn't add **FLAX Art & Design** (1699 Market, 415-552-2355, www.flaxart.com), *the* supply store for artists.

instant replay

• ***Play It Again Sports***
45 West Portal
415-753-3049
www.playitagainsports.com

This chain of individually-owned stores will buy your "gently used" sporting goods and pay on the spot. They'll let you trade up, too, or price your goods for sale on consignment. Play It Again makes a strong marketing pitch to parents of rapidly-growing kids, but hey, there's a kid in all of us, especially those of us with time on our hands.

"The place rocks," says Dane Larson. "I bought my golf clubs there. They happen to have a great selection of lefty clubs, very rare for even new sporting goods stores."

And how's the quality? Excellent, according to Dane: "Most used sporting goods stores carry a lot of crap, but Play It Again stocks only equipment in good condition, and generally not very old."

Fore!

SPORTING GOODS

If you're going to recreate, you might need to gear up. One category of exercise is so simple and straightforward that all you'll need is a good pair of shoes—and the right duds. This would be the walking-hiking-jogging-running category.

You'll find everything from trail shoes to track spikes at **On the Run** (1310 9th Avenue, 415-665-5311). Don't be overwhelmed by the variety of choices. Remember, you can only wear one pair at a time.

Lombardi's (1600 Jackson, 888-456-6223, www.lombardisports.com) is the favored choice for general sporting goods, with a strong selection of ski, snowboard, and all-around sports apparel. You'll pay full retail here, but they'll let you test drive a mountain bike by riding it around on their roof.

For discounted items and a good selection of athletic footwear, track down **The Sports Basement** (Mason Street, Building 610, the Presidio; 1301 6th Street, 415-437-0100, www.sportsbasement.com).

"If you haven't been to Sports Basement, you must check it out for yourself," says Kelli Elliott. "It's awesome!" But she adds, "Warning: do not visit unless you don't mind spending because they have such cool stuff, it's really hard to get in and out without lightening the wallet."

Kayaks probably don't top your "need to have" list, but if you're looking for a used one, try www.rummaging.com, which carries closeout, overstock, demo and liquidation kayaks at discounts up to 50%.

Roaring Mouse Cycles (1352 Irving, 415-753-6272, www.roaringmousecycles.com) comes highly recommended and sells road and mountain bikes, plus all the latest accessories. The spartan **Pedal Revolution** (3085 21st Street, 415-641-1264) peddles pedals and other parts that are both new and used, and offers a selection of new, custom-built and refurbished bicycles.

Out of the area sporting goods outlets include:

- ***Adidas Outlet,*** *2266 Monterey Road, San Jose*
- ***Any Mountain Outdoor Outlet,*** *2990 7th Street, Berkeley*
- ***Fila Outlet Store,*** *145 Park Lane, Brisbane*
- ***North Face Outlet,*** *1238 5th Street, Berkeley*
- ***Outback Outlet,*** *2517 Sacramento Street, Berkeley*
- ***Ujena Swimwear,*** *1400 Shoreline Road, Mountain View*
- ***Wildnerness Exchange,*** *1407 San Pablo Avenue, Berkeley*

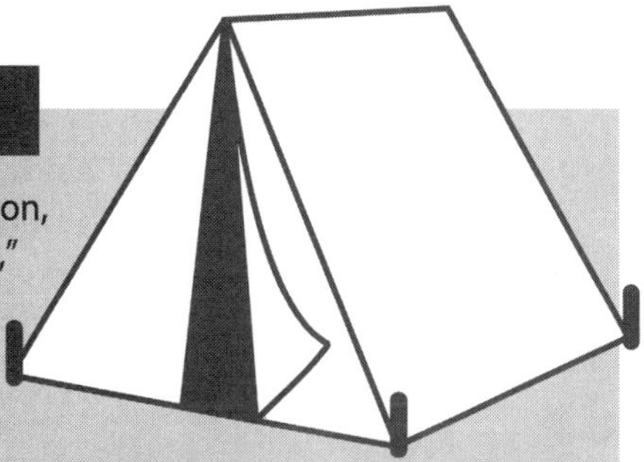

THE CAMPER'S CORNER

"If shopping for a polar expedition, the following doesn't apply," advises veteran camper Kelli Elliott, "but most of the time, ***Target*** (5001 Junipero Serra Boulevard, Colma, 650-992-8433; 133 Serramonte Center, Daly City, 650-755-2393) is hard to beat for the basics. They usually have great prices and a good selection of inflatable mattresses, ice chests, tents, lanterns, folding chairs, camp grills, and insect repellant. I was surprised and impressed by their sleeping bag selection last season."

If you'd rather rent your outdoor gear, ***Outdoors Unlimited Rental Center*** (near the corner of 3rd Avenue & Parnassus, 415-476-2078) is convenient and inexpensive. Located under the UCSF library, they rent tents, sleeping bags, stoves, lanterns—everything you need for a weekend away.

Seeking the requisite sunshower for your first Burning Man expedition? You can order one online at *www.shop-discount.com* or *www.campmor.com*, or check out a hard copy at ***G&M Sales*** (1667 Market, 415-863-2855, *www.gmoutdoors.com*), also good for backpacks, sleeping bags, and outerwear.

chinatown:
gifts for everyone!

Are there more Chinese-Americans in San Francisco than in China? There are certainly more t-shirts bearing likenesses of the Golden Gate Bridge. At five for $14, they make altogether appropriate gifts for your out-of-town friends. So do $2 slippers and $15 silk pyjamas.

Other treasures to be mined on the side streets: linen tablecloths, jade jewelry, plastic toys, herbal pharmaceuticals, paper lanterns, imported teas, and bargain-priced cookware.

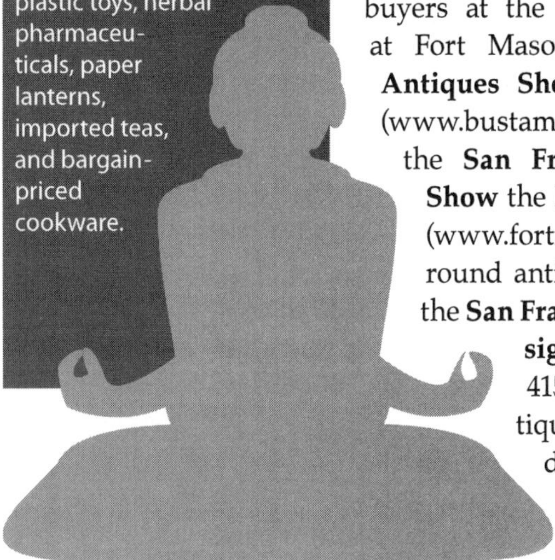

WINDOW SHOPPING

Almost any window in Union Square frames a pretty picture but for particularly tasty eye candy, loiter around **Neiman-Marcus** (150 Stockton, 415-362-3900, www.neimanmarcus.com) during the Christmas season, where the art of window display rises a notch above crass commercialism into—well, less crass commercialism. (There's a reason people call it Needless Markups!) Neiman's and others' window displays are archived online back to the year 1997 at www.fashionwindows.com.

Antiques make for pleasant perusing as well. Mingle with the browsers and buyers at the regular antique shows at Fort Mason Center: **Bustamante Antiques Show And Sale** in April (www.bustamante-shows.com) and the **San Francisco Fall Antiques Show** the last weekend in October (www.fortmason.org). Enjoy year-round antique people-watching at the **San Francisco Antique and Design Mall** (701 Bayshore, 415-656-3530), a giant antique, vintage and artifact dealer collective.

Ever wonder what Dianne Feinstein's living room looks like? We don't either. But if anyone has the good taste and personal wealth to purchase from the **San Francisco Design Center** (Two Henry Adams, Suite 450, 415-490-5800, www.sfdesigncenter.com), it would certainly be our esteemed local senator. SFDC's 100 showrooms are free and open to the public during your blessedly-free weekdays, and feature the best name brands in the latest styles. One can always dream! Their semi-annual sample sales, generally in May and November at the **Concourse Exhibition Center** (635 8th Street, 415-490-5800), are also open to the public and offer bargains for the whole family.

UNEMPLOYED SHOPPING GRAND PRIZE

And the winner is... the Mission District! A stroll down Valencia Street alone will take you past at least a dozen unemployed-friendly venues, such as:

Abandoned Planet Bookstore
518 Valencia, 415-861-4695
Features two resident cats and comfy chairs and sofas, even a piano.

Community Thrift
623 Valencia, 415-861-4910
CT donates part of your purchase price to whichever one of the 200 different charities on their list was designated by whomever donated your item.

826 Valencia Street
826 Valencia, 415-642-5905, www.826valencia.org/store
It's San Francisco's only independent pirate supply store!

Find tons of grocers on Mission Street itself, plus oodles of discount stores including the **99¢ & Over Discount Outlet** (2205 Mission, 415-647-9495), **Giant Value** (2558 Mission, 415-647-5382; formerly known as the "99 Cents Only Store" but not to be confused with the store above, trust us), and **One Dollar One Store** (1985 Mission, 415-626-1238), where everything really *is* just $1.

Wacky Mission District thrift stores include **Thrift Town** (2101 Mission, 415-861-1132), **Goodwill** (2279 Mission, 415-826-5759; Mission & South Van Ness, 415-575-2240), **Mission Thrift** (2330 Mission, 415-821-9560), and the **Salvation Army** (1500 Valencia, 415-643-8040).

The non-profit second-hand store **Nu2u** (2415 Mission, 415-550-0115) even trains Bay Area homeless youth.

SOMA: quirkiness

Of all that's off-beat South of Market, the ***Third Street Warehouse*** (2325 3rd Street) nabs top honors for its eclectic collection of shops, including ***House This*** ("one-of-a-kind doorknobs, candle holders, napkin rings"), ***City Limit*** ("posters, calendars, unique museum-style gifts") and the ***Hat Man*** ("outrageous hats, silk scarves and handbags").

Honorable mention goes to the ***San Francisco Flower Mart*** (640 Brannan @ 6th Street, www.sfflmart.com) where wholesalers supply morning shoppers with comfortably-priced fresh and dried flowers.

PACK IT UP

As the typical unemployed budget would dictate, you're not likely to head home from these expeditions with bushels-full of bargains. That's okay, now's the time to travel light. Find out how to turn your sabbatical into time on the road in the next chapter.

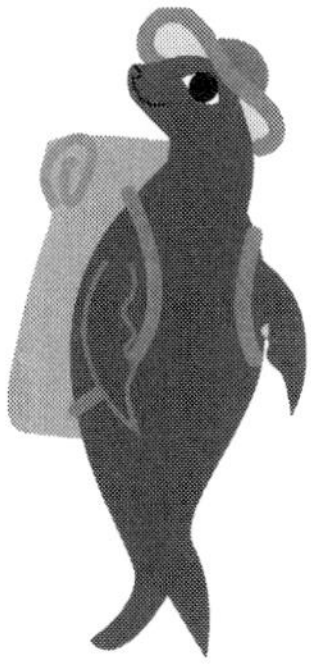

CHAPTER 5
TRAVEL

"...the grand tour is just the inspired man's way of heading home."

~Paul Theroux

UNEMPLOYMENT and travel were meant for each other. In fact, unless your work includes travel, you are by definition "out of work" *anytime* you're on the road—which we hope is a lot! We cannot stress this enough: if you can afford an extended trip, go. It's a great big world, and this is a golden opportunity to explore it.

How long should your trip be? Only you can decide, but keep in mind that many people have taken off a year or more and survived (and thrived) to tell the tale. Worried about marring your resume? Don't be. Savvy employers understand now more than ever that people need breaks from their day-to-day work.

Think you're too old to travel, or have too many commitments at home? You're not, and you don't. Couples and families go traveling all the time. Homes can be sold or rented, bills can be paid in advance, pets cared for, children shipped off to boarding school (okay, we're kidding here). The point is, you'll always find excuses for not going, but how will these excuses sound 10 or 20 years from now, when you find yourself wishing you'd gone while you had the chance?

This chapter does not purport to be a comprehensive travel guide; we merely make some humble suggestions to get you started, based on our own experiences and those of many other travelers. If none of them rev your engine, by all means—set your own itinerary.

Take off and go!

A Few Words About Sabbaticals

All right, we won't be *totally* bohemian. Few would fault you for wanting to have a job when you get back. If you have a job now, consider negotiating for a sabbatical.

Collaborate with your employer to create a win-win OOTO* spree: work extra hours before you leave, arrange to job-share, accept reduced pay, or take an unpaid leave of absence.

You can spend your time off in countless creative ways, from environmental volunteer programs in Antarctica to cooking schools in southern Italy. Lucky for you there are excellent books on the topic. One of the best is *Six Months Off* by Hope Dlugozima, James Scott, and David Sharp, replete with tips on negotiating and planning your sabbatical, as well as ideas on what to do if you *do* get the green light to go.

**That's "out of the office," in case it's been a while.*

THE ROOTS OF SABBATICALS

The modern sabbatical has its roots in academia, where the concept of checking out of the classroom is commonplace. Those nutty professors are at least smart enough to have figured out a way to regularly ditch work and keep their jobs!

Although it's taking them a while to come around, corporate America is beginning to grant its blessing to the notion of taking an extended break from the job. Consulting firm Accenture, for example, proposed a progressive sabbatical program in 2002 called "FlexLeave." FlexLeave allowed certain employees to take up to 15 months off at 20% pay plus benefits, and guaranteed their jobs on return. While the program may have been created specifically as an alternative to layoffs, it represents the increasing flexibility employers are offering their employees.

ROAD TRIPS

Finally, you're free! And you have piles of time on your hands—but maybe not piles of loot. Enter the good old American road trip, an economical way to spark the wandering spirit. With the right car, it's a cheap alternative to air travel that can relieve stress, clear your head and rejuvenate your spirit.

Matt Green, a former software executive, found his post-work road trips to the desert rather soothing, to put it mildly: "Staying in a rat-shit hotel, I slept better than I did in those $350-a-night first class hotels I stayed at when I was working."

America is one vast network of open roads, so the routes we suggest are only a starting point. And if your starting point isn't San Francisco? Fly out to ground zero and then buy or rent a car; invite friends who live near your launching point, and use *their* car; or use a vehicle transportation company (see "Road Trip Resources" p. 215).

Wherever you begin and whatever method you choose to get there, don't forget to make a few wrong turns. You never know where they might lead you.

The West Coast Trail

Drive time: 4 days (one way)
Distance from SF to starting points:
Vancouver, 950 miles; San Diego, 500 miles.

Pack up your vehicle and head out on the Pacific Coast Highway for a spectacular west coast tour. If you head south to San Diego from Seattle or even Vancouver, the climate will improve as you go. Take advantage of the many excellent coastal campsites along the way, and don't miss Mt. Rainier, Mt. Saint Helens, Hood River, Humboldt, Santa Barbara, or La Jolla.

Get Your Kicks...

Drive time: 4 days (one way)
Distance from SF to starting point:
Los Angeles, 385 miles.

Get hip to this timely tip: although it's no longer "The Mother Road" John Steinbeck described in *The Grapes of Wrath* (1939), Route 66 is still the iconic American road trip, showcasing Americana at its finest. Immortalized in song and TV, "Historic Route 66" has connected Chicago to Los Angeles for almost 80 years. Put on some Nat King Cole and do what the man says—get your kicks.

You can travel this time warp in either direction. For the best views—and the full historical experience—take a convertible, or even a motorcycle! To get yourself tuned up, motor on over to www.route66.com. To hook up with a phat Harley hog, see www.route66riders.com.

National Park Loop

Drive time: 10-12 days
(3-4 weeks total trip depending on route and number of parks)
Begin and end in SF.

There's a reason people come from around the world to see our national parks: they're arguably the best on the planet. Tour the parks of the west to see for yourself!

Kick off the giant loop about six hours north, at Redwood National Park, home to some of the world's tallest trees. Continue along the Oregon coast and into Washington, where Mount St. Helens (now a National "Volcanic Monument"), Mount Rainier, Olympic, and North Cascades National Parks await you. Then cut across to Montana's Glacier National Park, and finally down to Wyoming for Jellystone—er, Yellowstone—the granddaddy of them all.

The dazzling Grand Tetons beckon a short distance to the south. When you reach southern Utah, break out the mountain bike, and take your pick of parks, which include Arches, Canyonlands, Glen Canyon, Bryce Canyon, Capitol Reef, and Zion. The Grand Canyon lies across Arizona and it is, despite the crowds, undeniably spectacular.

If you're feeling super lucky when you reach Las Vegas, put your money on black and see if you can't double your leisure fund. If not, avoid its magnetic pull and point yourself southwest to California's Death Valley and its fantastic desert ecosystems. Continue north through Sequoia and Kings Canyon, and finish your park journey in Yosemite, the crown jewel of the national park system.

parks prep

Can't wait to gas up the ol' family truckster? Make sure the time is right. Tom Williams, professional tour director and resident road trip expert, recommends visiting in the fall. "The summer crowds are gone, the students are all back in school, and you get the great fall colors with cooler temperatures in the southwest." Avoid July and August, he says, unless you like it really hot.

MORE...

The Coast-to-Coaster

Drive time: 4-6 days (one way)
Distance to starting points:
Newport, Oregon (US-20), 640 miles; US-50 starting point in SF.

Everyone should drive across the U.S. at least once. For a speed run (set that radar detector), use the major interstates funded during the Eisenhower administration, such as I-70, I-80, or I-90. For a more leisurely trip, take a road less traveled, such as US-20, "The Oregon Trail," or US-50, "The Loneliest Road." The Oregon Trail follows paths taken by the earliest Americans, from the rugged crunchiness of the Oregon coastline to the sandy, highly refined shores of Cape Cod, with a little bit of everything in between. Say hey to Yogi as you pass Wyoming's Yellowstone National Park, but don't rent any barrels when you get to Niagara Falls. The two-lane US- 50 is less dramatic, but a fine and dandy sampling of small town America from San Francisco to coastal Maryland.

Southern Man

Drive time: 4 days (one way)
Distance to starting point: LA, 385 miles.

The southern states boast some of America's most distinctive cultures, from Texan to Creole to Old South genteel. US-80 (not to be confused with the larger Interstate-80), stretches from southern California to Georgia, and passes through just about every southern state in between. You'll traverse the great plains of New Mexico and Texas, then find the true heart of Dixie, from the Mississippi delta through the Appalachian Mountains, finishing near Savannah, Georgia.

Local Ted Wallace (name changed) recalls fondly his detours in southern Texas, "floating down the Rio Grande on inner tubes, and sneaking across the border into Mexico to drink at local cantinas." Time your trip right, and you can swing through New Orleans for Mardi Gras. Don't forget your banjo!

...CONT'D

Tom also advises getting a National Parks Pass ($50) with a Golden Eagle hologram ($15 extra) for entrance to any national park or land managed by U.S. government agencies. To buy one, or to research your journey, check out the ***National Park Service ParkNet*** (*www.nps.gov*) or one of the ***National Park Stores*** (Pier 39, Embarcadero @ Beach, 415-433-7221; Fisherman's Wharf, 75 Jefferson, 415-434-4622; 4 Embarcadero Center, 415-984-0640).

THE ULTIMATE ROAD TRIP

Bret Livingston and Patty Segar thought they'd go for a quick drive after they quit their jobs—across the North and South American continents! So they took a year, and hit the road.

Bret and Patty gassed up in northern Alaska and cruised the entire length of the Pacific coastline. They outrigged their Toyota truck with a camper shell, complete with sleeping quarters, a propane stove, camping supplies, food, water, surfboard and snowboard equipment, and other supplies they thought they might want on a leisurely one-year drive. Along the way, they encountered crazy bush pilots, plane crashes, gun-yielding banditos, over-sexed field workers, defective roof racks, extorting border personnel, ornery customs officials, stomach-churning ferry rides, and many dubious characters of questionable legal standing.

Despite the challenges, they say it was the trip of their lives, and wouldn't change the adventure for anything. What's more, it didn't cost them a dime, career-wise; they're each back at the same company they worked for prior to their journey. Let that be a lesson to the worry-wart in all of us!

Local Road Trips

If you don't have the time or the interest for a long road trip, you might enjoy a Sunday drive—or maybe even a *Monday* drive. You can make these road trip "quickies" in an afternoon or a weekend directly from San Francisco.

Santa Cruz

Drive time: 1-2 hours.

The drive from San Francisco to Santa Cruz along Highway One is curvy and coastal, and all the more exhilarating in a convertible or a Porsche (know anyone with a convertible Porsche?). You'll pass the scenic Pigeon Point lighthouse along the way, as well as the Año Nuevo nature reserve, home to California's largest population of elephant seals. The wonderful beach community of Santa Cruz boasts natural beauty and warmer weather than surrounding areas, plus an increasingly cosmopolitan nightlife.

Find out what to do in **Santa Cruz County** at www.santacruz.org.

Lake Tahoe

Drive time: 3-4 hours.

World class skiing and boarding in the wintertime; hiking, biking and camping in the summertime—Tahoe has it all, even ballooning! Stellar accommodations are available in all price ranges. Save money and increase fun by renting a cabin with a larger group. Any inch of the shore will do—the lake doesn't have a bad angle.

Explore virtually all that is Tahoe, including up-to-the-minute weather reports, at www.tahoe.com.

Point Reyes

Drive time: 1 hour.

Point Reyes National Seashore is a local treasure. Dozens of land and marine mammals and almost half of all North American bird species have been sighted within the boundaries of this biologically diverse coastal area. Hike, camp, or just crash out on the vast beaches, and be home in time for happy hour.

Find more information about Point Reyes on the **National Park Services** website: www.nps.gov/pore.

Wine Country

Drive time: 1 hour to Napa or Sonoma.

"Tempting beginning; full-bodied middle; long, strong finish," she purred with her eyes closed. A romance novel? Not quite. Just another connoisseur enjoying the sumptuous wines of Napa Valley. A single day spent visiting the wineries can improve your wine knowledge and have you expounding like the experts.

Be warned: most wineries charge for tasting these days, anywhere from $3–$10 for a flight of several wines. Tours, however, are generally free, and usually end with at least one healthy swig on the house.

For free tasting in Napa, try family-owned **Sullivan Vineyards** (1090 Galleron Road, Rutherford, 877-244-7337, www.sullivanwine.com). In Sonoma, swing by the **Benziger Family Winery** (707-935-3000, www.benziger.com) for their popular (and free) tram tour.

Plan your assault on either valley by typing its name into your browser: www.napavalley.com or www.sonomavalley.com.

hoping to stretch your travel dollar?

• Look up old friends. Surely they'll invite you to stay if you promise to do the dishes!

• Consider bed & breakfasts. *www.bedandbreakfast.com* lists over 27,000 B&Bs; see also *www.inntravels.com*.

• Arrange a domestic homestay. This might be a bit tricky if you're not a language student abroad, so scour the bulletin boards in cafés or community centers en route, if for no other reason than a fascinating glimpse into the local psyche.

• Contemplate camping. There are over 100,000 campsites in the U.S. alone. Bring a sun shower to freshen up in the morning, and you'll smell ahead of the game: *www.reserveamerica.com*.

• Load up the cooler! It'll shrink your food costs. Besides, where else are you going to keep your "cold ones" until the end of a long day's drive?

• Sing songs in the car. Will it save you money? No, but everyone likes a sing-a-long, and it's one way to keep the driver awake!

49-Mile Scenic Drive

Drive time: 2 hours (without stopping).

San Francisco's 49-Mile Scenic Drive is one of those city-sponsored tourist routes that attempts to "help" you see all the sights. But what the heck, the sights in San Francisco are many, and this is one way to pack them all into one afternoon.

The original 49-Mile Drive, designed for the 1939 Golden Gate International Exposition, began at City Hall and finished at the then newly-opened Treasure Island. Today's revised route is a giant loop with no real beginning or end. The blue and white seagull signs help fly you along, but aren't always reliable—several areas are tricky to navigate, and the signs don't always match published maps. The route does hit pretty much all the major City tourist sites, if that's your speed.

For a fitness adventure, try tackling the route by bicycle! See **Chapter 7** under "Biking" for details.

General Tips for the Road

A little bit of planning will drive you a long way on the open highway. Tom Williams recommends the organized tour companies for free ideas on itineraries. **Trek America** (800-221-0596, www.trekamerica.com), a company he's worked for, is one of his faves. After 30 years of running road tours across North America, they may have learned a thing or two. Better yet, says Tom, consider going on one of the treks yourself. "They are hidden gems for people in the U.S. The company markets primarily to international tourists, but the trips are a great way for us Americans to see our own country, and to meet people from all over the world at the same time."

Tom also recommends the off-season to avoid crowds, save money, and (sometimes) score better weather.

Road Trip Resources

Planning

The book *Road Trip USA,* by Jamie Jenson, can help drive your planning (check www.roadtripusa.com) but AAA is *the* resource for road trips. You'll get your $49 annual fee back several times over, with free maps, tour books, trip planning and other travel services, plus used car diagnostic checks and emergency road service for that inevitable breakdown on a lonesome highway. AAA's local affiliate is the **California State Automobile Association** (150 Van Ness, 415-565-2012, www.csaa.com).

Car Buying

Spare your own car the dings and dents by buying (and later selling) a used one. For deals on used cars, try **AutoBytel** (www.autobytel.com), **Craig's List** (www.craigslist.org), **PoliceAuctions.com** (www.policeauctions.com), or the old-fashioned classified ads: ***San Francisco Chronicle Classifieds*** (415-777-7777). The ***Kelly Blue Book*** (www.kbb.com) will tell you how much to pay—it's free (the site, not the cars). Look for a reliable make like a Toyota or Nissan, or something easy to repair (anything old and American).

driveaway into the wild blue yonder

If it was good enough for Jack Kerouac, it might work for you: drive someone else's car for a vehicle transportation company, sometimes referred to as a "driveaway."

It's pretty basic: you put down a security deposit (normally $300 cash), refundable upon "successful" arrival, and take one of their cars from point A to point B. They'll even pick up the first tank of gas! After that, you need only pay for gas and stick to a pre-determined time and mileage schedule, roughly 400 miles per day (which unfortunately won't get you to Mexico). Leisure Local Tim drove from Denver to San Diego: "I scored a brand-new Mustang convertible. It was so sweet!"

The biggest and best-known company, with offices throughout the U.S. and even a few in Canada, is:

- ***Auto Driveaway Co.***
  800-346-2277
  www.autodriveaway.com

  Bay Area office:
  28402 Century Street
  Hayward
  510-782-4999
  www.driveawayco.com

the green tortoise: an alternative to driving

The Green Tortoise has been running adventure travel buses since 1974, and "adventure" is truly the operative word here. The trips are known for their communal atmosphere, with custom sleeper coaches, group meals, and activities.

The Green Tortoise home base is San Francisco, where they also own and operate a youth hostel. Itineraries include regional, national, and international journeys. This is not your average Greyhound, so be prepared to have some fun on "the only trip of its kind."

- ***Green Tortoise Adventure Travel***
  494 Broadway
  415-956-7500 or
  800-867-8647
  www.greentortoise.com

Skipping The Road Altogether

Okay, so you can't drive forever. Eventually, you may tire of the wind in your hair, not to mention the bugs in your teeth.

For jumping around the U.S. by plane, the place to find deals on domestic airfare is San Francisco-based **Hotwire** (www.hotwire.com). Gregg Brockway, chief product officer and co-founder, says, "Americans are putting more of an emphasis on saving money. 'Cheap' isn't a dirty word any more. These days, cheap is like a badge of honor—people will talk endlessly about how they saved $20 on a hotel room or $50 on an airfare. They like to feel smart that they paid less than the next person." So go ahead, feel smart. Make our day!

INTERNATIONAL TRAVEL

Even a week abroad is better than none. If you have the ways and means, the world is waiting for you—take advantage. Pick any starting point on the globe and chart a course through new lands and cultures. International travel can teach you about yourself and what is important to you. We highly encourage taking off for several months or longer if you can.

All of our travel ideas would fill a different book; these are just a few with something unique for the leisure seeker—inexpensive travel, a sophisticated travelers' infrastructure, or opportunities for work or study.

As you travel, remember that you are both a pilgrim and an ambassador of leisure. Take some time to learn about your destination before you go; do some research on the **U.S. Department of State** website (www.state.gov, search for "background notes"). And take some time, period. Most of the world doesn't operate at the pace of the American office drone. Everything takes longer, especially when you don't speak the language. You're on a journey, and you're on your own time; enjoy it.

SISTER CITIES

Abidjan, The Ivory Coast
Assisi, Italy
Caracas, Venezuela
Cork, Ireland
Esteli, Nicaragua
Haifa, Israel
Ho Chi Minh City, Vietnam
Manila, Philippines
Osaka, Japan
Paris, France
Seoul, Korea
Shanghai, China
Sydney, Australia
Taipei, Taiwan

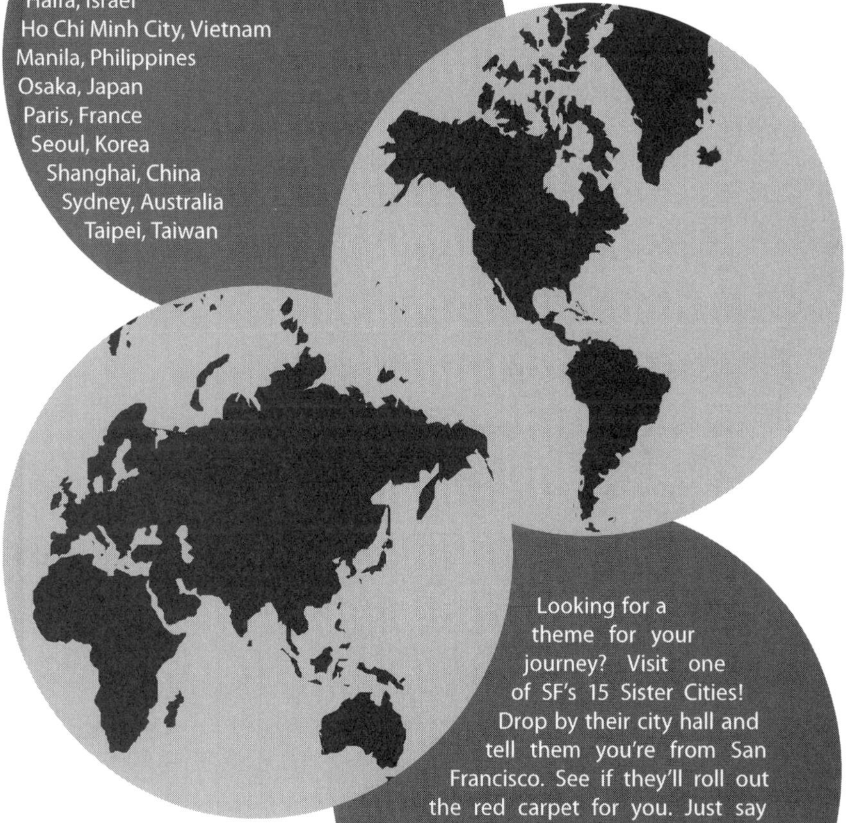

Looking for a theme for your journey? Visit one of SF's 15 Sister Cities! Drop by their city hall and tell them you're from San Francisco. See if they'll roll out the red carpet for you. Just say you're friends with "Da Mayor!"

Southeast Asia

Any seasoned traveler will tell you that Southeast Asia is one of the world's most fascinating and cheapest destinations. Tom "Mr. Travel" Williams sums it up: "The variety in Southeast Asia is just incredible. I can hike a volcano in Indonesia, stay in a $2 hut on the beach in southern Thailand, and eat extraordinary food in a Singapore street stall for $1. And as far as crowds go, there's always that next island out there that's still unspoiled."

Many parts of Southeast Asia, particularly Thailand and Malaysia, have an excellent travelers' infrastructure of inexpensive accommodations and transportation—perfect for stretching an unemployed budget. Bangkok, although noisy, polluted and altogether chaotic, is a backpacker's haven for cheap plane tickets and other transport. It's also an excellent place to connect with other travelers with like-minded interests—it won't be difficult to find your unemployed brethren here! Singapore is another major hub to launch from, well-served by major airlines.

Sister Cities:
Ho Chi Minh City, Vietnam
Manila, Philippines

For more information:
Asia Holiday Travel, Inc.
(567 Pine #203, 415-421-6630)

India/Nepal/Tibet

India could be your place if exploring your spirituality is one of your goals. Of all the places in the universe to visit, this region may offer a Western traveler the most consciousness-altering experience. Not an easy, relaxing realm, India has tested the mettle of even the most hardened travelers, but also provides the most rewarding revelations. Ross Taggart took a year off from teaching in the Bay Area to live, study and teach at a Tibetan monastery in Dharmsala, a city in northern India. "The whole experience was very intense," he says. "It changed my view on life forever."

The mountains of Nepal have long been a destination for international mountaineers and are home to some of the best trekking on the planet. Tibet, for its part, has persisted in relative isolation, and the Chinese government still requires visitors to obtain special travel permits. The region's mix of Buddhist and Hindu religions only adds to the richness for Westerners.

For more information:
India Tours & Travel (1533 Franklin, 415-673-2742)
M & K Travel (870 Market, Suite 350, 800-578-9207)
Consulate General of India (540 Arguello, 415-668-0662)

China

China demands its own separate mention from the rest of Asia, as it's more than just a country; it's an entire world in and of itself. From its urban industrial wastelands to its ancient imperial ruins, China is a land of contrasts. Beijing and Shanghai are fascinating cities, but let's not forget about Hong Kong, handed back over to the Chinese in 1997, which still maintains the busiest port in the world. Add to that the island of Taiwan and a country full of spectacular mountains, rivers and culture, and travel in China could fill up more than a year's itinerary (if you could manage to extend a visa for that long).

Marthe Stanek, an employment lawyer whose mother is Chinese, visited China in 1998. "It seemed to me the exact opposite of San Francisco. The human condition there is so overwhelming; it really makes you appreciate what we have here at home." Bring your Buddha nature as you will need it to navigate a country that welcomes visitors, but in a less than efficient way.

Sister Cities:
Shanghai, China
Taipei, Taiwan

Neighboring Sister Cities:
Osaka, Japan
Seoul, Korea

For more information:
China Travel Service (1523 O'Farrell, 415-921-3533)
China Travel Service USA Inc. (575 Sutter, 415-352-0388)
Chinese Cultural Center Taipei (832 Stockton, 415-982-4672)

Africa

Africa is not a single destination but a giant continent of countries to explore. One would do best to focus on just a handful. South Africa's beautiful coastline and world-famous game parks summon the leisurely wanderer in the post-Apartheid era. An extra bonus is the currently favorable exchange rates, making South Africa a "super-bargain." Ted Witt, an operations director from San Francisco who was laid off during the dot-com bust, spent one month in South Africa during a recent six-month journey. He tells us, "As long as all you're doing is surfing and hanging out, you can easily live like a king on $500 a month. You could pull it off even cheaper if you live more economically. Ostrich meat is really cheap, and low in fat!"

Tanzania and Kenya also offer adventure in abundance, be it surveying the Serengeti, climbing Kilimanjaro, or overlanding through some of the world's best game preserves. Dana Magenau, who spent several months in Africa during a recent one-year sabbatical, says Tanzania was easily his favorite of the four African countries he visited. He didn't make it to a few choice ones, though, like mystic Morocco in the northwest; the stable, wildlife-rich Botswana in the south; or enigmatic Mozambique in the southeast, along the Indian Ocean.

Sister City:
Abidjan, Côte D'Ivoire (Ivory Coast)

For more information:
Africa Tours (210 Post #911, 415-391-5788)

South Pacific

Nothing could be more leisurely than island-hopping in the South Pacific. The Society Islands (a.k.a., Tahiti), the Fijian island chain, the Cook Islands, and the islands in between all offer the region's distinct tropical flavor, with tall, swaying palms and gregarious, ultra-friendly locals. Dane Larson, a marketing consultant from San Francisco, surfed and lazed away several months in the Society Islands after a two-year stint of full-time work, and says, "Life there was so slow, I almost got bored. Almost."

Do yourself a favor while you're all the way down under, and continue to New Zealand, a land of vast, unspoiled nature. The country is an outdoor adventurer's dream. What the heck, you might as well throw in Australia as well, seeing as how it's one of the *greatest destinations on the planet*. Spend a year there without skipping a beat. We wouldn't blame you if you up and moved there!

In both Australia and New Zealand, the fully developed economy and English-speaking citizenry ease the task of securing an odd job, although acquiring a legal working visa is extremely difficult for Americans. Farming skills are particularly useful in New Zealand, where travelers can regularly trade farmhand chores for food and lodging. Peruse www.destinationdownunder.com and look under "Jobs For Backpackers" for more information.

Sister City:
Sydney, Australia

For more information:
South Pacific Express Travels (1586 Bush, 415-775-8989)

Western Europe

While it tends to be a more conventional destination than others, Western Europe still emanates an irresistible aura of history and culture. One can hardly deny the allure of sipping wine on a sunny afternoon at a sidewalk Parisian café or savoring the sumptuous cuisine of Sicily. The north offers the unflappable refinement of Scandinavia; the south, the hot, Latin rhythms of Spain and Portugal; and the middle, the canals and the seat of European government.

home sweet home

If you're a home owner, international home exchanges may be able to save you a bundle on accommodation. Check out ***Global Home Exchange*** (*www.4homex.com*) to get the complete skinny; annual membership cost $48 Canadian in 2003.

The budget can be tricky here. In general, prices fall with latitude: Greece, Turkey, Italy, Spain, and Portugal are going to be your cheapest bets, while Scandinavia is one of the world's most expensive regions. Unless you've got unlimited funds, you'd better plan to make friends up north who can double as hosts! Still, Western Europe's extensive hostel network and efficient train system have long made it a budget travelers' haven. The fact that English is widely spoken (much to the chagrin of the French) also makes travel relatively easy.

Western Europe may also be the region for you if you're interested in pursuing that studious sabbatical—say in art, language, or cooking. The combination of English-speaking schools and "old world" expertise in certain specialty fields can make for a rewarding educational experience. For more information on European schools, see *The Back Door Guide to Short-Term Job Adventures* by Michael Landes, a book full of ideas for taking time off.

Sister Cities:
Assisi, Italy
Cork, Ireland
Paris, France
Thessaloniki, Greece

Neighboring Sister City:
Haifa, Israel

For more information:
Europe Travel (447 Sutter, Suite 413, 415-395-9302)
Europe Vacations (944 Market, 415-837-0218)

Eastern Europe & Russia

From the well-traveled countries that are the Czech Republic, Poland, or Hungary, to more obscure destinations such as Slovakia, Yugoslavia, or Croatia, Eastern Europe has plenty to offer the adventurous traveler. No one can deny the elegance and intrigue of such sophisticated cities as Prague or Budapest, but less-charted locales, like Slovenia, Croatia, or the Baltic States of Estonia, Lithuania, and Latvia, all hide glorious treasures.

These days, the lines between Eastern Europe and Russia have blurred. Russia's mix of Old World, Eastern bloc nation and deregulated economy can be both fascinating and dangerous—crime and corruption interspersed with cultural gems. The Baltic States are a prime example, where Russian *mafiya* chat on cell phones in front of beautiful medieval churches.

Andis Blukis, a San Francisco engineer and writer, recently returned from Riga, Latvia. After jumping ship from a fast-sinking dot-com vessel, he sought refuge in the small country of his ancestors. Originally planning a summer break, Andis remained in Riga a full year, working periodically as a software engineer for a Latvian phone company. "I worked with and learned from engineers who were rebuilding an unbelievably large and complex, yet archaic phone call tracking system into Oracle as it simultaneously continued recording phone calls—the equivalent of rebuilding the engine of a 747 on the way across the Atlantic. Yet these same engineers also chose to haggle with an old bearded lady over the price of tomatoes, cream, and stinky cheese at the local medieval marketplace, rather than go to a modern supermarket." He lived well in Latvia on approximately $1,000 per month.

For more information:
Consulate General of Russia
(2790 Green, 415-202-9800)
Russart Travel Service
(291 Geary, Suite 511, 415-781-6655, www.russart4you.com)
SF's oldest Russian travel agency, full-service retail

DRESS FOR SUCCESS(-FUL TRAVEL)

For some mobile clothes that won't rumple your style, visit:

Andiamo Travel Clothes
1956 Lombard
415-546-2491

They carry pleasantly affordable wash and wear gear, from the everyday through the elegant; you can save your didge for the more important things, such as round-the-world plane tickets!

Latin America

"Latin America" is a broad term used to blanket a region of dozens of unique countries and cultures. From a travel standpoint, however, Latin America can be fairly divided into two primary areas: Mexico and Central America, for one, and South America, for the other.

The first region is almost as accessible by land as by air: Panama City is no farther from San Francisco than is New York, as the crow flies—or drives! Anyone who's been to the Mission District will recognize its amalgam of Spanish colonial and native American peoples. Bring your water gear, as two major oceans grace its shores; either side of the isthmus offers wonderful coastline to explore.

South America is more diverse, and the culture ranges from indigenous to a variety of northern European colonial influences. From the sophistication of Buenos Aires to the raw, colorful communities of the Bolivian highlands, the continent begs to be explored. Bargains are not hard to find either. Argentina, with its economic woes, is particularly well-priced these days.

Melissa Manwaring and Bryan Jadot, southward travelers in 2002, enjoyed four-course meals for two (including a nice Argentine wine) in Buenos Aires for just one $20 bill, and center orchestra seats at the symphony for only a fraction of that ($5). "Your dollar [in Argentina] now buys four or five times what it did a few years ago," Melissa told us, "so considering that Buenos Aires was once as expensive to visit as New York City, in many ways there's never been a better time to go. Plus, the Malbec is delicious!"

language study in latin america? ¡que bueno!

Seeking to dramatically improve her Spanish, Heidi Wells went directly to the source. For three months, she lived in Xela (a.k.a., Quetzaltenango), Guatemala, where she enrolled in one-on-one Spanish classes, five hours per day, five days a week.

"My instructor, Victor, doubled as my local tour guide," Heidi told us. "We'd go anywhere I could think of, from grocery shopping to trips to the pig farm. Everywhere we went, Victor grilled me on my Spanish and taught me new words." Her Spanish went from basic to keen in a Latin heartbeat.

Back stateside, Heidi kept the lessons going by tapping into Oakland's Guatemalan community—over cervezas at the neighborhood cantina.

¿Porqué no?

Sister Cities:
Caracas, Venezuela
Esteli, Nicaragua

For more information:
Buenaventura Travel
(2000 Van Ness, Suite 612, 415-777-9777)
Exito Travel
(800-655-4053, www.exitotravel.com)
a consolidator, which means cheap air tickets
The South American Explorer's Club
(New York, 607-277-0488, *www.samexplo.org*)
another top-notch organization
that publishes an extremely current
quarterly magazine and maintains clubhouses
in Ecuador (Quito) and in Peru (Lima & Cusco)

BE A RUNNER

Air couriers are the insiders' source for remarkably cheap international flights, provided you have the flexibility. These companies offer extreme discounts to someone (you, hopefully!) who will "courier" a shipment to its destination.

This isn't *Midnight Express;* passengers don't ever handle the shipment. They simply go through an extra administrative step with the air courier's agent upon departure and arrival. The courier normally sacrifices any checked luggage, and is only allowed only a carry-on. The return flight usually carries some time restrictions, ranging anywhere from seven days to six months.

In general, the closer to departure you purchase a courier flight ticket, the cheaper it is. One traveler we spoke with recently flew from San Francisco to Hong Kong round trip for $150, and another made it to Sydney and back for $200!

Listings with the ***International Association of Air Travel Couriers*** (*www.courier.org*) will cost you a membership fee of $45; browse the site first to decide if it suits your travel needs.

international trip resources

International travel guidebooks are many. Here are our favorites to read up with:

- ***Lonely Planet*** (510-893-8555, *www.lonelyplanet.com*)
- ***Rough Guides*** (U.K.-based, *www.roughguides.com*)
- ***Time Out*** (*www.timeout.com*)

To do more research and find maps, books, foreign-language dictionaries, and more, check the following agencies and stores:

- ***AAA Travel Agency*** 150 Van Ness 415-565-2141
- ***American Youth Hostels*** 425 Divisadero, Ste. 307 415-863-1444 *www.norcalhostels.org*
- ***Complete Traveler*** 3207 Fillmore 415-923-1511
- ***Get Lost Travel Books*** 825 Market 415-437-0529

more...

THEME TRAVEL

Ever ponder how Sir Francis Drake was able to complete his miraculous voyage circumnavigating the globe? Looking for a way to immerse yourself into a foreign community and hold normal conversations with the locals?

Add some pizzazz to your travels by finding a theme or a purpose for your journey. Theme-based travel gives you a vehicle for seeing the planet while granting you a fulfilling educational, cultural, physical—perhaps even metaphysical—experience. Your travels might revolve around a particular activity like mountaineering or surfing, or they could include studying language or history at a local university. Dive on in!

Study the Local Language

Nothing will ingratiate you to a foreign community like speaking the local language. The fastest way to ramp up your language skills is to "immerse" yourself in the dialect with in-country study. The learning process itself will be a terrific way to get to know people, as well as a heck of a lot of fun.

Some areas, such as Paris or Shanghai, are known for their language schools, but you should be able to find some form of instruction virtually anywhere you look (including truly virtual instruction: online).

For information on foreign language classes abroad, try **Berlitz Language Center** (180 Montgomery, 415-986-6464, www.berlitz.com), or **Language Study Abroad** (1960 5th Avenue, San Rafael, 415-454-9072).

You'll find plenty of assistance on the Web as well. Start with either **GoAbroad.com** (720-570-1702, www.goabroad.com) or **Languages Abroad** (800-219-9924, www.languagesabroad.com), and take it from there.

Teach English Overseas

Teaching English can be a groovy way to both make money while you travel and interact with locals. Lucky for you, San Francisco is a global center for getting certified to teach English, with hundreds of schools dedicated to ESL (English as a Second Language) or EFL (English as a Foreign Language) teaching certification.

A couple of the biggest are **Berlitz** (see previous page), and **St. Giles International** (One Hallidie Plaza, Ste. 350, 415-788-3552).

For an informative website with general ESL resources, also see **Dave's ESL Cafe** (www.eslcafe.com).

Sports, Music, and Other Hobbies

If you're a rock climbing or river kayaking fanatic, you probably don't need much persuading to pack your gear and seek out foreign climbs and rivers. But even if you're not an expert, choosing an activity outside of your own country will show you altogether different sights and experiences.

Music, for example, is a fabulous way to bridge cultural chasms. If you play an

...cont'd

- ***Rand McNally***
  Map & Travel
  595 Market
  415-777-3131

- ***Thomas Bros.***
  Maps & Books
  595 Market
  415-981-7520
  www.thomas.com

When you're ready to book your trip:

- ***Air Brokers International***
  685 Market, Suite 400
  415-397-1383
  www.airbrokers.com

  An airline consolidator for cheap wholesale airline tickets.

- ***Adventure Center***
  1311 63rd Street, Suite 200
  Emeryville, 800-227-8747
  www.adventurecenter.com

  A wholesaler for international organized adventure trips. Good for ideas, as well as if you want to travel with a group.

- ***Smarter Living***
  www.smarterliving.com

  Online travel booking.

- ***Cheap Tickets***
  www.cheaptickets.com

  Deals on international airline tickets and hotels.

instrument, strap it to the pack for jam sessions with local musicians. Bring your yoga, dance, or other "practice," and add some international flair.

Several people we spoke with took their bicycles with them and cycled cross-country, in places as diverse as Europe, Cuba, and New Zealand. They dealt with their share of challenges (harsh weather, breakdowns, and accidents, to name a few), but they also breathed in the culture, met residents, and even shared portions of their trip with local cyclists. "New Zealand was a great place to bike," Travis Johnson (name changed) told us. "The roads were good, without much car traffic, and the scenery was amazing. And if I ever got tired of biking in the rain, I would just pull off and stay at one of the thousands of guesthouses."

TRAVEL WON'T DETRACT FROM YOUR CAREER

Don't let your friends tell you that an extended hiatus will derail your career. Travel did exactly the opposite for Randy Risher, a successful Bay Area sales director. The 18-month journey he and his wife took around the world enhanced his standing in the eyes of more than one potential employer and ultimately helped him land a slot with a software company that went from rags to riches—and stayed there.

"I think people want to hire more well-rounded people," he told us. "I even interviewed for one position where I was extremely underqualified, yet almost got the job, all because the CEO loved the fact that I had traveled." Randy is now in early retirement, all thanks to that itch to explore.

A travel sabbatical worked for Dana Magenau, too. He scored a plum job as Director of The Grammy Foundation after climbing world mountains for 13 months. "I think they just figured if I could do something like that, then surely I could handle running a foundation," he jokes.

Work and Volunteer Travel

"Volunteer vacations" are quickly rising in popularity, and organizations now specialize in arranging them. Short of joining the **Peace Corps** (333 Market, 415-977-8800, www.peacecorps.gov) for two years

CAPTAIN COOK: A CAUTIONARY TALE

Captain James Cook and his crews were the first Europeans to visit much of the South Pacific, exploring the islands in three great voyages of discovery. On his third voyage, however, Captain Cook left his leisure mindset at home. Welcomed as a god in 1778, the Captain was killed by native Hawaiians in 1779 after weeks of ugly, non-guest-like behavior, culminating in a fight over a small boat. If you're following in Captain Cook's infamous steps, be sure to mind your manners.

(which you can of course always do), there are a surprising number of ways to incorporate work and volunteering into your travels.

Volunteer vacations run the gamut from remote environmental projects to inner-city teaching, and can range from two weeks to a year or more. For example, **Global Service Corps** (300 Broadway Street, Suite 28, 415-788-3666 x128, www.globalservicecorps.org) coordinates a program in Tanzania where volunteers can participate in HIV/AIDS awareness and prevention, either with a short-term or long-term project.

The **Sierra Club** (Outing Department: 85 2nd Street, 2nd Floor, 415-977-5522, www.sierraclub.org/outings) offers projects for the environmentally conscious. **Global Exchange** (2017 Mission, 415- 255-7296, www.globalexchange.org) provides what they call Reality Tours, in-country journeys designed to highlight global problems and "suggest ways in which people can contribute positive change."

Create Your Own Theme

Get creative and devise your own premise for a journey. Browse the annals of history for a topic that interests you, and design an itinerary around it. Your trip through Latin America could trace the conquests of Hernán Cortés, for example, or your South Pacific voyage could follow Captain Cook's (but be courteous—see above).

Another tried and true source of inspiration is literature: let Michener, Hemingway, or Theroux steer you through new and exotic lands. (Hemingway fans beware: more than a few have already made the pilgrimage to Pamplona.)

GREAT MOMENTS IN UNEMPLOYMENT

John Steinbeck
(1902–1968)

Not only did the Salinas-born writer John Steinbeck spend years of his life unemployed, partially-employed, or points in between, but woven throughout his most famous novels are persistent themes of unemployment, struggling workers, and the common man. The Grapes of Wrath, probably his most famous novel about labor, profiled the plight of dispossessed farmers during the Great Depression. • • • Steinbeck knew when to take a break. Fresh on the heels of Grapes' successful release in the spring of 1940, he sought refuge in Baja with close friend and marine biologist Ed Ricketts. The pair chronicled their adventures on the wild peninsula in *Sea of Cortez*, a journey of natural beauty, exploration, and science.

HOW TO TRAVEL WITHOUT LEAVING

Perhaps you don't have the budget for a big trip overseas, yet still would like to explore a new area or culture. Not to worry. The cosmopolitan San Francisco menu includes many exotic colors and flavors.

Language, for example, doesn't need to be studied in a foreign country. You can do it right here at home, and it's a great way to introduce yourself to a new region. Shake your international booty to some world music, and learn a thing or two about a regional dance in the process (find out more about local salsa options in **Chapter 4** or bellydance in **Chapter 10**). Globally orient yourself with seminars, events, and talks on a topic or region of interest; they take place all the time at venues such as:

- ***World Affairs Council of Northern California***
  312 Sutter, Suite 200, 415-293-4600, *www.itsyourworld.org*
- ***Abadá Capoeira San Francisco (Brazilian Cultural Center)***
  3221 22nd Street, 415-206-0650, *www.abada.org*
- ***Instituto Italiano di Cultura San Francisco***
  425 Washington, Suite 200, 415-788-7142, *www.sfiic.org*
- ***Russian Center of San Francisco***
  2450 Sutter, 415-921-7631, *www.russiancentersf.com*
- ***Alliance Francaise de San Francisco***
  1345 Bush, 415-775-7755, *www.afsf.com*
- ***United Irish Cultural Center***
  2700 45th Avenue, 415-661-2700
- ***Chinese Cultural Center of San Francisco***
  750 Kearny, 3rd Floor, 415-986-1822, *www.c-c-c.org*
- ***Japanese Cultural and Community Center***
  1840 Sutter, 415-567-5505, *www.jcccnc.org*
- ***Mission Cultural Center for Latino Arts***
  2868 Mission, 415-821-1155, *www.missionculturalcenter.org*

HOW TO SAVE MONEY BY TRAVELING

It may seem a paradox, but you can actually *save* money by traveling. If you're living off zero income, few places will deplete your savings faster than the good old U.S. of A. and San Francisco in particular. The dollar goes much farther in places like Southeast Asia, Latin America, or Eastern Europe.

If you're a renter, consider giving up your lease and storing your furniture, or subletting your place while you're gone. If you own a home, think about renting it out. The money you save (or make!) on rent could pay for months of roaming abroad.

You can also save significant money on daily living expenses such as food and lodging in regions where the cost of living is low, even after subtracting the cost of getting there. Presumably, you won't be spending nearly as much money on items like clothing, gas and utilities, nor burning through cash at fancy restaurants or bars. Amen to that!

Some sample monthly budgets for recent expeditions by Bay Area travelers:

South Africa: *$500 (60% off just for entering the country!)*
Central America: *$750–$1,000 (sailboat extra)*
Latvia: *$1,000 (includes payoff to local mafiya)*
Czech Republic (Prague): *$750 (tipping not required)*
Italy: *$1,500 (Chianti is extra)*
Argentina: *$500 (U.S. greenbacks are king)*

A Final Note

Travel can be enormously fulfilling, even life-changing. Unfortunately, in this modern era it also can be hazardous, particularly for Americans. The status and safety of different international regions is constantly changing. Use your best judgment when choosing a destination and take appropriate precautions when traveling to "hot spots". Consult the latest travel advisories from the **U.S. Department of State** (http://travel.state.gov).

IN YOUR OWN BACKYARD

If travel isn't your cup of tea but you'd still like to add some spice to your life, mine the following chapter, **Unemployment on the Edge**, for ideas on some colorful exploits—right here at home!

CHAPTER 6
UNEMPLOYMENT ON THE EDGE

"It is better to have loafed and lost than never to have loafed at all."

~James Thurber

UNEMPLOYMENT brings a certain freedom—freedom to do what you want when you want, freedom to stay out all night if you like, and in many cases freedom to experiment. Miss the opportunity to sample that recreational drug back in college? Now may be the time. Always wanted to explore the existential, spiritual or meditative worlds? There may be no better time than the present. Going out on a mid-week, all-night "bender" (defined more or less as drinking or partying until you see the sun coming up) is now not only possible, but in some cases highly advisable.

A large caveat—this chapter includes a few anecdotes about illegal activities. Our aim is neither to promote nor condemn breaking the law but merely to explore the full spectrum of unemployed culture. Gambling, drugs, and other illegal activities are as real a part of San Francisco life as cafés and museums.

Experimentation means different things to different people. "Living on the edge" could be as simple as going to a yoga class to practice vinyasas for the first time. It might imply the more risqué, such as watching a peep show or trying illicit drugs. Open yourself to new experiences, and you will likely find doors opening for you in return.

That said, only you know how far you can safely push the envelope. Freedom is as much about learning your limits as it is about charting new ground. If you don't know your limits, take this opportunity to find out. As Joe Gilmartin, infamous proprietor of the **Black Horse London Pub** (1514 Union, 415-928-2414) has been known to say, "You gotta say to yourself, 'Once a week.'"

DRINKING & DRUGS

If you're thinking about conducting some personal chemistry experiments, history is on your side. San Francisco's "drug-friendly" culture has earned the city notoriety since the opium dens of the 19th century. Beatniks read their poetry through a haze of marijuana smoke; students manufactured LSD in their bathtubs in the 1960s; Ecstasy fueled all-night club dances in the 1990s. As for drinking—let's just say the City's relationship with booze has lubricated the town ever since its origins as the village of Yerba Buena.

A Night on the Drink

With plenty of time to ride out a morning-after hangover, you'll find unemployment offers an ideal time to tie one on. Not that you necessarily need any guidance in this area, but a few basics will surely enhance any fun night of drinking.

One, don't drink alone—get yourself some "drinking buddies." Girls or guys, it doesn't matter, but no one should be drinking solo.

Two, don't drive—take cabs or get a designated driver, no exceptions. There's

liquid innovation

The fame of the City's watering holes dates back to Barbary Coast days. The martini, a drinker's drink if there ever was one, was reputedly born at the Occidental Hotel back in the 1860s, where a bartender made it for a patron who wanted something strong enough to last the ferry ride from San Francisco to "Martinez" (get it?). Today's ***Occidental Cigar Club*** in the Financial District (471 Pine, 415-834-0485), has inherited both the name and the art of martini making, and is one of those "owner occupied" establishments that allow you to puff away to your heart's content.

Other drinks attributed to San Francisco include the Irish Coffee brewed at the notorious ***Buena Vista Café*** (2765 Hyde, 415-474-5044), and the Mimosa, supposedly invented at the recently-closed Jack's Restaurant by none other than director Alfred Hitchcock and financier Louis Lurie.

absolutely no reason to get behind the wheel after a night of drinking in a city with as much transportation assistance as San Francisco.

Three, expand your horizons. Try some new and different places. There are thousands of bars within the city limits that have a heck of a lot more character than your run-of-the-mill yuppie bar (see **Dining & Nightlife** for inspiration).

Think there's no place like home? Save some money and host your own cocktail party. Stock up with proper cocktail gear: low and highball glasses, martini glasses, essential mixers, garnishes, a good bartending book (our personal favorite is *The Bartender's Bible*, by Gary Regan), and ice—always plenty of ice! Ask friends to bring over their booze of choice and voila! The party is on.

Whatever your choice, remember to drink plenty of water and take some aspirin before bed to help ease that morning pain.

A Day on the "Green"

No, it's not legal, but you'd be hard-pressed to find a major U.S. city that is more tolerant of marijuana use and cultivation. The City was among the first to allow the medical use of marijuana, passing Proposition 215 in 1996. Although at odds with federal lawmakers ever since, San Francisco has declared itself a sanctuary for the use, cultivation and distribution of medical marijuana.

So what does this mean to you, the edgy leisure seeker? Well for one, California maintains a more lenient legal policy on marijuana than most other states, calling it a "non-arrestable misdemeanor" (akin to a traffic ticket) for personal possession under 28.5 grams (roughly an ounce). It also means you will not have a difficult time locating high-quality pot from some reasonably reputable sources in and around San Francisco.

As local Ross Denny (name definitely changed) quips, "Weed will get you through times of no money better than money will get you through times of no weed." Well said! If you're experimenting for the first time, we're sure you can find friends for advice, support, and, er, collaboration.

You didn't hear it from us, but if you are so inclined, you may also be able to obtain your very own medical marijuana prescription for that which ails you. This is where those "doctor friends" can really come in handy. For more information and to learn about the risks involved, contact **California National Organization for the Reform**

of Marijuana Laws (CA NORML, 2215-R Market #278, 415-563-5858, www.canorml.org).

Cannabis clubs in San Francisco are frequently changing locations, and are notoriously reluctant to advertise exact addresses. Try the **Market Street Club** (2340 Market, 2nd Floor, 415-861-1864).

Rave Away

San Francisco hosts a thriving DJ and club scene, some of which (but not all) is tied closely to Ecstasy, as well as other so-called "club drugs." The merits and safety of "E" are debatable, but one thing is rarely disputed—paired with good dance music, the Ecstasy-taker will likely want to dance all night long. Make sure you stay hydrated!

For club and DJ music scenes, try **Ten Fifteen** (1015 Folsom), a big club that rotates themes each night of the week. For smaller venues, groove into **DNA Lounge** (375 11th Street, 415-626-1409, www.dnalounge.com), or **111 Minna** (111 Minna, 415-974-1719, www.111minnagallery.com).

GETTING EXTREME

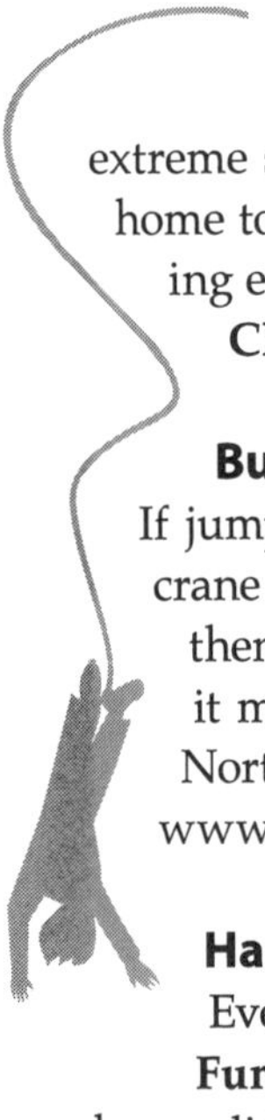

If you prefer the natural high of an adrenalin rush, try extreme sports. San Francisco often hosts ESPN's "X-Games" and is home to almost every imaginable risk-taking activity. If you're feeling extra edgy, do it all without health insurance! (Otherwise see **Chapter 3** for insurance resources).

Bungee Jumping

If jumping from a bridge, out of a hot air balloon, or off a giant crane attached to nothing but a giant rubber band appeals to you, then bungee jumping is for you. At a cost as low as $50 per jump, it makes for a relatively cheap thrill. For jumps in and around Northern California, contact **Bungee Experience** (209-295-6123, www.californiabungeee.com). Have a nice fall…

Hang Gliding

Ever wanted to fling yourself off a cliff and fly like a bird? **Fort Funston** (Highway 35 near John Muir Drive) is your place, where hang gliders and paragliders congregate and launch themselves over the edge of the Pacific Ocean. Another popular launching point, north of the City, is **Mount Tamalpais** in Marin County, where you can soar over Stinson Beach. **San Francisco Hang Gliding Center** (510-528-2300, www.sfhanggliding.com) provides lessons, rental equipment, and other hang gliding resources.

Sky Diving

There's no rush like falling out of an airplane, whether it's a one-time tandem jump or the first of many solos. **Skydive San Francisco** (707-894-9241, www.skydivesf.com) can serve your needs. Just remember, when "push" comes to "shove," you have to jump out of a plane strapped to a sack of silk. Bon voyage!

Auto Racing

You may always have dreamed of screaming around a racetrack at top speed. Or perhaps you want to test the limits of your own car. Okay, maybe you're just bored and need to get out of the house. It may be time to get behind the wheel!

Start out on cruise control for the three-hour drive to the race track at **Thunderhill Park** (in Willows, north of Sacramento, 530-934-5588, www.thunderhill.com). Then rev up your engine with their popular high performance driving school. You'll need your own street-legal car (we highly recommend a Porsche 911, but that's just us), a 3 point belt-harness for both front seats (i.e., the standard shoulder and lap strap), a Snell-rated helmet, and a cool leather jacket. Okay, the jacket's optional. For $195, you get an all-day training class on the track, lunch, and a much-coveted Thunderhill t-shirt. Plus, you get to brag about the day's events over beers afterwards with your new driving comrades.

bridge to bridge

Law-abiding citizens, avert your eyes now. We've heard a rumor that some drivers use local bridges at off hours to "determine" how far the needle spins on their speedometer.

The Bay Bridge *was* the bridge of choice, with its split upper and lower one-way levels, until the non-stop construction began. But there's an even bigger obstacle: the highway patrol is on the case. Patrollers often lurk at the Treasure Island on-ramp late at night, waiting to nab speedy drivers.

Westward to 280, perhaps?

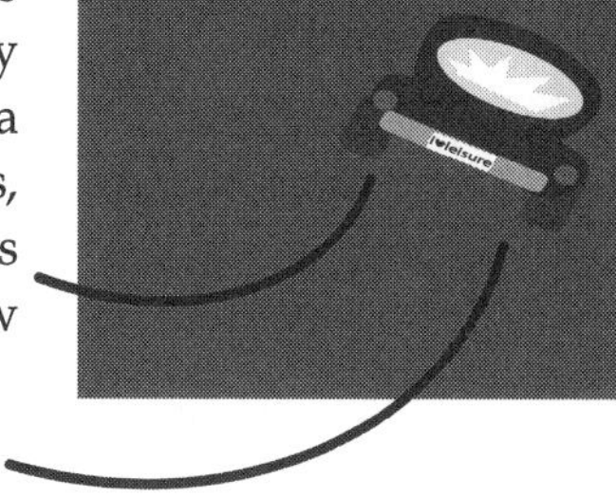

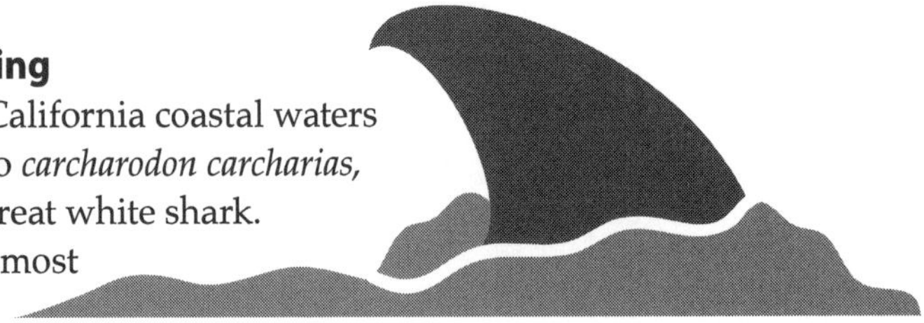

Shark Diving

Northern California coastal waters are home to *carcharodon carcharias,* a.k.a. the great white shark. One of the most densely populated great white habitats happens to be just off the coast of San Francisco, in the Farallon Islands. Spend the day on a Sanctuary Adventure with the **Farallones Marine Sanctuary Association** (www.farallones.org); kayak and boat tours offer close encounters with sharks, whales, elephant seals and sea lions, as well as many species of birds. To get even more edgy, don a wetsuit and jump into a shark cage for an up-close-and-personal glimpse of a great white. It's an experience you won't soon forget.

For info on whale watching trips (sans shark diving) to the Farallones, contact the **Oceanic Society** (415-474-3385, www.oceanic-society.org/pages/wwa.html). Day trips cost $66 per person Fridays and Mondays, and $69 per person on weekends. Several companies operate shark diving expeditions to the Farallones—curiously, all seem to be affiliated and use the same divemasters. Try **Incredible Adventures** (800-644-7382, www.incredible-adventures.com/shark_encounter.html). Save your pennies for this one, as the trips are not cheap, running $700–$1,000 per person!

SPIRITUALITY

Any situation that exposes one's core beliefs, material values, or immortal soul is an extreme activity indeed. If the Leisure Commandments don't move you, use your flexible schedule to explore your own personal spirituality. Don't go join a cult or anything, just investigate any longings for "The Infinite" you may have been suppressing. And remember: spirituality is found not necessarily within a group, but within an individual.

One-Time Dose of Church

Maybe you want to attend a single church service for a dose of religious culture or spiritual cleansing—or maybe you just need someplace to hang out on a Sunday morning! Whatever your motives, many local places of worship, even the famous ones, welcome "drop-ins."

Glide Memorial United Methodist Church

(330 Ellis, 415-674-6000, www.glide.org)

As those who've been there already know, Glide is more than going to church—it's a full-body experience. Every Sunday at 9am (and again at 11am), Glide rocks, breathes, and reverberates. For 40 years, Reverend Cecil Williams, who has "retired" but still manages to deliver plenty of sermons, has built and presided over one of the most recognized congregations in the U.S., whose parishioners include such notables as Oprah Winfrey. On any given Sunday you'll see yuppies jigging alongside the homeless, in what is best described as an "only in San Francisco" event. Religion aside, Glide also provides countless social services to the city of San Francisco, from hot meals for the homeless to high-tech job skills training.

Grace Cathedral

(1100 California, 415-749-6300, www.gracecathedral.org)

Grace is the Episcopalian center of San Francisco. It offers concerts and open services for anyone who "seeks God and is drawn to Christ." It's a hip church, as indicated by its web site (recent headlines included "Tales From the Crypt," and "Rolling Stones Rock San Francisco!"). A choral service is performed within the cathedral's beautiful walls every Sunday at 11am, and their classical concert series is extremely popular.

Judaism

Oy vey, are there ever a lot of resources for those looking to explore Jewish history and culture! Whether you're a goyim or a Yiddishe kop, begin at the **Jewish Community Center of San Francisco** (1808 Wedemeyer, 415-346-6040, www.jccsf.org; current location is temporary during construction of a new center at 3200 California @ Presidio, to be opened in January 2004). The JCC focuses more on culture and community than on theology, but offers many classes that can point you toward further study.

Beyt Tikkun Synagogue (415-575-1200, www.beyttikkun.org) describes itself as "a Jewish Renewal and Politics of Meaning oriented synagogue." It does not currently have a permanent location, but hosts a variety of events in San Francisco, Berkeley and San Rafael. **Chochmat HaLev** (2215 Prince Street, Berkeley, 510-704-9687, www.chochmat.org) is "an independent center of Jewish meditation" that offers healing and meditation services as well as Torah study classes. **Lehrhaus Judaica** (2736 Bancroft Way, Berkeley, 510-845-6420, www.lehrhaus.org) is a non-denominational Jewish studies school that offers seminars and courses throughout the Bay Area on Jewish history, philosophy, theology, and culture.

Catholicism

Catholicism, edgy? Consider the bundle of paradoxes that make up Holy Mother Church—from liberation theology to the stance against birth control, from the world's largest charitable organization to the gilded palaces of the Vatican—and yeah, you have yourself a religion on the edge.

San Francisco has a strong Catholic tradition, dating back to Fra Junipero Serra's 1776 founding of **Mission Dolores** (now at Dolores & 16th Street). Today, two other large churches dominate the City's Catholic community.

St. Mary's Cathedral (or rather, The Cathedral of St. Mary's of the Assumption, 1111 Gough, 415-567-2020, www.stmarycathedralsf.org) is a dramatic modern structure atop Cathedral Hill, and serves as the headquarters of the Archdiocese of San Francisco. Sunday Masses are at 7:30am, 9am, 11am and 1pm (in Spanish). If the sermon's boring, step outside and decide for yourself whether the Cathedral's roof was designed to look like the inside of a washing machine, or if the designer's real agenda was to cast a shadow in the shape of a woman's breast.

St. Ignatius Church (650 Parker, 415-422-2188, www.stignatiussf.org), part of the Jesuit-run University of San Francisco since 1914, remains an impressive San Francisco landmark. Its floodlit turrets light the night for miles around—a beautiful sight that gives neighboring landlords a built-in selling point.

Hinduism

San Francisco itself is not exactly a Hindu center, but temples are scattered throughout the Bay Area. **Chinmaya Mission** (1050 Park Avenue, San Jose, 408-998-2793, www.chinmaya.com/san-jose) is among the largest and most prominent, and noted for its strong children's programs.

Within city limits, one of the few Hindu-based temples is operated by the **Vedanta Society** (2323 Vallejo, 415-922-2323, www.sfvedanta.org). Although not strictly Hindu, the society offers personalized spiritual direction, as well as lectures on Sundays and Wednesdays.

Buddhism and Zen Centers

We bow to the late, great leisure master Bruce Lee: "The less effort, the faster and more powerful you will be." Heeding Bruce's wise advice (and San Francisco's Asian influences), a variety of local Zen and Buddhist centers are seeking to lead you to enlightenment.

The **San Francisco Zen Center** (www.sfzc.com) is one of the foremost Buddhist sanghas outside of Asia. You'll find classes, retreats and workshops at any of its three practice centers: the **Beginner's Mind Temple**, also known as **City Center** (300 Page, 415-863-3136); **Green Dragon Temple**, or **Green Gulch Farm** (1601 Shoreline Highway, Sausalito, 415-383-3134); or **Tassajara Zen Mountain Center**, also known as **Zen Mind Temple** (39171 Tassajara Mountain Road, Carmel Valley, 831-659-2229). Beginners can start with the Saturday 8:45am introductory session at City Center.

The Mission District's **San Francisco Buddhist Center** (37 Bartlett, 415-282-2018, www.sfbuddhistcenter.org) is an almost entirely volunteer-run organization that manages to put on an impressive number of classes, events, and retreats. Don't be discouraged if it takes them a few days to return your messages or e-mails; patience and kindness are essential to your Buddha nature.

retreats

The beautiful wilderness settings of the ***Green Gulch Farm*** and ***Tassajara Zen Mountain Center*** (see main text, this page) are especially conducive to meditation.

Green Gulch Farm offers a public program every Sunday that includes meditation instruction, a lecture, tea and lunch, all for a small requested "donation" of $8 for the lunch (participants are also asked to donate something to the temple).

Tassajara, a full-fledged Buddhist monastery, is closed to the public for much of the year but open to guests from May through August (reservations absolutely required). Inner-peace comes at a price if you stay on the premises. A cheaper alternative—for a limited number of day guests—is the $20 day pass ($10 for children), a real bargain when you consider it buys you full access to their excellent facilities, which include hot springs, steam rooms, sun decks, hot plunges, jacuzzis and showers.

burning man: a religious experience?

What began in 1986 as a small Summer Solstice celebration on Baker Beach has become a worldwide movement: ***Burning Man*** (*www.burningman.com*), an annual event that welcomed more than 30,000 participants in 2003.

Every year during the week prior to and including Labor Day weekend, attendees (many of them from San Francisco) make the annual pilgrimage to Black Rock Desert in Nevada. What transpires can be adequately understood only by those who experience the phenomenon in person. Suffice it to say, the event could qualify in any number of categories within this very chapter: drugs, sex, extreme activities, and, yes, even religion.

At its core, Burning Man is simply a pure celebration of creativity, community, and self-expression. There's only one rule: participate, don't spectate. If you go, strap on your safety helmet—you're in for a wild ride!

Islam

Most Bay Area Islamic organizations lie outside the city limits, with two notable exceptions. The **Islamic Society of San Francisco** (20 Jones, 415-863-7997, www.zayatech.com/32/) provides classes, counseling and special services, including marriages; the **Islamic Center of San Francisco** (400 Crescent, 415-282-9039) is a traditional mosque. In Silicon Valley, the **Muslim Community Association of the San Francisco Bay Area** (3003 Scott Boulevard, Santa Clara, 408-970-0647, www.mca-sfba.org) offers a wide range of events and programs, including an online job bank and apartment search service.

Personal Growth

Lisa: *I want you to shut off the logical part of your mind.*
Bart: *Okay.*
Lisa: *Embrace nothingness.*
Bart: *You got it.*
Lisa: *Become like an uncarved stone.*
Bart: *Done.*
Lisa: *Bart, you're just pretending to know what I'm talking about!*
Bart: *True.*

~The Simpsons

There may come a time in your life when it's time to hand over the keys to someone else, and let them take you for a little ride. With luck, you won't end up in a long Kool-Aid line in the middle of the jungle, or in a deep slumber in a San Diego bunk bed sporting a pair of Nikes! Despite the sensational press over these horrible aberrations, there are some very positive and effective self-help programs out there—just find the one that's right for you.

In San Francisco, try the **Gestalt Institute** (417 Balboa, 415-379-9848, www.gestaltinstitute.com). It has a legitimate reputation for helping both academics and working (and non-working!) professionals. Another option might be **Sedona Training Associates** (888-282-5656, www.sedona.com), which is good enough for Joan Collins as well as for many psychologists. Although it's headquartered in Arizona, it holds frequent seminars in San Francisco.

FROM FLOWER POWER TO CULTS

San Francisco and the Bay Area have long been magnets for anyone seeking spirituality, self-help, or self-actualization—which means they've also been magnets for cults.

During the "Flower Power" era of the 1960s, impressionable youth flooded the Bay Area, living commune-style around Haight-Ashbury and Berkeley. Ten years later, the infamous Jim Jones led his People's Temple congregation on that fatal pilgrimage from San Francisco to Georgetown, Guyana (see ***Chapter 4*** for the whole story).

Even today, you won't have to look far for a wide selection of cults in the Bay Area. One organization recently under scrutiny was the ***San Francisco Church of Christ***, affiliated with the industrious International Churches of Christ—but not to be confused with the mainstream Protestant "Church of Christ." The SFCOC reportedly had a habit of luring unsuspecting college students and young professionals, then using high-pressure tactics to convert them into "disciples." Former church members have in turn started their own non-profit organization: ***Reveal*** (*www.reveal.org*), chartered to disseminate truthful information about the church and help members leave if they want to.

Many local psychologists also specialize in personal growth services, so if one-on-one therapy is more appealing to you, try starting with the **San Francisco Psychological Association** (415-681-3063, www.sfpa.net) for a local referral.

If you find yourself suddenly in the "wrong" organization, there are groups that can help. Research the **American Family Foundation** (AFF, www.csj.org), whose mission is to study, educate, and assist people with relation to cults. Also see **CultsOnCampus.com** (www.cultsoncampus.com) for general information and resources on cults.

SEX IN THE TIME OF UNEMPLOYMENT

Sexuality and unemployment go together like—well, let's just say they go together. Sex and sexual pursuits take time, energy, and often a certain degree of (pardon the pun) flexibility. For this reason, time off offers the perfect opportunity to put some zest back into your sex life, be it within an existing relationship, or out in the risqué world of the San Francisco underbelly.

Ross Denny (name still changed), our resident green expert, agrees. "One of the nice side benefits to being unemployed and having carnal relations is that you can have a relatively sleepless night, see your lover off to their job in the morning, then go back to bed and catch 40 more winks." He is also a big fan of the dual leisure model. "If you find a partner who is also unemployed, then *every* night is like a Friday night!"

If it's sex you're looking for, San Francisco is a fruitful place. The City deserves its reputation as one of the most sexually liberated urban centers in the country. There are numerous sexual pursuits to be found in the area, both above and below board. From gay to heterosexual to every combination in between, chances are there are venues and opportunities to meet your needs.

Hooking Up

The good, old-fashioned one-night stand is a time-honored route to sexual satisfaction. Judgments aside, if you're so inclined, here are a few thoughts.

First and foremost, be safe and take responsibility for your actions. Second, you're going to need to pick a few places to go, and we feel obliged to throw out some suggestions.

As for bars, some notorious heterosexual single scenes by neighborhood include: **Matrix Fillmore** (3138 Fillmore, 415-563-4180) in the Marina. Bring your snazzy dress, and your wallet. The **Bluelight** (1979 Union, 415-922-5510) is another Marina haunt that's a little more casual, and heavy drinking is encouraged. In Russian Hill, try the **Royal Oak** (2201 Polk, 415-928-2303) for fraternity-like mingling.

North Beach has plenty of options, but the **Bubble Lounge** (714 Montgomery, 415-434-4204) is known as a swanky singles scene. In the Mission you can take your pick, but you might buzz by **Blondie's Bar & No Grill** (540 Valencia, 415-864-2419, www.blondiesbar.com), or across the street, by **Casanova Lounge** (527 Valencia, 415-863-9328). SOMA's **111 Minna** (you guessed it, 111 Minna, 415-974-1719) is a hip locale where a lot of connections are made nightly.

For same-sex hook-ups, the popular **Martuni's** (4 Valencia, 415-241-0205) is a warm and friendly piano lounge where patrons often sing along with the music. You can also try the **Bar on Castro** (456B Castro, 415-626-7220), which has a small dance floor and, fittingly, a well-stocked bar. Women will have better luck at the **Lexington Club** (3464 19th Street, 415-863-2052, www.lexingtonclub.com) for female-to-female mingling.

THE MARINA SAFEWAY: FACT OR FICTION?

Ever since Armistead Maupin's popular 1970s serial *Tales of the City* hailed it as *the* pick-up spot in the City, the ***Marina Safeway*** has held legendary status as a place to hook up. But is this "meat market" reputation still justified?

Many of its frequent patrons say the Marina Safeway's standing is more folklore than reality. Several San Franciscans, in fact, let slip that either location of ***Trader Joe's*** (3 Masonic, 415-346-9964, or 555 9th Street, 415-863-1292) is the preferred new spot for those looking to get their melons squeezed.

Bars not your scene? Try your local café, laundromat, or grocery store. People are generally much more approachable there than in the average bar. Try this as an opening: "Hi. I'm unemployed and having fun during my time off. Care to have fun with me?" Okay, so maybe save that line for the EDD office.

Enjoy a different kind of "suds" between wash cycles at **Brain Wash** (1122 Folsom, 415-861-3663), where you can even catch the occasional live band. Care for some appetizers, too? The **Marina Safeway** (350 Bay, 415-781-4374), has long been hailed as San Francisco's meat-market of choice (and we don't mean ground chuck!), yet its reputation appears to be waning (see box above). The **Castro Safeway** (2020 Market, 415-861-7660) is the shopper's choice for same-sex connections.

For café society, mingle with the beautiful people at **The Grove** (2250 Chestnut, 415-474-4843), or hang with young professionals and med students at **The Canvas** (1200 9th Avenue, 415-504-0070, www.thecanvasgallery.com). At **Café Macondo** (3159 16th Street, 415-431-7516) you can talk liberal politics with a decidedly international crowd.

Strip Clubs

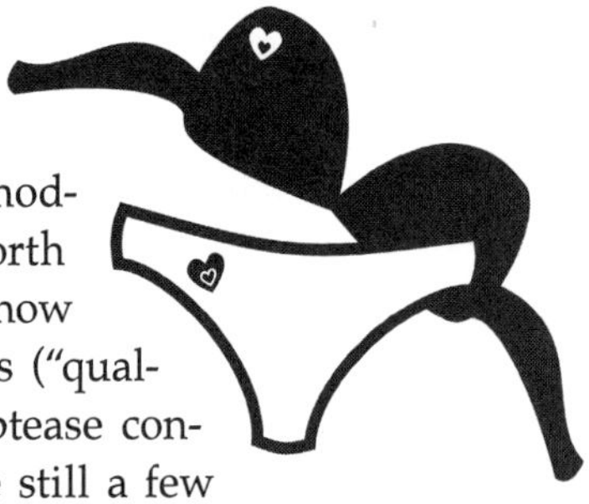

Strip clubs can be fun for boys and girls alike. Ironically, although the modern topless dance club was born in North Beach in the 1960s, San Francisco is now noticeably light on quality strip clubs ("quality" being a relative term here). Striptease connoisseurs need not despair; there are still a few nuggets around.

The **Gold Club** (650 Howard, 415-536-0300) is probably the cleanest and best option for food, drink and bare breasts. Bargain hunters note—the daily happy hour, from 3pm-7pm, includes free admission and drink specials.

For a strip club of a more, shall we say, "advanced" nature, the **Lusty Lady Theatre** (1033 Kearny, 415-391-3991) is the best value in town. Admission is always free, and private viewing rooms start as low as a quarter. It happens to be the first strip club in the country where all the employees, including the dancers, are unionized. You just can't beat union labor!

> **special performances**
>
> Once home to porn queen and sex educator Annie Sprinkle's provocative sex shows, ***848 Community Space*** (848 Divisadero, 415-922-2385, *www.848.com*) shows it all—and we *do* mean all. "We have done and will continue to do almost anything!" they say. It's not an understatement. Host to anything from yoga to literary smut to pagan rituals, 848 provides the most open of open forums. Check their calendar for a performance to match your taste.

Massage Parlors

This section speaks mainly (though not exclusively) to our male readers, so men, listen up: San Francisco is home one of the most extensive networks of Oriental massage parlors outside of Asia, serving a wide range of tastes and budgets. Two that our "experts" highly recommend are the **Golden Flower Steam & Sauna** (215 2nd Street, 415-546-6333) and the **Empire Health Club** (428 O'Farrell, 415-441-4133). Prices begin in the $50-60 range for a half-hour "house massage," rise to $100-150 for a massage with a "happy ending," and swell further from there. And if you have to ask what a happy ending is, might we suggest you skip the massage parlor altogether?

Erotica

Modern porn—at least the film variety—grew up in San Francisco (ah, the memories). The Mitchell Brothers founded their porn empire in the 1960s, making the City a hub for the X-rated film industry until everyone moved south to Los Angeles in the 1980s. You'll still find plenty of good "research" material (film and otherwise) for your sex-capades, but it varies widely in atmosphere and quality.

For some down-n-dirty porn emporiums, flip through **Frenchy's** in the Tenderloin (1020 Geary, 415-776-5940), or the venerable **Big Al's** in North Beach (556 Broadway, 415-391-8510), which claims to have the "best selection of DVDs in the City." For a brighter, more "couples friendly" atmosphere, the place to go is **Good Vibrations** (see box below).

For good old-fashioned film, try the landmark **Mitchell Brothers' O'Farrell Theatre** (895 O'Farrell, 415-776-6686) or any of the much cheaper but dicier adult theaters along Market Street near the Tenderloin.

GOOD VIBES AT GOOD VIBRATIONS

Back in 1977, sex therapist Joani Blank noticed a lack of resources for women seeking quality sexual information and products, so she created her own store to provide a pleasant, clean, and safe shopping experience for women as well as men. From this humble beginning, ***Good Vibrations*** (1210 Valencia, 415-974-8980; 1620 Polk, 415-345-0400; 2504 San Pablo Avenue, Berkeley, 510-841-8987, *www.goodvibes.com*) grew into what is now not only a San Francisco institution, but a nationally recognized resource for sexual education and merchandise. Sex-goody connoisseurs will delight in the Valencia Street location's Vibrator Museum, which takes visitors on a historical journey through the evolution of vibrators, as well as the store's infamous "Wall O'Dildos," which is, we trust, self-explanatory.

Sex Education

If you're serious about getting educated, you're in the right place, as it just so happens that the City is home to the **Institute for the Advanced Study of Human Sexuality** (1523 Franklin, 415-928-1133, www.iashs.edu). Harboring the largest collection of sexual materials in the world, the institute offers advanced degrees in sexology, including masters and doctorate programs. For more relaxed tutelage, try **Good Vibrations** (see previous page). They teach a range of evening classes, from safe sex workshops to BDSM role playing, which—the authors can attest—are both informative and fun.

If you're the shy type, bone up online with **San Francisco Sex Information** (877-472-7374, www.sfsi.org). Their well-maintained site and hotline is a non-judgmental, one-stop information clearinghouse on sex, and their volunteers are extensively trained.

PLACES

Everybody has a favorite outdoor romping ground (don't they?). If you don't, maybe it's time to get one. This list comes from our friends at the ***Bay Guardian*** (415-255-3100, *www.sfbg.com*), who have bravely done some research in the noble interests of journalism and public service. Some people return to these sites year after year—or, in some cases, night after night.

- ***Red Rocks*** (16th Street @ Roosevelt, near the Randall Museum). A little rock enclave above the Castro that's popular with hikers during the day; after dark, it becomes a slice of lurid heaven.

- ***Buena Vista Park*** (Haight @ Lyon). A popular spot at night for anonymous encounters, mainly of the male variety.

- ***Windmills at Golden Gate Park*** (West end of Golden Gate Park). For years known as a gay cruising area for anonymous sex, this spot gets downright seedy.

- ***Angel Island*** (415-435-1915, *www.angelisland.org*). Plan a date with your partner to this state park, and combine fabulous views with plenty of nooks and crannies. Weekdays are best, when it can be almost deserted.

Sex Clubs

If you're really looking to stretch your sexual boundaries, you might consider going to a sex club. San Francisco has several, all legally owned and operated. The only catch—alcohol and other drugs are strictly prohibited. God forbid people mix their alcohol with their orgasms!

Probably the best and most popular is the **Power Exchange** (74 Otis, 415-487-9944, www.powerexchange.com), which caters to just about every imaginable taste and gender. The venue is divided into two separate clubs: one exclusively for gay and bisexual men, and the other for couples and just about everybody else.

Both clubs used to operate seven days a week, but have recently curtailed to 4-5 nights per week (it seems times are tough, even for sex clubs). If a standard night is not wild enough for you, you can sample one of their special events such as the Fetish Ball & Slave Auction. Crack that whip!

Gay and bisexual men might also check out **Eros** (2051 Market, 415-864-3767, www.erossf.com), which emphasizes safe sex, or the overtly-named **Blow Buddies** (933 Harrison, 415-777-4323, www.blowbuddies.com), a private club that caters to a variety of fetishes.

MORE FUN WITH YOUR BODY

Many forms of cosmetic self-expression simply won't fly in an office environment, even if that office *does* have a ping-pong table. But if you're no longer reporting to The Man, it might be time for you to dye your hair a crazy color, stick a big ring in your nose, or get that cool snake tattoo you've been eyeing at the local ink parlor. Lower Haight and the Mission are your neighborhoods of choice in this department. A mid-week field trip can help you research these various body alterations.

Tattoos

Tatt' calling your name? You're in luck—San Francisco's tattoo artists are world-famous. One of the best parlors in town is **Sacred Rose Tattoo** in the Mission (491-A Guerrero, 415-552-5778, www.sacredrosetattoo.com). Just remember—tattoo removal is painful and expensive; anything inked into your skin at 25 should look just as good on you at 50.

Body Piercing

Conveniently located just around the corner from Sacred Rose Tattoo is **Body Manipulations** (3234 16th Street, 415-621-0408, www.bodym.com), where you can obtain any type of body piercing, branding, or "scarification" under the sun, some of which may make you squirm. Body Manipulations merits the distinction of being the oldest piercing studio in San Francisco, and also maintains the best reputation.

Hair

Nothing signifies a break from conventionality quite like fluorescent spiky hair. To get some groove back into your own, try **Edo Salon** in the Lower Haight (601 Haight, 415-861-0131), or **Glama-Rama** in the Mission (417 South Van Ness, 415-861-4526, www.glama-rama.com). Keep in mind when you're done with all that crazy hair, it was your idea, not ours!

WHEN LEISURE BECOMES SLEAZE-URE

What if you find yourself not only on the edge, but over it? Pay attention to your quality of life; these edgy adventures are supposed to improve your life, not detract from it. If you're concerned about whether you're overindulging in drink, drugs, alcohol, sex, gambling or any other vice, get some help.

Leisure Liz	Sleazure Larry
You like going out with your friends.	You no longer have any friends.
You wake up next to a stranger and say, "This could be the start of a beautiful friendship."	**You wake up next to a stranger and say, "Who the !$#@ are you, and what are you doing in my bed? Oh—we're not *in* my bed?"**
You usually have enough money to be able to pay for your entertainment of choice.	You constantly scrounge for jack to support your activities and owe several people money.
You enjoy telling your friends stories about what you did last night or last week.	**You're ashamed to tell your friends what you did last night or last week—assuming you remember it.**

Time to Go on the Wagon?

It's amazing how fast an open tab can drain the budget—especially a leisure budget. For now, consider a sojourn to sobriety. Amy O'Reilly (name changed) gave up drinking after her high-tech employer laid her off, so she "could keep a clear head, and not get too depressed." It worked.

Same goes for other drugs. Dr. Anthony Liguori, assistant professor working in Human Behavioral Pharmacology at Wake Forest Medical Center, has given his monkeys large daily doses of THC (no, you can't get the monkey job). Guess what—it turns out that the constantly stoned really *are* less motivated. If "wake and bake" has become your unemployed motto, it's probably time to give your lungs (and mind) a break.

KNOW WHEN TO FOLD 'EM

Gambling on the Academy Awards isn't going too far—is it?

Cinema fan and leisure connoisseur Dane Larson figured *A Beautiful Mind* and Ron Howard were locks for the 2002 Best Picture and Best Director Oscars. He borrowed on his credit card and bet big—thousands of dollars big—on those two categories. To maximize his potential gains, he also bet on the strong favorite for Best Supporting Actor, Sir Ian McKellen in Lord of the Rings, and tied all three bets together for a movie trifecta. Sadly, the Academy stiffed Sir Ian (so much for knighthood), and Larson's losses in that category wiped out his winnings on the other two awards. Poorer but wiser, he wound up several thousand dollars deeper in debt.

Gambling in excess can lead to financial catastrophe and dash your hopes for a long sabbatical. Day-trading online can too; it's really just gambling in fancier clothes. If you've built up a leisure fund, protect it.

Addictions

A pleasure becomes an addiction when you can't stop, even though you know you should and you aren't even enjoying it anymore. Almost any behavior can become addictive if you're vulnerable, especially if you're depressed.

Here are a few of the organizations that want to help you when you can't help yourself.

- ***Freedom from Smoking***
  800-LUNG-USA, *www.californialung.org*
- ***Nicotine Anonymous***
  415-995-1938, *www.nica-norcal.org*
- ***Gamblers Anonymous***
  800-287-8670, *www.norcalga.com*
- ***Overeaters Anonymous***
  St. Francis Hospital, 900 Hyde @ Pine, 2nd Floor
  415-436-0651, *www.oasf.org*
- ***San Francisco Alcoholics Anonymous***
  415-674-1821, *www.aa-san-francisco.org*
- ***Haight Ashbury Free Clinics***
  Alcohol Treatment Services:
  425 Divisadero #201, 415-487-5634, *www.hafci.org*
  Substance Abuse Treatment Center:
  529 Clayton, 415-565-1908, *www.hafci.org*
- ***Narconon***
  atop Mt. Madonna near Watsonville, CA, 800-556-8885
  www.california-drug-rehab.com

EXERCISE THE POWER OF CHOICE

Whoa, some sobering thoughts to end on. But time off is all about choice, edgy or otherwise. Unemployment can—and should—give you a level of control over your life you've never had before. Time off is the time to take charge, whether it's through experimentation or by setting new goals. If your new personal power includes the physical, read on for a guide to sports and fitness in the City by the Bay.

CHAPTER 7
FITNESS

"Leave all the afternoon for exercise and recreation, which are as necessary as reading. I will rather say more necessary because health is worth more than learning."

~Thomas Jefferson

LET'S face it, getting in shape doesn't happen overnight. Fitness takes time and dedication. But what better challenge to attack when you're unemployed?

Physical activity helps keep you out of the doctor's office, a boon if you're underinsured. It makes you look good. More important, it makes you feel good, and it's the perfect way to maintain a sense of achievement when you don't have an employer to reward your accomplishments.

In fact, staying fit will be more important than ever if you suddenly have fewer commitments. Exercise keeps you moving. Consider it a crucial obligation—to yourself. Others might come to the rescue if you blow your unemployed budget, but no one else can work out for you.

Experts prescribe a minimum of three sessions a week, so get on it! (Sorry, schlepping to Walgreens to buy new batteries for the remote doesn't count.) Set a modest goal if you're just starting—lose 10 pounds, run a 12K race—or simply look good naked. If you're already reasonably fit, choose something more aggressive like competing in a marathon or triathlon. Either way, shoot for a pattern that you can stick with whether your schedule is rigid or flexible. Maintaining a healthy mind and body is yet another key to the lifestyle of leisure.

THE GYM WORKOUT

Once you've committed to fitness, the next choice is where to work out. Gyms are a reliable option. "I got up at 5am every single day and went to the gym," Marsha Converse told us. "It was one of the best things I did for myself after I got laid off."

Private health clubs abound in San Francisco. Their luxury touches vary from the ear-splitting rhythms of **24-Hour Fitness** (eight San Francisco locations, www.24hourfitness.com) to an onsite spa and butternut squash risotto (zero calories, honest!) at the posh **Bay Club** (150 Greenwich, 415-433-2200, www.sfbayclub.com), but even the sparsest weight room will pump you up. Monthly dues vary accordingly.

LOCAL CLUBS	
Club One seven SF locations www.clubone.com	**Sports Club/LA** 747 Market, 888-891-2757 www.thesportsclubla.com
Gold's Gym 2301 Market, 415-626-4488 1001 Brannan, 415-552-4653 www.goldsgym.com	**Crunch Fitness** 1000 Van Ness, 415-931-1100 61 New Montgomery, 415-543-1110 www.crunch.com
Gorilla Sports 2324 Chestnut, 415-292-8470 2450 Sutter, 415-474-2699 2330 Polk, 415-292-5444 www.gorillasports.com	**Pinnacle Fitness** 345 Spear, 415-495-1939 One Post, 415-781-6400 www.pinnaclefitness.com

The deal at the **Embarcadero YMCA** (169 Steuart, 415-957-9622, www.ymcasf.org/embarcadero) may have the most muscle, with no up-front membership fee, no minimum time commitment and moderate monthly dues. The Y's four floors of fitness include a rooftop track, an indoor Olympic-sized pool and classrooms for cardiokickboxing and tae kwon do.

If you get your kicks from Pilates, try a small neighborhood health center such as **Body Kinetics** (2399 Greenwich, 415-931-9922), where classes are limited to four students per instructor. **Simply Balanced Fitness Studio** (2845 California, 415-567-4349) supplies yoga, dance therapy, and a tranquil atmosphere.

The university gyms also make good neighbors. Residents within a certain radius are eligible for annual membership at the first-rate **Koret Health & Recreation Center** (at USF, Turk & Parker, 415-422-6820, www.usfca.edu/koret). Koret's got it all: an Olympic-sized pool (see "Swimming" on p. 260), three basketball courts, five racquetball courts, a weight room, two aerobics studios and one sun deck—for tanning the old-fashioned way. Neighbors who live within the bounds of 3rd Avenue, Lyon, California & Haight can join for $545 per year. Others can buy fifteen-use or drop-in passes, good anytime except Monday through Thursday after 2pm, unless you're taking an aerobics or aquatics course—then any time the class is offered.

Millberry Center (at **UCSF,** 500 Parnassus, 415-476-1115, www.cas.ucsf.edu) is open to neighbors and the general public during liberal off-peak hours. Millberry members receive discounts not only on athletic classes and training, but across a whole spectrum of recreation, from concerts and movies to equipment rentals and outings from UCSF's **Outdoors Unlimited** (550 Parnassus, 415-514-1603, www.outdoors.ucsf.edu, and see the **Unemployed Shopping Guide**).

GYM SLUTTING

Can't decide where to work up a sweat? Try "gym slutting:" going from one free trial membership to another. Most chains offer two weeks gratis to first-time local guests. Hit up five of the franchises in the City, and that's 2+ months of gym membership—for free!

Dana Magenau did just that when he first came to San Francisco. "I felt it was in my best interest to thoroughly investigate the pros and cons of each and every gym out there," he told us with a wink.

The best introductory rates come from yoga and Pilates studios. If the first class isn't free, it's sure to be cheap, as low as a dollar a day on the "90 days for $90" plan at ***Sacred Space Healing Center*** (776 Haight, 415-431-0878, *www.sacredspace-sf.com*). By the time you're done making the rounds to other yoga open houses, you'll probably be back at work. At least with all that stretching, you won't be a corporate stiff.

MIND & BODY

Rough and tumble contact sports not your style? Then peace out through Tai Chi or yoga.

Tai Chi

The **Golden Gate Park Tai Chi Class** (Spreckels Lake, 36th Avenue & Fulton, www.ggptaichi.org) schools students on weekends, no charge. The experts rise, shine, and salute at 6:30am, and beginners join in a couple of hours later. This group also teaches at **City College of San Francisco** (John Adams Campus, Masonic & Hayes), **AP Giannini Middle School** (3151 Ortega, 415-759-2770), and cable Channel 29.

During the week, the faithful practice at Golden Gate Park's 6th Avenue cul-de-sac (a.k.a. **Roller Village**) and in its **Music Concourse** (surrounded by the Academy of Sciences, the closed DeYoung Museum and the former Asian Art Museum). Tai Chi'ers also favor **Washington Square Park** (Columbus & Union) in the wee morning hours.

burn, baby, burn

You might anticipate getting in the best shape of your life with all this time to pump iron. The funny thing is, you'd burn calories just reading, or sunbathing in the park—even rolling a joint! Your basal metabolic rate (BMR) measures how many calories you burn to maintain normal body functions like breathing, heartbeat, and staying warm, and it accounts for 60-70% of the calories you fire through each day.

So if you're firmly planted on the couch watching Oprah, why bother with exercise?

Here's why. Even at rest, a pound of muscle burns more calories than a pound of fat—*twenty-five times* more. True, you'd have to do some serious strength training to add more than five or ten pounds of muscle, but increasing your BMR by building muscle will still give you that extra edge in keeping in shape even when you're sitting on a chair behind a desk.

Calculate your BMR online at ***Global Health & Fitness*** (*www.global-fitness.com*, "Free Fitness Tools").

Their "BMR Calculator" will tell you how many calories you can consume without gaining weight. It takes into account the burn from key leisure activities such as Strolling (210 calories/hour), Golfing with a Pull Cart (300 calories/hour), and Square Dancing (350 calories/hour—yee haw!).

Yoga

Strike a pose with yoga, another way to ease into exercise. **Yoga Tree** (780 Stanyan, 415-

387-4707, www.yogatreesf.com) is a popular studio these days, and it has new locations sprouting up all over the City, including sites in the Mission, Hayes Valley, and the Castro. **The Mindful Body** (2876 California, 415-931-2639, www.themindfulbody.com) will indeed be mindful of your body as you partake in their large selection of Hatha and Ashtanga yoga classes.

Don't let them call it Hot Yoga, though, unless they're paying dues to Bikram Choudhury. He founded *and copyrighted* the routine of 26 Hatha yoga poses performed in a very warm room and known as Bikram Yoga. Bikram is not always a battle—many instructors tailor their sessions to newbies and pregnant women—but advanced practitioners revel in the more competitive environment.

particularly hot studios

Funky Door Yoga
1749 Waller, 415-668-2227
1334 Polk, 415-673-8659
186 2nd Street, 415-957-1088
2567 Shattuck Avenue, Berkeley, 510-204-9642
www.funkydooryoga.com

Global Yoga
2425 Chestnut, 415-292-9774
6300 California, 415-751-6908

Bikram's Yoga College of India
455 Judah, 415-753-8694
www.sunsetbikramyoga.com

THE GREAT OUTDOORS

How 'bout them outdoor workouts? Shuffle along amidst redwood, fir and eucalyptus trees, or whack tennis or croquet balls at **Sigmund Stern Grove** (19th Avenue & Sloat). The adjoining **Larsen Park** has both tennis and basketball courts, plus an indoor swimming pool (see **Sava Pool** in "Swimming" p. 260), although classes soak up most of the pool schedule. **Parkside Square**, also next door, adds a baseball diamond and a court apiece to the tennis and basketball rosters.

The **Presidio** is another free public "gym" available around the clock (see **Bay Area Ridge Trail** under "Biking" p. 268 and "Hiking" p. 271), but for sheer variety and expanse, no City land tops the green acres of **Golden Gate Park**.

Golden Gate Park (415-831-2700) is a one-stop workout shop! The wild and wooly park contains more than 1000 acres of athletic wonderland, compared to 25,000 square feet for a typical San Francisco health club (never mind that 74,999 other "members" will be working out with you on any given weekend). Here's the whole circuit:

• Smash and volley on the 21 recently resurfaced courts in the **Golden Gate Park Tennis Complex** (across JFK Drive from the Conservatory of Flowers, 415-753-7001). Reservations are required for weekends and holidays only; call on Wednesdays between 4-6pm. Get the scoop on rates, free youth tennis and the **Adult Beginning Drop-In Tennis Program** on Saturdays from the clubhouse (415-753-7100). • • Would you rather two-wheel it? Rent a **mountain bike** or **beach cruiser** from **Wheel Fun Rentals** (next to Stow Lake Boat House, 415-668-6699, www.wheelfunrentals.com) and cycle from the top of the Panhandle down to Ocean Beach. Middle Drive is closed to cars on Saturdays. • • Inline skaters should turn out on Sundays and holidays, when JFK Drive is closed to cars between Kezar & Transverse Drives. The **Golden Gate Park Skate Patrol** (volunteers trained in First Aid and CPR) services this emissions-free zone. Sundays attract roller skaters, too (takes you back, doesn't it?). DJ David G. Miles, Jr., a.k.a. the Mayor of Golden Gate Park and the founder of Skate Patrol, starts pumping the jams around noon at **Roller Village**, the park's freshly paved and expanded roller disco (Fulton & 6th Avenue, near the Rose Garden). • Reel down the tempo at the **flycasting ponds** (near JFK Drive & 36th Avenue and the Bison Paddock, 415-386-2630). You'll have to bring your own equipment, but the ponds require no reservation and are considered some of the best in the country. The nearby **Angler's Lodge** is free on Tuesdays, Thursdays, Saturdays and Sundays. • We could get into this no-reservations agenda. Are you with us? Walk right up to the publicly-priced nine-hole **Golden Gate Golf Course** (47th Avenue & Fulton, behind the Beach

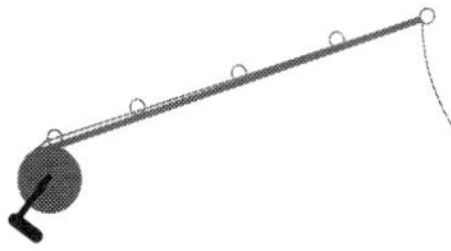

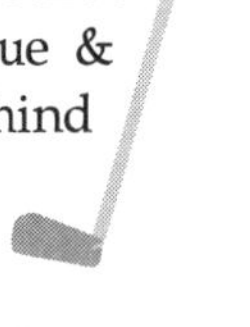

Bikers and bladers will like the smooth race track at the ***Polo Field*** (opposite 35th Avenue), also known as Golden Gate Park Stadium and familiar to many as the Bay to Breakers after-party site (see ***Fairs & Fests***). The Polo Field hosts soccer games and a par course, too.

Chalet, 415-751-8987). Ditto for the two indoor and two outdoor handball courts (on Middle Drive East between Martin Luther King Jr. & Bowling Green Drives, opposite 7th Avenue and north of the Big Rec baseball field). • The **archery field** (47th Avenue just off Fulton) provides bales of hay, but your real target is up to you. Rent equipment at the nearby **San Francisco Archery Pro-Shop** (3795 Balboa, 415-751-2776, www.bysel.com). • Rent a **boat**—row, pedal, or motor—and float around Strawberry Hill and past Huntington Falls in **Stow Lake** (Boathouse near JFK & Cross Over Drives, 415-752-0347). • Horseback riders have been out of their saddles since 2001, when the 130-year-old **stables** closed for renovation. Chaps your hide, does it? Then support the **San Francisco Stables Foundation** (155 17th Avenue, 415-255-2003) in lobbying for new non-profit stables, which would be unique in the City and would offer guided rides along the park's 12 miles of bridle trails. • Or use those trails for hiking. Both bridle and walking trails stretch to almost every corner of the park, including the **Senior Citizens' Exercise Course** (Fulton & 36th Avenue, behind the Senior Center). • Alterna-sportsters play Ultimate Frisbee at the **Kezar Triangle** (just west of Kezar Stadium) and also at **Sunbather Meadow** (across from the handball courts). •

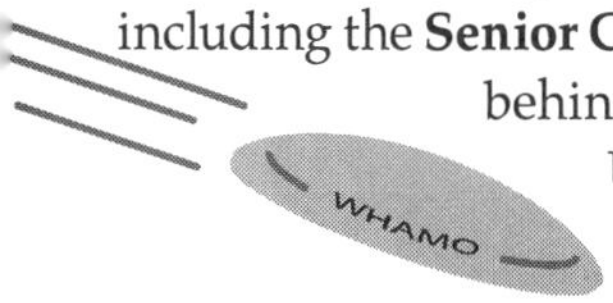

KEZAR STADIUM

Although the site dates back to 1922, the City rebuilt the original ***Kezar Stadium*** (on Frederick, near the Haight) after the 1989 Loma Prieta earthquake. And what a fine job they did! This former home of the San Francisco 49ers now seats 10,000 and houses all-weather track and field facilities for high school football games and other team sports, including ***rugby***.

• Want to join a team that's more conventional? (Hint: it's *not* the Leisure Team.) •  • Play baseball on the two diamonds at **Big Rec Ball Field** (north of 7th Avenue), softball in **Mother's Meadow** (at Waller & Kezar) or at **Speedway Meadow** (JFK Drive south of 24th Avenue), or soccer at the **Beach Chalet Soccer Complex** (just east of the windmill behind the Beach Chalet). The **Athletic Fields Reservation Office** is in **Pioneer Log Cabin** (near Stow Lake, 415-831-5510). • 
• Find feisty pickup basketball in the **Panhandle** (Masonic between Fell & Oak)—no reservations required, just "game." •

WATER SPORTS

Swimming

Hazel Langenour became the first woman to swim across the Golden Gate channel on August 11, 1911 (the same year Californian women won the right to vote). Enquiring minds want to know: did she train at a public pool?

The **Recreation & Park Department** (501 Stanyan, 415-831-2747 for the Aquatic Office, www.sfgov.org, search for "rec park") maintains plenty of heated and affordable public pools: only a dollar a swim for those in "economic need" and just one quid more for a lesson. Recreational swim hours vary by season and are limited at times to an hour a day, but most pools are indoor and large, 40'x100' unless otherwise noted. Facilities include showers, changing areas and bring-your-own-lock lockers.

The functional but spare city pools, however, pale in comparison to the City's best pool: at the **Koret Center** (see in "The Gym Workout" on p. 255). Koret features an Olympic-sized indoor pool (that's 50 meters, in case it's been a while since you've seen the summer Olympics), a competitive masters swim team, even certified lifeguards.

The **Dolphin Swimming & Boating Club** (502 Jefferson, Aquatic Park, 415-441-9329, www.dolphinclub.org) has been a San Francisco institution since 1877. Even local health guru Jack LaLanne is an honorary life member. Dolphins swim at Aquatic Park and escape from Alcatraz (see p. 262). They pay

public pools

Balboa Pool
San Jose & Havelock
415-337-4701

Coffman Pool
Visitacion & Hahn
415-337-4702

Garfield Pool
Harrison & 26th Street
415-695-5001
water aerobics

Hamilton Pool
Geary & Steiner
415-292-2001
masters workouts
water aerobics

King Pool
Carroll & 3rd Avenue
415-822-5707
75'x42' & kid's wading pools

Mission Pool
Linda & 19th Street
415-695-5002
outdoor, summer only

North Beach
Lombard & Mason
415-274-0200
two 90x25 pools
water aerobics

Rossi Pool
Arguello & Anza
415-666-7014
water aerobics

Sava Pool
Wawona & 19th Avenue
415-753-7000
masters workouts
water aerobics

a fair price to do so, but it's worth every penny and jar of petroleum jelly to Dolphin Club Polar Bears—swimmers who log in 40 miles or more during winter. Brrrrr!

GREAT MOMENTS IN UNEMPLOYMENT

Fitness maverick ***Jack LaLanne*** is world-famous for his tireless work ethic, even though he's never clocked in with an "employer" in his life. Instead, he chose a path of entrepreneurship at an early age. As a teen, he was inspired by a crusading nutritionist speaking in Oakland, and discovered the Berkeley YMCA soon after. At age 21—about 40 years ahead of his time—LaLanne opened an Oakland gym, the nation's first modern health club. • • • LaLanne came up with early designs for many of today's weight and exercise machines, and spread the gospel of fitness through a variety of products and media, including a television show that aired daily for an incredible 34 years. At 89, he's still going strong, threatening to celebrate his 90th birthday by swimming—handcuffed and shackled—from Alcatraz to Fisherman's Wharf, a feat he performed at age 60 while towing a 1000-pound boat. In fact, nutty local stunts have always been a staple with LaLanne: at age 40, he swam the length of the Golden Gate Bridge, underwater, with air tanks and 140 pounds of equipment; at age 44 he paddled 30 miles from the Farallon Islands to the San Francisco shore; and he's swum to shore from Alcatraz several times, typically with his limbs bound and thousands of pounds of cargo in tow. Why? To add to the challenge, of course. As LaLanne has shown over and over, ***"If your mind can conceive, your body can achieve."***

Triathlon Clubs

The in-house masters swim team of the **Golden Gate Triathlon Club** (www.ggtc.org) takes care of its water workouts at **Herbst Natatorium** (2001 37th Avenue). The first session is free, then it will run you $6 to drop in and $45 to swim all month. Individual membership in U.S. Masters Swimming is required, at $25 a year.

But why not go the whole nine yards? (Actually, it's a little longer than nine.) Triathlon training is all the rage in San Francisco, especially with women. **Beyond Limits Women's Sports** (415-533-3095, www.beyond-limits.com/triclub) invites athletes of any level to introduce themselves to the club with a free swim or running workout. The **San Francisco Triathlon Club** (www.sftriclub.org) doesn't dangle a freebie to newbies, but a $65 payment to this non-profit will get you 12 months of membership—and a water bottle! Pay $50 to the Golden Gate Triathlon Club (see previous page) to participate in running and biking workouts, as well as swimming, for a year from the day you sign up.

THE ESCAPE FROM ALCATRAZ TRIATHLONS

With all the ways to escape from Alcatraz these days, it's a good thing there's no longer a prison out there. Aside from various swim-only events, no less than three triathlons kick off at the Rock: (1) the ***"New Balance Escape from Alcatraz" Triathlon*** (in June, *www.tricalifornia.com*, 831-373-0678); (2) Envirosport's ***"Alcatraz Escape from the Rock" Triathlon*** (in June, *www.envirosports.com*, 415-868-1829); and (3) the private ***"Escape from Alcatraz"*** cosponsored by the Dolphin Club and its neighbor, the ***South End Rowing Club*** (in October, *www.dolphinclub.org*).

Although each is intense, it's the Dolphin's self-proclaimed "granddaddy of escapes" that's got us thinking. Thinking things like, "Who in their right mind would swim 1.25 miles in the Bay—without a wetsuit or fins—then bike 14 miles over the bridge to Mill Valley, and then run 13 miles over Mount Tam's Dipsea Trail to Stinson Beach and back?"

Dolphins, that's who. These urban polar bears have braved the 50°F-61°F Bay water since 1877, well before Aquatic Park opened to the public in 1939. Cold water swimming generates the development of white blood cells, which fight off disease. Polar Bear Peter Drino claims that no one gets sick at the Dolphin Club. What's another 27 miles of biking and running when you've got health like that?

What would *you* be thinking during the 35 to 100 minutes it takes to swim to shore from the Rock—worrying about sharks? No need. No one's been attacked inside the Golden Gate for over 130 years. Not that we're due or anything…

Rowing & Kayaking

Try the venerable **South End Rowing Club** (500 Jefferson, 415-776-7372) for rowing and swimming, or handball when you're in landlubbing mode. Like the **Dolphin Club** (see "Swimming" p. 260), South End charges non-members $6.50 a day. The Dolphin Club itself has 16 rowboats and several open-water shells, as well as kayaks and a second rowing facility at Lake Merced. **UCSF RecSports** (www.recsports.ucsf.edu) also has a rowing club at Lake Merced, where it rents its rowing equipment to the public for $230 per year.

For more sea kayaking, talk to UCSF's **Outdoors Unlimited** (see in "The Gym Workout" on p. 255)—they offer Ocean Beach outings and moonlight paddles to Angel Island. **Sea Trek** (415-488-1000) rents kayaks on Angel Island itself to those who have experience and a reservation.

skating on thin ice

Okay, so it's frozen, but ice is still H2O, which makes ice skating *sort of* a water sport. Figure your eights or skid to a hockey stop at the only outdoor rink in San Francisco: the **Kristi Yamaguchi Holiday Ice Rink** (Justin Herman Plaza, 415-956-2688), open in winter. (We're talking January here, not June!)

If you'd rather remain indoors, glide over to the **Yerba Buena Ice Skating Center** (above the Moscone Center, 750 Folsom, 415-777-3727, *www.skatebowl.com*).

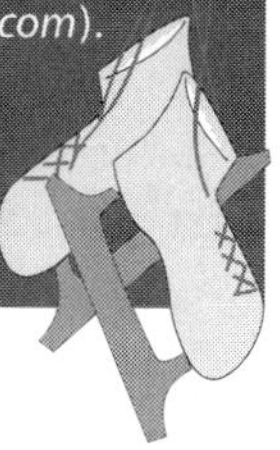

TENNIS

San Franciscans can play the budget-friendly sport of tennis year-round. You might even make a friend or two while you're at it. In fact, the three courts at **JP Murphy Playground** (1960 9th Avenue @ Ortega) boast the best "pick up" tennis in the Bay Area.

The pristine courts of the City's private tennis clubs are for members only. Not only do have you to be a member to use the 12 indoor or 12 rooftop courts of the **SF Tennis Club** (645 5th Street, 415-777-9000, www.sftennis.com), but you have to wrangle an invite from another member just to join. The club does offer *something* for nothing—the excellent pointers on their website!

HOLDING COURT

Rossi Playground Arguello & Anza 415-666-7011 (restored surfaces, new fencing and new benches)	***Mission Dolores Park*** Dolores & 19th Street 415-554-9529 (6 courts)	***McLaren Park*** Mansell & Visitacion 415-337-4700 (8 courts)	***Hamilton Rec Center*** 1900 Geary @ Steiner 415-292-2008 (a pool to splash around in after your match; table tennis, too)
	Moscone Rec Center Chestnut & Buchanan 415-292-2006 (4 courts)	***Mountain Lake Park*** Lake & 12th Avenue 415-666-7005 (ducks and geese)	

GOLF

You might assume that green fees would blow the unemployed budget. Guess again. For only $40/year, SF residents can buy a Golf Resident card and get significant discounts at five of the six city-owned golf courses. Pick one up at **City Hall** (Treasurer's Office, Room 140, 1 Dr. Carlton B. Goodlett Place).

Then tee off for nine holes at the par 27 **Golden Gate Park Golf Course** (see "Ultimate Gym" p. 259) or for a full 18 at the par 68 **Lincoln Park Golf Course** (34th Avenue @ Clement, 415-221-9911). Admire the flora and fauna from the 18 holes of par 72 **Sharp Park** (at the foot of Sharp Park Road off of I-280, Pacifica, 650-359-3380) or turn 9 holes into 18 by teeing off from different pins the second time around at **Gleneagles Golf Course** (in McLaren Park, 2100 Sunnydale, 415-587-2425). (Since Gleneagles is leased to a private management company, your resident card won't work here.)

The 18 holes at the newly renovated **Harding Park Golf Course** (99 Harding Road @ Skyline, near Lake Merced, 415-661-1865) are the crown jewel in the City's golf program. Unless the City totally shanks it, look for the PGA to tote a big pro tourney every three years to what is now being called one of the best municipal courses in the country. The City has also renovated the 9-hole **Fleming Park** (adjacent to Harding Park).

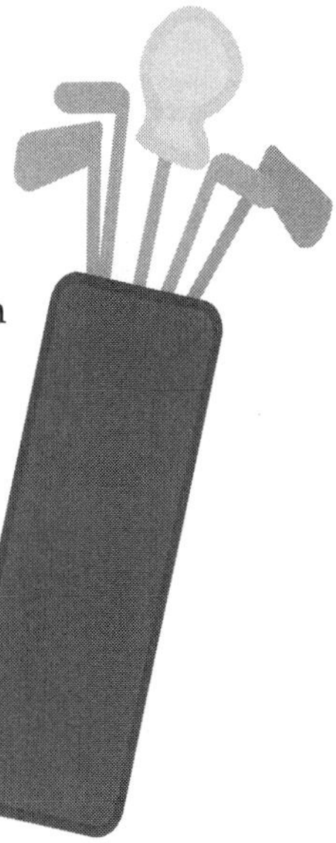

The 18-hole par 71 **Presidio Golf Course** (300 Finley Road @ Arguello in the Presidio, 415-561-4661, www.presidiogolf.com) is privately-owned but open to the public. The Presidio sports a practice center, golf shop, equipment rentals, free clinics—even late afternoon discounts as low as $45 on weekends after 4pm and $25 on weekdays after 5pm. Check online for the latest specials.

Mission Bay Golf Center (1200 6th Street @ Channel & 16th Streets, 415-431-7888) has a two-tiered, 300-yard driving range that's lighted at night, so swing away anytime. Bonus: the center has a bar and restaurant, and is chipping distance from the **Sports Basement** (see the **Unemployed Shopping Guide**), where you can stock up on gear.

BIKING

Swimming? Tennis? Golf? Enough already with the country club sports. It's time to change gears—into biking gear, that is.

If you don't own a bike, a rental will run you about $5/hour or $25/day. Shops providing sales, repairs, parts, and rentals are located throughout the city, but are concentrated around Golden Gate Park and around Fisherman's Wharf. The following stores rent bikes; some rent skates and blades, too.

Fisherman's Wharf Area

Bay City Bike Rentals & Tours
(2261 Taylor @ Beach, 415-346-2453, *www.baycitybike.com)*

Bike and Roll Adventure Bicycle Co.
(734 Lombard; Anchorage Shopping Plaza @ Jefferson & Jones, 415-771-8735, *www.bicyclerental.com*)

Blazing Saddles
(1095 Columbus; 2715 Hyde @ Aquatic Park; Piers 41 & 43; 415-202-8888, *www.blazingsaddles.com*)

Golden Gate Park Area

Golden Gate Park Bike and Skate
(3038 Fulton, 415-668-1117)

Surrey Bikes & Blades
(50 Stow Lake Drive, 415-668-6699)

Avenue Cyclery
(756 Stanyan, 415-387-3155)

critical mass

Despite a bit of road rage from gridlocked drivers and over-zealous cyclists, the "unorganized coincidence" known as ***Critical Mass*** (*www.critical-mass.org* or *www.talkfastrideslow.org*) still rolls through town each month, reclaiming public streets for bicycles with the rallying cry, "We're not blocking traffic, we *are* traffic!"

This two-hour holiday from cars starts from ***Justin Herman Plaza*** (foot of Market @ Embarcadero) at 6pm on the last working Friday of each month. Most participants cheer and holler through the Broadway Tunnel (or wherever else they roll that night) while most onlookers smile and wave them on.

From its humble beginnings with 48 riders in year one, Mass has spread to 300+ cities around the world. In its heyday, you could trace the route by watching where the TV choppers flew. More than 10,000 cyclists turned out to celebrate its tenth anniversary on September 27, 2002.

Find out more in *Critical Mass: Bicycling's Defiant Celebration*, an anthology edited by Chris Carlsson, one of the original riders.

The **San Francisco Bicycle Coalition** (415-431-2453, www.sfbike.org) offers general information on biking in the City, and cooperates with the **Department of Parking and Traffic** and the **Bicycle Advisory Committee** to provide the **San Francisco Bike Map & Walking Guide**. The Bike Map shows street grades, bike lanes, bike paths and three official bike routes—the "Waterfront" (15 miles), the "Tour of Parks" (25 miles) and the "City Loop" (30 miles).

Biking in San Francisco is so good that Henry Kingman wrote a whole book about it: *Short Bike Rides In and Around San Francisco*. Find history, pictures, detailed routing and mileage for rides like the "Sneaky Crosstown Route" and the "Midtown Mosey."

Mountain Biking

You're not obligated to mountain bike just because you live 20 miles from the sport's birthplace, but how can you not? "Downhill runs [are] the ultimate test of handling," according to Joe Breeze of **Joe Breeze Cycles** (P.O. Box 201, Fairfax, www.breezerbikes.com). Them there are fightin' words!

The dirt and rocks of **Mount Tamalpais** in Marin County prompted custom bike-manufacturer Gary Fisher and his friends to deck out their rides, which led to the first formal, timed downhill race and eventually seeded the growth of the whole industry (see box next page). Mount Tam remains one of the country's most visited mountain biking spots. Whether you're heading all the way up or only as far as the Headlands, find downloadable maps and recommended single track, advanced, and winter rides at www.marintrails.com/biking.

GO TELL IT ON THE MOUNTAIN

Otis Guy, Gary Fisher, Tom Ritchey, Joe Breeze and friends could hardly have predicted that their enthusiasm for chugging up Mount Tam's steep slopes (on one-speed bikes!) and barreling back down again would earn them a place in local lore. After all, they weren't the first ones to do it.

A group of cyclists known as the Canyon Gang held their earliest races on Mount Tam in 1971, aided by the "balloon tire:" a tire phat and knobby enough to handle the punishment of rapid off-road descents. Five years passed before the first official race on October 21, 1976, down the east face of Pine Mountain just north of Mount Tam. The blistering speeds so hammered the riders' coaster brakes that they had to re-pack their hubs with new grease in order to make the ride again. The trail itself became known as Repack, still a popular and intense 2-mile, 1300-foot downhill bomb for the fearless.

A San Jose manufacturer released the first mass-produced mountain bike in 1981—the Specialized Stumpjumper. Mountain bike sales tripled every year for several years after that, and annual unit sales since 1984 have averaged close to ten million. Even the Olympic Committee has cashed in on the action by offering a medal in cross-country mountain bike racing.

All because some Marin-ites had the need for speed.

touring

While they're nowhere near as ubiquitous as mountain bikers (or bike messengers, for that matter), long-distance riders do have a place in the City. Even touring tourist Lance Armstrong visits—along with the other top cyclists who compete in September's ***T-Mobile International*** (formerly the San Francisco Grand Prix; start and finish at Pier 1, *www.sanfrancycling.com*).

Those who'd rather pedal than spectate can spin along the local segment of the ***Pacific Coast Bicycle Route*** (*www.adv-cycling.org*, under "Bike Routes" then "Pacific Coast"). Route 95 stretches a full 1,830 miles from Oregon to Mexico, rolling through San Francisco along the way.

If you go off road (as you should) in Golden Gate Park, hit it on a weekday so you don't run into (or over!) pedestrians. Most of the trails are bike-legal, although you'll see tell-tale treads on a few no-bike zones anyway.

The Presidio, on the other hand, closes most trails to mountain bikes. The bikeable portion of the **Bay Area Ridge Trail** (415-561-2595, www.ridgetrail.org) in the Presidio runs a puny 2.5 miles. Yet, as **San Francisco Mountain Biking** (www.sfmtb.com) envisions it, an official Presidio Loop could be so much more—10.1 miles and an 1140-foot elevation gain. Download the *San Francisco Mountain Biking Map* from their site, plus see maps of challenging routes such as The San Francisco Epic (24.62 miles, 1661-foot elevation gain) and the Mount Davidson There-And-Back (over 18 miles and 1146 feet up).

What, you want *more?* Then snag a copy of *Mountain Bike! Northern California* by Linda Austin, which details 100 rides. If you'd like some in-person advice, chat with the nice folks at **Valencia Cyclery** (1077 Valencia, 415-550-6601, good for beginners to intermediates) or **American Cyclery** (858 Stanyan, 415-876-4545; 510 Frederick, 415-664-4545, www.americancyclery.com), which specializes in advanced riding gear.

Excursions

Some cyclists simply seek leisure. (Say *that* ten times fast!) For those who favor fun over fitness, we highlight three sightseeing rides.

The first is **49-Mile Scenic Drive**—map available online (www.sfvisitor.org, click on "Maps" then "Citywide Map") or in hard copy at the **San Francisco Visitor Information Center** (Hallidie Plaza, 900 Market @ Powell, 415-391-2000). It could take a while to bike this baby (4-6 hours of riding time, plus frequent beer, snack, and photo-op stops) so bring a lock. You'll want to replace the freeway stretches with some alternate streets so consult the map on that one. Beware of a few ambitious hills, including Twin Peaks, Land's End, and California Street on Nob Hill. If it suits you, don't hesitate to stretch the trek out over several days, as any *leisure connoisseur* would.

Make the much shorter jaunt across the Golden Gate Bridge any time of day or night. No schedule, that's leisurely too! The bridge ride covers only 1.7 miles, unless you tack on the climb to the Marin Headlands. You must ride on the east side path on weekdays between 6:30am and 3:30pm, and on the west side path at any other time. No pedestrians are allowed on the west side path, not ever, so if you're prone to collisions, that's the path for you.

Pedal from there to **Sam's Anchor Café** (27 Main Street, Tiburon, 415-435-4527, www.samscafe.com). The ride from the City is only half the fun! Follow the old Southern Pacific Railroad tracks (which used to connect to a ferry station in Sausalito) and then the scent of Eggs Benedict and Bloody Marys. Afraid you'll get a little tipsy while you're there? By all means, take the ferry back!

parcourses

With a name as dated as "Jazzercise," parcourses are indeed a throwback, but we'll bet you didn't know that they arrived in the U.S. via San Francisco. Back in 1973, a Bay Area real estate developer named Peter Stocker, after seeing similar courses in Europe, assembled the very first stations in ***Mountain Lake Park*** (the Presidio, near Park Presidio @ Lake) using handmade wooden signs.

Amazingly, a few remain around San Francisco (unlike Ripley's Museum, believe it or not!). Instructions on exercises like the Achilles stretch, log hop, vault-bar and up to two dozen others are evenly spaced throughout courses on ***Marina Boulevard***, in **Golden Gate Park** (around the Polo Field), and around ***Lake Merced***. For a quicker workout, ride your bike between stations. Or, roll your own par course: do calisthenics at regular intervals during a run.

ON FOOT

Walking

Walking is a great way to kickstart a lapsed cardio program. Take a walk in the park—any park—or, for a more urban adventure, stroll along the Embarcadero adjacent to the Financial District. What was once an industrial wasteland is now a delightful waterfront promenade, seven miles from end to end.

Another visually appealing and easy

waterfront walk is the Golden Gate Promenade, four miles from Aquatic Park past the Marina Green to Fort Point. Stock up on supplies at the (oh my gawd!) **Marina Safeway** (15 Marina @ Laguna). Perambulate past the kite-flyers on the **Marina Green** (Marina Boulevard between Scott & Webster), pass the volleyball players near the **Yacht Club**, and sail on into **Crissy Field** (see **Chapter 4**). If you're feeling ambitious, continue an extra 1.7 miles across the Golden Gate Bridge. Only the east side is open to pedestrians, but that's okay—you'll enjoy unobstructed views of the famous skyline.

Oh, did we forget to mention that hill? The foot of the bridge looms a couple hundred feet above Fort Point. Alex So (name changed) knows the route well. "I was on a serious walking regime after having a quintuple bypass," he told us, "but the hills were really killing me." Oh, the irony! Alex complained to his doctor. The prescription? More hills! "When I'm not trudging up to the bridge, I walk the crooked part of **Lombard Street** (between Hyde & Leavenworth)—backwards." See "Running Stairs" p. 272 if you're inclined to find more inclines.

Head back to the flatlands along the **Great Highway**. You'll have to share the trail with bicyclists and joggers, but the smell of the salt air will make any congestion worth braving. Starting at the south end (Great Highway @ Sloat Boulevard) and walking north will lead you to two national Landmarks just below the **Cliff House** (1090 Point Lobos, 415-386-3330, www.cliffhouse.com)—the **Giant Camera** (an antique camera obscura that produces 360-degree views of the Seal Rock area, closed for renovation until 2004) and the **Musée Méchanique** (also being renovated but filled with old-time coin-operated entertainment—player pianos and fortune-telling machines). If you've practiced on any of San Francisco's other steep streets, the ramp up from sea level to the landing above Seal Rock will be a breeze.

Hiking

What mountain biking is to touring, hiking is to walking. The same dirt trails allow for similar off-road adventure—just at a slower pace.

More than 50 miles of trails weave through the 6300 acres of redwood groves and oak woodlands in the **Marin Headlands** (just north of the Golden Gate Bridge). Those who conquer the climb to the 2571-foot peak of **Mount Tamalpais** (801 Panoramic Highway, Mill Valley, 415-388-2070) will be rewarded with amazing views and maybe even refreshments—the stand is open daily during summer and on weekends the rest of the year. The picnic tables stay put year-round.

Back in San Francisco proper, **Land's End** trails run from Seacliff to the former site of the **Sutro Baths** (near Point Lobos @ 48th Avenue). The trailhead for the Presidio's 2.5 mile stretch of the **Bay Area Ridge Trail** (see "Biking" p. 268) is near Arguello Gate and the Presidio Golf Course Clubhouse.

ANGEL ISLAND

Angel Island is the largest island in the bay, making ***Angel Island State Park*** (415-435-1915, *www.angelisland.org*) quite popular in summer for hiking, biking and camping. Its fire roads and foot trails include 8 miles of steep roadway and the 5-mile mostly-flat Perimeter Trail. If you're up for a little altitude adjustment, take the short but angular Northridge/Sunset loop trail to the Mount Livermore summit—the 360-degree view is fantastic.

You'll have to pack your gear up the same steep slope to reach the island's nine campsites, each equipped with a picnic table, food locker, running water, pit toilet, and BBQ (no wood fires allowed), but having the park to yourself after the last ferry leaves and being able to see the night lights of San Francisco and the Golden Gate Bridge right from your sleeping bag will more than make up for the cold, wind, and fog. Or so says Tom Stienstra, author of not only *California Hiking* but also *California Camping*. Call ***ParkNet*** (800-444-7275) for reservations.

Unless you're up for a frigid swim through a major shipping channel filled with sweeping currents, the way to get there is on the ***Blue & Gold Fleet*** (Pier 41, Fisherman's Wharf, 415-705-8200, *www.blueandgoldfleet.com*). It takes 40 minutes each way and costs $10.50 round trip, which covers the park entry fee.

Ferry service is slightly more frequent on the ***Angel Island-Tiburon Ferry*** (415-435-2131, *www.angelislandferyy.com*), at least on weekends, but you'll have to start from Tiburon. If you go this route, work up an appetite hiking first, then head over to ***Sam's Anchor Café*** (see "Biking" p. 269) for a refreshing adult beverage.

For more hiking routes, see the comprehensive alphabetical trail index posted on **San Francisco Bay Area Hiker** (www.bahiker.com), or find a copy of *California Hiking* by Tom Stienstra & Ann Marie Brown.

Jogging (Or Is It Running?)

Even though you can jog just about anywhere you can walk or hike, certain spots attract more joggers than others. The trail around **Lake Merced** (Harding Road off Skyline) is one of them, as is Ocean Beach at low tides when the sand is hard and flat. The Embarcadero is popular with the corporate set at lunchtime or after work.

Want a lane of your own? Circle a track at a high school or at **Kezar Stadium** (see "Golden Gate Park" p. 259). If you trot out to **Fort Point**, find the painted handprints (and doggie paw prints!) on the wall and give 'em ten. They're there to give you a sense of completion.

Stay fit (and meet people too) all for the low, low price of $0 with **Hash House Harriers** (415-409-4274, www.sfh3.com), or join the members of the **San Francisco Road Runners Club** (415-273-5731, www.sfrrc.org) on Tuesday nights or Saturday mornings, year-round. Although

an urban workout: running stairs

For a really intense workout, hustle up and down any of the City's more than 350 stairways.

At the pinnacle of difficulty is the set in the 'Set, a.k.a. the ***Temple of Doom*** (between 16th Avenue & Funston; Moraga & Pacheco), which features a series of steep stairs, ratcheting ever-skyward (they don't call it the "Temple of Doom" for nothing!). The Temple is frequented by runners and surfers, and includes a natural (unnatural?) chin-up bar over the first set of stairs for interval training.

No less difficult are the ***Lyon Street Stairs*** (ascending from Green to Broadway), which Marina-types ascend to stick closer to home. Should you miss the tourists on your way up the ***Coit Tower Stairs*** (Filbert @ Telegraph Hill Way) from North Beach, look for them as you trot back down the hillside via the ***Filbert Street Steps*** (from Sansome to Coit Tower) to the landscaped Levi Plaza.

Thank you sir, may I have another? Yes, you may. Locate all the stairs your heart (pumping, undoubtedly) desires in *Stairway Walks in San Francisco* by Adah Bakalinsky.

SFRRC's annual membership is not cheap, the first gallop is always free and drop-ins cost just $5—plus the ubiquitous liability-waiver form. Who needs rights when you can run with the fast crowd?

The **MetroSport San Francisco Run Club** (415-923-6453, www.e-metrosport.com) welcomes runners of all levels, even those who merely jog. Meet them on Wednesdays at the corner of Filbert & Fillmore for six to eight miles, no charge (just don't bogart the refreshments, they're for members only). World class athletes occasionally join similar Wednesday freebies of about five miles, no set route (but lots of hills), sponsored by the **Niketown San Francisco Running Club** (278 Post @ Stockton, 415-392-6453). Niketown's refreshments are free for everyone, plus they throw a monthly raffle and occasional seminars into the mix.

non-race footraces

Although it's not competitive for the vast majority of participants, San Francisco's ***Bay to Breakers*** (see FAIRS & FESTS) is the largest footrace in the world. In fact, the crowd is so dense for the first mile or two, you couldn't run it if you tried.

"Drinkfest" would be a better word than "footrace" to describe the ***Urban Iditarod*** (*www.urbaniditarod.com*). Still, this trek around the City by humans imitating canines does involve sneakers, a stop watch and a winner's stand. Throw in a few shopping carts and you've got yourself a race. Woof!

If you're old enough to remember Wayne Walker, you are way overdue for a sabbatical. This former 49er and local sportscaster threw down the gauntlet to Race the Cable Cars up Hyde Street. Beaten badly, Wayne was, back in the day when this kind of promo (for Rice-a-Roni?) was still original. Wait, it still is!

Running & Racing

Any doubts about when you graduate from jogging to running? A ticking clock and a number safety-pinned to your shirt will dispel them. It's a race. You paid money. You'd *better* be running!

Racing is a great way to measure progress, as well as augment your wardrobe. (Another t-shirt? At least this one doesn't scream "dot-com victim!") Challenges, ranging from short course to long, start with the 5K run/walk and 10K **Run to the Far Side** (Golden Gate Park, produced by RhodyCo Productions: 415-759-2690, www.rhodyco.com). Contestants, in costume or out, race through scenic Golden Gate Park in November. All racers gain free admission to the California Academy of Sciences.

Will you run faster in June when you **See Alice Run** (Golden Gate Park, produced by RhodyCo Productions: 415-759-2690, www.rhodyco.com)? Maybe the concerts and giant post-race party will sustain you through the 5 mile (8K) run and walk through Golden Gate Park. You'll have to push a little harder for the **Bridge to Bridge Run** (Bay Bridge to Golden Gate Bridge, 415-995-6868, www.bridgetobridge.com), a 12K sanctioned race (or 7K run and 5K walk). Everyone starts together in front of the Ferry Building.

The **San Francisco Half-Marathon & 5K** in January (415-333-4780, www.pamakids.org) is one of the nicest half marathons around, starting and ending in Golden Gate Park with a romp alongside the Pacific Ocean en route. If you're prepared to go the full distance, enter the **San Francisco Marathon** (415-284-9653, www.chroniclemarathon.com), the last Sunday in July.

friday night skate

So you're groovin' out at the ***Bus Stop***, imbibing a fine malt liquor and admiring your own hip-hugging boot-cut jeans. You sense a growing buzz, vaguely '70s and strangely familiar. The Bay City Rollers? (S, A, T-U-R, D-A-Y, *night!)*

No, this is *Friday* night, and the hum you hear is from the spinning wheels of the ***Midnight Rollers***, San Francisco's own neo-retro skate group.

Participating in a ten-year-old tradition, inliners and rollers alike gather from all over the Bay Area to make this crazy circuit-skate. The pre-skate dance commences at 8pm in ***Justin Herman Plaza***, rolls all around the City—even through the Broadway Tunnel—and ends up back where it began.

For more info on this and other City skating, contact David Miles (415-752-1967, *www.cora.org*).

TEAM SPORTS

Few endeavors fire up the competitive engines faster than team sports, where winning's not everything, it's the only thing—besides the beer and pizza after the game, that is.

Working out with others will keep you enthused about sports and focused on a group goal. You'll keep those sports metaphors current, too, in case you head back to a workplace where phrases like "dropping the ball" and "hitting a home run" are common parlance (see also "Bullshit Bingo" in **Chapter 12**).

Rec Leagues

League play in the City ranges from mainstream, at the **Golden Gate Sport and Social Club** (see **Chapter 8**), to

C-level, with **San Francisco Mullets Women's Basketball** (they're looking for a center; contact Julie Lane, jujulie_1969@hotmail.com). Organized street and roller hockey leagues compete at school playgrounds in the Marina (try **Bladium In-Line Hockey League**, 510-814-4999, www.bladium.com). If the words "full contact" excite you, play with the **Bay Area SheHawks (BASH) Women's Rugby Club** (www.bashrugby.com). And **Team SF** (www.teamsf.org) invites everyone under the sun (and the rainbow) to organize and/or participate in just about any sport imaginable (table tennis, anyone?). None of these catch your fancy? Then start a league of your own! If Madonna and Geena Davis can do it, you can too.

MAKE THE MOUNTAIN COME TO YOU

Rockclimbing at ***Yosemite*** (see ***Chapter 5***) is a world-class pursuit that you can practice far closer to home, at ***Mission Cliffs*** (2295 Harrison, 415-550-0515, *www.mission-cliffs.com*). By local climbers' accounts, Mission Cliffs rocks. "It's a great place to connect with other climbers and plan outdoor excursions, as well as learn the basics if you're new to the sport," says climber Heather Emigh.

Mission Cliffs boasts a 50-foot lead wall and a bouldering cave, as well as a fully-equipped weight room, locker room, and sauna. Day passes run $10 on weekdays before 3pm, $18 at other times. Rent equipment for $5 more. The $100 you drop on a one-month pass (or the $160 for ten visits) can be applied toward the initiation fee if you later decide to join.

Pickup or Drop In

Can't handle the obligation of an organized league? That's perfectly natural. It's a symptom of *job churn*—a condition brought on by a little too much structure.

Play pickup or drop in instead. The eligibility rules for the **UCSF Drop In Leagues** (www.recsports.ucsf.edu) couldn't be simpler: just show up and pay! Women's basketball runs $20 per quarter, and volleyball and badminton are each $18 for 5 drop-ins. The tennis club charges $20 per person per quarter, student or not, to cover the cost of reserving the courts.

For pickup basketball—if you've got game—travel to the courts in the **Panhandle** (between Fell & Oak near Masonic), at **Duboce Park** (Scott & Duboce), or on many other playgrounds. **Potrero Hill Recreation Center** (801 Arkansas, 415-695-5009) also sports courts, as well as a gymnasium, a baseball diamond, tennis courts, and a playground, plus an O.J. Simpson mural (which you can revere or throw tomatoes at, depending on your perspective).

Jackson Playground (17th Street between Carolina & Arkansas, 415-554-9528) fields baseball, a playground, and yet more basketball, both indoor and outdoor. Soccer is a little harder to find, but try the new fields at **Dolores Park** (Church/Dolores & 18th/20th Streets, 415-551-3660).

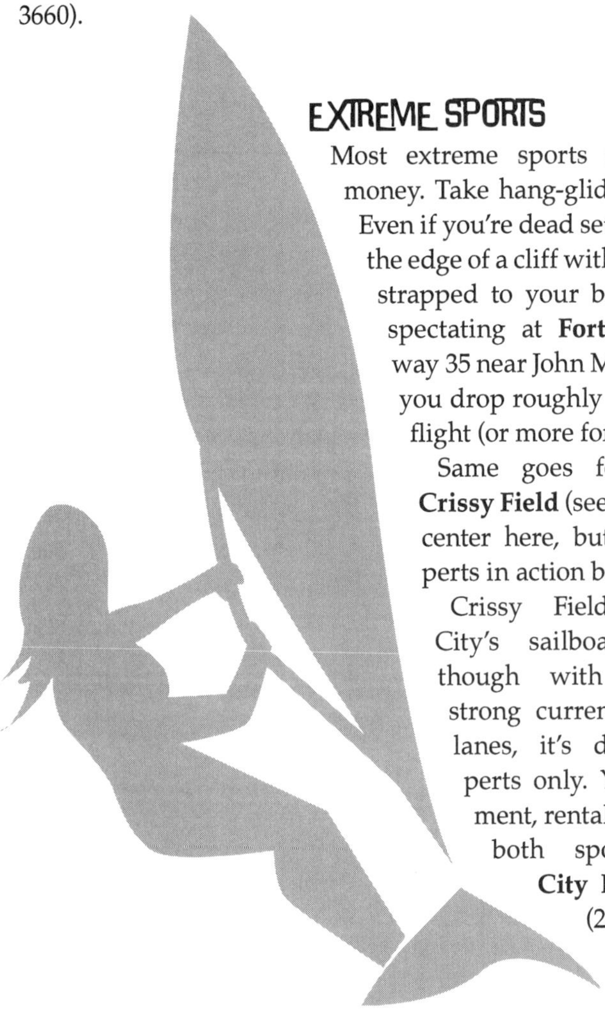

EXTREME SPORTS

Most extreme sports require extreme money. Take hang-gliding, for example. Even if you're dead set on careening off the edge of a cliff with synthetic wings strapped to your back, think about spectating at **Fort Funston** (Highway 35 near John Muir Drive) before you drop roughly $300 per tandem flight (or more for lessons).

Same goes for kiteboarding: **Crissy Field** (see **Chapter 4**) is the center here, but observe the experts in action before you dive in. Crissy Field is also the City's sailboarding hub, although with heavy winds, strong currents and shipping lanes, it's definitely for experts only. You'll find equipment, rentals, and lessons for both sports at nearby **City Front Sailboards** (2936 Lyon, 415-929-7873).

Surfing

Want an experience that's as leisurely as it is extreme? Go surfing. "Surfing was made for unemployment, and it's no coincidence that the two go hand in hand," says local surfer Ted Witt. "You can cruise up and down the coast endlessly looking for the best possible spot, wait out the swell or tide, and stay out as long as you want."

Surfing **Ocean Beach** (Great Highway from Balboa to Sloat) could be considered a pretty good workout, experts only. For training, some surfers paddle there from **Aquatic Park** (see "Swimming" p. 260)—the recklessly ambitious kick off from the Bay Bridge—then head through the Golden Gate and around. Tip: try to stay with the tide.

For the best selection of boards and wetsuits, drop into **Wise Surfboards** (800 Great Highway, 415-750-9473); for cool clothes to go with, hit **Aqua Culture Surf & Snowboard** (2830 Sloat, 415-242-9283); and for the underground connection, slide into **SF Surf Shop** (3809 Noriega, 415-661-7873).

Skateboarding

"Skating is not a crime!" so goes the rally-cry. In SF, however, many sidewalk areas remain "legally" off limits to skaters. That doesn't seem to quell the City's strong skate culture. Bullet down **Fell Street** for an adrenalin-pumping downhill run (if you can time the lights, that is). For street skating, cruise along the **Embarcadero** or in and around **Kezar Stadium**. To get more space, local downhill carver Chris Flesher prefers the Sunset slopes out towards the beach. "I like to come down Ortega when the sun is out because you get a good look at the ocean with the afternoon sun shining on it." Watch out for those stop signs!

Skates on Haight (1818 Haight, 415-752-8375, www.skatesonhaight.com; 1219 Polk, 415-447-1800, www.skates.com) is *the* preeminent skate shop in town. The Haight Street location can outfit all of your skateboarding needs and provide in-line rentals, while the Polk Street virtual store (internet orders only) will roll you through the in-line world.

Adventure Clubs

The list of extreme adventures is extremely long. Sample them all—bungee jumping, skydiving, cave crawling, snowboarding, rafting—with an adventure club:

- ***Bay Area Outdoor Adventure Club***
  415-954-7190, *www.outdooradventureclub.com*
- ***Adventurous Woman Sports***
  Pier 38, Suite 1, 415-397-7678, *www.adventurous.com*
- ***Outdoor Action Fitness***
  415-383-3186, *www.outdoorfitness.com*
- ***Absolute Adventures***
  415-505-5964, *www.absoluteadv.com*
- ***girlsAdventureOUT***
  510-465-0016, *www.girlsadventureout.com*

GET OUT THERE

As the Bay Area Outdoor Adventure Club says—try new sports, meet new people! Mine the next chapter for even more ideas on how to add a little pizzazz to your social calendar.

CHAPTER 8
FAMILY & SOCIAL LIFE

Nobody sees a flower—really—it is so small it takes time—we haven't time—and to see takes time, like to have a friend takes time.

~Georgia O'Keeffe

IF you're like many hardworking, career-oriented individuals, your social life suffered during your last bout of over-employment. Long hours, the daily pressures of demanding jobs, and work-related travel conspire to sap our relationships.

Time off, on the other hand, provides an excellent opportunity to revitalize your social life, whether you're married or single, young or old. Even if you're gainfully employed, you can still make the time to improve your relationships. After all, our social connections are truly the juice of life!

So what are you still doing at home? Get out there!

San Francisco is a mad city—inhabited for the most part by perfectly insane people whose women are of a remarkable beauty.

~Rudyard Kipling

GET OUT AND MEET SOMEONE!

Flirting Before 5pm

People are surprisingly more approachable during the day. As an alternative to the typical night spots (i.e., bars and nightclubs), try cafés, retail shops, or galleries during daytime hours. Choose places where you're comfortable, and have other reasons for being there.

Chapter 4 lists our favorite "hanging out" cafés, but not the **San Francisco Museum of Modern Art** (151 3rd Street, 415-357-4000, www.sfmoma.org), a great place to meet other art aficionados. The affiliated **Cafe Museo** (415-357-4500) right next door provides an easy transition step for that chance encounter. Try the first Tuesday of *every* month, when admission is free.

Union Square is an untapped wellspring for new acquaintances or a worldly romance. Thousands of shoppers, both international and local, descend upon this downtown area daily. Should you make a connection while trying on that coat at Macy's, amble over to **Café Claude** (7 Claude Lane @ Bush, 415-392-3505), a hip joint just off Union Square. For a more swanky atmosphere, try afternoon tea or a cocktail at the **Compass Rose Lounge** in the lobby of the **Westin Saint Francis Hotel** (335 Powell, 415-397-7000).

Enroll in Activities

That old adage is trite but true: you'll meet people who share your interests when you go do things you like to do. So sign up for a class, join a group, or take up a new sport.

Marina Sarmiento, a single attorney in San Francisco, touts organized dancing as a no-hassle way to make new friends. She swings into action at something called *Lindy in the Park*, a swing dance group that meets every Sunday from 11am–2pm at the **Band Shell (**near the

California Academy of Sciences). "It's a great way to meet people, and you don't have to worry about getting turned down to dance," Marina tells us. "There's a swing dancing etiquette, so you don't get that meat market feel."

Straight male leisure seekers take note: yoga classes have great gender ratios, primarily filled with women! Plus, the atmosphere is soothing and relaxed. Just don't intrude on others' space during their practice. Particularly social studios include the Stanyan Street location of **Yoga Tree** (780 Stanyan, 415-387-4707, www.yogatreesf.com), and **Global Yoga** (2425 Chestnut, 415-292-9774; 6300 California, 415-751-6908), which specializes in Bikram Method Yoga. Both are top studios in the fitness sense as well (see **Chapter 7** under "Yoga").

Single women, don't despair; team sports tilt the odds back in your favor, whether you're watching or playing. Sports bars during football season are packed on Saturday and Sunday afternoons; tackle them all, and then bring your own game to a local sports league. **Golden Gate Sport and Social Club** (415-921-1161, www.ggsportandsocialclub.com) is the premier organization for adult sports leagues in San Francisco, and offers everything from softball to street hockey. Coed football teams match five men with three women—see, your odds are already improving!

Artsy types looking for a queer connection may prefer the **Queer Cultural Center** (www.queerculturalcenter.org), a virtual organization that showcases and promotes queer artists' work. Its site lists local gay art events, among other information.

scrumming

If the words "tight scrum" are enough to get you sweaty, take the word of same-sex seekers who tell us that rugby is a fruitful way to "interact" with other gays. The ***San Francisco Fog*** (415-267-6100, *www.sffog.org*) is a club that is, by their own description, "principally composed of men of color and gay men," so there you go.

Women wanting to run and scrum can look into the ***San Francisco Golden Gate Women's Rugby Club*** (*www.geocities.com/sfwomenrugby*), or the ***Bay Area SheHawks*** (510-433-7187, *www.bashrugby.org*). Note that neither club explicitly promotes itself as a lesbian rugby club.

Host Parties

Now's the perfect time to throw that dinner or cocktail party. Ask your friends to invite some new people, and you can do the same. Small gatherings are a great way to make new acquaintances. The more ambitious can host an "unemployed" theme party: have everyone bring their best (and worst) unemployed stories, and play games such as Layoff Lamenting (or the "How I Got Laid Off" one-upping game), or Travel Challenge—whoever has the best travel story wins.

Marina Sarmiento, our resident swing dancer, became legendary among friends for her enticing singles parties. "I got the idea from 'Sex and the City.' They had a 'recycling' party, but I didn't want to call mine that. So I named it 'The Single, Mingle, Tingle, Wine Soirée.' Everyone was required to bring a single friend and a bottle of wine, or they weren't allowed through the door." The parties are on hiatus now: Marina's first four were so successful, she's had a boyfriend for more than a year.

Dating Services and Social Clubs

We know, we know—modern dating services and social clubs aren't for everyone. But several of you have claimed success, or at least positive experiences, so we're going to pass along a few recommendations.

Not surprisingly, tech-savvy San Francisco is very open to the whole online dating phenomenon. The pre-eminent service is **Match.com** (www.match.com), where users can search through thousands of potential "matches." This includes any combination of gender matches—boy meets girl, girl meets boy, girl meets girl, boy meets boy (but not anything in between!). It takes a while to go through all the postings but hey, time is (hopefully) what you got.

Be warned: the City is a small community, and your anonymity isn't assured. Make sure you're comfortable with others knowing you're using the service. Just ask Kurt Fenton (name changed), a technology strategist in San Francisco, whose degree of separation from a woman he met on Match.com was just one: "I couldn't believe it—I had just started using the service. I went out on one date, and it turns out the girl was my friend's roommate!" He still recommends the service, though.

A singles' group exclusively for the Bay Area is **Table for Six** (888-640-4646, www.tableforsix.com). Members dine with others of like interests in groups of six at restaurants throughout the Bay Area. Everyone pays for their own dinner, avoiding any awkwardness surrounding the bill. Check, please?

Urban Diversion (1329 Columbus, Suite B, 415-776-7455) is a social adventure club that aims to divert from the norm by throwing folks together through sky diving, river rafting, and other pulse-quickening activities. Member Marcus Ronaldi likes the departure. "Urban Diversion puts the emphasis on fun, not on treating dates like job interviews." The coolest part? They have their own clubhouse hideaway for members, complete with a tiki bar!

Single women can look into **Spinsters of San Francisco** (415-437-4990, www.sfspinsters.com), an all-women's philanthropic group that isn't a singles group *per se* (or so they say), but one that definitely has a strong social emphasis. The sorority-averse need not apply. The **Bachelors of San Francisco** (P.O. Box 26237, SF, CA 94126), the oldest social club in the City, is also mixing and mingling—often with the Spinsters. Send them a postcard if you want to hang out. Adventurous gay men and women can give **San Francisco Gay Singles** (www.sanfranciscogaysingles.com) a whirl.

the need for speed

Speed dating is a new idea that might be zooming to a bar near you. An LA rabbi invented the concept in 1999 to help connect Jewish singles, and it's now blossomed into a full-fledged industry.

Single men and women of pre-determined age ranges go to a bar and meet each other through a series of rapid "dates," usually ten minutes or less. After the meetings, potential matches indicate whether they'd like to contact the other person; if both parties agree, they share contact information.

San Francisco bachelor J.J. Dillon recently experienced this social phenomenon. "Any woman who asked me what I did outside of work stayed on my list," he told us, "and any woman who asked what kind of car I drove did not."

Believe it or not, dozens of companies would like to whisk you around the dating block. One of the biggest and best-run is ***8minuteDating*** (*www.8minutedating.com*), which boasts five event organizers in SF alone. Another homegrown escort is ***Impact Date*** (*www.impactdate.com*), which floats among the swankiest joints in town.

Volunteer

That's right, volunteer; the hidden perk is social interaction. Work at an event you couldn't otherwise afford, such as the Cystic Fibrosis Foundation's Great Strides event, or one of the American Cancer Society's evening galas. You'll meet a ton of new people, usually in a relaxed setting. Plus, you get the bonus of knowing you're helping a cause.

Valerie Britt started the **A-List Special Events Calendar** (415-567-3165, www.thealist.info) e-mail list in 1998 to provide a select list of the "very best parties, charity galas, and special events in and around the San Francisco Bay Area." Sign up for her e-mails if you want to stay in the know.

josh finds his muse

"As a writer, you always need fresh ideas to play with," says San Franciscan Josh McHugh. "The ideas that come to you via media, whether TV, print, or even the Web, are, by definition, processed and, as a result, a bit stale. The good stuff comes from live conversations."

Josh recently spent the better part of a Friday tooling around Fillmore Street in Pacific Heights, with ***Tully's*** (2455 Fillmore, 415-929-8808), a hub of community activity, serving as ground zero. Among those he met were a construction foreman, a professional musician, a dot-com-forced-retiree-turned-coffeehouse-manager, and a baby-toting mom doubling as a caterer and taking her own baby steps—as a home IT network administrator.

"Talking with humans, face to face, is by far the best way to get brand-new ideas bouncing around," Josh reports. "Plus, shooting the shit with people in a coffee shop is a lot more fun than squinting at a screen."

Be Open at All Times

A horse with blinders only sees the racetrack; an overemployed San Franciscan only sees the job. Downtime rips those blinders off, leaving us open to new encounters. Once you're open, you might be overwhelmed with opportunities.

The anonymous J.D., an attorney in San Francisco, finally had the energy to meet new people during a recent period between law firms. He chose to focus on dating, so much so that he found himself dating two women at the same time—something he doesn't necessarily recommend!

You might be surprised at how many new people you can meet on any given day and how little you know about the people you've already come across. Try this exercise: during your daily routine, whatever it may be, introduce yourself to each and every person you interact with and spend a moment to learn something about them. Start at the coffee shop in the morning; include the bus driver if you take public transportation, the gas station attendant, the florist, the bartender, and so on. Josh McHugh, a San Francisco-based writer, took the opportunity to do just that during a recent break between assignments and found it refreshing—and a good muse! (See previous page.)

RECHARGING YOUR RELATIONSHIPS

How many times have you heard your significant other tell you, "I never see you anymore?" Have you forgotten your dog's name? If you're like most of us, juggling full-time work and relationships is a challenge. Whether you're married, just beginning to date someone, or somewhere in between, take this opportunity to recharge your relationship. Here are some ideas to get you started.

Cook For Your Partner

Cooking for someone (assuming that you enjoy it) is a wonderful way to show them you care. Use extra time in the early evening to prepare a scrumptious meal, so when your significant other is done with work, you can enjoy dinner together. You'll save money, spend quality time in the privacy of your own home, even be able to choose your own music! For some altogether luscious ideas about cooking and romance, check out **Sex and the Kitchen** (www.sexandthekitchen.com), a web site dedicated to culinary and romantic delights.

Plan a Weekend Getaway

Choose a place you've both wanted to go: the mountains, the coast, or maybe wine country? Make it a surprise and you'll be a star in your partner's eyes for sure. You have literally thousands of choices, particularly if you're willing to spend some cash. If you're not, some less expensive—albeit alternative—escapes are within striking distance of San Francisco.

Coast south along Highway One to two of our favorites that won't drain the budget. **Pigeon Point Lighthouse Hostel** (210 Pigeon Point Road/Highway One, Pescadero, 650-879-0633, www.norcalhostels.org)

is spectacularly stationed along the San Mateo coastline, about an hour's drive south of San Francisco. It has both shared and private rooms, and a hot tub cradled in the cliffs above the Pacific Ocean. **Point Montara Lighthouse Hostel** (16th Street at California Highway One, Montara, 650-728-7177, www.norcalhostels.org), is only thirty minutes from the City, and is also perched atop cliffs along the water. Private rooms (with shared bath) at both hostels ranged from $50–$60 per night for two in 2003, and reservations are mandatory, best made well in advance. Because these are run as hostels, they do come with their share of rules—such as curfews—so be sure to check those out ahead of time.

Twenty minutes north of San Francisco, nestled on Mount Tamalpais, lies another alternative getaway: **The West Point Inn** (Mount Tamalpais, Marin, 415-388-9955, 415-646-0702 for reservations). This rustic mountain cabin is hike-in only, and what it lacks in refinement it more than makes up for in character and breathtaking vistas. Guests pack in their own food and bedding, and have a choice between stand-alone cabins or rooms inside the inn itself. The cost in 2003 was $30 per person for either type of accommodation.

For a more upscale weekend, you might consider staying at a bed & breakfast. Although not always cheap, they usually offer better value than your average hotel. Good sources for finding B&Bs in Northern California include the book *Absolutely Every Bed & Breakfast: Northern California,* by Carl Hanson, and the excellent web resource **Bed & Breakfasts Online** (www.bbonline.com).

Out to Lunch

Stop by your partner's workplace (if there is one!) for an impromptu lunch date. Eating lunch together is an unusual event for most couples so it makes for a nice treat. You'll score major brownie points, maybe even impress the coworkers. Add to that the possibility of additional networking opportunities, and you might make this a regular occurrence!

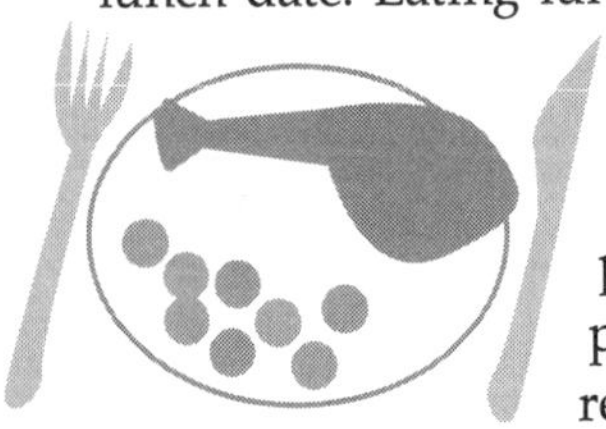

Think Romance

Love is eternal, but romance takes time. With some extra hours you can plan all sorts of little surprises. Surprise your loved one by decorating the house with candles, preparing a fragrant bubble bath, or offering your services as a masseur or masseuse. Or take your partner somewhere special in nature, perhaps to the beach to watch the sunset, or on a picnic in the woods (Golden Gate Park has plenty of great picnic grounds). As clichéd as it may sound, the simplest efforts are often the most romantic.

UNEMPLOYMENT AND POPPING THE QUESTION

Ted Witt, who worked as a project director in San Francisco, credits his recent stint of unemployment with taking his relationship to the next level.

Although he fell in love with his wife, Shauna, while they were working for the same company, both were subsequently laid off. She found another job relatively quickly but he continued to be unemployed for a full year, albeit most of it by design. Rather than put a strain on their relationship, Ted's unemployment helped both of them put more energy into their romance and Ted actually ended up asking Shauna to marry him while he wasn't working. Though concerned about how his jobless status would look to his father-in-law to be, Ted did secure his blessing (ok, so he fibbed a little about some "consulting" projects) and then had plenty of time to plan the engagement, before and after he popped the all-important question.

Shauna and Ted are now living in Corte Madera, happily ever after!

LOVE IN THE TIME OF UNEMPLOYMENT

What's that, you say? No time for love? If you're not working, you no longer have that excuse. And if you are working, then you'll just have to make the time, because love requires it. Think about the last time you fell in love with someone. Somehow you found the time to dream, plan, hope, and strategize about your blossoming relationship. You might not have even realized it at the time, but you probably dropped many other things in order to focus on the new person in your life.

In researching an article on unemployment and relationships, Ann Marsh, a freelance writer from Los Angeles, found several young career-driven individuals who had either put off serious relationships or neglected them altogether. It was only after they became disillusioned with their jobs or got laid off (or both) that they finally got involved in a serious relationship. Considering her own status, Marsh took these words to heart (see "Dating as a Full-Time Job" below).

Erik Wohlgemuth, an environmental consultant in San Francisco, was working a flexible twenty hours a week when he first met his girlfriend Arah who, in turn, had recently left her job at Booz Allen. He says they probably wouldn't have ended up together if they hadn't had that free time. "We both had recently gotten out of serious relationships, and were enjoying our new-found freedom," Erik told us. "Arah and I were also able to take off on more spontaneous dates, such as a last-minute visit to New York over the holidays, and a romantic road trip to Bend, Oregon."

DATING AS A FULL-TIME JOB?

No one ever said that dating couldn't be a full-time job. After getting laid off from her job as a staff writer for *Red Herring* magazine, Ann Marsh decided the time had come for her to have a serious relationship. Tired of not meeting the right men, Ann took to the task at hand. Using an ambitious, systematic dating strategy, she went about the process of finding the right man with all the zeal of an industrious entrepreneur. Six months later, she claimed to have gone on dates with no fewer than one hundred men! The work paid off, as Ann and her boyfriend Johanne have now been together for over a year and a half, and just announced their engagement. For his part, Johanne feels secure (and rightly so!) in the fact that Ann has definitely explored her options.

RECONNECTING WITH FRIENDS

Like all relationships, good friendships require time, energy, and nurturing, yet we too often neglect them when we're busy with work. We might want our platonic relationships to be like they are on *Friends*—jovial camaraderie, back-slapping good times, everyone always there for each other—but good friendships take a lot of work.

Your friendships may take on new dynamics. If your friends traditionally identified you with your work or career, they may now rediscover you in a different light. This can have a snowball effect, teaching you more about your friends outside their own work environments.

Organize rallying events for yourself and your companions: a weekly "friends dinner," for example, or a movie night, or simply a trip to the local café. Consider a leisure retreat with other friends who also have flexible schedules, letting you and your cohorts get to know each other in a different environment. Road trips allow ample bonding time (see **Chapter 5**). Backpacking, spas, sporting events, camping—all are great ways to rally a small group and spend dedicated time together.

Rob Darren (name changed) organized a weekly guys' movie night with his friends, many of whom weren't working, choosing a different theme each week. "It was a great way to get everyone together," he told us, "although you could definitely tell who was working and who wasn't. We'd host it on a weeknight, and the employed guys wouldn't drink much and would slip out relatively early. But those of us who weren't working, we'd sometimes tear it up into the wee hours, and we definitely bonded around that."

SF's Unemployed Communities

Speaking of unemployed bonding, the Bay Area's economic climate has created a new category of social events that revolve around unemployment. Not only are these great ways to share experiences with your fellow unemployed, but they're also excellent opportunities to meet new people.

Several of these groups have either evolved into job search services (e.g., the pink slip parties) or waned away, but a few remain. **Bojon.com** (www.bojon.com) is one such survivor, throwing quarterly parties to celebrate the "Kingdom of Bojon." Signing up for

all together now

SF was made for the friendly, so gather yours together for some good clean fun.

Relax and rejuvenate midweek at The City's favorite spa, ***Kabuki Springs & Spa*** (Japan Center, 1750 Geary, 415-922-6000, *www.kabukisprings.com*). The communal baths are reasonably priced at $15 Monday through Friday, before 5pm; $18 evenings and weekends. Tuesday is the only coed day, clothing required (bummer!); otherwise, the baths are gender-divided by day of the week.

Or, rally the troops for bowling night at ***Presidio Bowling Center*** (in the Presidio, corner of Moraga & Montgomery, Building 93, 415-561-2695), an old military bowling alley that is now open to the public. Heck, join a league! "We got our favorite bar to sponsor us," says J.J. Dillon, "and beers were on the house every night we won a game."

the Bojon mailing list will score you invitations to join other leisure seekers at official Bojon festivities. **Craig's List** (www.craigslist.org) serves as a *de facto* community for the unemployed. In particular, check out the sections on "jobs" and "community," as well as the "personals" section (if you're so inclined). **Oddtodd.com** (www.oddtodd.com, see **Chapter 3**, also "Great Moments" next page) of Internet layoff fame is a place to connect digitally with like-minded leisurely folks (or at least watch some funny cartoons!). Check out **Laid Off Land**, a Yahoo discussion group linked from the Odd Todd home page.

THE TAO OF BOJON

"What's better than your dream job?" asks the King of Bojon. "No job!" The ***Bojon*** site (*www.bojon.com*), created and maintained by San Franciscan Tom Haan, has created a community and local buzz among laid-off high tech workers.

Brian Cox, Tom's friend's little brother, coined the term "bojon" in the early 1990s. A sophomore in college in Wrightsville Beach, NC, surrounded by upperclassmen boasting about the great gigs they had lined up for after graduation, Brian wanted to sound equally sophisticated. He told his brother's friends he was going to work for Bojon. "It's a French company," he claimed. And it's also "no job"—spelled backwards!

Tom is quick to set his site apart from those that express bitterness about being laid off. Bojon is not an ephemeral concept. "Somebody who is uptight about not having a job and who is running around pressing resumes is not truly bojon," Tom explains. "Conversely, somebody who loves his profession and is passionate about his work can be bojon." Tom quotes the Chinese philosopher Chang Ch'ao: "Only those who take leisurely what the people of the world are busy about can be busy about what the people of the world take leisurely."

The Buddha couldn't have said it better himself.

GREAT MOMENTS IN UNEMPLOYMENT

CREATIVELY ODD

What to do when you've been laid off, have no real work or social life to speak of, and sit around and watch television all day? No problem: take your creative energy, combine it with some minimal Flash development skills and a wicked sense of humor, and create the most popular Internet cartoon series ever. Set up a tip jar on the site, and sit back and watch the money roll in, along with book and other development deals.

Odd Todd (*www.oddtodd.com*) did just that, and may be the one having the last laugh. His site has received more than one million hits from over 40 different countries, and Todd Rosenberg has become a media darling, appearing on CNN and the *Today* show, among others. His new book, *The Odd Todd Handbook: Hard Times, Soft Couch* may further solidify his position as a true leisure legend.

UNEMPLOYMENT & FAMILY

We have some idea of who *you* are—unemployed or *aspiring unemployed*—but little knowledge of your family. You all had parents, of course (and some of them were even human!). Perhaps you're from a family of six with lots of aunts and uncles and several sets of grandparents. Think of all the leisure loan potential!

Your family can be a tremendous source of support during time off, be it weeks, months, or even years of unconventional living. But keeping up the role you filled when you had a job can be trying. Your spouse, parents, or even kids may have certain expectations of you, and taking time off doesn't always fit neatly within those parameters. Maybe you never want to go back to work. What would your family think about that?

It could be time for you (like Chevy Chase) to load up the "family truckster" and hit the road on the way to Wally World (but please, leave your crazy aunt at home). Or, if you're still unattached, perhaps you'd prefer to drift in your parents' pool, contemplating your future (á la Dustin Hoffman).

kids

One could hardly argue against spending more time with your kids. Of course, some of you with little terrors may be looking for just the opposite: reprieve! Kidding aside, it's been a delight and inspiration to hear of so many people who've taken sabbaticals to get closer to their little ones.

Steve Wozniak of Apple Computer fame has long preached the virtues of society's paying more attention to children. After taking a rather extended period "off" from Apple (way back in 1985!), Woz actively helped found several local organizations supporting children and education, including The Tech Museum and the Children's Discovery Museum of San Jose.

Stacie Parker, an entrepreneur who owned two shops on Union Street, sold both to focus on raising her children. "Retail is no life for a parent," she said. "I had a 24-hour-on-call schedule. And I poured myself wholly into the daily grind, traveling to tradeshows and working late nights and weekends in the stores. But at 35, I had waited a long time to be a mom. So at that point I felt no guilt in giving up my business."

Whatever avenue you choose to get some quality time with your family—kids, spouse, parents, siblings or others—make sure you get it while you can, understanding that it might take an extra effort to adjust. Below are some suggestions on how to relate, where to take your children in San Francisco, how to organize family activities, or how to take a family vacation, Griswold-style!

Husbands and Wives

Is life different for married couples when one or both aren't working? Remember *Ozzie and Harriet? Leave it to Beaver?* Dad earned the dough and Mom spent it—on the family and the home, of course! While that may now seem archaic, it did give couples the luxury of more free time, or at least the appearance of it. We can debate gender roles and family values, but the bottom line is that the spouse who is not working will have more time and energy to focus on relationship and family.

Scott Philips, who negotiated a partially paid sabbatical with his employer, Accenture, was able to spend valuable time with his Czech-born wife in her home country, much of it at her family's home in the woods of Bohemia, such an appropriate place for leisure! According to Scott, "We got to know each pretty well over the last year, without all of the job-related stress in the way. I think it's made us a stronger couple. In terms of shared experiences, it was like having five years of American time together."

Adjusting

As beneficial as it can be, being out of work can also cause domestic turmoil. The myth that equates unemployment with laziness or underachievement can strain a couple, creating a lack of respect and understanding, and ultimately animosity. Ironically, according to career counselor Rochelle Teising, dual-income couples are likely to feel this tension the most: the partner that's still working full-time perceives the other to be loafing at home. It's hard for anyone living with a partner who is enjoying time off not to be jealous, Teising says.

Matt Green experienced this firsthand, admitting it was tricky to be around his family all the time after he quit his job. "Now that I'm not working, my wife Val's life hasn't changed," Matt says, "but I'm out riding my motorcycle, meeting my friend for a beer, and that's something I have to be sensitive to. Jealousy's too strong a word, but she's thinking, 'I still have to do what I do and you get to go play.'"

Matt's wife eventually asked him to take on more of the household responsibilities. The transition was difficult, as Matt didn't feel he was skilled at anything around the house. Take doing laundry, for example. "During this motorcycle trip I was just on, I thought about going to a laundromat, and I said, nah, I'm going to wear what I have on for three days and then go back to Vegas and just buy new clothes. And that's what I did."

But once Matt was able to relax and show more patience, the family was able to slip into a comfortable routine, and he was able to spend more quality time with his wife and kids—which had been his ultimate goal.

Family Activities

Now that you've made the effort to take more time for your family, what are you going to do with them? Sitting around the house watching *Oprah!* is hardly quality time. Even a city as cosmopolitan as San Francisco has plenty of better kid-friendly activities.

For outdoor adventures during the daytime, one option is to take the kids to Crissy Field. **Parks as Classrooms** is a joint program of the National Park Service and Golden Gate National Recreation Area, and **Crissy Field Center** (Building 603, Mason & Halleck in the Presidio, 415-561-7690, www.crissyfield.org) is its local education center. Enroll your children in one of their excellent programs, or simply take the family to the park and enjoy the beautiful setting.

Another outdoor option is a kid-friendly hike. Your sprites will enjoy Mount Tamalpais in Marin or Tilden Park in the East Bay as much as you do. For thorough information on hiking with children in the Bay Area, including tips and recommendations, visit **Bay Area Hiker** (www.bahiker.com, link to "Hiking with kids").

Yerba Buena Gardens in San Francisco's SOMA district (899 Howard, www.yerbabuena.org) have just about everything you could possibly imagine to occupy the little rascals' short attention spans (or just get them out of your hair for a few minutes!). One part of Yerba Buena called **The Rooftop**, located on the City block bordered by Mission, Howard, 3rd & 4th Streets, is a kids' mecca. Start with **Zeum** (4th Street & Howard, 415-777-2800, www.zeum.org), a wonderful art and technology center for children of all ages. The Children's Garden is also a small tyke's dream come true, with ladders, slides, a sandbox, a maze, and all sorts of other fun "stuff." Exhausted chasing the little ones around? Hit the **Yerba Buena Child Development Center** (790 Folsom @ 4th Street, 415-820-3500, www.southofmarketchildcare.org) when your patience has worn thin and you're ready to let someone else take care of the kids for awhile. Actually, it's a diverse children's center that offers a variety of programs, but unfortunately you'll have to enroll ahead of time.

The **Metreon** (101 4th Street @ Mission, 415-369-6000, www.metreon.com) entertains children well into their teen years. The more cultured (and ambitious) can try the **San Francisco Museum of Modern Art** (see "Flirting Before 5pm" p. 280). Last but not least is the **Exploratorium** (3601 Lyon, 415-561-0360, www.exploratorium.edu), an SF treasure that will delight both adults and kids from grade school on up.

tykes & travelin'

California teachers Karin & Joe Dixon didn't let parenthood slow them down. Karin pursued a Fulbright scholarship in Stockholm and Joe came along for the ride to take care of their infant son, Amos, who was eleven months old at the time. They traveled through parts of Norway and Germany in addition to living in Stockholm, all the while toting Amos along in the Baby Björn.

For preparation, Karin and Joe recommend *Lonely Planet's Travel With Children* by Cathy Lanigan. Karin also recommends taking a high-quality stroller, a good plastic pouch bib, backpacks instead of suitcases, and plenty of emergency snacks. She says breastfeeding, for those still nursing, can make traveling more leisurely for parent and child.

A notable online resource for San Francisco family outing ideas is **GoKid.org** (www.gokid.org), a nonprofit online guide dedicated to kid-friendly stuff in the City.

If you're looking for restaurants that stimulate the imagination as well as tolerate plenty of screaming and food throwing, it's hard to beat **In the Night Kitchen** (in the Metreon Center, 415-369-6079). The restaurant has brought to life the Maurice Sendak book of the same name, and the affiliated toy store next door, **Where the Wild Things Are** (415-369-6008), is stocked with plenty of life-sized wild things. Both kids and adults will enjoy the casual, diner-style atmosphere of the **Fog City Diner** (1300 Battery, 415-982-2000).

Family Vacations

If life's a journey you take with your family, why not hit the road for real? Although traveling with your family can be trying, it can be extremely rewarding, too. We subscribe to the Nike school of thought in this department: "Just do it."

Travel for Kids (www.travelforkids.com) is a helpful web site for kid-friendly travel preparation as well as ideas for international and local destinations. Their San Francisco section includes a thorough list of local ideas, too.

Maternity/Paternity-Leave

Surely one of the most important reasons to take time off from work is to care for and raise a small child. This is hardly a new concept, but the values and the process have evolved over the years. The federal Family and Medical Leave Act (FMLA) of 1993 stipulates that certain employers (generally, public agencies and businesses with fifty or more employees) must grant eligible employees up to twelve weeks unpaid leave for the birth and care of an employee's newborn child. For more information on the FMLA, check with the **Department of Labor** web site at (www.dol.gov).

Most employers offer paid maternity-leave benefits, whose features vary by company. Andrea Ghez, a professor and scientist at UCLA, took advantage of the university's flexible maternity-leave benefits, and used a combination of time off and flex-time during her baby's first six months. "There wasn't much precedent for me to follow. If you can believe it, I was only the second woman in my department to take maternity leave as an active, full-time professor."

CONGRATULATIONS ON THE BABY!

(NOW WE HAVE TO LET YOU GO)

Micki Karrer's maternity leave had a rude beginning. Then-head of marketing for telecom startup Sigma Networks, Micki got laid off two weeks before she was to go on leave—right before her due date! Because the company shut down soon thereafter, she lost her health insurance as well.

Lucky for the whole family, Micki's husband's insurance kicked in to cover most of the maternity expenses, and much to her credit, she was able to adapt quickly. In retrospect, she sees the sudden time off as a blessing: "The timing worked out great, as I was able to take about nine months off, which was perfect. Also, with a baby on the way, I had more perspective than many of my colleagues did, and could just focus on being a mother."

Unfortunately for everyone, this type of benefit is usually available only to mothers. Some companies may offer personal leave above and beyond the federal law. Maureen Feeney works at Agilent Technologies, one of the more progressive employers in the Bay Area; she recommends pro-actively negotiating with an employer. She did just that, received ten weeks of paid maternity leave, and was able to tack on another six months of unpaid leave, for a total of nearly nine months. Her husband Jeff, however, who also works for Agilent, wasn't so lucky; he had to use his vacation time in order to get paid time off. Unfair!

We encourage all mothers *and* fathers to ask for extended leave during their newborn's first year and beyond. Look at it this way: you're not just asking for yourself, you're setting a precedent for all your future-parent colleagues. Your employer may surprise you; many are if not sympathetic, at least open to negotiation.

Some terrific books on the subject go into much greater detail. *Everything a Working Mother Needs to Know About Pregnancy Rights, Maternity Leave and Making Her Career Work for Her*, by Anne C. Weisberg and Carol A. Buckler, for years has been the bible. Also cherished is *Life After Baby: From Professional Woman to Beginner Parent*, by Wynn McClenahan Burkett, which focuses on professional women entering parenthood.

Single Parents

A single parent might not have much wiggle room when it comes to taking time off, but that doesn't mean it can't be done. Careful planning and a strong support network of friends and family will help.

Adrianna Moore (name changed) spent many months taking involuntary time off in 2002. As a single mother of two, she didn't enjoy her time off so much as survived it, but she did feel it was important to present her situation positively to her children. "I didn't feel guilty, but I was worried about finances—and my kids noticed I was sad." She managed to maintain a positive outlook during a challenging time, in part by working out "a ton." Go Adrianna!

Marsha Converse, also a single mother, lost her job with Northpoint Communications during company-wide layoffs. Despite serious financial and personal turmoil, her son says she emerged from the experience "less stressed and more level-headed." She says, wisely, "I feel like getting laid off made me a human being again. I feel like I now know what's important."

LASTING CONNECTIONS

Heavy stuff, to be sure, but unemployment, whether forced or voluntary, gives countless people new perspective on their relationships, with universally positive results. If you care to share that positive impact, take the next chapter to heart, and get out there and volunteer. Now that you've completed your unemployed odyssey, it's only right for you to start sharing the leisure!

LEISURE CITY

PART THREE

SHARING THE LEISURE

CHAPTER 9
VOLUNTEERING

We make a living by what we get, we make a life by what we give.
~Winston Churchill

Unless someone like you cares a whole awful lot,
nothing is going to get better. It's not.
~Dr. Seuss, The Lorax

NOW that you've played to your heart's content, you want to start sharing the leisure. Kudos to you! Welcome to the wide world of volunteering.

Volunteering can improve the world for so many people, including you! While you're helping others, you can:

- work outdoors and then sleep like a rock
- enjoy free food and drink
- augment your t-shirt collection
- scam on babes
- meet new neighbors
- explore new neighborhoods
- have an office to go into and a phone to use

All that, plus you can meet influential people, explore career interests, and learn new skills. Good gravy! It's a wonder we're not volunteering all the time.

Volunteering is a San Francisco tradition. Each immigrant community leaves its own legacy of giving, such as the Jewish immigrants who founded the Eureka Benevolent Society in the mid-1800s to feed and shelter widows and children. San Franciscans were also at the forefront of AIDS fundraising before the epidemic was even in the news (see box below).

Now is the time to carry that tradition forward. "We've gotten a lot of great volunteers who are temporarily unemployed," says Natasha Glushkoff, who runs the volunteer program for **San Francisco Architectural Heritage** (2007 Franklin, 415-441-3000, www.sfheritage.org). "A few have always wanted to volunteer but have 'always been so busy.' So far, all have stayed active or at least stayed connected with us even if they found jobs again."

HISTORY OF THE AIDS QUILT

In 1987, a small group of activists and citizens met in a San Francisco storefront with the goal of creating a lasting memorial for those who had died of AIDS. The meeting served as the genesis and foundation of both the NAMES Project and The AIDS Memorial Quilt.

The quilt is now housed in Atlanta when it's not touring the rest of the country, and it serves as a powerful reminder of the enormity of the AIDS epidemic. It's composed of approximately 48,000 panels commemorating over 88,000 individuals, weighs close to 54 tons, and has been put to good use by the ***NAMES Project Foundation*** (404-688-5500, *www.aidsquilt.org*), whose mission is "to preserve, care for, and use The AIDS Memorial Quilt to foster healing, heighten awareness and inspire action in the struggle against HIV and AIDS." NAMES has raised more than $3 million for AIDS service organizations throughout North America.

WHERE TO START

With all the worthy causes in San Francisco, it's a challenge just deciding which ones to support. Fortunately, some centralized resources can help you choose.

A good starting point is **The Volunteer Center of San Francisco** (1675 California, 415-982-8999, www.vcsf.org). The Center's website includes information on group volunteering, special events and other one-day opportunities. The center will even help you form your own nonprofit.

The **Bay Area Volunteer Information Center** (www.volunteerinfo.org) is a more grassroots clearinghouse. Their "Volunteer Opportunities Hotlist" helps fill jobs from repairing computers to picking fruit to making sandwiches.

Do you have a particular date or a certain skill in mind? The web engine at **SF Bay Area Volunteer Solutions** (www.volunteersolutions.org/sfbay), sponsored by the United Way, lets you search by your skills, interests and availability. **VolunteerMatch** (www.volunteermatch.org) is another highly recommended online resource.

If you want to volunteer but aren't sure how much time you'll have, reach out to **Hands on San Francisco** (330 Townsend, Suite 137, 415-541-9616, www.hosf.org). They publish a monthly calendar of projects that don't call for any minimum commitment. Their nights and weekends projects accommodate even those with a day job. Find more "done-in-a-day" projects through **Community Impact** (721 Central Avenue, Mountain View, 650-965-0242, www.communityimpact.org). Projects will occasionally require an orientation, but otherwise you don't need any experience or ongoing commitment.

volunteer etiquette

True, volunteer jobs don't pay and you can't really get fired. That doesn't mean the normal rules of courtesy don't apply. People are counting on you! Call if you're going to be late or have to cancel. If you have to bow out of an ongoing commitment, try to find a replacement. It's only right, plus the MC at that fundraiser dinner you just flaked on might reappear across the table—at your next job interview!

BUILDING SKILLS

Do you want to get into event planning but need more experience? Would you like to improve your salesmanship? Use volunteering to build your resume. Team up with a non-profit and help them raise money, or volunteer to organize a special event for a philanthropic organization. Countless non-profits will provide you with skills training in return for your time and effort.

Take, for example, this invitation to potential volunteers from the **San Francisco Choral Society** (236 West Portal #775, 415-566-8425, www.sfchoral.org):

> *Admit it—at some point you've thought about making a few fundraising calls but then it dawned on you, "I can't even ask for extra ketchup; how could I ask for a donation?" Guess what? You don't actually have to know how. We'll train you. This free training will be conducted by a professional development consultant. You gain marketable skills, the chorus gains donations and everybody is happy.*

We couldn't have said it better ourselves! This pitch is certainly more persuasive than being begged and cajoled.

SFCS is not the only nonprofit that dangles the training carrot to attract quality volunteers. Natasha Glushkoff reports that docents of the Haas-Lilienthal House tours enjoy "all sorts of fabulous lecturers" in a "really awesome" nine- or ten-week class. Other volunteers receive free **Heritage** (see p. 302) membership.

Dane Larson volunteered at the **Cystic Fibrosis Foundation** (1939 Harrison Street, Suite 207, Oakland, 510-267-9699, www.cff.org/northerncalifornia.htm) and was surprised to find it helped build his sales skills. "They had me on the phone every day, asking companies to donate prizes for their auctions and special events. It got to the point where I wouldn't take no for an answer. Of course, it helped that it was for a charity because I could really lay on the guilt trip."

For more on (leisurely) skill-building, jump ahead to **Chapter 11**, where you'll find all sorts of unorthodox job hunting ideas.

GET OUT OF THIS HOUSE

Environmental groups have long made San Francisco their home, including the venerable **Sierra Club** (85 2nd Street, 2nd Floor, 415-977-5500, www.sierraclub.org). Naturalist John Muir and others founded the Sierra Club in 1892, and in 1893 they set up their first office at the California Academy of Sciences in Golden Gate Park. The headquarters has remained in the City ever since.

Everybody needs beauty as well as bread,
places to play in and pray in, where nature may
heal and give strength to body and soul alike.
~John Muir, *The Yosemite* (1912)

Go out and celebrate San Francisco's environmental heritage. Enjoy the great outdoors and spruce up its appearance at the same time. Here are some links to organizations with regular volunteer days:

Volunteers in Parks Program
www.cal-parks.ca.gov
click on "Volunteers in Parks"

Trail Center
www.trailcenter.org
click on "Volunteer!"

Greenbelt Alliance
www.greenbelt.org
choose "Get Involved" then "Volunteer/Intern Opps"

Several organizations sponsor beach cleanups at Ocean Beach, including the **Surfrider Foundation** (www.sfsurfrider.org), and the **California Coastal Commission** (www.coastal.ca.gov, search "coastal cleanup").

Golden Gate National Parks Conservancy (415-561-3034, www.parksconservancy.org) wants *you* to steward some parks. Get involved with the Presidio through **Presidio Park Restoration** (Park Stewards Volunteer Hotline, 415-561-3034, ext. 3445). More than 2,000 volunteers help restore the Presidio's open spaces each year. Call for information on upcoming workdays.

Perhaps you revel in napping under big shady trees? Enjoy the crunch-crunch of pine needles and branches under your feet? If so, **Friends of the Urban Forest** (Presidio, Building #1007, 415-561-6890, www.fuf.net) would like to speak with you. "FUF" is a community-based group that works to expand and protect San Francisco's urban forests, also known as "trees." Join FUF for a one-day planting binge—they'll even provide lunch! If rescuing our ailing leafy friends is more your speed, join their "treeage" program (get it?) and cruise the streets of San Francisco looking for TIT's (Trees In Trouble). They need your help!

Be a park hero by donating some time to the **Golden Gate National Recreation Area** (Volunteer Coordinator, Fort Mason, Building 201, 415-561-4755, www.nps.gov/goga/vip/). Not only is the GGNRA the largest urban park in the world, but it's home to some of the most spectacular open space in the country. Get the insider scoop on this tremendous resource by collecting data on wildlife, growing native plants, or protecting endangered species. All volunteers receive free orientation and training.

FORCED VOLUNTEERING

Sometimes, volunteering just makes common sense. Those inconvenient times when you're facing a jail sentence, for example. Be sure your lawyer is familiar with the ***San Francisco Pretrial Diversion Project*** (SFPDP, 567 7th Street, 415-626-4995, *www.sfpretrial.com*), a program formed to provide first-time non-violent misdemeanor offenders the opportunity to perform community service in lieu of prosecution (sorry, you repeat offenders are out of luck). Volunteering might never look so appealing!

Project 20 (as it's otherwise known) was formed in 1976 by socially conscious lawyers, judges, and citizens, and is now one of the most infamous programs offered by SFPDP. Under Project 20, beleaguered parking and traffic offenders work off their tickets by performing visible Department of Public Works projects such as painting over graffiti, cleaning city streets, or sweeping sidewalks. Like most things related to parking and traffic in the City, the program has a lot of rules. Read up on them at *www.sfpretrial.com/project20*. Happy cleaning!

ACTING LOCALLY

Helping your neighbors might not have the glam appeal of a volunteer vacation or a stint monitoring an overseas election, but it sure can put your own problems in perspective.

Reading Aloud

If you've gotten this far, we know you can read. Help others learn to read too, through **Project Read** (San Francisco Public Library, 100 Larkin, 415-557-4388, www.projectreadsf.org), the adult literacy program of the San Francisco Public Library. Volunteer tutors attend an orientation and twelve hours of tutor training—not a bad perk if you're also looking for paid tutoring work. This project requires a commitment to tutor the same person for one year, once or twice a week. In return, you'll receive up to six ongoing tutor trainings.

Are you good at reading out loud? Here's your chance to speak out—on air. The **Rose Resnick Lighthouse for the Blind** (Volunteer Coordinator, 214 Van Ness, 415-431-1481, www.lighthouse-sf.org) needs volunteers to read the daily news to their blind or visually impaired radio audience. The Lighthouse could use your practical services as well, helping campers enjoy summer swimming, hiking, and horseback riding at Enchanted Hills Camp in wine country. You receive training, room and board, and campers gain independence and confidence in their abilities.

Nurture Your Neighbors

Consider yourself fortunate if you are not suffering from abuse or AIDS, and doubly fortunate if you can help those who are.

Join forces with the respected **Riley Center** (415-255-2894, www.rileycenter.org) to help abused women get out of a bad situation. Volunteer roles include Crisis Line Advocate, Children's Activities Volunteer, and language translation.

Get involved with local healing by assisting the **UCSF AIDS Health Project** (415-476-3890, www.ucsf-ahp.org). Help people reduce the risk of HIV transmission, cope with emotional challenges of HIV infection, or support friends and family. AHP offers not only volunteer opportunities, but also a formal post-baccalaureate internship program for the truly inspired.

Teach tech to Tenderloin residents at the Computer Training Center of the **San Francisco Network Ministries** (559 Ellis, 415-928-6209, www.sfnetworkministries.org). The Reverend Cecil Williams would also like your help at **Glide Memorial Church** (330 Ellis, 415-674-6000, www.glide.org) and one of its many volunteer service programs, from meals to health to education. **Dolores Street Community Services** (938 Valencia, 415-282-6209, www.dscs.org) is another grassroots group founded to help working immigrants and AIDS sufferers.

If you prefer to dress down while socializing, try a one-time group project, like building a house with **Habitat for Humanity** (78 Ocean, 415-406-1555, www.habitatsf.org).

weekday specials

Feel like riding a bike? Join ***Trips for Kids of Marin*** (415-458-2986) on a Wednesday or Thursday for a mountain bike trip through the Marin Headlands with inner-city youths. You'll need your own gear and a sack lunch. Riders meet at ***Re-Cyclery*** (610 4th Street, San Rafael, 415-458-2986).

Project Open Hand (730 Polk, 415-447-2300, *www.openhand.org*) provides meals to impoverished HIV/AIDS sufferers and seeks volunteers seven days a week who can "slice and dice," are "good with a shopping cart," or can take "meals with love out on the road and deliver."

Environmentalists can contact the ***Rainforest Action Network*** (221 Pine, Suite 500, 415-398-4404, *www.ran.org*), who, in their own words, are "not your typical tree-huggers." Volunteers are needed in RAN's SF office Monday-Friday, 9am-5pm, for general office work, data entry, mailings, and banner- and sign-making. Every Thursday from 6pm-10pm you can mail your way to pizza bliss with their Bulk Mail Pizza Parties! RAN also offers a variety of internships, from media outreach to research.

Still thinking globally? Whet your international appetite by helping **Global Exchange** (2017 Mission, Suite 203, 415-255-7296, www.globalexchange.org) with international human rights issues and policies. Their programs include study tours, retail stores promoting alternative trade, educational development, media outreach, and human rights campaigns.

WORKING WITH KIDS

Perhaps no one deserves your charitable attention more than children in need. If teaching is your bag, help the kids through **San Francisco School Volunteers** (601 McAllister, 415-749-3700, www.sfsv.org), who will set you up to tutor students, read to children or chaperone field trips. Volunteers can tutor math and reading through community organizations too, such as the **Hunter's Point Boy's and Girl's Club** (729 Kirkwood, 415-822-7140) and the **San Francisco Senators, Inc.** (1351 42nd Avenue, 415-665-0770).

Bond more deeply with children (and make more of a commitment) at **Big Brothers Big Sisters of San Francisco & The Peninsula** (600 Townsend, 415-503-4050, www.bbbsa.org), and the **Columbia Park Boys and Girls Clubs** (nine locations including 450 Guerrero, 415-864-2724; 163 London, 415-334-2582). They provide clubhouses around the City where kids learn arts and crafts, sports and health, character, leadership and other good citizenship skills.

If you seek a rewarding challenge, contact **SFCASA** (833 Market, Suite 1004, 415-398-8001, www.sfcasa.org), an organization that pairs up volunteers one-on-one with children living in foster care. "CASA" stands for Court Appointed Special Advocate. Each volunteer advocate becomes a sworn court officer who works to understand the interests and legal needs of the child they represent, and to make sure that lawyers, the courts and social services agencies are protecting them. Becoming a CASA advocate is an intense but important commitment. If you are going to stick around San Francisco, now might be a good time to get the 36 required hours of training under your belt.

COMMUNAL GIVING

Volunteering was more than a temporary diversion for Dave Casuto. He burned up his volunteer hours at the ***Burning Man*** office (see "Participate" at *www.burningman.com*) and enjoyed it so much that he continued volunteering on weekends even after he found a full-time job. "It was a great way to connect to an amazing community," Dave told us.

You can contribute to the Burn at the event itself, too, by making playa signs, working the ticket gate, or performing any number of other activities. Just remember to come back to your hometown playa when it's all over!

WORKING WITH SENIORS

The elderly have made their contributions to the community, so why not give them something in return? Benefit from the wisdom of experience by befriending a senior through **Little Brothers—Friends of the Elderly San Francisco** (909 Hyde, Suite 628, 415-771-7957, www.littlebrothers.org/sanfrancisco). They organize programs ranging from volunteer visits to special events and parties. And get this, they offer skill-building internships, in areas such as database management, non-profit management, and event planning.

To help deliver the basic necessities of life to the elderly, hop on board with **Meals on Wheels** (1375 Fairfax Avenue, 415-920-1111, www.mowsf.org), one of the most successful charities around. Donate a lot or a little, and see clear and immediate results. The "How to Help" section of their website lists opportunities such as grocery shopper, meal server, or even lunchtime performer! What better opportunity for budding musicians to gain a dedicated audience and to strut their stuff? (A word to the wise: go easy on the grinding speed metal or punk rock lyrics.)

WORKING WITH ANIMALS

Today's urban dogs and other animals have it tough. For one, they can no longer feast on plump peacocks in Golden Gate Park! (See the story of Connemara, **Chapter 4**.) For another, their numbers continue to grow without a corresponding increase in homes or services.

Plenty of wayward pets and animals need your assistance. First stop should be the **San Francisco SPCA** (2500 16th Street, 415-554-3000, www.sfspca.org), a group focused on saving our homeless canine and feline friends, and providing them with care and treatment. Search the SPCA website under "Help Us" for details on cat socializing, dog walking, or adoption counseling.

San Francisco Animal Care and Control (1200 15th Street, 415-554-6364, www.sfgov.org/site/acc_index.asp) is the official city agency charged with assisting our animal companions. Several other non-profits partner with them, including **Reunion Rescue** (415-586-8229), who would like you to adopt a homeless pet. City agencies need friends, too, so the SFACC has enlisted the **Friends of San Francisco Animal Care and Control** (1200 15th Street, 650-757-0842, www.fsfacc.org), who invite you to join them in supporting the goals of the SFACC.

WORKING THE ROOM

Want to meet and greet while you're volunteering? No problem. The concept of "singles volunteering" is popular and highly refined in San Francisco.

At the center of social volunteering is the unique group **Imgood.org** (www.imgood.org). A combination of clearinghouse and singles club, the site enables "Do-gooders" to set up "doGOODates" with other "do-gooders" and benefit a worthy cause in the process. Who can argue with all that goodness being spread around?

Other particularly social groups include the **Commonwealth Club's INFORUM** (595 Market, 415-597-6700, www.commonwealthclub.org) and the **World Affairs Council's Young Professionals International Forum** (312 Sutter, Suite 200, 415-293-4600, www.itsyourworld.org). Both openly discuss the sometimes-controversial issues relevant to the 21- to 40-year-old set, and offer opportunities to organize events that benefit their parent organization. As an added bonus, get elected to chair the Council's International Forum and you'll sit on the board—alongside well-connected San Franciscans.

swanky parties

Day-of assistance with special events is fun, on site, and very social. It often helps to raise boatloads of money. Sound like your scene? Then don your tux or evening gown, and help the rich and notable loosen their grip on their wallets. Start with:

- the ***San Francisco Volunteer Center*** (*www.vcsf.org*), which lists one-day events under "Special Event Volunteering"
- the swanky events of the ***American Cancer Society*** (235 Montgomery, Suite 320, 415-394-7100, *www.cancer.org*), which can double as great networking opportunities
- the ***Cystic Fibrosis Foundation*** (1939 Harrison, Suite 207, Oakland, 510-267-9699, *www.cff.org*), which uses special events as one of its primary fundraising vehicles, and is always looking for volunteers

Want to support the arts instead? Check out the **San Francisco Opera's Bravo! Club** (301 Van Ness, 415-861-4008, www.sfopera.com), dedicated to building a young audience for the opera. Young singles support dance too, through the **San Francisco Ballet's ENCORE!** (455 Franklin, 415-553-4634, www.encoresf.org).

GIVING AND LIVING LEISURE

That's a lot of giving going on! But as the cliché goes, you get what you give. The more good vibes you share through volunteering, the safer the world becomes for leisure.

Keep that "Share the Leisure" feeling in mind as you transition out of pure recreational mode into your next big life endeavor, be it heading for the halls of academia or (ack!) going back to work.

CHAPTER 10
BACK TO SCHOOL

"Woo-hoo! I'm a college man! I won't need my high school diploma any more! I am so smart! I am so smart...S-M-R-T! I mean, S-M-A-R-T..."

~Homer Simpson, Homer Goes Back to College

SOONER or later, many people reach a crossroads: get a new job or… go back to school!

Higher education can serve as a panacea for what ails the leisure seeker. Where else can you ditch the pressures and responsibilities of a job while appeasing the productivity clan? Graduate school, my friend, graduate school.

Being job-free is not the only benefit of going back to school. Have you always wanted to study history? Now's your chance. Looking to change careers? A new degree can open doors as well as minds. Maybe it's a trade that appeals to you. Become a certified bartender. Go to beer school!

You can never learn too much. If you can fund more school, get thee to thy registrar and get those neurons firing.

THE PERPETUAL STUDENT

Can't get your socks to match, or harbor a secret propensity for wearing corduroy sport coats? Whether it's a convenient hiding place or a passionate extension of your life's mission, academia allows you to dress as you like, create your own schedule and philosophize until the wee hours of the morning. Sabbaticals are not only allowed, but encouraged!

Academia can make a superb cocoon for the *leisure connoisseur.* "Gradual" programs can go on for years and years, all under the guise of "work." Not bad, considering how numerous the funding and sponsorship possibilities are. You could even focus your studies exclusively on the subject of leisure, as has Professor Benjamin Hunnicutt (www.shorterworkhours.com) at the University of Iowa—perhaps the most scholarly *leisure seeker* in the nation!

If you're intent on completing a full-bore Ph.D. program, more power to you. Be advised that while academia can appear to be "the life" looking from the outside in, it too has its share of organizational politics, bureaucracy and inflexibility.

leisure studies

The scholastic study of leisure is multi-disciplinary, drawing from fields such as history, sociology, economics and politics to describe how people spend their free time. Many reputable universities have Leisure Studies departments, including ***San Francisco State*** (Department of Recreation and Leisure Studies, 1600 Holloway, Gym Building, Room 207, 415-338-2030). The department offers bachelor's degrees in Recreation and master's degrees in Recreation Administration. You can even specialize in "therapeutic recreation" to become nationally certified as a recreation therapist.

Now *that's* a program we can get behind!

more leisure...

GETTING STARTED

Going back to school full-time is a major decision, especially if it means leaving a high-paying job. Debt and career derailment can loom large. Will your investment pay off?

Very likely, in the long run. Think about it this way: you'll have the rest of your working life to earn dollars, but you might never have a better chance to get a graduate education. Most fellow earthlings won't ever have the chance. From that perspective, consider it a real opportunity and privilege.

Lisa Turner decided to apply to a graduate journalism program after getting laid off from her dot-com job. "The prospect of giving up a big salary to go back to school was daunting," she told us. "But coming from a position of unemployment or self-employment, it was more realistic."

Robert L. Peters' book *Getting What You Came for: The Smart Student's Guide to Earning a Master's or a Ph.D.* can help you weigh the pros and cons of becoming a student again. But don't limit your calculus to the practical; some of life's most enriching experiences result from factoring in the whimsical, too.

...more leisure

If you think leisure might be the field for you, try your hand at an actual course. Heidi Wells took one as an undergrad at San Francisco State. "I got a 'C' on my first paper," she told us. "A 'C' in leisure? I couldn't let that happen. It was odd taking leisure so seriously, but I ended up with an 'A' in the class." Heidi graduated at the top of her leisure class, recently completing her third extended trip abroad.

Research

You'll find comprehensive information on programs in the U.S. and abroad at sites like **GradSchools.com** (www.gradschools.com). The site is funded by sponsoring universities, which means the information is free, but might be skewed in favor of those sponsors. **Peterson's** (www.petersons.com) produces another free education portal with a good search engine; just be prepared for them to hardsell you one of their many books on the topic!

A more neutral source of U.S. graduate program rankings is ***US News & World Report*** (www.usnews.com, "Rankings & Guides," then "America's Best Graduate Schools").

The Admissions Process

Applying to grad school and getting accepted are two different steps entirely. Be it for an MBA program at a top ten university or a certification course in holistic medicine, the admissions requirements and application process will be more stringent and involved than for undergraduate study. Don't be intimidated—you won't be the first or the last to go through the process. In fact, guiding applicants through the admissions maze has become its own thriving industry.

If you have your eye on the business world and making tons of money, for example, you can buy the book by Matt Symonds and Alan

Mendonca, *ABC of Getting the MBA Admissions Edge.* If you aspire to heal others, check out Andrew Goliszek's straightforward but useful *The Complete Medical School Preparation and Admissions Guide.* And if you advocate justice for all, pony up for *Law School Admissions Adviser* by Ruth Lammert Reeves.

Entrance Exams

No institutional process would be complete without good old fashioned standardized tests. Welcome to the wonderful world of acronyms: GRE, GMAT, LSAT, MCAT, TOEFL...Y-I-K-E-S! Those who dwell in the neo-acronym world of high tech will feel right at home.

Again, there are companies that can help—for a not-so-nominal fee. **Kaplan** (800-527-8378, www.kaplan.com) and **The Princeton Review** (800-273-8439, www.princetonreview.com), the preeminent test preparation companies, offer live and online courses for all common standardized tests. Live course fees start at a whopping $1,000. Even the more economical online courses and self-study materials will soak up anywhere from $100 to $500 of your leisure bucks. If you're the self-disciplined type and you want to be more frugal, you can go with materials from the bookstore. **Stacey's Booksellers** (581 Market, 415-421-4687, www.staceys.com) has an extensive selection of test prep texts.

Are the pricey courses worth the money? Ted Witt bumped his GMAT score by only 30 points (from 560 to 590) after taking a live course. He admits, though, that he might have been a little preoccupied—his second try was only six days before his wedding!

"I decided to take the test again four weeks later with no studying, and scored a 700—a 110 point difference," he told us. Guess it took a while for the course info to sink in, or maybe the test is just that random. Ted's final answer? "Prepare with books or a class, and if you aren't happy with your score, take the test again."

WHO'S GONNA PAY?

These days, most graduate programs require serious cash. First stop: the parents. Paying tuition is a legitimate use of their money, right? Wrangling financial aid from your family can take some persuasion, however.

Mary Mangold's father was skeptical when she asked for a loan to go to film school, so Mary got creative. "I brought Dad to an open house at [SF State's] College for Extended Learning downtown," she said. "My future film teacher was so inspiring, my dad agreed to support me."

When you're making your pitch, highlight the ways that the university experience will make you a better person and increase your earning power in the long run. Don't forget to mention how it could boost your ability to care for your elders in their retirement: a little leisure for you now means greater leisure for them later. Isn't it nice how that works?

Scholarships

Parental sponsorship not an option? Then think "scholarship." Scholarships are fantastic, untapped resources, many of which garner little competition. These treasures won't stay hidden for much longer, though. The Web makes it infinitely easier to ferret them out.

Scholarships.com (www.scholarships.com) is one of the least commercial sources of information. A sophisticated search engine helps you manage their extensive database. **BrokeScholar** (www.brokescholar.com) is another good source, boasting a database of more than 900,000 scholarships worth over $3 billion. **FastWeb** (www.fastweb.com), owned by the career website Monster.com, also lets you search for colleges as well as scholarships, for free.

the scholarly bay

The Bay Area's university scene doesn't match Boston's in terms of density, but it does in terms of prestige and variety. The graduate schools at Berkeley and Stanford consistently rank among the best in the country. Together, the region's research universities number 24 Nobel laureates among their faculty members. That's no shortage of brain power! (How many Nobel laureates *does* it take to change a light bulb?) Venture capitalists credit this environment with creating a fertile nesting ground for technology and innovation.

Universities within the city limits include San Francisco State University (SFSU), University of San Francisco (USF), University of California San Francisco (UCSF), Golden Gate University, and the Academy of Art College. Berkeley, Stanford, San Jose State, and Santa Clara Universities loom within striking distance.

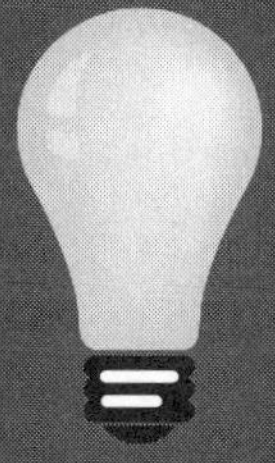

Closer to home—and not solely in cyberspace—is **The San Francisco Foundation** (225 Bush, Suite 500, 415-733-8500, www.sff.org), one of the nation's largest and most prestigious community foundations. Peruse regionally-based scholarship options on their site under "grantmaking," then "scholarships" or visit their brick-and-mortar site in person on weekdays.

For information on general financial aid within the state of California, see the website of the **California Student Aid Commission** (www.csac.ca.gov), which focuses primarily on grants and loans. Many of their programs are geared towards low-income students and families.

Student Loans

If you've squeezed out whatever scholarship or family money is available and you are still short on tuition, consider a student loan. Most are offered at exceptionally low interest rates, many are subsidized by the federal government, and repayment schedules are usually flexible.

A loan is still a loan, however, no matter how attractive the terms. Do the math and make sure you're comfortable with how much you'll owe once you've earned your degree. Consult the **U.S. Department of Education** (www.ed.gov under "Financial Aid") for information on grants and Direct Loans from the federal government.

MONEY FOR NOTHIN'

While there's always Fulbright or Rhodes, you might be surprised at who else awards scholarships, and for what purposes. For example, ever heard of the ***National Wool Growers Memorial Fellowship***? (Memorial Fellowship, 6911 South Yosemite, Englewood, CO 80112-1414, 303-771-3500). It's awarded to "further the advancement of the sheep, lamb and wool industries." That's right, sheep—and sheep-related graduate studies. Shearing, anyone?

If it's outdoor adventure you're after, scout out the ***Explorers Club's Exploration Fund*** (46 East 70th Street, New York, NY 10021, 212-628-8383, *www.explorers.org*). Grants in amounts of up to $5,000 are available to graduate students each year for an oh-so-modest mission: "to broaden our knowledge of the universe." The narrow-minded need not apply.

GOING TO SCHOOL OVERSEAS

Did you miss out on that undergraduate semester abroad? Go now! Take the opportunity to study overseas, and you'll reap the benefits of travel and education in one neat package.

Brian Pollack went on exchange to Madrid for six months during his MBA program at the University of Washington. "It was one of the best times of my life," he says. "Madrid is an amazing city, and the Spanish culture suited me perfectly." Most universities offer overseas exchange options to their graduate students in addition to their undergrads.

Not matriculated in a degree program? Don't despair. Any number of fields offer stand-alone international programs. An exceptional starting point for research is the **Bechtel International Center** (422 Lagunita Drive, Stanford, 650-723-1831, www.stanford.edu/dept/icenter) at Stanford University. Here you'll find information on all things international, from overseas education to global employment opportunities. Online, check out **Studyabroad.com** (www.studyabroad.com) for a comprehensive directory of programs abroad.

loans that can bring you to tears

About six months after joining her first-choice law firm in San Francisco, Erica Madison (name changed) found herself crying in her office one night. "Practicing law was nothing like studying it," she told us, "and I realized I was handcuffed to working at this place I didn't like, in order to pay off the huge private loans I took, in order to get the education I got, in order to get this job—that I didn't like!"

All's well that ends well, though: Erica devoted a huge portion of her salary to paying off those loans as fast as she could, knocking off almost *a hundred thousand dollars* in less than three years.

Two years later, she changed careers and has now happily returned to academia, working for a university while earning her Masters in Education.

TRADITIONAL PROGRAMS

While not everyone wants to become a doctor, lawyer, or executive, few can deny the broad-reaching benefits of a professional degree. Counting Berkeley, Stanford, UCSF, and Hastings, there's no shortage of top programs here in the Bay Area, along with stiff competition. Win entrance to any of these local programs and you'll make mom and dad proud.

Business School

All of you future titans of industry can earn an MBA at virtually any local school, but you won't be alone. According to the Graduate Management Admission Council, applications nationally were up an average of 34% in 2002. The good news is that they declined some in 2003. The bad news is that the decrease was mostly just a fallback from the record spike of applicants in 2002. The bottom line: you'll have some company applying to business school.

For overall quality of program, the **Haas School of Business at UC Berkeley** (510-642-1405 for full-time program, www.haas.berkeley.edu) and the **Stanford Graduate School of Business** (650-723-2146, www.gsb.stanford.edu) stand well above the rest of the pack. The 2003 *US News & World Report* survey ranked Stanford number one in the nation for full-time MBA programs, and Haas number ten.

Peter Johnson, co-director of admissions at Haas, says they're seeing more recently laid-off applicants than in past years. "Job opportunities in technology are fewer and the venture capital market for entrepreneurs is not good at present," he says. "As a result, many people feel that it is an ideal time to step out of the work force and enhance their management skills while they wait for the economy to improve." Amen to that!

Medical School

While insurance companies continue to put the squeeze on the entire medical profession, becoming a doctor remains a noble calling. Acquire the power to heal at the world-class **UCSF School of Medicine** (415-476-9000, www.ucsf.edu), where you can study alongside Nobel Prize winners. The **Stanford School of Medicine** (650-723-4000, www.med.stanford.edu) ain't half bad, either. The two schools excel in both research and medical practice, and have joined forces in many endeavors.

Law School

If you've always dreamt of arguing your case in front of a jury or suing the pants off of your neighbor, consider getting a law degree first. Hang out at San Francisco's other "beach"—the concrete deck at **Hastings College of the Law** (200 McAllister, 415-565-4600, www.uchastings.edu). **Stanford Law School** (650-723-2465, www.law.stanford.edu) and **UC Berkeley's Boalt Hall** (510-642-1741, www.law.berkeley.edu) will also wise you up to the ways of the law, albeit in a less urban environment. All three are highly regarded programs, with Stanford and Berkeley again ranking near the top.

LOVING THE STUDENT LIFE

Working in an unstructured atmosphere, on your own time schedule, in a creative learning environment—it sounds terrible, doesn't it? Jay Drake worked for six years before returning to law school, where he reveled in the student lifestyle. He found the youthful, academic environment energizing. "I was always amazed at how some law students cried about how hard it was being in school," Jay told us. "Having been in the working world for a number of years I would laugh, remind them that being a student has many advantages, and that if they think school is hard to wait until they start the daily grind of the working life with all of its stresses and frustrations." Jay is now an attorney in San Francisco, with fond memories of his student hiatus.

NIGHT SCHOOL AND CONTINUING EDUCATION

If a full-time program doesn't fit the bill, maybe a part-time program will. We're biased towards full-time programs (no work!), but if you absolutely must, consider night school or continuing education. You can customize most programs to accommodate your (pending?) work schedule.

Executive/Part-Time MBA Programs

Executive MBA programs, which allow a student to earn an MBA without quitting the day job, are increasing in popularity. Just think, you get to work full-time *and* go to school—double the fun! A word of caution: most executive programs charge as if an employer were footing the bill.

East Coast tradition embraced West Coast innovation in 2001, when the University of Pennsylvania's highly regarded Wharton School opened **Wharton West** in San Francisco (101 Howard, Suite 500, 415-777-1000, http://west.wharton.upenn.edu). Early enrollees have given high marks to both its executive MBA program and its open enrollment executive education courses at the historic Folger Building. Now *that's* good coffee!

student discount, please!

You didn't hear it from us, but City College will issue you a student ID on the spot when you register for a class. If you later cancel your registration, you'll still have your ID. What you do with that ID is up to you, but you might consider getting a few discounts on movies, museums, and the like. No one ever said a student had to be under 25....

The Professional MBA for Executives program at **USF School of Business and Management** (2130 Fulton, 415-422-6771, www.usfca.edu/sobam) offers a solid curriculum to support those with regional business aspirations. **SF State College of Business** (1600 Holloway, 415-338-1276, http://cob.sfsu.edu), the local workhorse university, presents its version as an Accelerated MBA. Finally, **Golden Gate University** (415-442-6500, www.ggu.edu/schools/business/emba.html) offers a Strategic Executive MBA (SEMBA—sounds like a Latin dance!) program.

Outside the City, the **Haas School** (510-642-0292 for part-time programs) offers both weekend and evening MBA programs. Both are excellent values, and thus are highly competitive. *US News and World Report* recently ranked its part-time program seventh in the country. Haas has combined forces with **Columbia Business School** to offer an executive MBA program on the Berkeley campus (510-643-1046, www.berkeley.columbia.edu), which also ranks well nationally. Down in San Jose (do you know the way?), **San Jose State University's College of Business** (408-924-3400, www.cob.sjsu.edu) offers two evening MBA options, with the added advantage of strong ties to the Silicon Valley business network.

Law School at Night

Not everyone who wants to study law can afford to study in a full-time program. If you can't seem to break away during the day, it *is* possible get your law degree in the evenings. Thank goodness there's still a way to get more attorneys out there!

The part-time evening program at **Golden Gate University School of Law** (415-442-6630, www.ggu.edu/schools/law) is the most flexible, and can arrange for you to attend day classes part-time after you're admitted to the night program. The **USF School of Law** (415-422-6586, www.usfca.edu/law) has a part-time, mostly evening, JD program. Unfortunately, neither Stanford nor Hastings nor Boalt offers a part-time program.

Continuing Education

Continuing ed can spark your intellect and open up new cerebral worlds—or it can teach you how to taste wine, repair your car, or do your taxes. Either way, it expands your horizons, and that's a big part of the practice of leisure.

Almost all of the local universities offer some form of continuing adult education. **UC Berkeley Extension** (510-642-4111, www.unex.berkeley.edu) has two campuses in San Francisco (425 Market; 55 Laguna, although the Laguna campus is, unfortunately, slated to close after the Fall 2003 semester due to budget constraints), in addition to locations in Berkeley, Oakland, Fremont, Redwood City, and San Ramon. Their courses include certificate and special programs as well as a broad variety of general ed classes. Some of the spicier courses from their Spring 2003 catalog included "Love, American Style: A Cultural History of Sexuality in the United States" and "The Greatest Wines in the World."

SF State College of Extended Learning (1600 Holloway; 425 Market, 2nd Floor, 415-405-7700, www.cel.sfsu.edu) has a fine selection of continuing education courses, with an additional location in Oakland (2201 Broadway Street).

SFSU's pioneering **Multimedia Studies Program** (425 Market, 2nd Floor, 415-405-7700, http://msp.sfsu.edu/home.html) was at the forefront of the Internet boom and vaulted countless local students into the world of multimedia and the Web.

At just $18 per unit, courses at **City College of San Francisco** (415-239-3000, www.ccsf.edu) might be the best bargain around. For-credit courses are available on just about any subject imaginable, and non-credit division courses are tuition free. That's right, free. Students need only show up on the first day of class and buy their own books and supplies.

take two

Susan Logas, a 52-year-old mother who retired early from a career in telecommunications, returned to school at City College to study computer science. Several years later, she had completed certificate programs in Unix System Administration and Web Administration.

"I love going to City College," Susan told us. "I love being an adult student—it's a whole different perspective. I know how to study. I know how to listen. And I know how to support the teachers." Susan's now contemplating re-entering the workforce as a system or web administrator, thanks to her fine new education.

ALTERNATIVE EDUCATION

"Alternative education" is a peculiar expression, really—sort of like "alternative rock." What exactly constitutes "alternative?" Who decides what is "alternative" versus "mainstream?" Damned if we know. In any event, we feel compelled to share some options you might not find in your average Ivy League course catalog.

Vocational Schools

If you want to acquire a set of skills quickly, vocational schools can get you where you want to go. They usually specialize in a focused trade, such as technology, design, or culinary studies.

The nationwide **University of Phoenix** (185 Berry, 800-448-6775, www.phoenix.edu) presents a variety of practical programs for working adults, including business, technology, healthcare and education. Another option is **Heald College** (350 Mission, 800-755-3550, www.heald.edu), which offers associate degrees and certificate training, primarily in technology.

If the above say nothing but "yawn" to you, jump to some more vivacious options, below.

Drop-In Schooling

The loosely-defined concept of auditing classes gained popularity in the 60s. Needless to say, it's a very cost-effective method of study. You

THE AUDIT ARENA

Not surprisingly, UC Berkeley tends to be lenient in the audit arena, although gone are the days when just about any inquisitive soul could sit in on their class of choice. Jeremy Cantor audits at least one class there a semester. Of course, it helps that he works for the university! Despite Jeremy's insider advantage, he trusts that most professors will be happy to accommodate an auditor if the class has space, and you approach them early, with a genuine interest in the subject.

Jeremy recently audited a graduate-level course in Public Health Policy with the professor's permission. "It's a great way to break up my week," he told us. "A good class is a stimulating, challenging environment and when you audit, there's no required work. I've been able to check out a number of career and grad school possibilities."

can study what you want and the admission requirements are quite lax—as in, nonexistent!

Policies vary among universities and professors, so you might have to check around a bit before choosing your "major" but generally speaking, the larger the university and the bigger the class, the easier it will be to audit.

If you ask the professor up front if you can audit the class, you risk being asked for proof that you're enrolled in the university. This is where holding on to that old student ID card would come in handy! Stealth mode might be an option for larger classes, but that means skipping exams and other graded assignments. Whether you have the professor's permission or not, one major drawback of auditing is that there's no chance for credit or to bring home an "A" on your report card (no extra allowance for you!).

Mom, Dad—I Want to be a Chef

San Francisco is a culinary mecca and home to several internationally recognized culinary academies, a boon if soufflé is "ze way" you'd like to make your living.

The **California Culinary Academy** (625 Polk, 800-229-2433, www.baychef.com) offers not only instruction for students but gourmet dining for the public at very reasonable prices (see **Dining & Nightlife**). The world-renowned cooking school cranks out chefs who go on to cook at top venues around the globe.

If you'd like to bake like the masters, perfect your (spring-) form at the **San Francisco Baking Institute** (480 Grandview Drive, South San Francisco, 650-589-5784, www.sfbi.com), "where better baking begins" (but where, pray tell, does it end?). The well-respected **Culinary Institute of America at Greystone** (2555 Main Street, St. Helena, 800-333-9242, www.ciachef.edu) is just a stone's throw away in nearby wine country, and well-worth the commute—chefs from here land sweet gigs at the most chic restaurants around.

Another Round?

Bartending can make for a lively career or merely a quick cash stop-gap. The evening hours assure plenty of lounge time during the day.

Higher education in the field is available at the **American Bartenders School** (55 New Montgomery, 800-532-9222, www.barschool.com), which offers degrees in the time-tested field of "mixology." It could be just the medicine that the doctor ordered. As one giddy graduate on their website attests, "I was laid off from my job because the company was losing money. I needed a skill that I could learn quickly, and I could make money. I took the class at American Bartenders School, and one week later I was a certified bartender. I now work in an upscale restaurant. I make good tips and eat great food. I am a happy guy."

But wait, there's competition in the world of cocktail education. The **National Bartenders School** (870 Market, Suite 828, 800-556-6499, www.nationalbartending.com) is home-grown and eager to train you. So, too, is the **San Francisco School of Bartending** (760 Market, Suite 833, 415-362-1116, http://sfbartending.com), which touts a classroom replica of a bar, "except for the hangover." Woo-hoo! Bartending courses at the different schools cost from $500 to $1,000 and will have you drink-ready in about two weeks.

A new concept has hit the City like a cool draft: beer school. Educate yourself in the art of brewing fine hops and malts at **21st Amendment** (563 2nd Street, 415-369-0900, www.21st-amendment.com), a restaurant and brewery near SBC (Pac Bell) Park. "Professor Nico" will take you through the history and craft of different beer styles, and each one-night course comes complete with a syllabus, appetizers, and (but of course) plenty of liquid samples. The whole keg consists of five courses; tuition is $20 a night.

so you've always wanted to be a...

• *Mechanic* •
Break out the tools in the Automotive Technology program of ***City College of San Francisco's Office of Vocational Education*** (415-550-4440, *www.ccsf.edu/Services/Vocational_Education [note the capital letters here]*, locations throughout San Francisco). Students can earn certificates in mechanics as well as body and fender repair.

• *Esthetician* •
Get the skinny on all kinds of beauty training at the ***San Francisco Institute of Esthetics and Cosmetology*** (1067 Folsom, Suite 200, 866-734-3244, *www.sanfranciscoinstitute.com*) in their programs for cosmetologists, estheticians, and nail technicians (hey, it's technical!).

more...

HOLISTIC SERVICES

Have you always dreamt of laying your hands on others? Poking needles through someone else's skin? (Minds out of the gutter, please.) You might be a born holistic healer with the untapped potential to treat your fellow human. The following dynamic programs can help you help others.

Massage Therapy

Who doesn't like a massage therapist? (Especially one you are dating!) They spread more joy than perhaps any other class of professionals, and feed off of that joy in return. Liz King, a massage therapist from Pacifica, says her career is very fulfilling. "I know that I am positively influencing people's lives, and helping them relax."

If you want to become this popular and get paid for it to boot, you'll need training. There are countless school listings to massage through, including the **San Francisco School of Massage** (1327 Chestnut, Suites A & B, 415-474-4600, www.sfsm.net), and the **Western Institute of Science and Health** (78 1st Street, 415-543-1833, www.westerni.org), which specializes in advanced degrees and training from Shiatsu to Hydrotherapy.

...cont'd

• *Pilot* •
Take off into the wild blue yonder if you must, but please—take some lessons first! Crissy Airfield now harbors snowy egrets, not planes, so buzz on down to the San Carlos Airport and ***Bel-Air International*** (795 Sky Way, San Carlos, 650-596-9900, *www.belairintl.com*). There you can train for anything from piloting a private plane to commandeering a jumbo jet.

• *Veterinarian's Assistant* •
If you're not up for the commitment of a veterinary program like the one at UC Davis, then pony on up to ***Santa Rosa Junior College*** (1501 Mendocino Avenue, 800-564-7752, *www.santarosa.edu*) and enroll in their Animal Science Certificate Program. Their courses will prepare you to be a veterinarian's assistant (or ranch manager—giddyup!). Imagine the possibilities—you might win that coveted sheep scholarship after all.

Teaching Yoga

New yoga schools are popping up like flies in and around the City, and schools need teachers. Stretch your boundaries by teaching others to stretch theirs. You'll keep a fit mind and body while you're at it.

Barbara MacMillan, a self-proclaimed yoga fanatic, enrolled in an intensive four-week program at **Greenpath Yoga** (2242 Lombard, 415-775-7545, www.greenpathyoga.org) and now teaches at several studios in Mill Valley. She also offers private lessons at her home. "The best part of teaching yoga is that it provides the most fulfilling work atmosphere I've ever had," she says. "The energy is positive and everyone leaves the lesson feeling better than when they arrived."

Other notable instructor schools include **It's Yoga** (848 Folsom, 415-543-1970, www.itsyoga.net), which specializes in Ashtanga, and **Yoga Center of Marin** (142 Redwood Avenue, Corte Madera, 415-927-1850, www.yogacenterofmarin.com), which bases its courses primarily on Iyengar. Some programs offer scholarships or a tuition payment on a sliding scale.

citizen's academy

Do you aspire to be a better citizen and contribute more to your community? You can train in the fine practice of citizenship through the ***City of Oakland's Citizen's Academy*** (Office of the City Manager, Oakland, 510-238-3301). The purpose of the program is "to engage Oakland citizens with their City government by providing an interactive forum to learn first hand how the City of Oakland is structured and managed." You have to apply (and be accepted), and the weekly classes are held on weekday evenings and Saturdays.

Walk the beat with the SFPD through their ***Citizen's Police Academy*** (350 Amber, 415-401-4701, *www.ci.sf.ca.us/police,* "Citizen's Academy"). This program, predictably, focuses more on municipal policing, and aims to "develop a closer understanding and working relationship between the San Francisco Police Department and communities served." Classes meet on Monday nights for 13 weeks in a row, and participants are expected to attend all classes. Those with spotty criminal records need not apply.

Chinese Medicine & Acupuncture

Are you a stickler for acupuncture? This and other alternative health practices have flourished in the U.S. during the last 20 years, as more and more people explore the healing power of ancient Chinese therapies.

In the Bay Area, the two most prominent acupuncture schools are the **American College of Traditional Chinese Medicine** in Potrero Hill (455 Arkansas, 415-282-7600, www.actcm.edu) and, across the Bay, the **Academy of Chinese Culture and Health Sciences** (1601 Clay Street, Oakland, 510-763-7787, www.acchs.edu). Both are accredited by The Accreditation Commission for Acupuncture and Oriental Medicine (ACAOM).

San Francisco's own Chinese medicine guru is author and wellness pioneer **Doc Misha** (www.docmisha.com). Her site on Traditional Chinese Medicine features books, clinics and all sorts of other "wellness" goodies.

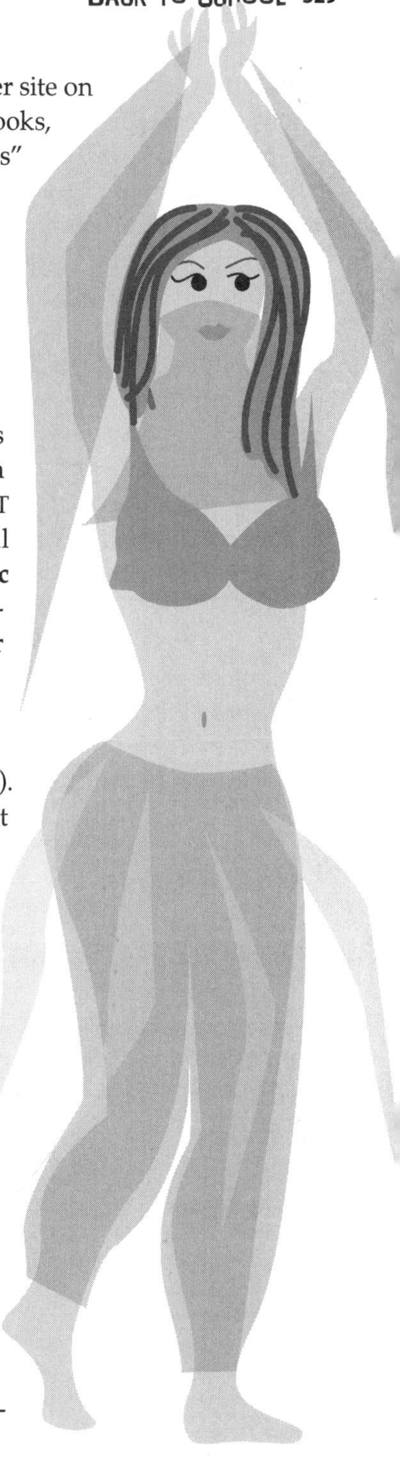

Chiropractic

Are chiropractors truly medical doctors? It's debatable. Go to school and then decide for yourself whether you've become a "real" doctor or not.

Cracking the code on chiropractic schools in the Bay Area is a bit of a challenge, with surprisingly few focused purely on SMT (that's Spinal Manipulation Therapy, for all you neophytes). Try **Palmer Chiropractic West** (90 East Tasman Drive, San Jose, 408-944-6000, www.palmer.edu), renowned for its focus on sports medicine and training, or **Life Chiropractic College West** in the East Bay (25001 Industrial Boulevard, Hayward, 800-788-4476, www.lifewest.edu). And remember—it's not "cracking" but "spinal manipulation."

Belly Dancing

Last but not least, we come to the study of belly dancing. What back-to-school discussion would be complete without touching on this incomparable art? And you thought all those dancers at Kan Zaman were *born* with rolling stomachs and gyrating hips. Au contraire, mon frère—those dancers trained for years in order to master their craft.

Belly dancing has its roots in Middle Eastern culture and the traditional dance is quite conservative. Practiced by women for other women only under the guise of a fertility ceremony, it was reputedly taught to young girls as a way to strengthen their abdominal muscles in preparation for childbirth.

Leave it to western culture to add the erotic touch. Apparently the hip and abdominal movements were too risqué for conservative western views at the end of the 19th century, so the dance was branded as immoral. This only piqued the public's interest. Hollywood latched onto the dance and contributed the seductive costumes and naval jewelry that prevail among belly dancers today.

Why the heck do we care about the history of belly dancing? We're not really sure. All we know is that we like it, and we're all for the modern sensual versions too. Further, we encourage the leisurely study and practice of the art.

Curious students can contact **Fat Chance Belly Dance** in the Mission (670 South Van Ness, 415-431-4322, www.fcbd.com), which specializes in American Tribal Style Bellydance. The **San Francisco Dance Center** (26 7th Street, www.linesballet.org/dance, 415-863-3040) also lists belly dancing courses on their docket. Liz King takes regular lessons at **Downward Dog Yoga** in Pacifica (94 West Manor Drive, Pacifica, 650-355-9642, www.downwarddogyoga.com) and hopes to begin performing soon. "It's not just a workout," she says. "It's a reconnection to my femininity."

FINAL EXAM

Powerful stuff indeed. Whether reconnecting with your femininity or your ability to mix drinks, studying queuing theory or organic chemistry, you'll never go wrong furthering your education. However, if you must (and we do mean must) go out and get yourself a job, read on to learn how you can find fulfilling work without giving up your hard-earned sense of leisure.

CHAPTER 11
THE LEISURELY JOB HUNT

"Find a job you like and you add five days to every week."

~H. Jackson Brown, Jr.
Author, Life's Little Instruction Book

WHY would a book about savoring time off focus its last two chapters on work? Talking about jobs in a book on leisure might seem ironic but most people not only need to work, they *want* to work—as long as that work is something they feel good about. So when you're good and ready to take the plunge back into the working world (or are just in dire need of a steady paycheck), turn to this chapter for some informal job search ideas that will stave off the *post-sabbatical blues.*

Nontraditional tactics range from going to parties to taking ski weekends to playing golf. Sound like fun? Sound leisurely? It can be. No one ever said searching for a job had to be a drag. Leave the career fairs to those who feel the need to don a business suit and stand in a long line with resume in hand.

Take the time to envision your ideal job, too. Do you want to work for yourself or someone else? Big organization or small? Business, non-profit or other? If all you want to do is fund more leisure, this meditation won't take long. If you're ready for deeper career soul searching, no job hunt guide tops the classic *What Color Is Your Parachute,* by Richard Bolles. Either way, look for work that will feed your spirit as well as pay your bills, because nothing anchors a life of leisure more than a job you can't wait to get to each day.

THE ZEN APPROACH TO JOB HUNTING

Job searches, like dating and other quests in life, obey a natural rule: the harder you search, the more elusive the result. We've all experienced the phenomenon of being more attractive to others when we are already involved in a relationship. The same holds true in the work world: potential employers find us more attractive if we are already involved with another organization.

Great, but what if you *don't* have a job? Remember that you don't have to *be* taken to *seem* taken—or at least desirable. By conveying that you aren't desperate for a job, you'll come across as confident, secure and in demand, whether you really are or not. This is, of course, easier said than done.

Whatever your circumstance, keep reminding yourself that you are a valuable, unique asset—because you are! The job search is all a matter of figuring where that asset fits within the work world, not about whether you are able to get hired by a particular industry or organization.

So don't *look* for a job, at least in the traditional sense. Let the job come to you, O Zen master. Let employers know that you're a survivor—even though you're searching for work, your world won't end if they can't or won't hire you.

leisurely work & the wisdom of the ages

Work is love made visible.

~Kahlil Gibran

• • •

Let the beauty of what you love be what you do.

~Rumi

• • •

Your work is to discover your work, and then with all your heart to give yourself to it.

~Buddha

Staying calm about your job search doesn't mean you can sit and wait for the phone to ring. It just means that job-searching is not a competition that you win or lose. You won't earn points for talking to the most HR people, scheduling the most interviews or landing the most offers. You will score by landing a job that you love.

"What Do You Do (For Fun)?"

Do you like parties? Find some! But don't stop there, go out and have fun at whatever else it is that you like to do too. Depriving yourself of your favorite activities or interests in favor of an extra hour in front of the computer is hardly going to benefit your search. Indeed, driving yourself crazy with the job hunt is not only detrimental to your frame of mind, it can actually hinder your search.

If you like to snowboard, go snowboarding. If you like to golf, get a foursome together. Better yet, invite a friend to bring along an associate who might be a good contact.

It's remarkable how many people find a job or at least a connection leading up to it by pursuing their natural ambitions. Gary Brockway's (name changed) passion was playing the stock market so now he's a self-employed day-trader. "I turned something that was a hobby (trading stocks) into a lifestyle and profession," Gary says.

Mine Your Friends & Family

Surprisingly, a lot of people shy away from reaching out to friends and family while they're job hunting. This, at a time when they could most use their help.

Don't be shy. Ask those closest to you for help with your job search. You'll surely return the favor when *they* need help. Get them working for you and follow up with them diligently. Your friends and family are your emissaries as well as your support team and can make your "job" a lot easier. Who better to market your value than the people who know you best?

Don't make the mistake, however, of relying on loosely-based contacts to go to bat for you. While casual contacts are important for gathering information, they'll rarely risk their reputation

put on your party hat

Sitting at home watching reruns of *Sex in the City* is not going to broaden your network or expose you to new career possibilities (although it might expose you to something else...). So, get out and socialize, be it at a bar in the evening, an aerobics class in the morning or any other activity where other people will be around.

House parties are a job-search gold mine, particularly those thrown by your friends. The guest list itself embodies a subtle screening process, and you'll enjoy a trust based on the fact that you're all friends of the host. Talk with people about their jobs and let it be known that you're looking for work yourself. Don't walk around with your resume, but be receptive when others offer information. They almost certainly will if they feel they're able to help. Remember, people want to work with other people they like. If they like you in a social context, they're more likely to help you out when it comes to working for their company.

to promote your skills. Rely mostly on your closest allies. You could be surprised to discover the friends they have in influential places.

Adrianna Moore (name changed), an attorney who was *limbo-employed* for six months, asked her friends and family for honest feedback on her strengths and weaknesses. "It got them involved without blatantly asking for their Rolodex," she said, "and it helped them to understand better to whom and to where they could recommend me."

seek the zone

Pay attention to what you do with your time when you can do anything you want, and ask yourself, "Can I translate any of this into a paying job?" Maybe not, but then again—maybe you can.

In sports psychology speak, seek "the zone." Look for those moments when time disappears and not a thought enters your mind except what you're doing at that moment, then look for a job that includes those activities and skills.

"If you have to settle for less than your dream job in the short term," counsels Joel Garfinkle, career coach and founder of ***Dream Job Coaching*** (Oakland, 510-655-2010, *www.dreamjobcoaching.com*), "stay committed to what you ultimately want to create in this world."

Seek Employment by Osmosis

Much like a groupie backstage at a rock concert, you too must be a "hanger-on" to the employed set. As much as we laud the cafés and other weekday hangout spots in the leisurely sense, you might want to curtail those three-hour coffee sessions now (we know, it seems like sacrilege!). When your goal is to find an employer, you need to share a table with someone who's working. Call it employment by osmosis.

Short of hanging out in your best friend's office all day, try timing your meals to catch the working set during morning coffee, lunchtime or happy hour. Find out if any of your friends need a date to a company cocktail hour or holiday party and volunteer your services. If you can afford it, join a health club, a social club or a (shhhh...) secret society. Anything to get yourself out of the house and around those with jobs! Find more ideas in "A Guide to Local Networking" on p. 338.

Work For Free

Why would you want to work free? Because, on a short trial basis, it can be an ideal way for you and a potential employer to decide whether there's a good match.

Say you're attempting a lateral transition. Even though you're confident that your skills will cross over, your future employer might not be. Mitigate the risk by offering to work unpaid for a 30-day trial period. If both you and the employer are pleased, you'll be hired. Put this agreement in writing ahead of time if you can. Even if you're fully qualified for the job, an unpaid trial period might be the way to go in a tight market. Think of it as *pre-re-employment.*

Eliminate Expectations

Dealing with expectations poses a real challenge in any employment re-immersion process. If you have a strong idea of what you want to do next, set yourself free to pursue your goals. Let go of your salary expectations. Be ready to sacrifice responsibility or stature in return for greater personal fulfillment.

Victims of the tech crash, in particular, have had to take several steps backwards before moving forward. Tim Whiting (name changed) was the co-founder of an Internet startup and worked as head of operations for nearly four years. Despite this experience, he had a difficult time transitioning to a different industry.

"People look at being at a dot-com as a joke," he told us. "As far as potential employers are concerned, it's as if those years didn't even exist." Once Tim released the memory of his old salary and status, however, he landed a gig in organic produce, an industry he's always been interested in.

GET CREATIVE

According to a 2002 survey by ***The Creative Group*** of Menlo Park, California (888-846-1668, *www.creativegroup.com*), job seekers use some downright wacky tactics to stand out in the crowd during a tight job market.

Advertising and marketing executives were asked the most unusual tactic they had seen a job hunter use. Among the responses: singing telegrams, resumes written on softballs, and lottery tickets included in place of cover letters. One eager interviewee even followed up by sending a pair of socks to the hiring manager. Their lucky interview socks, perhaps? We just hope they were washed!

LOST TIME ON THE RESUME

Are you worried about holes in your resume? Don't be overly concerned. Monster.com reminds us that one out of every five workers is out of work at some point each year. Odds are, that crowd includes some of your potential employers. If that doesn't make them sympathetic to your situation—we forbid you to work for them!

Kidding aside, the sad truth is that not everyone who receives your CV will see time off for the major accomplishment that it is. *We* know that you weren't just on vacation during your time off, you were building leadership skills through travel and outdoor adventures, presentation skills through karaoke... But it might take some ingenuity to convey the extent of your dedication to your future employer. Hang in there!

When you look back at how you've spent your time, get creative when filling in those resume gaps. How creative is ultimately up to you, but the following tongue-in-cheek suggestions should help to get the hamster wheel spinning.

WINE, DON'T WHINE

Will Eagle's hourly wage fell from $135/hour for high-tech consulting to $8/hour selling wine at retail, but Will's passion for wine kept him going. He rapidly earned buying power at ***The Wine Club*** (953 Harrison, 415-512-9086, *www.thewineclub.com*), met more people in the industry, and expanded his already impressive knowledge of fine wines. Drank his fair share of them, too! Will eventually landed a job in wine public relations but The Wine Club lured him back to work for management and do in-house public relations.

"Sometimes you've just got to look around," Will says. "I was in The Wine Club making a purchase one day, and there was a 'help wanted, no experience necessary' sign on the back of the door. When the clerk asked if there was anything else he could get me, I responded, 'Not unless you want to get me an application...' I was working there within a week, and I considered it a tremendous education. The only bad thing is, now everyone hands me the wine list when we go out!"

Leisure Larry
1392 La Playa
San Francisco, CA 94122
415-564-9894

Key Qualification: Master of Leisure
Objective: To marry my passions with my work.

PROFESSIONAL EXPERIENCE

Dec 2003	**Marine Biology Researcher** [*Translation:* sat on the beach]
Nov 2003	**Public Speaker** [*Translation:* karaoke bar junkie]
Oct 2003	**Restaurant Management Intern** [*Translation:* sat at the bar]
Sep 2003	**Construction General Contractor** [*Translation:* built a rolling bar for Bay to Breakers race]
Aug 2003	**Volunteer Worker** [*Translation:* constructed papier mâché palm trees for Burning Man theme camp]
Jul 2003	**Change Management Consultant** [*Translation:* helped best friend get over breakup]
Jun 2003	**Subject of Monitored Health Study** [*Translation:* friends watched me drink too much and then fall down]
May 2003	**Employed by the State** [*Translation:* collected Unemployment Insurance]
April 2003	**Employed by the State** [*Translation:* incarcerated]
Mar 2003	**Freelancer** [*Translation:* "freelancer"]
Feb 2003	**Healthcare Consultant, Financial Counselor, Expert Time Manager and Personal Assistant to Busy Executives** [*Translation:* raised a family]
Jan 2003	**Teacher** [*Translation:* taught little brother to snowboard]

EDUCATION
Training [surfed the 'net]
Continuing Education [surfed the 'net]
Executive Education [surfed the 'net]
Adult Education [slept around]
Cultural Exchange Student [ordered margaritas in Cabo]

A GUIDE TO LOCAL NETWORKING

Every person and every book you turn to when you're looking for a job will stress the value of "networking." You might get sick of hearing it. While we don't dispute its value—even "hyper-networking" has its place—not all networking was created equal. Here's the local spin on where to meet people in the best position to help you.

Bars & Restaurants

Many a professional connection has been made over an adult beverage at the corner tavern. Of course, we would *never* endorse drinking just to get drunk (would we?) but alcohol does serve as a so-called social lubricant… so when it's time to find a job, you need to graduate from the coffee house to the bar.

For "Financial D" networking (investment bankers, legal eagles and the like), **The Royal Exchange** (301 Sacramento, 415-956-1710, www.royalexchange.com) is simply an institution. Here you'll find suits mixing with khakis, lawyers mixing with bankers, and the occasional miscreant mixing with—the stir stick? The crowd tends to be on the younger side, but the place does see its share of "suit" veterans. Right next door is **Harrington's Bar & Grill** (245 Front, 415-392-7595), a good place for a boozy lunch during the week. You'll see button-up business types coexisting with mechanics and construction workers.

For an old school, cigar-smoking crowd, try lunch or cocktails around the corner at **Tadich Grill** (240 California, 415-391-1849), which also happens to be the oldest restaurant in California, dating back to 1849 (note the phone number). Moving slightly south of Market, the newer **Cosmopolitan Café** (121 Spear, 415-543-4001), joins financial types and technology folks.

For a completely different scene, **111 Minna** (111 Minna, 415-974-1719, www.111minnagallery.com) hosts a raucous happy hour that attracts tech folks and creative hipsters. While some decent new-economy banter flies around there, the techies network best at **Café Mars** (798 Brannan, 415-621-6277), given that several software companies, including Macromedia, HQ just down the street.

Lalita's Distinctive Thai (96 McAllister, 415-552-5744) is a drinking hangout for Hastings law students and practicing litigators alike. Criminal trial attorneys, however, frequent the **Absinthe Brasserie and Bar** (398 Hayes, 415-551-1590) near City Hall.

Literary and creative types seek like-minded souls at **Vesuvio Caffe** in North Beach (255 Columbus, 415-362-3370), or across the alley at **City Lights Bookstore** (261 Columbus, 415-362-8193). If politics and city government are your thing and you can afford an $8 cocktail, try **Jardinière** (300 Grove, 415-861-5555) where "Da Mayor" and other city bigwigs hang out.

membership groups

You need not belong to the highly exclusive and secretive ***Bohemian Club*** (415-885-2440) to network through social organizations (although you're welcome to give it a go—good luck!).

Consider other less "gentried" groups, such as the ***Commonwealth Club*** (see ***Chapter 9*** under "Working the Room"), which bills itself as the "nation's oldest and largest public affairs forum." Over the years, it has hosted such luminaries as Teddy Roosevelt, Bill Clinton, and Bill Gates. The $110 annual membership could be well worth the investment.

The ***World Affairs Council*** (also from ***Chapter 9***, "Working the Room"), another member organization, hosts over 200 events a year on international politics, business, education, and art. An individual membership will set you back $85.

These orgs might cost ya' but remember—membership does have its privileges.

Networking Organizations

On the more formal side, organizations exist for the sole mission of bringing people together for professional purposes. The **Churchill Club** (www.churchillclub.org) touts itself as Silicon Valley's premier business and technology forum. A $125 annual membership fee entitles you to program discounts, but you don't have to be a member to attend events. The **San Francisco Chamber of Commerce** (235 Montgomery, 12th Floor, 415-392-4520, www.sfchamber.com) has all kinds of good stuff designed to connect you up, from international mixers to Business After Hours, a monthly networking forum. See their website under "Programs & Events" for the full scoop.

One of the better online organizations is the fairly new **Ryze** (www.ryze.com), a national networking group with a strong contingent in the Bay Area. The tools on their site help connect people both professionally and socially. Visitors to **Craig's List** (www.craigslist.org) can connect with just about any type of community, as well as peruse the job board and events listings. Women interested in technology can unite around **San Francisco Women on the Web** (www.sfwow.org) and partake in a host of gatherings such as their colorfully named "Scrappy Hours," which rotate among City bars every few weeks (not to worry, the bars themselves are not all that "scrappy"). For those entrepreneurs out there, **WorkIt** (www.workit.com) is a Bay Area focused group dedicated to professionals working at technology startups.

Great Moments in Unemployment

Richard Bolles, author of ***What Color Is Your Parachute***, wrote his best-selling treatise on job hunting after a budget crunch cost him his own job as canon pastor at Grace Cathedral in San Francisco. No sooner did he find another position than he recognized the same career anxiety among the campus ministers he was now supervising. To help them with job switching and procurement, Bolles self-published 100 copies of his 168-page job hunter's "bible" in 1970 and handed them out for free.

Over 30 years later, ***Parachute*** sells 15,000 to 20,000 copies each month and, in 1995, made the Library of Congress's Center for the Book's list of "25 Books That Have Shaped Readers' Lives." Bolles pioneered the concept that the best way to find a job is to focus on the skills and talents you want to use and then find an organization that needs them. An ordained Episcopalian priest, Bolles is considered the father of career soul-searching.

GETTING SOME COACHING

Career Counselors

Back in high school, Mary Mangold sought advice on how to make use of her talents. "I always knew I was creative but I never knew how to get there," she said. "I talked to my high school career counselor about all the things I wanted to do. When I stopped talking, he looked at me—stared at me—and said, 'You have just got the longest eyelashes I've ever seen.'"

Thank goodness that most of today's career counselors are more professional. If you're having a difficult time charting a new career path or finding the right job, consider hiring one. They're not "headhunters" but trained professionals who focus on counseling and coaching. Services range from low- or no-cost job placement assistance from volunteers to in-depth life coaching that requires a significant financial commitment. Choose your guidance wisely, as there's a range of advice available, not all of it useful.

One the most well-respected organizations in San Francisco is the **Bay Area Career Center** (57 Post, Suite 804, 415-398-4881, www.bayareacareercenter.com). Started by former members of the Alumnae Resource Center, the BACC offers counseling, workshops, and other career-assistance services from a veteran staff.

Free Help

If you're out looking for work, chances are you're in serious cash-conservation mode. Before shelling out big bucks for a full-blown analysis from a Ph.D., check out what's available for less. Several San Francisco organizations gear their services towards lower-income job seekers.

Experience Unlimited (745 Franklin, 415-771-1776, www.eu-sf.org) is funded by the California Employment Development Department. It's right next door to the **San Francisco EDD** (801 Turk, 415 749-7503)—in fact, you might feel like you're *at* the EDD. You become a "member" by volunteering 16 hours per month, and attending two general meetings and one department meeting per month. A tad bureaucratic, perhaps, but often an effective way to get leads.

Sponsored by the SF Chamber of Commerce, **The Job Forum** (235 Montgomery, 12th Floor, 415.392.4520, www.thejobforum.org) has a mission to "provide ideas, advice, counsel and encouragement to job seekers (and career changers) in the San Francisco Bay Area." It's not an employment agency, but a forum to support the job search process through weekly evening meetings. **One Stop San Francisco** (www.onestopsf.com, click on "Job Seekers") provides a directory of the City's major employment and training programs, including the City College of San Francisco. There are also three affiliated **Career Link Centers**, the best of which is in the Mission (3120 Mission, 415-401-4800) and boasts a computer facility, free internet access, and a helpful staff.

SELF-EMPLOYMENT

Even when you're not working, you probably come up with countless ideas on how you would do things better than your old boss. Here's your chance! Time off can spur you to start your own venture and see where it leads.

In fact, times of high unemployment correlate directly with times of increased entrepreneurial activity, a phenomenon that academics call the "shopkeeper effect"—workers are in transition, labor is cheap and abundant, and many people are forced into self-employment. So there you go. While it won't necessarily lead to owning the next Microsoft (then again, you never know), going solo carries many of the same advantages as creating a fully-staffed company.

One outstanding perk is that even though no one else reports to you, you're still your *own* boss. Self-employment is often a one-way street for that very reason. "I don't think I'll ever work for someone else again," Lisa Turner, principal at **Word Inc.** (www.word-inc.com), said after breaking free from corporate life to become an independent marketing and public relations consultant. "I finally came to terms with the fact that it never was my style and likely never will be."

Gary Brockway (name changed) found that the biggest benefit of working for himself was setting his own agenda. "If I want to go surfing that day, I can go surfing," he told us. "I don't miss working in an office at all." Deanndra Eggers, sole proprietor of the specialty pet supply store **Puppy Cat** (289 Divisadero, 415-621-5911) seconds the sentiment. "As much as I liked the company I worked for, it was still Cubicle World. Just a maze of cubicles. Not looking at those walls, that drab tan and gray—that's one thing I like about working for myself."

STARTING YOUR OWN BUSINESS

The shopkeeper effect can spawn more than self-employment (or self-*un*employment). People who have either quit a job or stopped looking for a new one often start full-blown companies, complete with employees and overhead. This means that the current economic climate is ripe for your budding inspiration.

Still think the timing's not right? There's truly no time like the present (and no present like the time). Deanndra Eggers received plenty of warnings from well-meaning friends not to start a business in a down economy, but she did it anyway. "People will always need to feed their pets," she told us, "and I always wanted to open a pet store, so I did. I figure it's a risk whether the economy is down or not." A well-calculated one, it seems—barely six months into operations, she received a *"Best of San Francisco 2003"* nod from the *San Francisco Weekly.*

Local resources to help you on your way include **Nolo Press** (950 Parker Street, Berkeley, 800-728-3555, www.nolo.com), with a great selection of "how to" books to help the blossoming entrepreneur, and the **Small Business Administration** (455 Market, 6th Floor, 415-744-6820, http://www.sba.gov/ca/sf), which can assist with loan guarantees and advice. The SBA has an excellent on-site facility and library, and offers free small business seminars, a "getting started" checklist and a model business plan outline. The SBA also guarantees loans of up to $50,000.

If you're just starting out, rest assured that you won't necessarily need a huge bankroll or a loan. You will have to make some sacrifices. "You can start a business on peanuts," says Joe Gilmartin, proprietor of the **Black Horse London Pub** (1514 Union, 415-928-2414, www.sf-blackhorse.com). "My beer license was only $450. I sold my motorcycle for $500 and slept on a friend's couch for a year."

Was it worth it? Joe thinks so. "The bottom line is, I have job security," he says. "I can control how long I'm going to have a job."

a beautiful loan

"The most beautiful thing about the SBA loan," says Joe Gilmartin, "is that you don't have to pay principal for the first two or three years. You pay interest only, so you have time to get ramped up."

Joe secured an SBA-backed loan to grow his business. "The SBA might tell you differently," Joe said, "but loan approvals take 3-6 months. The Catch-22 is that they'd rather you have an existing business that you want to expand, versus just a concept for a new business."

Be prepared to log in some serious hours if you start a company. "You gotta have that mental game that you're willing to work around the clock for very little," Joe advises, "but the longer you stick with it, the better your chances are going to be to make it. All big businesses have to start as a small business."

Don't be surprised to find that all this effort is a labor of love, either. "Finding work that aligns to you will make work feel more like leisure, because you'll be doing what you do naturally and effortlessly," says career coach Joel Garfinkle. "It brings you fulfillment, and allows you to feel lighter about your life and what you want to give to this world."

What the professionals predict, the entrepreneurs live: "I think I work the same amount in seven days that I did in five," Deanndra told us, "and I don't have any days off, but it doesn't feel like work. I am very relaxed."

How very leisurely!

CHAPTER 12
LEISURE BACK TO WORK

There is something wrong with my eyesight.
I can see going to work.

~Teddy Bergeron

YOU knew this day would come eventually: you're going back to work. You're *re-employed*. Income! If you've gotten close to the bottom of your leisure bucks stockpile, the thought of a regular paycheck is probably a welcome relief. Still, anxiety of a different kind might be nagging at you now—the fear that your days of leisure have come to an end and you'll revert to being a *slave.*

Fortunately, that doesn't have to happen. You *can* create a more leisurely environment at work, whether that environment is an office, the outdoors, an emergency room or a classroom. This knowledge is the key to fully savoring your last days off.

The practice of leisure will take a slightly different form at work. "Leisurely work" implies that the stress and tension is manageable, and that you're relaxed and fulfilled because your job draws on your natural passions and talents. As career coach Joel Garfinkle reminds us, "Finding your dream job brings you fulfillment. It allows you to feel lighter about your life and what you want to give to the world."

Ease into leisure mode at a new job if you want to create a good first impression. Promote leisure for the benefit of the organization, use the tips we offer only when they will fly in your workplace, and choose your leisure "battles" as carefully as you chose your employment.

WORK SMART, NOT LONG

One of the toughest aspects of shifting from full-time leisure to work is the feeling that you've lost control of your agenda. Being constantly in reaction mode is quite un-leisurely. Lend more order and sanity to your day with the following "work smart" tactics.

Start Work Before Working Hours

There's no need to start your day with an emergency. Yet, in many jobs, if you arrive at the official beginning of "office hours," the red light on your voice mailbox will already be lit and people may even be lined up at your door. Try getting in 15 or 30 minutes early, and don't answer the phone or take any appointments before 9am (or whenever the regular shift starts). Maybe you'll be able to return one of those voicemails with a message saying, "Thanks for calling about that project. It's done."

Even better, start tomorrow's work yesterday—take fifteen minutes at the end of each workday to set six goals for the next day so when you come in, you won't get sidetracked fighting fires. Prioritize and stick to your plan. You'll sleep well for it.

Leave on Time

Just like getting in early, staying late can allow you to work without interruption. However, most of us are just "done" by 5pm. We have friends to see and so much leisure to enjoy! Develop a reputation for leaving on time, and people will learn not to task you at 4:30pm. They will come to you sooner in the day with their requests. You'll have some peace to wrap up your day before you leave.

Stay Late on a Friday Night

Leave work on time but spend a weekend night at the office? It might be counterintuitive, but finishing your work week at your own pace can allow you to enjoy Saturday and Sunday to their fullest. Unfinished tasks won't nag at your conscience all weekend. You won't be harried and rushing out to a Friday night dinner with friends who are probably just as tired as you are. Wouldn't it be more relaxing to get together on a Saturday night instead?

You can even take some time for yourself: pay bills, answer some personal e-mails, read a magazine. Doing things on Friday night that you'd normally put off until Sunday can leave you feeling calm and rested as the weekend comes to an end. We're not suggesting spending *every* Friday night at the office, just every once in awhile. It could be the most peaceful time you'll spend at work, even if it means missing a cocktail hour every now and then.

mix it up

Can't decide if you're a morning or a night person? You don't have to. Vince Crivello, a Director at Schwab, thinks you should mix it up instead. Take a page from his day planner:

"One could come in early and leave early—maybe go for a swim, a hike in the headlands, a drive down Lombard Street. Or pick a morning to hang out: read the paper, go for a run, make a breakfast burrito, whatever. Leave late if you need to, but mix up the routine. It gives you something to look forward to, especially if you don't do any travel for work."

Beware of False Deadlines

Jane once stayed in her office literally all night finishing a project for some dud who'd put her on a deadline, only to admit later that he'd just wanted her to work on his project first. He went on to boast that he ended up not needing her work at all. Jane then lost even more precious hours plotting her revenge!

Don't be a Jane. If your coworkers are well-intentioned but prone to panic, ask what will happen if the task is not done by tomorrow. Take a moment, light a candle and chant this mantra: "There is nothing, and I mean nothing, that cannot wait until tomorrow." Surely you can work together to set a more reasonable deadline. And if your colleagues really *are* that devious? Consider keeping a copy of Sun Tzu's *The Art of War* on hand.

ANTI-DEADLINE MANTRAS

"There's nothing that can't wait 'til tomorrow."

"I can help you later, but not right now."

"I'm afraid I can't meet that deadline."

"There's probably someone else who can do this sooner."

Delegate

If you want something done right, do you really have to do it yourself? Mastering control over your working hours means regularly asking yourself, "How important is *right* versus *done*?" If you're facing a task that only you are genuinely qualified to do, so be it. If you're keeping work to yourself out of short-term expedience, coach someone else on your team to take on the project. Taking those few extra minutes now will save you time in the long run, especially for recurring tasks.

Not incidentally, delegating will help you move up the ranks by multiplying your productivity and freeing yourself up to learn new skills. This concept is nothing new, but it's key to creating a leisurely workday.

Schedule Down Time

Working smart and not long includes scheduling breaks. "Taking breaks allows you to get the perspective to make decisions that support and honor you," Coach Garfinkle says. At least you won't sit there stalled, trying to force inspiration on yourself.

Instead of frittering away work hours on procrastination, use that time to do something more satisfying. See a matinée, go home an hour early and garden, or take a class. Jeremy Cantor has a friend who schedules at least two hours into her Palm Pilot each week for pure down time. "Now I do it too," Jeremy says. "It's great. I take it as seriously as any other appointment."

You can schedule breaks inside the office as well as out. If you have a desk job, set aside 30 minutes a day to answer personal e-mails or surf the net. You're going to do it anyway. This way, you'll know it's coming up. You'll be less distracted thinking about personal tasks or entertainment when you could be getting work done. Whatever you do during a break, plan your day to take plenty of them.

don't let this happen to you!

A business executive in England was spotted drifting from lane to lane at 70 MPH, driving after dark with his interior light on. The reason? He was reading a book propped up on his steering wheel—to catch up on work! This stunt got him reported, and then convicted of dangerous driving, for which he temporarily lost his license. Is any work that important? We don't think so. If you have a choice (and you always do), don't bring work home with you. Leave it at the office.

Catch a Leisure Nap

What do you miss most about your work-free days? For Andrew Riley, that would be naps. "I miss my naps even more than my previously inflated salary," he says.

So why not nap at work? Fewer than one percent of American employers promote it, yet 36 percent of Americans say they do it, according to a recent human resources management study. We endorse each one of these sleepy rebellions. If the stars of *ER* can hide in the back office of the emergency room and catch some short-term winks, why not the rest of us?

Several government agencies use nap programs for employees who work in high-risk environments. Naps can increase alertness, reduce errors and absenteeism, improve effectiveness and generally keep a smile on your face. "Workplace napping is a natural, no-cost way to increase worker productivity," say Dr. William Anthony and Camille Anthony, the authors of *The Art of Napping at Work*.

A nap can be as simple as a 15-20 minute siesta in your office, or a few minutes of zoning out while appearing to study your e-mail. Naps can be taken while you're "on the phone" too. Find more tips on how to nap and how to lobby management in favor of napping at www.napping.com. And on the first Monday after we spring forward into daylight savings time, don't forget to celebrate National Workplace Napping Day!

bosses need naps too

Howard Echsler (name changed) wasn't a big fan of annual reviews, but who is? He had accomplished a few things that year, so he wrote himself some notes, entered the boss's chambers and began to recite. It got quiet. He looked up and saw his boss's head nodding—further, further—until he was out! Howard waited quietly for a full fifteen minutes, just about the perfect length for a refreshing snooze. Then his boss woke up. "Anything more?" his boss asked. "Nope," Howard said. Howard left his "review," and two weeks later, got a raise!

Care For Your Mental Health

Remember all those personal chores you took care of during the day when you weren't working? Who has to know that they're all done? Translate "doctor's appointment" into "mental health break" and take a few hours off. Savor a late breakfast, catch a Giants day game or relax at Baker Beach. Go ahead, play hooky now and then.

In fact, take a whole weekday off. Don't go anywhere. Just hang out. Or, if you want to take a daytrip—say to Tahoe—you can avoid the weekend crowds. If your company allows for telecommuting, take two weekdays—in Napa or somewhere else close enough to work from remotely, just as if you were working from home.

Not all of this has to be off the record. Wouldn't your boss allow you a short respite after an exceptionally hard stint of work? You never know until you ask.

Keep your breaks clean in this sense, though: don't squander your leisure time. If you already take lengthy lunches or fritter away hours at the water cooler, realize that you're just extending the amount of time you spend at the workplace overall. The more you focus on work while you're *at* work, the more you can get away from it entirely and enjoy the rest of your life.

LEAVE WORK AT WORK

Let Your Brain Work Without You

You can go one better than finishing the day's work on Friday: try planning ahead for the next week, too. It takes only minutes to make a list of things to do first thing Monday. The act of writing a list can plant ideas in your subconscious that will stir around even after you've left the office, but you won't even feel it! This is the magic of the subconscious mind. Come Monday, you'll somehow be full of creative solutions to problems that seemed insurmountable the week before. While you're at it, make a list of your key accomplishments during the week. A little pride never hurts!

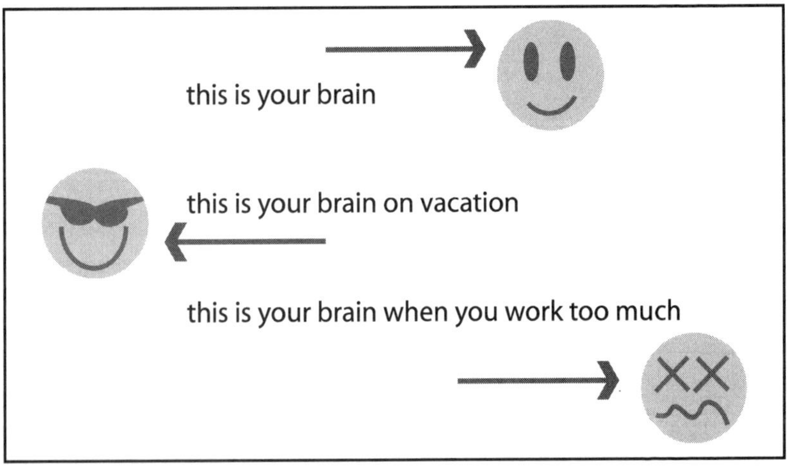

Keep 'Em To Yourself

Speaking of weekends (or whatever your regular days off are), we suggest you keep them to yourself. A normal full-time schedule is not supposed to include work seven days a week. Whenever you're tempted to go into the office on a Saturday or a Sunday or, even worse, you think about taking work home, repeat a variation on the anti-deadline mantra: "There is nothing, and I mean nothing, that can't wait until Monday." Really think about it. How many times have you panicked over some fire at work and realized later that with a little reflection, you could have come up with a more efficient solution?

If a short-term deadline makes it imperative that you work on a weekend, trade out that weekend day for a weekday off. If your corporate culture doesn't support that, rally your colleagues together and see if you can't change the tide.

ask for unpaid leave

Many companies will be amenable to granting you extra vacation days if they're unpaid. One single mother we know has negotiated an extra week's leave into every job offer she's ever had, and she spends it with her kids during their summer vacation.

If you didn't negotiate time off up front, ask for it now. Propose a couple of weeks off at a time when your department is trimming its budget. What boss could say no to that?

Keep your ears open too for sabbatical packages. Scott Phillips took his company's offer of 20% pay during a 12-month break and has now finished writing a novel and lived for a year with his wife in her native city of Prague, where 20% of a US salary goes a fair distance.

Use All Your Vacation Days

Vacation days should be enjoyed, not stockpiled. If you're fortunate, your management will feel the same way.

"One owes it to themselves, their family and their company to plan and take their vacation," says Bill Coleman, founder of BEA Systems, Inc. "While I was CEO of BEA, I encouraged my staff to take, at least every other year, a two-week or longer break during which their business voice mail and e-mail were turned off. Vacation time for me is where I can get perspective. In fact, my best epiphanies came when I was off for at least two weeks." BEA's use-it-or-lose-it vacation policy backs this up: employees cannot accrue more than 150% of their allotted annual vacation.

Although there are plenty of trips you can't take while fully employed, you can still cover some ground in the usual two weeks off.

office exercise

Your leisure gear (see below) will come in handy for keeping your blood pumping at work. Stretch in the doorway. Dance around. Stand up (sit down, fight fight fight!). Does your company have a gym? Use it in the morning to get your energy up and your endorphins going, and invite others to join you. No gym? Never fear. "I used to lie on my back and do stretches while talking on the phone," says Dane Larson, an avid surfer. "It helped a lot when my back hurt, and often sparked some good conversation."

Office Yoga, by Darrin Zeer, seeks to "inspire you to take good care of yourself at the office and throughout the day" with all kinds of tips on how to relax and keep breathing at work. May all its readers reach the promised Office Nirvana!

Whether or not you have a trip planned, spend some weekdays out of the office. Better yet, tell everyone you're taking a trip but then stay at home. You'll enjoy completely unscheduled time to yourself, and you'll be able to relax and enjoy your own city for a change. "Commit to your vacation days at the beginning of the year," Coach Garfinkle advises. "Make them as important as you would the birth of a child."

FOSTER A CULTURE OF LEISURE

All these suggestions sound great in theory, but could be hard to implement if you can't get others around you (your boss, maybe?) to buy into the concept. Peace of mind starts with you, to be sure, but to change more than yourself, you'll have to win over others to the cause. Don't be shy about sharing your philosophy with your friends, your co-workers, and even your boss. Big changes can happen when people band together. Here are a few ideas to inspire your colleagues to adopt the leisurely "'tude" at work.

Tote Your Leisure Gear

Relaxation is infectious, so dress for the part. Keep a scrapbook open to the best photo from your last trip. Surround yourself with symbols of leisure and your hobbies, and coworkers are bound to wonder why you always seem so relaxed. At a minimum, it will give pause to those who constantly feel the need to escalate a crisis.

"Scuba doesn't make the work go away," says ex-pat Marlo Sarmiento, "but it sure does make me happy." That shows in the underwater photos he displays in his office. Licensing attorney Karen

Kouris (name changed) burned scented candles while she worked. "I got some grief from the salespeople for it," she said, "but it sure kept the room from getting too gamey during those marathon contract negotiations."

Build Your Own "Leisure Team"

Don't hoard your techniques, share the leisure! Although company perks like in-house massage therapy and pool tables might be part of a bygone era, creating an atmosphere of camaraderie will always be in vogue. "Workers who care about each other want to support each other," reminds Coach Garfinkle, "which creates an atmosphere of, 'I want to be here.'"

John Greene, a software support engineer and rock keyboardist, was recruited on his first day of work by his company band, the "Low Hanging Fruit." "We played several company parties including a couple of Hornblower gigs on the Bay," John recalls. "While the management-promised soundproof room never materialized, we do still have a piano and a drum kit in the rec area. LHF got the crowd dancin' and the bodies shakin'."

Socializing with people you like to work with (and can get things done with) can only bring more leisure to your day. Friday afternoon Happy Hours aren't too hard to pull off—rotate sponsorship of them through different departments to foster some friendly competition.

LINGO BINGO
and other reindeer games

The heyday of office pinball machines, pool tables, and aromatherapy might have passed, but that doesn't mean there aren't still games to be played. Even if you can't convince your boss to officially endorse games at work, there's always "Lingo Bingo"—a sure way to pass the time in a boring meeting. Listen for meaningless jargon like "stakeholder," "think out of the box," and "step up to the plate," and as soon as you hear five in a row—BINGO!!! Find four pre-printed gamecards at *www.workingwounded.com.* See also the "bullshit generator" housed at *www.dack.com/web/bullshit.html,* where users can combine any number of verbs, adjectives, and nouns to create true "bullshit." Unfortunately for most of us, these phrases will sound eerily familiar.

In fact, choose any activity or topic of conversation that takes you away from work for a moment. "I keep a lot of toys in my office," says Jeremy Cantor. "Balls, hacky-sacks, other things to toss around. People play with them when they come in to visit." Needless to say, Jeremy's got a lot of companionship at work!

This kind of grass roots effort is bound to be more effective than any top-down, contrived "team building" exercise, plus it's free. What manager could say no to that? On that note, make sure your team includes your boss. If your boss isn't an ally, try to get one who is.

GET POLITICAL

As many ways as there are to make your own workday more leisurely, you can't change the whole world all alone. So how can you change the rules of the game itself?

Join forces with the **Shorter Work Hours Movement**, for starters. The goals of organizations who support it run the gamut from "providing a range of services to enhance and improve workplace practices" (**New Ways to Work**, 425 Market, Suite 2200, 415-995-9860, www.nww.org) to "challenging America's workaholic culture, public and workplace policies" (**Shorter Work-Time Group**, in Massachusetts, 617-628-5558, www.swt.org).

Shorter Work Hours advocates believe that gains in productivity can be used to reduce hours instead of increase

take back your time

It's widely known that Americans work more than Europeans—350 more hours a year, on average. Translate that into work days, start from the end of the year and count backwards, and you'll hit October 24: the date in 2003 that workers around the world celebrated the first "Take Back Your Time Day."

The activists who organize this annual consciousness-raising event hope to "challenge the epidemic of overwork, overscheduling and time famine" in this country by encouraging national conversations on the topic. Of course, you'll have to play hooky to do so!

For more information, check out *www.timeday.org* and the new book, *Take Back Your Time* (ed. John de Graaf).

income, that involuntary unemployment would go down if working hours were shorter, and that shorter hours would lead to higher productivity. That could shorten hours even more, creating a cycle of endlessly increasing leisure!

Many U.S. companies have gotten better results at no extra cost by shortening the work day or week, including:

Kellogg's

Replaced eight-hour shifts with six-hour shifts at the start of the Great Depression. The six-hour day created jobs, increased production by 3-4%, raised morale, and lowered accident and insurance rates. Six-hour pay rose to eight-hour pay in just one year, and the six hour day survived in some departments until 1984.

Medtronic

Paid employees at the 40-hour level for 36 hours of work. Even without hiring more workers, output increased.

Ideal Industries

A four-day, 38-hour week at 40-hour pay decreased absenteeism.

United Service Auto Association

As hours went down, so did turnover and mistakes. Sales, morale, and efficiency all went up.

Nestlé

The work week ended on Fridays at 2:30pm. While some employees worked until 5pm anyway, no one could schedule a meeting for Friday at 3. Employees used that time to see the doctor, drop by the grocery store or beat it out of town for the weekend.

An innovative program designed by workshift analyst Ronald Healey of **The 30/40 Company** (in Indiana, 317-852-6800) has employees working thirty hours a week for forty hours pay. It has been adopted in manufacturing and is beginning to move into health care and government. Other U.S. companies have shortened workweeks without loss in pay during slow periods, allowed partners at accounting and law firms to work less than full time, and supported telecommuting, going so far as to reimburse employees who install high-speed communications lines in their homes.

Despite the success of these experiments, the Shorter Hours Movement in this country could use some help catching up with the movement in Europe. There were certainly enough overworked San Franciscans in the last boom economy—surely some of us who've taken sabbaticals are now sold on having a better balance in life.

Petition Management

You can change your own workstyle and you can speak out individually or in a group, but systemic change has to come from the top. If you're not a decision maker yourself, press your case with those who are. Did you know that MRI scans of fatigued brains look exactly like ones that are sound asleep? Slip that factoid into your next conversation with your boss, then make a request for a leisure-friendly policy like company-wide meeting-free hours. Find more ammunition in *Work To Live,* by Joe Robinson, founder of the Work To Live campaign.

LEISURE EVERYWHERE

We'll consider this chapter a success if any of its ammunition helps you make the case for more leisure at work. Speak up and speak often: leisure belongs everywhere, even in the office.

CONCLUSION

To be for one day entirely at leisure
is to be for one day an immortal.

~Chinese proverb

WE'RE *almost* ready to rest our case for leisure. Have we inspired you to take a break? If you've been plotting your getaway from the confines of your cubicle during your lunch hour, we have succeeded. We've done our job too if your layoff was easier to handle or your sabbatical a little jazzier. If you've discovered something new about yourself or San Francisco, all the better.

We hope you'll practice the *art of leisure* both at work and at play. Plan vacations with your friends and take them. Host leisure parties. Share this book!

Are you still not persuaded to lose a job at least once in your life? Then we'll leave you with some words of inspiration from our friends. Instead of overworking, you could be reaping all sorts of benefits from leisure—like they and countless others have.

FIND FOCUS

like Mary Mangold

"Sometimes it will seem like your unemployment is not temporary but it is. I'm glad I got laid off, in the end. If I didn't, I'd still be working on junk mail for E*TRADE."

SURPRISE YOURSELF

like Maureen Brown

"The biggest surprise was how un-bored I am. I thought I'd go crazy with nothing to do. Now I'm wondering how I'll ever have time to work again."

GAIN PERSPECTIVE AND CONFIDENCE

like Marsha Converse

"For six months, I thought it was me. Then I had an accident, I lost a finger—that shook me out of my fog. Now I know that if this contracting gig ends tomorrow, I'll have no money but I'll work it out. I'm not afraid of starting at the bottom again and working up because I know I can do it."

VOLUNTEER

like Dave Casuto

"I do enjoy time off… and I'm pretty good at it! I feel more connected to the City because I get to do a lot and participate in so many things, like volunteering."

FALL IN LOVE

like Ann Marsh

"We have an over-employed society in general. People who work too much don't have the time to be good significant others. When that changes, people have time to fall in love, like I did!"

TIE THE KNOT

like Lynn Yuen

"When I first got laid off, I was a wreck. So sad, depressed and the world was one black cloud. After a year-and-a-half of travel, surfing, going to the gym, lounging, seeing friends and a therapist, reading, having time to date—and now with Mr. Right who just went ring shopping last night—well, it all worked out."

CREATE YOUR OWN JOB

like Eddie Foronda

"It doesn't look like there's a whole lot happening, initially, but you have to tap into what you can do and your interests and just do it. Craig's List charges you nothing to start a business."

IMPROVE YOUR HEALTH

like Alison Madden

"I cut out alcohol and ramped up my hot yoga practice. It led to better health and balance by lessening stress, and helped me drink more water and get more sleep."

LEARN TO RELAX

like Jamie Alfaro

"Work has been my primary focus my entire adult life. All of my enjoyment was centered around work. I want to learn about what relaxing actually is."

LIVE ON LESS

like Dave Scheff

"If I were a millionaire, I wouldn't be living any better—except maybe I'd have a pool."

TAKE ANOTHER SABBATICAL

like Matt Green

"There is not a day that I look in the mirror and say, 'Matt, you gotta get back to work.' As soon as you get enough money to take three months off, do it. You take time off and if you don't like it, then you know you're about work. But if you like it, you see your family in a different light, then that tells you something too. It's risky quitting but there's so much more to your experience in living than a job. The more scary it is, the more important it is to do it."

SHARE THE LEISURE

like the Leisure Team!

ACKNOWLEDGEMENTS

THANKS to every member of the original Leisure Team! Without you, this book would not be here, and it's better thanks to all of your efforts.

Our All-Star "Staff"

★ **Jennifer Birch,** proofreading ★ **Heather Emigh,** tax expertise and advice ★ **Eddie Foronda,** photos, e-survey and web set-up ★ **Chris Hession,** webmaster ★ **Sara Irvin,** page set-up, illustration ★ **Ellen Clair Lamb,** editing, advice and more editing ★ **Jamie Leap,** book design, web design, all kinds of design ★ **Mary Mangold,** production scout and un-employment expert ★ **Melissa Manwaring,** trademark consulting ★ **Leah Piscopo,** fact checking

Most Valuable Players

• **Susan MacTavish Best,** PR brainstorming • **Alayne Brand,** substitute teaching "school" • **Neil Brown**, financial planning and slacker advice • **Rob DeWaters,** edgy leisure • **Karin Dixon**, how to travel with kids • **Hank "Mister SF" Donat,** all things San Francisco • **Anne & Horace Enea,** proofing, research, jokes • **Bridget Fonger,** publishing wisdom and lazy inspiration • **Joe Gilmartin,** corporate HQ, snailmail services, liquid encouragement • **Glenn Goffin,** proofing • **John de Graaf,** advice and the gift of time • **Nina Greeley,** proofing • **Matt Green,** more liquid encouragement • **Tom Haan,** "Bojon" inspiration • **Jill Hannemann,** proofing • **Darcy Hanson,** psychology referrals, general cheerleading • **Deirdre Hussey,** PR • **Jennifer Jeffrey,** editing, industry intel • **Sue & Peter LaTourrette,** proofing • **Ben Marcus,** cinema fan and Giants fanatic • **Karen Palmer,** PR • **Marcus Ronaldi,** happy hours and more happy hours • **Michael "Smitty" Smith, Jr.,** editing, overseas ally • **Rochelle Teising,** encouragement, psychology expertise • **Lisa Turner,** Writeshop master, deadline enhancement • **Chet Van Duzer,** resources, research, editing, source of much knowledge • **Ethan Watters,** support, advice, and encouragement • **Lynn Yuen,** most well-connected leisure seeker • **Steve Yung,** proofing, serious home-town tourist

The Rooting Section

Thanks to everyone we interviewed; to all the survey participants; to our friends and families for their title votes, wicked write-ins and keen feedback; and to our fellow scribes from the WriteShop. Thanks especially to Bill Ralph and Jeff Stamper at Malloy.

Our "Landlords"

Thanks for the Internet access, eternal patience and tasty 'ffeine!
• The Canvas • Central Coffee • Cole Valley Café • Cup-A-Joe Coffee House on Hayes • Java Beach Café • Jumpin' Java Coffee House • Kalmanovitz Library at UCSF • Notes From Underground • Oh! Java Café • Royal Ground on Clement • Samovar Tea Lounge

GLOSSARY OF

LEISURE LINGO

WHAT *is* Leisure Lingo, exactly? It's an attempt to remedy the serious lack of on-the-mark definitions for many of the concepts described in this book. Clearly, taking time off work, whether planned, forced or otherwise, is a poorly-defined notion in our work-centric culture. Leisure Lingo was born out of necessity, to add some clarity (as well as some fun) to those non-working times.

ART OF LEISURE		
(mainstream) None. Leisure is not an art.	***(Leisure Team)*** The skill, craft or phenomenon of creating a fulfilling life of leisure; making the easy way appear even easier.	***(example)*** Although it took a lot of hard non-work for him to master it, Alex felt he was well-schooled in the *art of leisure* after traveling the world for a year.
ASPIRING RETIRED		
(mainstream) None.	***(Leisure Team)*** Someone who's waiting for their options to vest or has saved up money and when the time is ripe, will jet off the job for good.	***(example)*** The company committee on Functionally Allocated Business Processes was chock full of *aspiring retireds*.
ASPIRING UNEMPLOYED		
(mainstream) None.	***(Leisure Team)*** Someone who's working way too much, observing their unemployed friends and thinking the grass seems a whole lot greener on the other side.	***(example)*** Mary, an *aspiring unemployed*, spent long afternoons staring out of her downtown office window at the sailboats drifting by on the Bay.

COASTER		
(mainstream) A round object, preferably composed of semi-porous stone, upon which to set a cold drink to keep it from sweating into the table.	***(Leisure Team)*** Someone who has enough money to sustain a healthy period of time off but not enough to retire, so is mastering the art of leisure before returning to a paying job.	***(example)*** Karen and Isidro had so many *coaster* friends, they decided to get married in Hawaii. The reception lasted three weeks.

CONSULTING		
(mainstream) Offering your expert opinion or advice in exchange for pay.	***(Leisure Team)*** A loosely-conceived term on a resume used to describe a multitude of activities including volunteering, networking, traveling, meeting with friends to drink coffee and discuss new business ideas and meeting with friends to drink beer and pontificate on the lagging economy.	***(example)*** Six months after getting laid off, Tara had accumulated so much *consulting* work that the local brew pub started charging her rent for her barstool.

FRICTIONAL UNEMPLOYMENT		
(mainstream) Short-term joblessness associated with mobility. A person who leaves a job to find something better is considered frictionally unemployed. This type of unemployment also characterizes workers in industries subject to seasonal fluctuations, e.g., construction, agriculture or winter recreation.	***(Leisure Team)*** Unemployment that causes unnecessary friction within one's family or oneself. Common among Type A personalities and those who don't plan ahead. Can be increased by pressures imposed by others.	***(example)*** Jerry realized how *frictionally unemployed* he was when his father asked him repeatedly at Thanksgiving, "So what *are* you going to do with your life, son?"

Job Churn		
(mainstream) Jobs are created and destroyed all the time. If more jobs are being created than destroyed, the unemployment rate goes down and we feel good about our economy, because it looks like it is growing. If fewer jobs are being created than are being destroyed, the unemployment rate goes up and we head to the unemployment office.	***(Leisure Team)*** The feeling you get in the pit of your stomach when you think about going back to work. Can be cured with heavy and continual doses of leisure.	***(example)*** When he thought about how close to the end of his sabbatical he was, Scott got a serious case of *job churn*. Fortunately, bringing leisure back to work with him kept his *job churn* in check.

Layoff Blues		
(mainstream) None.	***(Leisure Team)*** When you play them backwards, you get your job back.	***(example)*** Janice used to croon the *layoff blues* but she changed her tune once she started practicing leisure.

Leisure Connoisseur		
(mainstream) None.	***(Leisure Team)*** One who's gained wide experience in the various classes of leisure, including world travel, creative self-employment, music and athletic challenge. Most comfortable on sabbatical, in the company of other ladies or gentlemen of leisure, or spreading the word on the art of leisure.	***(example)*** Sam knew he'd become a true *leisure connoisseur* when he could no longer remember what day of the week it was.

Leisure Patron

(mainstream) None.	***(Leisure Team)*** A patron of the art of leisure. Can come in the form of a rich uncle, a government grant or a corporate sponsor.	***(example)*** Sarah was able to extend her on-location study of fine Bavarian beers when her German uncle donated to the cause, becoming her *leisure patron*—and new favorite uncle!

Leisure Seeker

(mainstream) None.	***(Leisure Team)*** One who pursues a life of relaxation and personal fulfillment. An enlightened one!	***(example)*** Bill knew he had become an advanced *leisure seeker* when he chose to take a year away from work in order to travel, instead of accepting a promotion at a job that he hated.

Limbo-Employed

(mainstream) None.	***(Leisure Team)*** Not quite working on a career but stymied in the full-time practice of leisure by the need to pay bills. Related terms: underemployed, misemployed.	(example) Tom's on-again, off-again consulting gigs left him stuck in the mire of *limbo-employment*.

McJob

(mainstream) None.	***(Leisure Team)*** What a writer, actor, or musician has to support a creative career.	***(example)*** Until Caleb's band gets a record deal, he's keeping his *McJob* at Starbucks.

MISEMPLOYMENT		
(mainstream) Forced career change or temporary work taken just to pay the bills.	***(Leisure Team)*** Settling for work that is unsatisfying and unfulfilling.	***(example)*** An artist at heart, Sheara was suffering from a horrible bout of *misemployment*—working long hours at an investment banking house with no time to spend the beaucoup bucks she was making.

POST-SABBATICAL BLUES		
(mainstream) None.	***(Leisure Team)*** A type of dirge, commonly performed on a 12-string guitar and most emotionally played when dealing with the harsh reality of going back to full-time work.	***(example)*** Working with headphones on at his new desk job, Carter suddenly realized he'd been singing the *post-sabbatical blues* out loud while his co-workers listened in.

PRE-RE-EMPLOYED		
(mainstream) None.	***(Leisure Team)*** Not looking for a job right now but expecting to do so in the near future.	***(example)*** Rob frequented Baker Beach more and more as he entered his *pre-re-employment* stage, bagging rays and thinking deep thoughts about leisure.

PROTESTANT LEISURE ETHIC		
(mainstream) A moral mandate to avoid idleness and convert all downtime into so-called productive leisure, such as a hobby.	***(Leisure Team)*** A well-intentioned but incomplete ethic that reflects an American obsession with output and success.	***(example)*** The *Protestant Leisure Ethic* drove Amy to squander her European sabbatical marching diligently through museum after museum taking copious notes.

Protestant Work Ethic		
(mainstream) A term coined by Max Weber to describe the productivity-oriented culture giving rise to capitalism in Western Europe and later the United States. The ethic that spawned what Weber called the "spirit of capitalism."	***(Leisure Team)*** Does not compute.	***(example)*** Leisure connoisseur Carey stared blankly from the bow of the boat as her friend, Blythe, recited the history of the *Protestant Work Ethic*. "Huh?"
Puritan Social Ethic		
(mainstream) An ethic prevalent in the Massachusetts Bay Colony, which dictated that wasting time was evil. Its more benign tenets include living simply and being thrifty.	***(Leisure Team)*** Say again?	***(example)*** Not applicable. Incorrect when used in writing or speaking, according to the grammar of Leisure Lingo.
Re-Employed		
(mainstream) Would you believe it? This word is not in the dictionary yet. We'll take a leap of faith that it would be defined as "employed again."	***(Leisure Team)*** Entering back into the workforce, and dealing with the "culture" shock that comes with it. Not unlike a spacecraft re-entering the earth's atmosphere and heating up from the friction and stress.	***(example)*** Jeri was having trouble getting to household chores like laundry now that she was *re-employed*, so she stocked up on a lot of new underwear and socks.

RETIRED		
(mainstream) Withdrawn from one's occupation, business, or office; having finished one's active working life.	***(Leisure Team)*** Happy! Leisurely! Free! Hallelujah!	***(example)*** Jamie threw a hearty fiesta in celebration of his newly *retired* status after his technology startup went public. Unfortunately, he quickly had to become *re-employed* six months later when his stock dove underwater.
SABBATICAL		
(mainstream) A leave usually taken every seventh year. In Jewish antiquity, it refers to the sabbatical year in which the Israelites were commanded to suffer their fields and vineyards to rest or lie without tillage.	***(Leisure Team)*** A godsend!	***(example)*** Sharon awarded herself a masters degree in Leisure after her long-awaited one-year *sabbatical* studying at a culinary school in Tuscany—and threw some stellar dinner parties for her friends, too.
SELF-EMPLOYED		
(mainstream) Earning one's livelihood directly from one's own trade or business rather than as an employee of another.	***(Leisure Team)*** Fulfilled! Self-actualized! Free! (But possibly working too much.)	***(example)*** Darryl couldn't have been happier now that he was *self-employed* as a landscape architect. His only challenge was keeping up with his growing client list!

Self-unemployed		
(mainstream) None.	***(Leisure Team)*** Refers primarily to someone who is starting a business but not making any money yet.	***(example)*** So Neil, howz work these days? Oh, well I don't do it any more, I am *self-unemployed.* Neil, did you get laid off? No, I made a choice, I am *self-unemployed.* How are you paying the bills without a job? Well, *self-unemployment* brings a whole new perspective to bills.
Sit		
(mainstream) To rest with the torso vertical and the body supported on the buttocks.	***(Leisure Team)*** A verb that describes the placid state of someone who's "between jobs." One of the primary pastimes of a leisure connoisseur.	***(example)*** LC: "Yo, whassup?" Slave: "I'm workin'. You?" LC: "I *sit.*" Slave: "True."
Slave		
(mainstream) Unpaid and involuntary worker. One who works extremely hard. One bound in servitude as the property of a person or household.	***(Leisure Team)*** Paid yet reluctant worker. Someone who works for The Man. In Leisure Lingo, to "slave" is to work extremely hard at a job that you don't like.	***(example)*** Alyssa tried to convince herself that her new software job would look good on her resume but deep down, she knew she was just a *slave.*

UNDEREMPLOYED		
(mainstream) Someone who wants to work but has stopped looking or is employed part-time but wants full-time work.	***(Leisure Team)*** A term that reflects the misconception that everyone should work full-time; a malaprop brought on by peer pressure or financial constraints.	***(example)*** Michael thought he was *underemployed* until he learned to stop overspending; then he realized that his work paid more than enough to finance his leisure.

UNEMPLOYED		
(mainstream) Out of work, especially involuntarily. Jobless. Not being used. Idle.	***(Leisure Team)*** Blissful! At ease! Emancipated! (but maybe a little worried about money).	***(example)*** Larry was *unemployed.* Larry was happy.

UNEMPLOYED HONEYMOON		
(mainstream) None.	***(Leisure Team)*** The euphoric period immediately after leaving a job when the world is new again, every sight and sound speaks to you and the leisure possibilities are boundless.	***(example)*** Liam and Marissa left their jobs at the same time and shared substantial bliss during their *unemployed honeymoon.* Unfortunately, once the honeymoon ended, so did their relationship.

UNEMPLOYED ODYSSEY		
(mainstream) None.	***(Leisure Team)*** The quest one embarks on after leaving full-time work, whether the unemployment is elective or imposed. A journey to the promised land.	***(example)*** Trevor took off from work for several "mental health" days so he could plot his upcoming *unemployed odyssey.*

Wasted Leisure Time Syndrome		
(mainstream) A particular kind of work spillover in which exhausted and drained workers can do little more with leisure time than engage in undemanding, unfulfilling and empty activities, as coined in 1973 by the late Swedish Professor Bertil Gardell.	***(Leisure Team)*** *Wasted* leisure time?!	***(example)*** Join the Leisure Team and help eradicate *wasted leisure time syndrome* from every city and town on the planet!

THE LEISURE LIBRARY

SELECTED SOURCES & FURTHER READING

Books

1. *21st Century Leisure: Current Issues,* by John R. Kelly and Valeria Freysinger (Allyn and Bacon, 2000).

2. *ABC of Getting the MBA Admissions Edge,* by Matt Symonds and Alan Mendonca (The MBA Site Ltd., 2001).

3. *Absolutely Every Bed & Breakfast: Northern California,* by Carl Hanson (Sasquatch Books, 1999).

4. *The Art of Napping at Work,* by Camille and William Anthony (Larson Publications, 1999).

5. *The Art of War,* by Niccolo Machiavelli (DaCapo Press, 2001 edition).

6. *The Art of War,* by Sun Tzu (Clearbridge Publishing, 1999 edition).

7. *The Back Door Guide to Short-Term Job Adventures (3rd edition),* by Michael Landes (Ten Speed Press, 2002).

8. *Bargain Hunting in the Bay Area (13th edition),* by Sally Socolich (Chronicle Books, 2000).

9. *The Bartender's Bible,* by Gary Regan (Harper Mass Market Paperbacks, 1993).

10. *Beating the Success Trap,* by Ed Brodow (HarperCollins, 2003).

11. *Blindsided: Financial Advice For The Suddenly Unemployed,* by Edie Milligan (Alpha Books, 2001).

12. *¡Burritos! Hot on the Trail of the Little Burro,* by David Thomsen and Derek Wilson (Gibbs Smith, 1998).

13. *The Cafés of San Francisco,* by S. Green, R. Green, and A.K. Crump (TCB-Café Publishing, 2002).

14. *California Camping: The Complete Guide to More Than 1,500 Tent and RV Campgrounds (13th edition),* by Tom Stienstra (Foghorn Press, 2003).

15. *California Hiking: The Complete Guide to More Than 1,000 of the Best Hikes (6th edition),* by Tom Stienstra & Ann Marie Brown (Foghorn Press, 2003).

16. *The Complete Medical School Preparation and Admissions Guide (3rd edition),* by Andrew Goliszek (Healthnet Press, 2000).

17. *Critical Mass: Bicycling's Defiant Celebration,* ed. Chris Carlsson (AK Press, 2002).

18. *Eat This, San Francisco,* by Dan Leone (Sasquatch Books, 1999).

19. *Everything a Working Mother Needs to Know About Pregnancy Rights, Maternity Leave and Making Her Career Work for Her,* by Anne C. Weisberg and Carol A. Buckler (Main Street Books, 1994).

20. *F'd Companies: Spectacular Dot-Com Flameouts,* by Philip Kaplan (Simon & Schuster, 2002).

21. *Finding Funding: The Comprehensive Guide to Grant Writing,* by Daniel M. Barber (Daniel M. Barber, 2002).

22. *The Future of Leisure Services: Thriving on Change,* by Geoffrey Godbey (Venture Publishing, 1988).

23. *Getting What You Came For: The Smart Student's Guide to Earning a Master's or a Ph.D.,* by Robert L. Peters (Noonday Press, 1997).

24. *Go Away Just For The Health Of It,* by Mel Borins, M.D. (Wholistic Press, 2000).

25. *Grants and Awards Available to American Writers,* by John Morrone, Victoria Vinton and Anna Jardine (PEN American Center, 2002).

26. *Histories of Leisure: Leisure, Consumption & Culture,* ed. Rudy Koshar (Berg Publications Ltd., 2002).

27. *Hobbies: Leisure and the Culture of Work in America,* by Steven M. Gelber (Columbia University Press, 1999).

28. *I'll Grant You That,* by Jim Burke and Carol Ann Prater (Heinemann, 2000).

29. *The Joy of Not Working (3rd edition),* by Ernie J. Zelinski (Ten Speed Press, 1997).

30. *The Joys of Unemployment,* by Jim Hayes (Piquant Publishing, 1998).

31. *Law School Admissions Adviser,* by Ruth Lammert-Reeves (Kaplan, 2000).

32. *The Lazy Person's Guide to Happiness,* by Ernie J. Zelinski (Thomas Moore Publishing, 2001).

33. *The Lazy Woman's Guide to Just About Everything,* by Judie O'Neill & Bridget Fonger (Elephant Eye Press, 2001).

34. *Life After Baby: From Professional Woman to Beginner Parent,* by Wynn McClenahan Burkett (Wildcat Canyon Press, 2000).

35. *Life or Debt,* by Stacy Johnson (Ballantine Books, 2001).

36. *Lonely Planet San Francisco (3rd edition),* by Tom Downs (Lonely Planet, 2003).

37. *Mountain Bike! Northern California,* by Linda Austin (Menasha Ridge Press, 2000).

38. *Office Yoga: Simple Stretches for Busy People,* by Darrin Zeer (Chronicle Books, 2000).

39. *The Overworked American: The Unexpected Decline of Leisure,* by Juliet B. Schor (BasicBooks, 1992).

40. *The Right to Be Lazy and Other Studies,* by Paul LaFargue (Fredonia Books, 2002).

41. *Road Trip USA (3rd Edition),* by Jamie Jenson (Avalon Travel Publishing, 2002).

42. *San Francisco Bizarro,* by Jack Boulware (St. Martin's Press, 2000).

43. *San Francisco Secrets,* by John Snyder (Chronicle Books, 1999).

44. *Scenarios For Success: Directing Your Own Career,* by Rochelle Teising (Rudi Publishing, 1999).

45. *Secret San Francisco,* by David Armstrong (ECW Press, 2001).

46. *Short Bike Rides In and Around San Francisco,* by Henry Kingman (The Globe Pequot Press, 1996).

47. *Six Months Off,* by Hope Dlugozima, James Scott, and David Sharp (Henry Holt, 1996).

48. *Smart Couples Finish Rich: 9 Steps to Creating a Rich Future for You and Your Partner,* by David Bach (Broadway Books, 2002).

49. *Stairway Walks in San Francisco (4th edition),* by Adah Bakalinksy (Wilderness Press, 2003).

50. *The Story of Leisure: Context, Concepts, and Current Controversy,* by Jay S. Shivers and Lee J. deLisle (Human Kinetics, 1997).

51. *Take Back Your Time,* ed. John de Graaf (Berrett-Koehler, 2003).

52. *The Theory of the Leisure Class,* by Thorstein Veblen (Dover Publications, 1994, originally published by Macmillan, 1899).

53. *Time For Food San Francisco* (Thomas Cook Publishing, 2001).

54. *Time for Life: The Surprising Ways Americans Use Their Time,* by John Robinson and Geoffrey Godbey (Pennsylvania State University Press, 1997).

55. *Time Off From Work: Using Sabbaticals to Enhance Your Life While Keeping Your Career On Track,* by Lisa Angowski Rogak (John Wiley & Sons, 1994).

56. *Time Out San Francisco (4th edition),* by Penguin Books (Penguin USA, 2002).

57. *The Tourist: A New Theory of the Leisure Class,* by Dean MacCannell (reprinted by University of California Press, 1999).

58. *Travel With Children,* by Cathy Lanigan (Lonely Planet, 2002).

59. *Try! A Survival Guide to Unemployment,* by Karen Okulicz (K-Slaw Inc., 1995).

60. *What Color Is Your Parachute?* by Richard Nelson Bolles (Ten Speed Press, 2003 edition).

61. *Work To Live,* by Joe Robinson (Perigree, 2003).

62. *Your Rights in the Workplace,* by Barbara Kate Repa (Nolo Press, 2002).

Other Leisurely Reading

63. "Active Unemployment—A Leisure Pattern for the Future?" by T. Kay, *Loisir et Societé/Society and Leisure* 12 (1989): 413-30.

64. "Building Wealth," by the Federal Reserve Bank of Dallas, www.dallasfed.org, search for "Building Wealth."

65. *The Dollar Stretcher Newsletter* (Jan. 20, 2003, volume 8, number 3, editor@stretcher.com).

66. "Extras! Extras! Read All About It!" by Edward Guthman, *San Francisco Chronicle,* April 21, 1998.

67. "Japan's Young Slackers: Youth prefer part-time employment," by George Wehrfritz, Deborah Hodgson, and Hideko Takayama, *Newsweek International,* June 4, 2001, p30.

68. *San Francisco Bike Map & Walking Guide* (Rufus Graphics, 2001).

69. "Totally Hooked: The weird and wonderful world of eBay," by Eric Wetzel, *Book Magazine,* May/June 2002.

70. "Unemployment and Free Time, the Role of the Protestant Work Ethic," by Boas Shamir, *Leisure Studies* 4 (1985): 333-45.

71. "Why All Those People Feel They Never Have Enough Time," by Trish Hall, *New York Times,* January 2, 1988.

INDEX

B

C

D

E

F

G

H

I

J

K

L

N

O

P

Q

R

S

T

U

V

W

JOIN THE LEISURE TEAM!

GREAT MOMENTS IN UNEMPLOYMENT

12

LEISURE TEAM FOUNDED!

Leisure Team Productions (LTP) is a media production company that promotes the art of leisure through books, magazines, events and film.

LTP came to life in 2002, founded by two unemployed former classmates over several rounds of cask-conditioned ales at the Black Horse London Pub (coincidentally, the site of their original corporate headquarters). Tired of misguided perceptions of unemployment and the national obsession with work, Leisure Team decided to join hands with other organizations and individuals who have found more balance in life, to feature them in a deservedly flattering light, and to throw some raucous fiestas in the process.

Time Off! The Unemployed Guide to San Francisco is LTP's first celebration of leisure, and is the first in a series of leisure team™ guides.

Do *you* want to join the Leisure Team? You can! All it takes is an address. Sign up now at *www.leisureteam.com*. To give us feedback or to talk about working together, contact us at:

Leisure Team Productions, LLC
1392 La Playa
San Francisco, California 94122

feedback@leisureteam.com
www.leisureteam.com

ABOUT THE AUTHORS

THE founders of leisure itself??? Well, not quite. Dean LaTourrette and Kristine Enea were both born in the Bay Area, grew up in the same hometown and have lived in San Francisco for the past 15 years. Both worked in the technology industry during its peak and subsequent bust. They have been successfully unemployed since 2001, pursuing creative interests and attempting to perfect the leisure lifestyle. Leisure Team Productions and *Time Off! The Unemployed Guide to San Francisco* were born during this time.

Kristine Enea

Kristine funded her leisure excursions by negotiating deals in the software industry. These days, she can be found either writing or trying to get more stamps in her passport. Her most recent international treks were from SF to Panama City and back—by car—and through the jungles of Bolivia via raft and small plane. On the domestic front, her ventures have included a foray into the world of video production with a notable stint as a powdergirl for HigbieVisual Productions. In addition to co-authoring *Time Off!*, Kristine heads up operations for Leisure Team Productions, managing book production and paying the bills.

Dean LaTourrette

Dean has worked primarily in marketing in the San Francisco Bay Area, on and off for the past 13 years. "On," as in when he has been fully employed with a variety of companies, and "off" during which time he has taken extended hiatuses to pursue his passions of travel, surfing, and writing. Dean has written for several publications, including *Citysearch*, *Surfer Magazine,* and *The Surfer's Path*. Dean swears that the idea for this book came to him while he was sneaking a nap at work, which only reinforced his desire to quit his job and write it. He's also responsible for sales, marketing, and schmoozing for Leisure Team Productions.

ORDERING INFORMATION

To purchase individual copies of *Time Off! The Unemployed Guide to San Francisco,* shop your leading Bay Area bookseller or order directly over the Web by visiting us at www.leisureteam.com.

For distributor inquiries or bulk orders, please call our office at 415-564-9894 or send an e-mail to: orders@leisureteam.com.

leisure team productions

share the leisure!